White's Dictionary of the King James Language

Volume 1
A — E

Title Page from the 1611 Authorized Version

White's Dictionary of the King James Language

(Understanding Bible Words as they were used in 1611)

Volume 1
A — E

By
Steven J. White
2004

Revised 2005

ISBN 0-9735309-0-1

Cover design by Stacy Smith (Faith Baptist Church, Tacoma, WA)

This book forms Volume One (letters A – E) of 'White's Dictionary of the King James Language'. We anticipate Volumes Two and Three to be printed within 12 to 24 months following this printing. Should the reader have a comment or suggestion that might help improve this dictionary, they are encouraged to send an email to the author at: info@whitesdictionary.com.

Visit us at www.whitesdictionary.com

NOTE:
The use of bibliographical sources in this book does not necessarily imply author endorsement in their entirety.

For
MONICA
my wife, whose endless love and encouragement has helped me all through life, and who did more behind-the-scenes work on this book than anyone will ever know.

For
BECKY
my daughter, who gave many tireless hours on the computer doing data input.

For
DAVID
my son, whose 'behind-the-scenes' help was indispensable.

For
DAVID COTTON
my Latin teacher, for his proof-reading and valuable suggestions, and friendship.

For
The **LORD** my **God**
Whom I first met in Montreal, on April 6, 1975. If it wasn't for Him, this dictionary would never have happened.

Thank you, Lord.

Zec.4:6, "...Not by might, nor by power, but by my spirit, saith the LORD of hosts."
Jam.1:5, "If any of you lack wisdom, let him ask of God, that giveth to all men liberally, and upbraideth not; and it shall be given him."

(the Bible verses that I depended on so many times while writing this dictionary)

Preface by the Author

Since my first pastorate in 1981, like many men in the ministry, I have delivered thousands of sermons, Bible studies and devotionals; I have read hundreds of books on Bible subjects; I have listened to countless sermons on various Bible topics; and I have spent many years digging, probing, questioning and searching out the truths of God's Word. Nevertheless, when I stand back and survey the years, it always comes back to *understanding the words*, even for people who are very good in English! Words - like tiny droplets of water - make up the streams and rivers of communication; and it's to these 'words of the King James Bible' that I owe my life.

For as long as I can remember, I have been interested in words and their meanings. As a pastor, I would read a commentary on the Bible where the author would say something like, "*Now the KJV uses the word 'charity', but a better translation would be 'love'.*" At this point, I would ask myself, "*Did they not have the word 'love' back in 1611?*" A quick study revealed that they had the word 'love'. This sent me deeper into study, asking the question, "*Then why did the translators of 1611 use the word 'charity'?*" The results of my study amazed me, proving to me that the words they chose were indeed proper words and did not need to be improved upon... if only we clearly understood them. In fact, how can we be "rightly dividing the word of truth" (2Tim.2:15) if we really don't know what the words mean, nor very little about the grammar?

As time went on, I began to realize that some Bible teachers were trying to 're-invent the wheel'. One problem in doing this is that, by constantly coming up with new words to explain the words that are there, people get the impression the Bible is not trustworthy, or it's too hard to understand so why bother. It is my belief that readers of the KJV Bible don't need new words, but instead, *they need to know what the existing words actually mean*. ▶***NOTE***: This does NOT mean we should ignore the original languages of the underlying texts! In fact, we often refer to them to give us a better understanding why the translators chose the words they did. Again let me say this, "*If you can work with the Hebrew, Aramaic and Greek languages, then by all means do it.*" But just remember that some of the world's most brilliant minds have already done this for us and have chosen English words that adequately translate the Scriptures. We just need to understand what the English words mean.

Although there are many excellent scholars who are of a variant opinion than my own, I have put together this dictionary upon the belief that the translators of the 1611 were superior in their scholastics than what we are today, and had access to documents that may be inaccessible today. While it is true there are minor variances between some KJV texts (see section entitled, 'Are There Problems in the King James Bible?'), there is certainly not enough to discourage one from viewing the words of the beloved KJV as Scripture, and therefore precious. Hence, great importance is placed upon each word, along with a great deal of time in research to ensure the accuracy of its meaning, according to how it was understood in the minds of the translators.

One of my many interests is in ASL (American Sign Language), which I use when speaking with deaf people. Often I have interpreted another preacher's sermon for the deaf (as it is being preached), which is both an honor and a challenge. But doing this has taught me many things regarding the transmission of words and concepts from the 'invisible spoken' into the 'visible seen' language of the hands and face. "Quit you like men" (1Cor.16:13) is an example of this. At first glance, it appears to be a contradiction of terms, yet the 1611 translators chose these words to adequately translate the present-middle-imperative Greek word, ανδριζεσθε (*andrizesthe*). The problem involves the modern-use of the word 'quit', but when we understand that the word was used in 1611 to mean 'bear or conduct', the problem clears itself up. (See 'Quit' for a deeper explanation.)

God has burdened my heart with the study of His Word and with languages, which include: French, Hebrew, Greek and Latin. My Bible of choice, for various reasons, has always been the King James version of the Bible. I have also discovered that as people gain a deeper understanding of the words of the King James language, the Bible becomes a whole new world of excitement! This is especially true with people for whom English is a second language.

'White's Dictionary of the King James Language' is the result of many years of general labors, and several years of specific labors, comprising many thousands of painstaking hours, and yet, to echo the words of Jacob, *"... and they seemed unto him but a few days."* (Gen.29:20) The words of the Bible are a consuming passion of my heart. *"How sweet are thy words unto my taste! yea, sweeter than honey to my mouth!"* (Ps.119:103). It is the desire of my heart, and goal of my life, to always remain faithful to God's Word through honest and diligent study.

There is a saying, among the archeologists, that one stands on the shoulders of the one before him. This tends to be true of etymology (the study of words) as I owe a debt of gratitude to those who have labored before me (see Jn.4:38), and, at times, I can feel their shoulders beneath my feet. So, to those whose names and works are written in the bibliography, I say a deep and heartfelt, *"Thank you for your precious labors."*

Choosing which words would be included in this dictionary was both easy and difficult. Surely there will be a word the reader hopes to find, but does not, and there will be a word the reader does not expect to find, but is pleasantly surprised. Such is the inherent problem with choice. Perhaps, in a future edition, we may be able to include every single word used in the KJV as well as all the variant forms.

Bible verses, giving examples of the word-entries have been

carefully chosen to help convey the fullest possible meaning of the word. In some places, for the sake of space and brevity, only part of a verse has been given.

As much as is possible, I have researched (at great length and expense!) using the finest grammatical and etymological resources I could find, to provide definitions of key Bible words. These definitions are according to my own understanding of the evidences, and as much as is possible, in my own words. I have taken every effort to ensure this dictionary to be of the highest quality and free from error. **Should the reader find an error, or have a suggestion for an improvement, then I would greatly like to know about it. Please contact me directly.**

It is my personal prayer and desire that this 'labor-of-love', together with the Holy Spirit of God, will abound in blessing for all who read it, and will become a key to help the next man after me to stand on my shoulders and further unlock "*... the depth of the riches both of the wisdom and knowledge of God!*" (Rom.11:33).

May the Lord bless you richly in your study of the Bible.

CAUTION: *This book was NEVER intended to be a weapon of warfare to divide God's people and cause divisions amongst brethren. This book was simply meant to be another "tree planted by the rivers of water" to give refreshment and strength to the weary pilgrim. There are far too many people ready to fight their 'private wars' using any weapon within their grasp, and I NEVER want this book to be drafted into the 'Army of the Flesh', nor used in any fashion which is not both humble and teachable.*

S.J. White
Author

Table of Contents

Introduction

Explanation normally comes 'after the fact', and this is absolutely true of a dictionary. In other words, sometime after a certain word has been devised and used, it then finds its way into a dictionary where the meaning is explained. A dictionary, therefore, is a compilation of words (usually from a single language) after those words have been in use for some time, with definitions as to how they have been used.

Through the years, the meanings of words can change, or they can even have variant meanings depending on geographic and sociological conditions, and so a good dictionary will make note of these changes and differences. The purpose of this dictionary is to examine the language of the King James Bible and understand the words as the translation committee of A.D. 1611 understood them. This is an important note, and MUST be kept in mind at all times.

There are many words in the Bible that have great theological meaning, but the purpose of a dictionary is not so much theological as it is etymological*. Compared to a body, words are like the bones; theology is the flesh and skin; the Spirit of God gives it life; and the preacher dresses it in the clothes he deems it ought to have. Please don't expect to find a lot of flesh in a book on bones, nor a lot of theology in a book on words. Yet, I humbly suggest, that without the bones, the flesh (and skin, and life and clothes) cannot stand, let alone walk. (As a note of interest, an adult human body has 206 different bones, more than half of which are found in the hands and feet.) Because the translators of the 1611 were also men of theology, some 'theological flesh-and-skin' has been added to a few of the bones.

*Etymology is the study of word-origins and their generally understood meanings at any given time.

With a total vocabulary of over 12,000 different words (including word variations), the King James Bible is a 'Mount Everest' to climb. Many of these words are still used in everyday speech, which makes our climb that much easier, and others are easy to understand 'variations' of a word we already know. However, to ascend the heights and plumb the depths, we must examine the words as they were used, and understood, in the minds of the 1611 translators and its early readers. This includes archaic words, such as 'thee' and 'ye', as well as more familiar (but less understood) words such as 'silly' and 'charity'.

This dictionary will be of special benefit to those people to whom English is a second language. There are also many people (for whom English is their mother tongue) whose vocabulary is limited, and this dictionary will be a special blessing to them. However, **TO GET THE MOST FROM THIS DICTIONARY**, it is strongly advisable to read all the preliminaries BEFORE actually getting into the words. It is suggested that the reader keep referring back to the section on 'Symbols, Abbreviations and their Definitions' till he/she can read [the words in brackets] as if they were a smooth sentence. Also, the reader will find, many times, the notation 'NOI'. (Note Of Interest). These are meant to pique the interest and refresh the mind as one plods along, in study, through this dictionary.

►**Please note** that while the sources of information contained in this dictionary are many and varied, they are simply that – sources of information. Some of the writers lived questionable lifestyles, and had personal practices that many today might shun, yet they are referred to only as far as their usage of words. In fact, with the exception of the Bible itself, this author in no way endorses all the writings of all the writers mentioned in this dictionary.

IMPORTANT HISTORY

How Did We Get Our English Language?

About 2,000 years ago, that area we know as England, was once inhabited by a group of people known as the 'Celts', who spoke Celtic languages. These same people also inhabited a great part of Western Europe including Gaul, Spain, western Germany, and Northern Italy. In A.D. 43, Emperor Claudius of Rome successfully conquered the Celts in the area of England, and introduced Roman ways as well as the Latin language. Latin was further introduced as the Roman Catholic Church began sending its missionaries into England in the 5th and 6th centuries. (NOI. The Celtic language is still spoken by a few people in the remote corners of France, the British Isles and elsewhere, and seems to be gaining in popularity.)

In about A.D. 410, the Romans began leaving England, and in about A.D. 449, Germanic tribes began their invasion of Britain and became the founders of what we know as the English nation. These tribes, according to historian Bede, in A.D. 731, included the Jutes (who established themselves in Kent), the Saxons (who settled in Sussex and Wessex (places such as Essex (meaning East Saxons) and Middlesex (meaning Middle Saxons) still bear their name)), and the Angles (who founded the Anglian kingdom in A.D. 547, north of the Humber River).

Over time, the Angles and the Saxons formed 'Anglo-Saxon' communities, while the Celts were pushed more and more (but not totally) out of England. Although there were several different Germanic tribes in England during these early years, the early Latin writers referred to all of them as either Saxones or Angli, and their language was called English (< OE. **Engle**, which is derived from the name of the 'Angles'). Likewise, the people and their land were called 'Anglecynn' (pronounced 'Angle-kin' and meaning 'race of the Angles'). Then, in about A.D. 1000, it became known by the name 'Englaland' (the land of the Angles), which shows the success of the Angles over the Saxons in their push for supremacy.

The mixture of the Germanic dialects in England resulted in the definite beginnings of the English, which is spoken today, and this is why we see many similarities between English and German. Over the years, there developed three main divisions of the English language: Anglo-Saxon or 'Old English' (OE. from about A.D. 450 – 1066); 'Middle English' (ME. from about A.D. 1066 – 1500); and 'Modern English' (E. from about A.D. 1500 till today). The differences between the three divisions involve changes in spelling (including certain letters that are no longer part of the Modern English alphabet), pronunciation, changes in grammar and the introduction of new words. In fact, the changes are so vast, that without special training, an English speaking person today could not possibly read or converse in Old English. The changes in language from OE. to ME. were so dramatic, that it has been estimated about 9 out of ten OE. words fell out of use. Bear this in mind next time a film is shown depicting life in the ancient days of 'King Arthur'.

Then came the event that literally changed the whole course of the English Language... in A.D. 1066 William the Conqueror came to England and defeated King Harold, thus winning the 'Battle of Hastings'. William brought into England a new ruling class of people from France and, for the next 300 years or so, French was the dominant language of the courts, as England developed its own Anglo-French aristocracy. Included in this time was the addition of new words, derived from both French and Latin.

Interesting changes in grammar were forthcoming. Old English grammar was based largely on noun and verb endings, similar to languages such as French. However, throughout the Middle English period, these endings began to disappear, and in Modern English we have but a scant few endings for verbs, such as adding 'ed' or 'ing'. Grammarians call this a change from a 'synthetic' language to an 'analytic' language.

Though hard for us to understand, the English language was considered, during those 300 years, to be an inferior and 'crude' language, not fit for the translation of the great literary works, including the Scriptures. Latin was, without question, the superior language at the time. (NOI. There was a desire by some powerful people to keep the Bible out of the hands of the common people, and the argument that 'English was an inferior language' was used to their benefit.) And so, there arose strong arguments both for and against the translation of the Scriptures into English, but, alas, those against the translating of the Scriptures (during those 300 years) had won out for the time being. It seemed that the English language still needed improvement in order to properly convey the meanings of the words of the Scriptures. (NOI. Even the 'comma', that we take for granted, was not used in English until it was borrowed from the French language in about A.D. 1520. Until then, writers separated their words in a sentence by using an oblique line, like this /.)

But the English language was developing, and in A.D. 1382, Wycliffe published a good translation of the Scriptures into English. Yet still, the language continued to grow and develop and soon a brilliant Christian scholar by the name of William Tyndale (1495 – 1536) risked his life to translate the New Testament into the English of his day. He said that he wanted the plowman to know more Bible than the priests he had met. King Henry VIII was set against any English version, so Tyndale went into exile where he wrestled with the English language and grammar to produce a very good translation in A.D. 1525. In 1534, he produced a revised version of his work and had begun work on the Old Testament when, sadly, he was betrayed by an Englishman, arrested and, on October 06, 1536, burned at the stake. Before he died, his last words were, "*Lord, open the eyes of the King of England*". God answered Tyndale's prayer by having the king grant permission for Miles Coverdale to complete his Old Testament translation and publish it in A.D. 1537 under the name "The Matthew Bible" (perhaps to spare embarrassing the government over Tyndale's death).

God was also answering Tyndale's prayer in yet another way, for during the period from about A.D. 1530 – 1660, the language literally exploded with the growth of new words, many of which were 'borrowed' from Latin. Sir Thomas Elyot (A. D. 1490 – 1546) was responsible for many Greek and Latin borrowings. Approximately 26,000 new words were added in the fields of theology, philosophy, architecture, law, navigation, commerce, technology, biology and medicine. This represents the fastest period of growth in the history of the English language. (NOI. The 'Church of England' came into being in A.D. 1534 after Henry VIII broke off relations with the pope, and proclaimed himself the 'sovereign head' of the English Church. This act alone required new theological words in English. The Church of England's 'Book of Common Prayer' has followed this growth pattern almost exactly. It was completed and published in A.D. 1549 and revised up until A.D. 1662. For the etymologist, its major benefit is that it shows how certain words were used and understood.)

From about A.D. 1580 onward, the argument that 'the English language is inferior' was no longer true. No one could say that English was inadequate in which to translate the Scriptures. This was due to four reasons: 1) important literary works had now been translated into English; 2) the vocabulary had grown to provide adequate words; 3) English was made eloquent by its new ability for rhetoric (the art of public speaking, such as Shakespeare's plays); and 4) the solid beginnings to establish word spellings and rules of grammar. Throughout England, there were various dialects of the language being spoken, but the purest form of English was being spoken in the king's court, which now made the perfect setting for the translating of the Scriptures.

Although actual English dictionaries and grammar books were practically non-existent until the late 1600's (which seems like having automobiles but no repair manuals), they still did fairly well. They had dictionaries for Latin-English equivalents, but no one thought they needed one just for English. The earliest actual English dictionary was called 'A Table Alphabeticall' by Robert Cawdrey, published in A.D. 1604. It had 2,500 words with very brief descriptions of each word. (Compare that with modern English dictionaries of over 500,000 words!) In A.D. 1676, Elisha Coles published a major dictionary of 25,000 words, which indicates the tremendous growth in the language.

In A.D. 1828, Noah Webster (America's greatest lexicographer* and able to read about 20 different languages) published a definitive work with numerous Biblical references, entitled, 'An American Dictionary of the English Language' (containing 12,000 words), which was adopted as the national standard by Congress in A.D. 1831. Today, many pastors and Bible scholars still refer to it constantly. (NOI. In A.D. 1833, Webster published his own version of the Bible. Using the KJV as his base, he tried to correct grammar and replace words that were no longer used.)
*A lexicographer is a writer or compiler of a dictionary.

Today, Global Reach (www.glreach.com) estimates that almost 37% of the world speaks English (NOI. All air traffic controllers of the world conduct all their communications with airplanes in English.) Estimates at the number of English words are now well over one million (some estimates are over two million, but even one million is more than any other language). The mix of various other languages in English was estimated in 1973 (by Thomas Finkenstaedt and Dieter Wolff in a publication entitled, "Ordered Profusion") to be approximately:

- Latin, including modern scientific and technical Latin: 28.24%
- French, including Old French and early Anglo-French: 28.3%
- Old and Middle English, Old Norse, and Dutch: 25%
- Greek: 5.32%
- No etymology given: 4.03%
- Words derived from proper names: 3.28%
- All other languages contributed less than 1%

▶**Please note**, concerning this dictionary, that while great efforts have been taken to indicate the first recorded date that a word was used in English writing, these should be regarded only as 'approximates', as different sources will have conflicting dates.

Who was King James?

(A.D. 1566 – 1625)

On June 19 in A.D. 1566, Mary, Queen of Scots, gave birth to a son...his name was James. On July 29, in the year A.D. 1567, upon the abdication of his mother (who by then was in prison), young James Charles Stuart became King James the VI of Scotland at 13 months of age. He was raised by relatives in Scotland and, religiously, had a Presbyterian influence. On February 8, in the year A.D. 1587, at 20 years of age, his mother Mary was beheaded for plotting against her cousin, Queen Elisabeth of England. (NOI. Mary, Queen of Scots is not to be confused with 'Mary Tudor', the zealous Catholic who reigned briefly on England's throne. Mary Tudor became known as 'Bloody Mary' for the hundreds of Christian martyrs slain in her zealous attempt to bring England back under the Roman Church. Mary Tudor died in November A.D. 1558.)

On November 23, 1589, at 23 years of age, James married 15 year-old Anne of Denmark, who bore him 3 sons:

1. Henry (February 19, 1594 – November 6, 1612),
2. Charles (November 19, 1600 – January 30, 1649), who succeeded James in A.D. 1625,
3. Robert (January 18, 1602 – May 27, 1602);

and 4 daughters:

1. Elizabeth (August 19, 1596 – February 13, 1662),
2. Margaret (December 24, 1598 – March 1600),
3. Mary (April 8, 1605 – September 16 1607),
4. Sophia (June 22, 1606 – June 23, 1606);

and one 'still-born' son (in May 1603). (Anne later died on March 4, 1619 at 44 years of age.)

Although he struggled with physical infirmities throughout his life, James seems to have been keenly interested in God and the Bible. As well as being a serious scholar, he was also fluent in Greek, French and Latin, though he himself did not translate a single word of the Bible, nor originate the idea of a new translation, let alone one with his name on it.

Queen Elisabeth of England, after a 45-year reign, lay on her deathbed and named James as her successor, because she had no children of her own. So, on March 24 in the year of our Lord 1603, James VI of Scotland (at 36 years of age) also became King James I of England, hence the titles King James

VI & I. At this point, James had become the first King of what he called 'Great Britain', because he was able to join the crowns of England and Scotland.

In 1604 after meeting with a counsel of England's clergymen, James gave his permission for the translating of a new Bible for the English-speaking people. This became known as the 'Authorized Version' because King James authorized it. (NOI. The publishing rights of the Authorized Version are still vested in the crown of England today.)
James survived numerous plots against his life. One of these was in 1605 by 8 men, including a man named 'Guy Fawkes', who planted 36 barrels of gunpowder in the basement beneath Parliament, which Fawkes planned to blow up when James was sitting in Parliament. The plot, however, was found out and all 8 men, including Guy Fawkes, were put to death. Although the plot was an organized retaliation over the 'anti-Roman Catholic laws', it has been assumed that, had James been killed, the work on the Authorized Version would have stopped, and there would have been no King James Bible. (NOI. 'Guy Fawkes Day', sometimes called 'Gunpowder Day', is still celebrated in England every November 5, in honor of James' survival. Some historians claim that it's from this name that we get our slang term 'guy', which they claim was used as a derogatory reference to someone. Eg. "That 'guy' over there.")

In 1612, his 18-year old son, Prince Henry, who was next in line for the throne, died. (NOI. The same year, Shakespeare published his 'King Henry VIII'.)

King James, himself, died peacefully on March 27, 1625 at 58 years of age, and was buried in Westminster Abbey. His second son, Prince Charles, succeeded him as king. Incidentally, three months later, Charles married 15 year-old Henrietta Maria, the daughter of France's King Henry IV. Years later, Charles was arrested and tried by British Parliament on charges of treason and executed on January 30, 1649. (NOI. Our modern-day 'Prince Charles' has an ancestry that dates back to this same King James.)

How did we get the King James Bible?

After ascending the throne of England, King James held a court conference in Hampton in January A.D. 1604 to help settle some church related problems. The previous century had witnessed the birth of the Church of England and the Reformation, both of which had come out of the Catholic Church. Add to this the zeal of the Puritans (who believed in nothing but the Bible only, and who had managed to gain some political clout) and it's easy to see that James had inherited a religious time bomb, just waiting to explode! His desire was to assemble a conference of bishops, clergymen, college professors and Puritans and try to resolve differences. Although a new Bible translation was not on the agenda for discussion, Dr. John Reynolds (president of Corpus Christi College at Oxford) proposed the idea that a new Bible translation would help appease the situation. Apparently, some of them held to the 'Great Bible' of A.D. 1539 (which some of them called 'corrupt') while others held the 'Geneva Bible' of A.D. 1560 (which was filled with marginal notes and references, and some thought this detracted from the Scriptures. The Geneva Bible was also the first Bible to be brought to America.). Thus, under pressure, the King gave his approval for a new translation to begin, which was to become known as 'The Authorized Version', and later, 'The King James Bible'.

In July 1604, King James wrote to Bishop Bancroft requesting him to select 54 learned and able men to the task of translation. Of this group, a couple died before beginning the work and a few were unable to participate because of commitments. The 47 remaining scholars were (according to Eldred Thomas in his book 'Bible Versions') comprised of six Bishops and 41 were university professors, of which 30 held doctorates and 23 were unusually gifted in Hebrew and Greek. The 47 were appointed and divided into six groups (two at Westminster, two at Oxford and two at Cambridge) who worked under some 15 stringent guidelines, one of which was that they were to keep the old ecclesiastical words. For example, 'church' was not to be translated 'congregation'. Apparently, none of the translators received any pay for their work, as they gladly volunteered their time.

In A.D. 1611, the work was finally completed and about 2,000 copies were printed in London by Mr. Robert Barker. The very first printing became known as the 'He Bible', because the typesetter left off the letter '**S**' in the 3rd person pronoun 'she', thus rendering it 'he' (emphasized in the following verse). Rut.3:15. "Also he said, Bring the vail that thou hast upon thee, and hold it. And when she held it, he measured six measures of barley, and laid it on her: and **he** went into the city." This was corrected in the A.D. 1613 printing, which became known as the 'She Bible'. (NOI. The author owns a digitally scanned reproduction of the complete 'He Bible'.)

The King James Bible was first printed by Cambridge in A.D. 1629 and was later 'reworked' a couple of times to correct spelling mistakes, which crept in because of early printing methods. The Cambridge Edition Bible that we use today is based on the corrected edition of A.D. 1769. It contains 66 books, which have 1,189 chapters, which have a total of 31,102 verses, which have 789,314 words in them, which are made up of 3,221,202 letters.

Are There Problems with the King James Bible??

►**IMPORTANT NOTE**: **This dictionary is based on the A.D. 1611 Authorized Version of the Holy Bible (sometimes known as the**

'He Bible' – see above) using the Cambridge text of the KJV (as opposed to the Oxford text). This is important to note because there are a few slight differences between the 1611 Bible and the KJV of today. There are even two or three minor differences between some modern KJV Bible editions, so the reader may find a variation of a word that is not in his or her KJV. Do not despair.

Some people believe the KJV is archaic and full of problems. It is the opinion of this author that, although there are certain minor differences between the A.D. 1611 and the modern KJV, there are no doctrinal problems or errors as such. Rather, the modern KJV is an accurate and trustworthy duplicate of the 1611 with only minor exceptions. (This opinion considers the 66 Books of the Bible only (39 in the OT, and 27 in the NT), without the apocrypha, the reading schedules or any notes of any kind.)

As strange as it may sound, various publishers of the KJV have a few slight differences in their Bibles. (Bear in mind that the Cambridge and Oxford texts are basically the only two sources for all the editions of the KJV.) For example, the Oxford spells the pl. 'cherubim' without a final 's', whereas the Cambridge spells it 'cherubims'. Furthermore, the Oxford has at least three other differences from the Cambridge: Jer.34:16 "he" (Cambridge "ye"), 2Chr.33:19 "sins" (Cambridge "sin"), and Nah.3:16 "fleeth" (Cambridge "flieth"). Various publishers, such as Broadman, Holman and Zondervan will follow either Cambridge, or Oxford, or will mix them both. For example, one Zondervan Bible tends to follow the Oxford text, except in Nah.3:16, where it follows the Cambridge. However, this Bible, in Phil.4:4, uses "always ", whereas the Cambridge says "alway". It is the opinion of this author that the Cambridge text is the correct one, however these differences do not alter any doctrine.

The reader should be aware that there are perhaps 76 verses with word 'differences' between the A.D. 1611 and today's KJV, but these involve things like a few adjectives and pronouns, words being plural or singular, etc. Listed below is a small sampling of the differences:

- Gen.39:16 (1611) "her lord" (KJV) "his lord".
- Lev. 20:11 (1611) "shall be put to death" (KJV) "shall surely be put to death".
- Jer.4:6 (1611) "set up the standards" (KJV) "set up the standard".
- Eze.24:7 (1611) "she poured it upon" (KJV) "she poured it not upon".
- Dan.3:15 (1611) "of a fiery furnace" (KJV "of a burning fiery furnace".
- Mt.12:23 (1611) "Is this the son of David?" (KJV) "Is not this the son of David?"
- 1Tim.1:4 (1611) "rather than edifying" (KJV) "rather than godly edifying".
- Heb.3:10 (1611) "err in their hearts" (KJV) "err in their heart".

Having said this, it is IMPORTANT to bear in mind that these differences are minor only and do not destroy the doctrines of the Scriptures. The KJV we use today is <u>not an exact replica of the 1611</u>, as there may be up to 140 minor word-differences (not counting spelling changes and the removal of the Apocrypha), but it is still an accurate and trustworthy duplicate as far as the actual text of the 66 books of Scripture is concerned.

To view the word-differences in graphic terms, imagine that a man, standing six feet tall (72 in., or 1.82 m.), were divided by 750,000 units of equal height (the approximate word-count of the KJV), and then had 140 of these units changed (the approximate number of differing words). The result would equal the thickness of dust on the soles of his feet (about .0134 thousands of an in., or 0.34 of a mm.). That's about the amount of difference there is between the 1611 and the modern KJV.

Nevertheless, where did the word-differences come from? The answer lies in how the early printers went about their jobs. Serious study of early printing methods deserves a large, complete book by itself, but here is a thumbnail sketch of what went on:

> From the time Gutenberg invented the printing press in A.D. 1455, printers have used moveable wood or metal letters. Considering that the 1611 Bible has almost 750,000 words (about 3,566,480 letters!), setting them in type was a mammoth job. Furthermore, no printer could afford to set and keep all the letters for all the pages, it was just too costly and too difficult to store. Instead, they would set the type for several pages, print thousands of copies, then dismantle the type and use it to set up for the next several pages. They continued doing this until they had printed the entire Bible.
>
> Compiling the pages was a job sometimes assigned to a lowly wage-earner who may not have been able to read (remember, not everyone in the 1600's could read, though some estimates put the reading percentage of the population as high as about 50%). So, in the bottom right corner of every page they printed the very first word of the following page. This helped insure that the compiler could find his way and not mix up the pages.
>
> Some printers often 'farmed out' some of the printing to other printers (so as the job could be completed faster) then sent back to the original printer for compiling, trimming and binding. Future Bibles were printed using a previous copy as a guide for the words, punctuation and layout.
>
> This, then, is how a few slight differences crept into print.

Any mistakes, however, were quickly discovered and remedied. For example, in A.D. 1631, King Charles (successor to his father James) ordered 1,000 Bibles from his printer, Mr. Robert Barker (the original printer who followed the methods described in the above paragraphs), but Barker's typesetter made a grievous mistake in Ex.20:14 and accidentally left out the word '**not**', making the commandment to say, "Thou shalt commit adultery". The king ordered this 'Wicked Bible' to be recalled and destroyed, and he fined Mr. Barker £300 English Pounds (an astronomical sum in those days!). In other printings, there were other such mistakes that were quickly caught, so it's easy to see why the typesetters trembled with fear when they printed a Bible!

The spelling of early modern English words could easily fill a book, because most words were spelled several different ways! (People would spell their words the way they sounded to them.) The 1611 Bible was actually the first major step towards solidifying the spelling of English words and rules of grammar, however the 'f' was still pronounced like 's' and the 'u' like a 'v', etc. By the 1700's, spelling rules were properly developed and by the 1800's, the spellings of most English words were finally established. For example, 'wee' was changed to 'we'; 'fheepe' was changed to 'sheep'; 'sayth' was changed to 'saith' and 'euill' was changed to 'evil'. (NOI. Photostat and digitally reproduced copies of the actual A.D. 1611 first edition are available on the market, for a modest price, in which the readers can see these differences for themselves.)

Because spelling rules were not established in the 1600's, and typesetting was still a laborious effort, the typesetters often took liberties in their work, making use of the variant spellings to their advantage in order to balance a string of text on a page. For example, when there wasn't sufficient space in a line, words such as 'and' would be shortened to a mere symbol, while 'the' was shortened to a 'y' with a tiny 'e' over top.

Often the letters ‘n’ and ‘m’ were left off the end of words and replaced with a symbol over the last vowel. Eg. ‘upon’ would be printed as ‘upô’.

An interesting example of balancing a line of text is with the word ‘diddest’ (see ‘Diddest’), which was a common spelling along with ‘didst’. (Other early modern English writings, such as the ‘Book of Common Prayer’ (A.D. 1559), used both spellings.) Both words meant the same thing and the 1611 uses ‘didst’ almost exclusively over ‘diddest’ except in Act.7:28, where it is presumed the typesetters needed a bit more space in the line of text, and so chose ‘diddest’ instead of ‘didst’.

A similar oddity is found in Mt.4:3, “If thou be the sonne of God…” and in verse 6, “If thou bee the sonne of God…” Both ‘be’ and ‘bee’ were acceptable spellings and were used wher-ever they fit. In fact, ‘sonne’ and ‘son’ were also acceptable, as seen in Mt.9:2, “Son be of good cheere”.

Other oddities include the ‘j’ and the ‘i’. These were printed with the same letter in both lower and upper case, and the ‘?’ looked more like a full colon (:) with the upper dot smudged. Nevertheless, spelling variations are not a problem in the KJV because there are no changes in doctrinal accuracy.

The science of printing has changed in marvelous ways since the 1600’s. What used to take a day can now be done in a minute, with no typesetting problems. The average home computer and printer can produce perfect documents that would make the printers in the 1600’s gasp in unbelief! But considering the fact that Satan has long tried to destroy the Word of God, it’s quite amazing that the printing of the 1611 Bible turned out as well as it did. But then, God has promised to preserve His Word (Ps.12:6-7; Mt.5:17-18; 24:35; 1Pt.1:23-25.)

Note: There may be those who use a copy of the King James Bible as edited by Dr. F.H.A. Scrivener in A.D. 1873. Dr. Scrivener spent many years comparing early copies of the KJV, and made certain minor changes that he thought would make it more accurate. His work became the basis for a concordance entitled, "The Strongest Strongs" (see Bibliography), therefore the reader may find a few minor differences between the statistics of this dictionary and the Scrivener edition of the KJV.

A PRIMER ON ENGLISH GRAMMAR

English Grammar

(Grammar is the 'dissection' of language into its logical parts.)

Please understand that this section is not meant to be a complete course on every aspect of English grammar, as it would require many entire books to do it justice. In fact, all that this dictionary examines are the words of the King James Bible and the grammar thereof. This means, primarily, a study of words that occur from about A.D.1066 to 1611 (though some will pre-date 1066) and the grammar of about A.D. 1600.

►**Important Note:** some English words are used as both a noun and a verb, but this dictionary is only concerned with the words of the KJV and how they are used. For example, consider the word 'abjects'. Although in English it can be used as either a noun or a verb, in the KJV it's only used as a noun, hence, it is listed and explained that way.

►**Also Note:** when many Latin (and some Greek) words are broken into their pieces (prefix, root and suffix), there are often slight differences in the spellings. In other words, the spelling of the compound word may be slightly different from the spellings of the individual words when broken up. Eg. *delectare* (= 'delight'), *de* + *lacere*. This is not a spelling mistake, but illustrates how spellings can change with compound words.

The rules of English grammar are basically the same as Latin grammar (from whence they came), consisting of 8 traditional parts of speech. These 8 parts include: 'Noun', 'Pronoun', 'Adjective', 'Verb', 'Adverb', 'Preposition', 'Conjunction' and 'Interjection'. After this we will deal briefly with 'Case', 'Punctuation', the 'Prefix' and the 'Suffix'.

Grammar is important because it guides the meaning and interaction of words. However, there are many people who struggle with trying to understand grammar, and often give up in frustration. Do not be discouraged. Take this section slowly – one part at a time – and go over each part several times until you understand it, then go on to the next part. Slowly, the petals of the 'flower of grammar' will open for you and you will enjoy the sights and sounds and fragrance of the language as never before!

The Eight Basic Parts of English Speech

#1. The NOUN

NOUN (n.) [A.D. 1398, < AF. *noun*, < OF. *non* < L. *nomen* = 'name'] Thus, a **noun** is 'a word used as the name of a person, place or thing'. Consider this statement, "A man, near the city, set up a stone." There are three nouns in this sentence, namely, man (a person), city (a place) and stone (a thing). Proper nouns (pn.) are names of particular nouns, rather than nouns in general, and begin with a capital letter. 'Samuel' is a pn. because it is the name of a particular man. 'Mizpeh' is a pn. because it is the name of a particular city, and 'Ebenezer' is a pn. because it is the name of a particular stone. See 1Sam.7:12.

CASE

'Case' is used to show how nouns (including pronouns and proper nouns) function in a sentence. Inflectional languages (such as Hebrew, Greek and Latin) show their case by different endings on a noun, whereas English shows case by how the noun is used and where it is put. English can also show the 'genitive case' by adding a 's to the end of a noun, as in 'Bob's car'. Normally, the nominative is put first, or near the beginning of a sentence, then the verb, and finally the accusative. To this may be added other parts of speech, as listed in this section, but this is a very common word order in English. Koine Greek has 8 case forms; and Latin has 6 case forms. Old English had 5 case forms (nominative, accusative, genitive, dative, and instrumental), whereas Modern English has only 3 (nominative, accusative and genitive).

1. Nominative (nom.): refers to the subject of a sentence. Eg. **Jim** hit Bob's car. 'Jim' is nom.
2. Accusative (acc.): refers to the object of a sentence. Eg. Jim hit Bob's **car**. 'Car' is acc.
3. Genitive (gen.): refers to the ownership in a sentence. Eg. Jim hit **Bob's** car. 'Bob's' is gen.

#2. The PRONOUN

PRONOUN (pro.) [A.D. 1530, < F. *pronom* < L. *pronomen*, *pro* = 'in favor of' (see L. prefix '*pro*-'[1]) + *nomen* = 'name' (see 'Noun')] Thus, a **pronoun** is 'a word used in place of a noun'. Eg. "The Pharisees went out." Here, 'Pharisees' is a noun, but the sentence could also say, "*They went out.*" The word 'they' is a pronoun, taking the place of the noun 'Pharisees'. There are 7 different types of pronouns.

1. Personal (represents people or things. See also section below on 'KJV Pronouns'.)
   a) first person singular (1st pers. sing.) – I, me, my, mine; (plural) – us, we, our
   b) second person singular (2nd pers. sing.) – thee, thy, thou, thine; (and plural) – ye, you, your
   c) third person singular (3rd pers. sing.) – he, his, she, her, it; (plural) – they, their
2. Demonstrative (demonstrates a point) – this, these, that,
3. Indefinite (no one in particular) – all, anybody, anybody, nobody, each, most, etc.
4. Interrogative (asks a question) – who, why, which, what, whose, etc.
5. Possessive (shows ownership) – his, hers, mine, yours, etc.
6. Reflexive (reflects back to someone or something) – myself, yourself, himself, etc.
7. Relative (relates one part of a sentence to another) – whom, which, that, etc.

KJV Pronouns

(See also section above entitled 'Case')

The following 11 personal pronouns are by no means unique to the KJV, but these days, the first five of them tend to be, so they are listed together as such. Pronouns used in the KJV are very important as they give precise meanings within the sentences.

1. Thou – pro. 2nd pers. sing. nominative case. Eg. "Thou art the man."
2. Thee – pro. 2nd pers. sing. accusative case. Eg. "I say unto thee..."
3. Thine* – pro. 2nd pers. sing. possessive case (used predicatively). Eg. "For Thine is the kingdom..."
4. Thy* – pro. 2nd pers. sing. possessive case (used attributively before a noun) Eg. "Thy will be done...", (or used attributively before an adjective, which is before a noun). Eg. "Thy first father...".

* Some people believe the only reason for using one or the other depends on the word following it. In other words, they believe that **thine** is used before a word beginning with a vowel (a, e, i, o, and u), while **thy** is used before a word beginning with a consonant (b, c, d, f, g, etc.). However, this is not always true. Consider: "thy affliction" (Gen.16:11); "thy exceeding" (Gen.15:1); "thy issue" (Gen.48:6); "thy oliveyard" (Ex.23:11); and "thy Urim" (Deut.33:8). Clearly then, **thy** can be used before a vowel. On the other hand, **thine** is only found before nouns beginning with a vowel, and prepositions, pronouns and conjunctions (such as 'be, for, to they, with'). However, all that is needed to connect 'thine' with a noun, beginning with a consonant, is to re-arrange the words, as in Ps.74:16, "The day is thine, the night also is thine: thou hast prepared

the light and the sun." Although **thine** and **thy** may appear similar, there is an important distinction between them, the difference being a greater or lesser emphasis on ownership. While both show ownership of something (i.e. the 'possessive case'), **thine** is far more emphatic (or 'predicative') and calls attention to this 'owner-relationship'. On the other hand, **thy** shows the simple quality (or 'attributive') of ownership. Put another way, **thine** shouts out ownership, while **thy** simply mentions the fact of ownership.

5. Ye – pro. 2nd pers. pl. <u>nominative</u> case. Eg. "Ye must be born again."

6. You – pro. 2nd pers. pl. <u>accusative</u> case. Eg. "I bare you on eagles' wings."

7. Your – pro. 2nd pers. pl. <u>possessive</u> case (used attributively). Eg. "Comfort ye your hearts."

8. Me – pro. 1st pers. sing. <u>accusative</u> case. Eg. "The serpent beguiled me."

9. Mine* – pro. 1st pers. sing. <u>possessive</u> case (used predicatively). Eg. "Mine Angel shall go before thee."

10. My* – pro. 1st pers. sing. <u>possessive</u> case (used attributively). Eg. "Am I my brother's keeper?"

* See note above on '**Thine**' and '**Thy**' because the same rules apply to '**My**' and '**Mine**'.

11. His – pro. 3rd pers. sing. neuter and masculine. Eg. (as a neuter) Gen.1:11, "... and the fruit tree yielding fruit after his kind." (NOI. 'Its' is never used in the Bible, except in one occurrence in Lev.25:5 – but in the 1611, the reading is 'it'. It was common in Middle English to use 'his' when referring to a neuter object. Today, in Modern English, we normally only use 'his' in reference to a male human or animal.)

Here are three case forms that are important to know (when understanding KJV pronouns):

1. Nominative – indicates the subject of the sentence. Eg. "Thou shalt not steal." 'Thou' is the subject.
   'I', 'thou', 'he', 'she', 'we', 'ye', (and sometimes) 'it' and 'they' are all nominative.
2. Accusative – indicates the object of a sentence. Eg. "I will come for thee." 'Thee' is the object.
   'Thee', 'you' and 'me' are all accusative.
3. Possessive – indicates who owns the object or verb in a sentence. This is shown in two ways:
   a. predicatively – makes a strong assertion or statement of 'owner-relationship'.
      Eg. "And if thine eye offend thee..." or "And all mine are thine..."
   b. attributively – indicates an attribute or a quality of ownership (similar to how an adjective behaves) but not as strong a statement as the 'predicative'.
      Eg. "Upon thy belly shalt thou go..." or "Reach hither thy finger, and behold my hands..."

'Thine', 'thy', 'your', 'mine' and 'my' are all possessive.

#3. The ADJECTIVE

ADJECTIVE (adj.) [A.D. 1414, < L. *adjectivus*, *ad* = 'to' (see L. prefix '*a–*') + *jecere* = 'to throw or add'] Thus, an **adjective** is 'a word that is added in order to modify (i.e. limit or explain) a noun'. Eg. "A red horse." Here, the adj. 'red' explains something about the n. 'horse'. It's not just any horse; it's the 'red' horse.

#4. The VERB

VERB (v.) [A.D. 1388, < OF. *verbe* < L. *verbum* = 'word' (i.e. 'the chief word')] Thus, a **verb** is 'a word that expresses some type of action on behalf of the subject'. Verbs can take on many different forms in order to let us know the time frame, who or what they're referring to, etc. Eg. "And Noah went in..." Here, the v. 'went' expresses the action of Noah.

Verbs are broadly divided into two classes: regular and irregular (also called 'mutant'). A regular verb will express 'time and condition' (tense) and 'attitude' (mood).

TENSE [A.D. 1315, < F. *temps* < L. *tempus* = 'time'] Thus, **tense** is 'the time frame in which the action took place'. There are five parts of **tense**. The first three parts of **tense** show when the action of the verb was performed.

1. 'Preterit' (pret.). [< L. *praeteritus*, (which is pp. of) *praeterire* < *praeter* (= 'past') + *ire* = 'go' (i.e. bygone)]. A 'preterit' expresses time that happened in the past. Eg. "*I went...*"
2. 'Present' (pres.). A 'present' expresses time that is currently happening. Eg. "*I am going...*"
3. 'Future' (fut.). A 'future' expresses time that is yet to happen. Eg. "*I will go...*"

The last two parts of **tense** show the 'state or condition' of the action of the verb when it was performed.

4. 'Perfect'. A 'perfect' expresses an action that has been completed. Eg. "So Moses finished the work."
5. 'Imperfect'. An 'imperfect' means the action of the verb, having begun in the past, is continuing, or has continued results, into the present. Eg. "... for he had married an Ethiopian woman."

MOOD [A.D.1374, < E. **mode** < OF. *mode* < L. *modus* = 'measure, manner or form']. Thus, **mood** (or 'mode') is 'an expression of the writer's attitude in what he is saying, whether it's a positive statement, a command, etc.'

Early Modern English (as used in A.D. 1611) still had a few special 'inflectional endings' on verbs to show TENSE (eg. pres.), MOOD (eg. ind.), PERSON (eg. 1st.) and NUMBER (eg. sing.). These are also listed under 'English Suffixes' below, but they include the following:

'–edst' Shows pret. ind. 2nd pers. sing. Eg. 'diggedst', 'filledst', 'paintedst', etc.

'–est' Shows pres. ind. 2nd. pers. sing. Eg. 'deckest', 'eatest', 'mayest', etc.

'–eth' Shows pres. ind. 3rd pers. sing. Eg. 'crieth', 'doeth', 'lieth', etc.

'–st' Shows (some pres. and some pret.) 2nd pers. sing. Eg. 'canst', 'dost', 'hast', etc.

Sometimes verbs are not 'regular', but often will 'mutate' into a slightly different form. These 'irregular' or 'mutant' verbs include participles, verbal nouns (also called 'gerunds') and infinitives. Given below is a brief description of each.

PARTICIPLE (p.) [A.D. 1388, < OF. *participle* < L. *participium* = 'a sharing'] Thus, a **participle** is 'a verb that is used as an adjective (it 'shares' the qualities of an adjective), in order to modify a noun or a pronoun'. Eg. "**And my people are bent to backsliding from me.**" Here, '**backsliding**' is the participle (in this case a 'present participle'), used as an adjective to modify the noun '**people**'.

There are two basic types of participles:

1. Present Participle (prp.) expresses present-tense or continuous action in conjunction with a form of the verb 'to be' (i.e. 'I am', 'you are', 'he, she, it

is', etc.). This is normally done by adding the suffix '–ing' to a verb such as 'go', as in "*I am going*". However, not all words ending in '–ing' are participles. Eg. "Over every creeping thing." Here, 'creeping' is an adj. and not a participle at all, because it modifies the noun thing.

2. Past Participle (pp.), usually formed by adding the suffix '-ed', '-d', '-t', '-en' or '-n'.
   The pp. expresses one of two things:
   a. past tense or completed action, in conjunction with a form of 'have' (i.e. 'I have', 'You have', 'He, she, it has', etc.). Eg. "We have climbed".
   b. passive voice (meaning the subject receives the action), in conjunction with a form 'to be' (i.e. 'I am', 'You are', 'He, she, it is', 'they were', etc.). Eg. "The waters were abated."

►**Note:** A participle may sometimes be used in one place as a prp., and then in another place as a pp. In such cases, the word is simply listed in this dictionary as a p. The information provided above is sufficient for the reader to determine what type of a participle is being used in each individual case. Also note that the 'future tense' may also employ a prp. or a pp. Eg. "I will be laughing."

VERBAL NOUN (vbl.n.) (also known as a 'gerund') [A.D. 1513, < L. *gerundium* < *gerere* = 'to carry on'] Thus, a **verbal noun** is 'a verb with the suffix '-ing' '. Though it has the nature of a verb, it acts like a noun in that it represents a 'thing'. Eg. "Naaman saw him running..." 'Running' is a verbal noun.

INFINITIVE (inf.) [A.D. 1470, < LL. *infinitives, in* = 'not' + *finitivus* = 'defining' or 'definite' (< *finire* = 'boundary or limit')] Thus, an **infinitive** is 'an open-ended verb in which no limits are given as to its duration'. Their normal construction is: the word 'to' + verb. Eg. 'These shall stand upon mount Ebal to curse'. 'Curse' now becomes an inf. because of the addition of the word 'to'.

▶**NOTE**: There are other varieties of verbs, and all are important as they define exactly what an author is saying, but for our purposes here, we will advise the reader to pursue other books on English grammar, such as are listed in the Bibliographical section at the end of this dictionary.

#5. The ADVERB

ADVERB (adv.) [A.D. 1530, < F. *adverbe* < L. *adverbium*, *ad* = 'to' (see L. prefix '*ad–*') + *verbum* = 'verb'] Thus, an **adverb** is 'a word that points directly to a verb', and is used to modify (limit, qualify or further explain) the meaning of that verb. Adverbs help answer questions about the verb, such as how, when, where and why? Eg. 2Ki.9:20, "...he driveth furiously." Here, 'furiously' is the adv., explaining the verb 'driveth', as if answering the question, "*How did he drive?*"

#6. The PREPOSITION

PREPOSITION (prep.) [A.D. 1000, < L. *praepositio* < *praeponere, prae* = 'before' + *ponere* = 'to place or put'] Thus, a **preposition** is 'a part of written speech (such as 'by', 'from', 'in', 'to') that is placed before a noun (or pronoun, or proper noun)' and shows its position or relationship to some other word or phrase within the sentence. Eg. 2Tim.3:1, "This know also, that in the last days perilous times shall come." Here, the prep. 'in' shows the relationship between 'perilous times' and 'the last days.'

#7. The CONJUNCTION

CONJUNCTION (conj.) [A.D. 1388, < L. *conjunctio* < *con-*

jungere, con = 'together or with' (see L. prefix '*co-*') + *jungere* = 'to join'] Thus, a **conjunction** is 'a part of written speech (such as 'and', 'if', 'or') that joins together two words or two phrases'.

There are two kinds of conjunctions in the KJV.

1. Coordinating – Eg. "Mary and Joseph." Here, the coordinating conj. is 'and '. It is called 'coordinating' because it joins together two similar nouns.
2. Subordinating – put at the beginning of 'dependent' clauses (which are short sentences having a subject and verb, but needing something else to make them understandable.) Eg. "Except the LORD build the house, they labour in vain that build it." Here, the subordinating conj. is 'Except'. Other such conjunctions include 'after', 'because', 'before', and 'inasmuch as'.

#8. The INTERJECTION

INTERJECTION (int.) [A.D. 1430, < F. *interjection* < L. *interjection* < *interjicere, inter* = 'between' + *jacere* = 'to throw'] Thus, an **interjection** is 'something thrown in between, or introduced abruptly', and reveals emotions such as surprise, sorrow, etc. Eg. "Alas! for that day is great, so that none is like it..." A few more interjections include 'Ah!', 'Aha!', 'Behold!', 'Lo', and 'Ha!'

Punctuation

PUNCTUATION separates the words on a page and forms intelligible thought and makes the meaning clear. Without punctuation, we would not know what was being communicated. The following are the basic rules of KJV English punctuation.

▶**Important Note:** it must be understood that there are some slight differences between the punctuation of the 1611 and our KJV, but no doctrine has been compromised. Eg. Compare: "O LORD heale mee," (Ps.6:2 in 1611, original spelling), and "O LORD, heal me;" (Ps.6:2 in KJV). Notice the comma after LORD and the semi-colon after 'me' in the KJV. They are slightly different but not so as to change the basic meaning.

The basic punctuation marks and their meaning:

- period (.) – shows the end of a complete sentence.
- comma (,) – shows a slight separation of ideas within a sentence.
- semi-colon (;) – shows a separation of ideas greater than a comma, but less than a period.
- colon (:) – shows the most separation of ideas within a sentence. It usually introduces another clause of equal importance, often as a further explanation of the first. Eg. the time of a clock might read '12:01'. The numbers on both sides of the colon are equal, in that they are both expressions of time, yet the second set of numbers helps to explain the first, and narrows its meaning.
- question (?) – shows the thought before it to be of a questioning nature. It was very common to see these in the midst of a sentence, which explains why the following word was not capitalized. Today, a question mark will finish a sentence, but in A.D. 1611, it could separate two or more clauses within a sentence.
- exclamation (!) – shows the thought before it to be of an emotional nature, such as surprise, lament or anger. It was very common to see these in the midst of a sentence, which explains why the following word was not capitalized. Today, an exclamation mark will finish a sentence, but in A.D. 1611, it could separate two or more clauses within a sentence.

<u>A basic 'clause' and 'sentence':</u>

<u>CLAUSE</u> – [A.D. 1225, < OF. *clause* < ML. *clausa* (= 'enclose') < L. *claudere* = 'to shut or close'] Thus, a **<u>clause</u>** is 'a group of words containing a subject and a predicate (a predicate is the word or words in a sentence, which expresses what is affirmed or denied about the subject), which form a distinct portion of a writing,' such as a part of a speech or part of a sentence.

<u>SENTENCE</u> – the same as a 'clause', but forming an expression of:

#1) declaration (eg. "*Bob went to church.*");
#2) interrogation (eg. "*Did Bob go to church?*");
#3) exclamation (eg. "*Bob went to church!*");
#4) command ("*Bob, go to church.*").

A sentence may contain more than one clause.

The Prefix and the Suffix

The PREFIX

<u>PREFIX</u>. [A.D. 1420, < L. *praefixus* < *praefigere*, *prae* = 'before' + *figere* = 'to fix or attach'] Thus, a **<u>prefix</u>** is 'something that is put before the beginning of a word'. In grammar, it can be a word, or a syllable (a 'syllable' is a vowel, such as 'a' or a vowel and consonant, such as 'en'), or a number of syllables, put at the beginning of a word in order to qualify the meaning of that word. Eg. 'proclaim'. Here, the prefix 'pro' (= 'to go before') is placed before the word 'claim' (= 'to cry out or to shout'). Thus, proclaim means 'to go before and cry out', similar to what a town-crier would do in making a public announcement.

The following is not a comprehensive list of all known prefixes, but rather, a list of prefixes used in this dictionary.

English Prefixes

a- (in OE. sometimes 'on-'.)

1.a) a 'motion onward' (as in going away from a position). Eg. 'A-far', 'a-fore' and 'a-way'.

1.b) an 'intensity' (with the idea of 'on', 'in', 'up' or 'into'). Eg. 'A-bide', 'a-rise' or 'a-wake'.

2. the idea of 'towards' (in the direction of). When combin ing prepositions (such as 'on', 'in' or 'at') with nouns or verbs (such as 'shore' or 'fresh') the prefix 'a' forms words such as 'a-shore' (meaning 'on or at the shore') and 'a-fresh' (meaning 'a fresh start' or 'beginning').
3. one (used as an article). Eg. 'A boat' (meaning 'one boat').

be- (also 'bi-')

1. a closeness such as 'by' or 'near'. Eg. 'Be-fore'.
2. an intensive thoroughness. Eg. 'Be-wail'.

de-

1. a 'downward motion'. Eg. 'De-scend'.
2. an outward motion 'off' or 'away'. Eg. 'De-fend'.
3. a motion 'completely to the bottom'. Eg. 'De-clare'.
4. an evil action such as 'putting down' or 'taking away'. Eg. 'De-ceive'.

em- (also 'en-') (note that many OF. words use '*en-*' as a prefix, with a similar meaning) Means 'in' or 'into' and often has an intensity involved. Excluding proper nouns, 'em-' is only used before words beginning with 'b', 'm' and 'p'. Eg. 'Empower'. As for 'en-', excluding proper nouns, it is never used before words beginning with 'b' or 'p', and is only used before 'm' in the word 'enmity'. Sometimes ME. words had multiple spellings (because people spelled the word as it sounded good to them). This can be seen in 'envy' (the more common spelling) and 'invye' (not used in the KJV). Both prefixes 'en-' and 'in-' mean the same thing.

with-
Meaning 'close to', as in 'up against' or 'alongside'. Eg. 'With-out'.

Greek Prefixes

α- (a-)
Adds a negative to the word. Similar to L. '*in*' or E. 'un'.

επι- (epi-)
Shows a direction of 'up to' or 'on top of'

εκ- (ek-) or **εξ-** (ex-)
Shows a position from where the action proceeds. Eg. 'Out of', 'from' or 'away from'

Latin Prefixes

ab- (also '*a-*' and '*abs-*')
1. motion toward in an intense way, as in 'to' (see also '*ad–*').
2. motion outward, as in 'away from'. Eg. 'Abuse' (*ab* = 'away from' + *usus*= 'to use') = 'to use in an improper way'.
3. motion downward. Eg. 'Abject' (*ab* = 'down' + *jectus* = 'cast') = 'to be cast down'.

ad- (also '*a-*', '*ac-*', '*af-*', '*ag-*', '*al-*', '*am-*', '*an-*', '*ap-*', *ar-*', '*as-*', and '*at-*')
Shows motion 'towards or near' as in 'to', but adds intensity to a word. Eg. 'Ad-vent' (*ad* = 'to' + *venire* = 'to come').

co- (also '*cog-*', '*col-*', '*com-*', '*con-*', '*cor-*' and '*cum-*')
Expresses 'together' or 'with', but also gives a suggestion of intensity and thoroughness.

de-
1. 'down' as in a direction (i.e. 'down to the bottom').
2. 'down' as in a very negative sense (i.e. 'to put down').
3. 'away from, without or completely'.

dis- (also '*di-*')
'utterly apart' or 'asunder' (see 'Asunder') and carries a strong intensive, negative feeling. Eg. 'Dis-belief'.

ex- (also '*e-*', '*ef-*' and '*es-*')
'from', 'out' or 'out of'. Eg. 'Exalt' (< L. *exaltare*, *ex* = 'out' + *altus* = 'high') = 'to raise up or elevate'.

in- (also '*im-*')
1. the negative 'not' (similar to E. 'un-' or the Gk. 'α' (*a*-). Eg. 'Inexpensive' = 'not expensive') or the idea of 'against'.
2. an intensive 'in', 'into' or 'on'. Eg. 'Incase'. Sometimes spelled in E. 'en' (eg. 'enslave') or in OF. '*em*' (eg. 'embellish').

o- (also '*ob-*', '*oc-*', '*of-* ' and '*op-*')
'against' or 'toward'.

pre- (also '*prae-*')
'before' (in front of). Eg. 'precept' (< L. *praeceptum*, *prae* = 'before' + *ceptum*, < *capere* = 'to take') = 'something taken before hand', as in 'a primary rule, commandment or admonition'.

pro- (also '*pos-* ')
1. for', as 'in favor of'. Eg. 'Pronoun' (< L. *pronomen* = 'in favor of a noun').
2. 'before' ('in front of'). Eg. 'Protect' (< L. *protegere* = 'to go before and cover').

re-

1. 'back' or 'backwards'. Eg. 'Revoke' (< L. *revocare* (= 'to call back') < *re* = 'back' + *vocare* = 'to call'.
2. 'again'. Eg. 'Rebuild'.

sub- (also *'suf-'*)

'beneath' or 'under', or 'at the end'. Eg. See 'Suffix' (below).

The SUFFIX

SUFFIX [A.D. 1604, < L. *suffixum* < *suffixus* < *suffigere, suf* = 'sub' or 'below or at the end' (see L. prefix '*sub—*') + *figere* = 'to fix or place'] Thus, a **suffix** is 'something that is put at the end of a word'. It is exactly like a prefix only at the end of a word instead of at the beginning. Eg. The word 'godly'. Here, 'god' is the word, and 'ly' is the suffix, in this case indicating 'the manner of' (see E. suffix '-ly').

English Suffixes

-able (also '-ble' and '-ible')

Changes verbs to adjectives and indicates 'capable of being' or 'worthy to be'. Eg. 'Honourable', 'capable of being honoured' or 'worthy of honour'.

-age

This has become a favorite ending of certain nouns and verbs to indicate 'that which pertains to its root'. Eg. The noun 'pilgrim' (the root) becomes 'pilgrimage' (things pertaining to the pilgrim). Also 'passage' (things pertaining to the 'pass' or 'the way'); 'courage' (things pertaining to the 'cour' (= 'heart') < L. *cor* = 'heart').

-ance (also '-ancy' and '-ence')

Gives a word the nature of both a verb and an adjective and

shows the quality, condition or state of being. Eg. 'Assistance', 'arrogancy' and 'prudence'.

-ate

Forms adjectives, nouns or verbs. Eg. 'Elaborate' (adj.), 'advocate' (n.), or 'meditate' (v.).

-ed (also '-d' and '-t')

1. Used on a verb to form a preterit (pret.) (i.e. a past-tense). Eg. "And he cried unto the LORD".
2. Used on a verb to form a present participle (prp.). Eg. "*I am amazed*".
3. Used on a verb to form a past participle (pp.). Eg. "*He was amazed*". (NOI. Verbs ending with 'd', 't', 'en' and 'n' become pp. and not pret.)
4. Used on a verb to form a participle (p.). Sometimes called a 'participial-adjective'. These can be either prp. or pp. See above examples. (This notation is given when a word in the Bible is used sometimes as a prp. and sometimes as a pp. See section on Grammar (Verb – Participle)).
5. Used on a noun to form an adjective (adj.). Eg. "Crookbackt".

-edst

Used on verbs only and makes them preterit indicative 2nd pers. sing. nom. (used only with 'thou'). Eg. 'Anointedst', 'defiledst', 'killedst', 'longedst', 'stretchedst', and 'vowedst'. (NOI. The verb 'didst' is the only exception to the '-edst' ending. 'Didst' also normally precedes an infinitive verb (such as 'laugh'). Eg. "... And he said, Nay; but thou didst laugh.")

-en

1. Used on a verb to form a participle (p.). Eg. 'Baken', 'beaten', etc.
2. Used on a noun to form a plural (pl.). Eg. 'Children',

'oxen', etc.

3. Used on a noun to form an adjective (adj.) with the idea of 'having the nature of'. Eg. 'Golden'.
4. Used on adjectives to form verbs (vb.). Eg. 'Hard' is the adj. and 'harden' is the v.

-er

Changes verbs into nouns, and identifies a person according to their occupation. Eg. 'Diviner' (= 'one who divines'), 'instructer' (= 'one who instructs').

-est

Used on verbs only to form present indicative 2nd pers. sing nom. (used only with 'thou'). Eg. 'Camest', 'comest', 'eatest', 'gavest', 'meanest', 'standest' and 'wouldest'.

-eth

Used on verbs only to form present indicative 3rd pers. sing. (used with: 'he', 'she', 'it', 'whosoever', or 'which') Eg. 'Compasseth', 'creepeth', 'crieth', 'doeth', 'findeth', 'goeth', 'lieth', and 'moveth'.

-ing

1. Forms nouns of action or 'verbal nouns' (vbl.n.). Eg. 'asking'. See section on Grammar – (Verb – Verbal Noun.)
2. Changes a verb into a noun. Eg. 'Build' > a 'building' (i.e. 'house').
3. Forms a 'present participle' (prp.), which expresses action in 'present-time' and modifies a n. Eg. A 'wayfaring man'. This is also known as a 'participial adjective'.

-ise (also '-ize')

A special ending for nouns, of Greek origin, to form verbs. The emphasis of these verbs is on the product or end result, as a state of being. Eg. 'Baptize' and 'chastise'.

-ish

1. Added to nouns to make adjectives that now show 'a belonging to' or 'a characteristic of' the n. it modifies. Eg. 'Foolish'.
2. Added to verbs of French origin as an ending. Eg. 'Perish'.

-ity (also '-ety')

Forms nouns expressing state, condition or quality. Eg. 'Enmity', 'iniquity', 'surety', safety'.

-ling

Added to nouns to mean 'one belonging to or concerned with'. Eg. 'Firstling', 'dwelling'.

-ly

1. Forms adjectives that show 'the appearance or characteristics of'. Eg. 'Heavenly' and 'worldly'.
2. Forms adverbs that can show:
   a. manner. Eg. 'Quickly'.
   b. extent. Eg. 'Thoroughly'.
   c. place or direction. Eg. 'Inwardly'.
   d. time. Eg. 'Lately'.

-ment

Changes verbs into nouns and shows the 'result or product of an action'. Eg. 'Refreshment'; 'atonement'.

-ness

Attached to adjectives and past participles to form nouns which express a state, quality or a condition. Eg. 'Darkness', 'brightness' and 'righteousness'.

-ous

Forms an adj. with the idea of 'abounding in', 'overflowing with', 'given over to' or 'characterized by'. Eg. 'Covetous'. (NOI. This suffix is also used in chemistry to imply a larger proportion of the element to which the '–ous' is attached. Eg. 'Sulphurous' = 'characterized by much sulphur'.)

-st (also '-t')

Used on verbs only to form present or preterit verbs, 2nd pers. sing. nom. (used only with 'thou'). Eg., 'Dost', 'seest', 'saidst', 'hast' and 'wast'. (NOI. The verb 'didst' is the only exception, and is actually another form of the ending '-edst'.)

-t (see E. suffix '–ed')

-th

Used on verbs and adjectives to form abstract nouns of state or condition. Eg. 'Strength' and 'breadth'.

-tion (also '-ion', '-ation' and '-sion')

Changes a verb into a noun, which now shows a state or condition. Eg. 'Acceptation'(= 'the state or condition of accepting'), 'visitation' (= 'the state of visiting').

-ure (also '-our')

Used on pp. stem of verbs to form nouns that indicate the idea of a process, an action or the result of an action. Eg. 'Scripture', 'pleasure', 'saviour' and 'armour'.

-ward

Used on adverbs, nouns, prepositions and pronouns to indicate 'direction' or 'tendency'. Eg. 'Back' (adv.) > 'backward'; 'seat' > 'seatward'; 'on' (prep.) > 'onward; 'thee' (pronoun) > 'thee-ward'.

-y (also '-ey')

1. Means 'in the manner of' or 'having the characteristics of'. Eg. 'Crafty'.
2. Means 'very' or the idea of 'more'.

ABBREVIATIONS & PRONUNCIATIONS

Symbols, Abbreviations, and their Definitions, Used in this Dictionary:

1611 1611 Bible (first printing). The very first printed copies of the King James Bible were known as the 'He Bible' because the typesetters left off the 's' on 'she' in Rut.3:15. This was corrected in the second printing. (See section on 'How Did We Get The King James Bible?')

? Questionable. Used to indicate that some piece of information may or may not be accurate. Eg. A.D. 825(?).

A.D. Anno Domini. (Latin) 'In the year of our Lord' (i.e. 'counting from the year in which Christ was born').

adj. adjective. See section on Grammar ('Adjective').

adv. adverb. See section on Grammar ('Adverb').

AF. Anglo-French. From about A.D. 1066 – 1500. This was the French that was spoken in England. It also formed much of the legal language in England.

Ar. Arabic. The Arabic language.

ASG. Anglo-Saxon Gospels. A translation of the four gospels into the Wessex dialect of OE. in about A.D. 1000. Used as such 'A.D. 1000(ASG.)' means the word entry was first recorded in the English language by the Anglo-Saxon Gospels, along with other possible sources*.

ASP. Anglo-Saxon Psalms. A translation of fragments of the Psalms into the Wessex dialect of OE. in about A.D. 1000. Used as such 'A.D. 1000(ASP.)' means the word entry was first recorded in the English language by the Anglo-Saxon Psalms, along with other possible sources*.

AT. Aelfric Translation. Aelfric was a Catholic monk (A.D. 955 – A.D. 1020) who translated many Scriptures from L. into OE. Used as such, 'A.D.1000 (AT.)', means the word entry was first recorded in the English language by the Aelfric Translation, along with other possible sources*.

BB. Bishop's Bible. In A.D. 1568, Queen Elizabeth ascended the throne of England and later commissioned the bishops of the Church of England to translate the Scriptures into E., which was translated in A.D. 1568. Used as such, 'A.D. 1568(BB.)', means the word entry was first recorded in the English language by the Bishop's Bible.

B.C. Before Christ. I.E. before He was born into this world.

c. century.

CB. Coverdale Bible. A revision in A.D. 1535 by Miles Coverdale of Tyndale's New Testament (and portions of his Old Testament), as well as Luther's German Bible, the Swiss Bible and the Itala Bible. Used as such, 'A.D. 1535(CB.)', means the word entry was first recorded in the English language by the Coverdale Bible.

Celt. Celtic. A generic term for an ancient people who inhabited the central and western parts of Europe, having their greatest expansion in the 3rd c. BC. Their language was of the Indo-European family, and their dialects influenced, among others, Irish, Scottish, Gaelic, Welsh and Cornish.

cm. centimeters. One hundredth of a meter, or about 0.3937 of an inch.

conj. conjunction. See section on Grammar ('Conjunction').

Cp. Compare. (also written as cp.)

Du. Dutch. The Dutch language.

E. Modern English. From about A.D. 1500 – present (although some grammarians divide it into Early Modern (1500 – 1800) and Late Modern (1800 – present).

EG. Exempli gratia. (Latin) 'example given'. (also writ ten as eg.)

etc. et cetera. (Latin) 'and the rest' or 'and so forth'.

Fr. French. From about A.D. 1600 till present.

Frank. Frankish. West Germanic language of the Franks of Gaul from A.D. 400 – 800.

ft. foot or feet. As in '12 inches per foot' (30.48 cm.).

fut. future. As in 'future-tense'. See section on Grammar ('Verb – Tense')

gal. gallon or gallons. As in U.S. gallons

GB. Geneva Bible. Printed and re-printed from A.D. 1560–1644. Used as such, 'A.D. 1560(GB.)', means that the word entry was first recorded in the English language by the Geneva Bible. (NOI. This was the first English Bible on American soil.)

Ger. German. The German language.

Gk. Greek. (NT. Gk.) also known as 'Koine Greek' from about B.C. 300 – A.D. 100

Goth. Gothic. Language of the 'Goths' from about A.D. 300 – 500.

Hb. Hebrew. OT. Hebrew of the Masoretic Text, used from about A.D. 500 – 900.

HB. He Bible. The first printing of the 1611. Used as such, 'A.D.1611(HB.)', means that the word entry was first recorded in the English language by the 1611 Bible.

HP. Hampole Psalms. A translation of the Psalms into ME. by Richard Rolle (A.D. 1290 or 1300-1429), who lived in Hampole, near Doncaster, South Yorkshire, England. Used as such, 'A.D.1340(HP.)', means that the word entry was first recorded in the English language by Richard Rolle of Hampole in A.D. 1340., along with other possible sources*.

Ice. Icelandic. The language spoken in Iceland and

Greenland from about A.D. 900 – 1500.

I.E. *Id Est.* (Latin) = 'that is'. (also written as i.e.)

in. inch or inches. (2.54 cm.)

ind. indicative. I.E. 'pointing out something as factual'.

incl. including.

inf. infinitive. See section on Grammar ('Verb – Infinitive').

int. interjection. See section on Grammar ('Interjection').

intru. intrusive. Meaning a letter that has crept into a word (usually by poor pronunciation) that has no etymological reason. (Eg. see 'Advantage'.)

It. Italian. The Italian language.

kilo. kilograms. As in a weight of 1,000 grams per kilogram (0.45 lb.)

KJV King James Version. The King James Bible we use today underwent spelling changes in A.D. 1769, but it's basically the same Bible as the 1611 except there is no 'Apocrypha' in it. Distinction is made between the KJV and the 1611 for spelling and minor changes. The KJV used in this dictionary is the 'Cambridge', as opposed to the 'Oxford'. (See section entitled, 'Are there problems in the King James Bible?')

km. kilometer. As in a distance length of 1,000 meters (1100 yards).

L. Latin. Also known as 'Classical Latin' from about 100 B.C. – A.D. 200.

lb. libra. (Latin) = 'pound or pounds' (shortened form of *libra ponda* = 'pound of weight') As in a weight of 16 oz. per pound.

LfG. Lindisfarne Gospels. A translation of the gospels into Latin by a monk named Eadfrith, around A.D. 700, in a place called Lindisfarne (off the north east coast of England). Then, in about A.D. 950-1000, a word-for-word translation into OE. was added in between the lines by a man named Aldred. Used as such, 'A.D. 1000(LfG.)', means that the word entry was first recorded in the English language as a hand written marginal note of the Lindisfarne Gospels, along with other possible sources*.

LG. Low German. Languages spoken in the coastal and lowland regions of Germany from about A.D. 500 until present.

Lit. Literally (or literally). 'To be verbally exact, according to the letters of the original'.

LL. Late Latin. From about A.D. 200 – 500.

LP. Lambeth Psalter. A translation of the Psalms into Latin with a word-for-word OE. translation added in between the lines. Used as such, 'A.D.1000(LP.)', means that the word entry was first recorded in the English language in the Lambeth Psalter, along with other possible sources*.

LV. Latin Vulgate. A Latin translation of the OT., NT. and Apocrypha by Jerome in A.D. 390 and called *versio vulgata* = 'common translation'.

LXX. The Septuagint. The Greek translation of the OT. done in about the 3rd century B.C. Tradition says it was translated in Alexandria, Egypt, by 72 scholars in 72 days. *Septuaginta* is L. and means 'seventy'.

m. meter or meters. As in a length of 100 centimeters per meter.

ME. Middle English. From about A.D. 1066 – 1500.

MF. Middle French. From about A.D. 1400 – 1600.

mil. milliliters. As in 1/1000 of a liter.

ML. Medieval Latin. From A.D. 500 – 1500.

mm. millimeter. As in a length of 1/1000 of a meter.

n. noun. See section on Grammar ('Noun').

NOI. Note Of Interest. Sectioned by round brackets ( ) and points out something of interest concerning the word entry.

Nor. Norwegian. The language brought to England by the Vikings from about A.D. 1000 – 1300.

NT. New Testament. Comprising the 27 books from Matthew to Revelation.

obs. obsolete. Means the word is no longer in use.

OE. Old English. From about A.D. 450 – 1066.
OED. Oxford English Dictionary. See Bibliography in the back.
OF. Old French. From about A.D. 900 – 1400. (NOI. More than 90% of it was from L.)
OHG. Old High German. From about A.D. 800 – 1050.
OIr. Old Irish. From about A.D. 600 – 900
ON. Old Norse. From about A.D. 1150 – 1350.
oo. obscure origin. This means that the word cannot be traced to a definite root or source. In such cases, similar words in other languages are shown, if possible, and suggestions are made.
OS. Old Saxon. From about A.D. 700 – 1100. The earliest written form of Low German.
OT. Old Testament. Comprising the 39 books from Gene sis to Malachi (no Apocrypha).
oz. ounce. As in a weight of 1/16 of a pound (28.35 grams).
p. participle. (can be either pp. or prp.). See section on Grammar ('Verb – Participle').
pers. person. As in 1st person, 2nd person or 3rd person.
pg. page. (or pages).
pl. plural. 'Two or more', as opposed to singular.
pn. proper noun. A name designating a particular noun. See section on Grammar ('Noun').
pp. past participle. See section on Grammar ('Verb – Par ticiple').
prep. preposition. See section on Grammar ('Preposition').
pres. present. As in 'present-tense'. See section on Grammar ('Verb – Tense').
pret. preterit. See section on Grammar ('Verb – Tense').
pro. pronoun. See section on Grammar ('Pronoun').
prp. present participle. See section on Grammar ('Verb – Participle').
ps. postscript. The extra words added to the very end of some books of the Bible.
RG. Rushworth Gospels. A Latin translation of the four

gospels in about A.D. 821 by a monk named Macregol, with an OE. translation added between the lines in about A.D. 975 by two men (Farmen and Oweun). It went missing for the next 700 years until John Rushworth (A.D. 1659-1701) found it and gave it to the Bodleian Library in Oxford. Used as such 'A.D. 975 (RG.)', means the word entry was first recorded in the English language by the Rushworth Gospels, along with other possible sources*.

Rus. Russian. The Russian language.

Sans. Sanskrit. The classical Indian literary language from about 400 B.C.

sing. singular. As opposed to plural.

Teut. Teutonic. The earliest known language of the Germanic tribes beginning in about B.C. 400 and continuing till about A.D. 700.

TNT. Tyndale New Testament. Translated by Tyndale in A.D. 1525. Used as such, 'A.D. 1525(TNT.)', means the word entry was first recorded in the English language by Tyndale in his translation of the New Testament in A.D. 1525, or a later printing date.

tot. total. Indicates a total word count of the word being examined including all of its varied forms. It is put within the fancy brackets at the end of the section of a word entry. (Eg. {tot. = 11x.}). When this does not appear, it means that the word count right after the word entry is also the total count.

trans. transliteration. [A.D. 1861, < L. *translitera*, *trans* = 'to cross over' + *litera* = 'a letter'] Thus, **transliteration** means 'to change letters over into the corresponding letters of another alphabet'. Sometimes a word in Hebrew or Greek will be transliterated or 'sounded out' in English. This is true of proper names and some verbs. Such words are, for the most part, not found in this dictionary; however, brief reference is made to a few. For the purposes of this dictionary, only words directly from Hb. or Gk. into E. will have the 'trans.' notation.

v. verb. See section on Grammar ('Verb').

var. variation. A change or alteration of a word.

vbl.n. verbal noun. A noun expressing action. Eg. 'babbling'.

VL. Vulgar Latin. The Latin spoken by the everyday peo ple, rather than Classical Latin.

VP. Vespasian Psalter. A translation of the Psalms into Latin, written in Canterbury, England in A.D. 825, with OE. words written over top of the Latin words. Used as such, 'A.D. 825(VP.)', means the word entry was first recorded in the English language in the Vespasian Psalter of A.D. 825, along with other possible sources*.

vs. verse. A verse of the Bible, as in (vs. 23).

WB. Wycliffe Bible. A translation of the Latin Vulgate into English by Wycliffe. NT. finished in A. D. 1380 and entire Bible finished in A.D. 1382. Revised by Richard Purvey in A.D. 1388. Used as such, 'A.D. 1382(WB.)', or 'A.D. 1388(WB.)', means that the word entry was first recorded in the English language by the Wycliffe Bible of A.D.1382 or 1388.

x. times. The number of times a certain word is used in the KJV.

* Sometimes other documents (i.e. poems, stories, etc.) from this same time period will also have the word entry listed. In such cases, we have given preference to the Scriptural source first and have acknowledged the fact that there are probably other legitimate sources that have also recorded the word.

Pronunciation of certain Old English (OE.) letters

ǽ like the ‘a’ in ‘bat’

é like the ‘a’ in ‘fate’

í like the ‘e’ in ‘seed’

ó like the ‘o’ in ‘boat’

ð like the ‘th’ in ‘that’

Abbreviations For The Old Testament Books Of The Bible:

Gen.	Genesis	Ecc.	Ecclesiastes
Ex.	Exodus	SoS.	Song of Solomon
Lev.	Leviticus	Isa.	Isaiah
Num.	Numbers	Jer.	Jeremiah
Deut.	Deuteronomy	Lam.	Lamentations
Josh.	Joshua	Eze.	Ezekiel
Jud.	Judges	Dan.	Daniel
Rut.	Ruth	Hos.	Hosea
1Sam.	1 Samuel	Joe.	Joel
2Sam.	2 Samuel	Amo.	Amos
1Ki.	1 Kings	Oba.	Obadiah
2Ki.	2 Kings	Jon.	Jonah
1Chr.	1 Chronicles	Mic.	Micah
2Chr.	2 Chronicles	Nah.	Nahum
Ezr.	Ezra	Hab.	Habakkuk
Neh.	Nehemiah	Zep.	Zephaniah
Est.	Esther	Hag.	Haggai
Job.	Job	Zec.	Zechariah
Ps.	Psalms	Mal.	Malachi
Pr.	Proverbs		

Abbreviations For The New Testament Books Of The Bible:

Mt.	Matthew	1Tim.	1 Timothy
Mk.	Mark	2Tim.	2 Timothy
Lk.	Luke	Ti.	Titus
Jn.	John	Phi.	Philemon
Act.	Acts	Heb.	Hebrews
Rom.	Romans	Jam.	James
1Cor.	1 Corinthians	1Pt.	1 Peter
2Cor.	2 Corinthians	2Pt.	2 Peter
Gal.	Galatians	1Jn.	1 John
Eph.	Ephesians	2Jn.	2 John
Phil.	Philippians	3Jn.	3 John
Col.	Colossians	Jude.	Jude
1Ths.	1 Thessalonians	Rev.	Revelation
2Ths.	2 Thessalonians		

- Words in *italics* indicate quotes or words in other languages (other than OE., ME. and E.) such as Latin, Greek, etc.
- Words in **bold** indicate the KJV word entries, defined in this dictionary in alphabetical order.
- Words that are **bold and underlined** indicate the word entry (after its etymological explanation), followed by an easy-to-understand explanation.
- Root words in OE., ME. and E. are emboldened in the CasablancaAntique font.
- Words that are simply underlined indicate the author's emphasis.
- Square brackets [ ] follow the **bold** key word and give the detailed etymological explanation of the word.
- Rounded brackets ( ) indicate an alternative word or phrase to the one just mentioned, or a smaller explanation within a larger explanation.
- Fancy brackets { } always come at the end of an entry and indicate alternate variations of the word, as found in the KJV. The absence of these brackets indicates that there are no other variations.
- Single quotation marks ' ' are used to show 1) colloquialisms (informal phrases of speech), such as 'water off a duck's back'; 2) alternative words or definitions; 3) syllables; 4) root words, or 5) part of a root word, such as a prefix or suffix.
- Double quotation marks " " are used to show a precise quotation, such as "Come unto me, all ye that labour and are heavy laden,"; or a single word from a quote such as, "come".
- Three periods in a row, within a quote, indicate there are more words in the quote, but have been left out for the sake of brevity.

+	and or compounded with.
<	derived from (i.e. it comes from another root word).
>	becomes.
=	equivalent to.

WEIGHTS AND MEASURES

The following table is designed to give the approximate equivalents of the most usual measurements and, should not be taken as absolute science.

When you know:	Multiply By:	To Find:
inches	25.0	millimeters
feet	30.0	centimeters
yards	0.90	meters
miles	1.60	kilometers
centimeters	0.39	inches
meters	1.10	yards
kilometers	0.60	miles
ounces	28.0	grams
pounds	0.45	kilograms
grams	0.035	ounces
kilograms	2.20	pounds
fluid ounces	30.0	milliliters
pints, US	0.47	liters
pints, Imp.*	.568	liters
quarts, US	0.95	liters
quarts, Imp.*	1.137	liters
gallons, US	3.80	liters
gallons, Imp.*	4.54	liters
liters	2.10	pints, US
liters	1.76	pints, Imp.*
liters	1.06	quarts, US
liters	0.88	quarts, Imp.*
liters	0.26	gallons, US
liters	0.22	gallons, Imp.*

NOTE: Imp.* = "Imperial" and refers to the British unit of measure.

How To Read A Word-Entry

Many features have been added to each entry in this dictionary, but, in order to save space on the page, they are key-coded. Below is a typical word-entry with several key-codes. Let's examine each part of the entry so that we understand exactly what is being said.

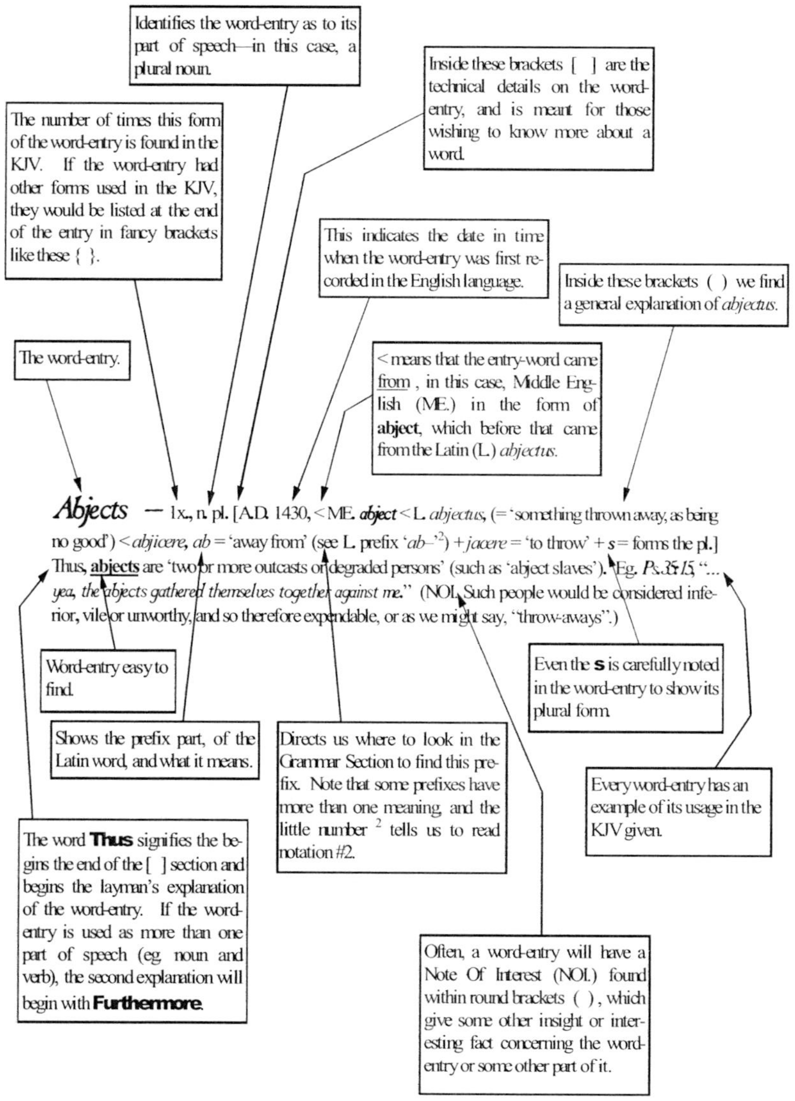

A

Abase – 4x., v. [A.D. 1393, < OF. *abaissier, a* = 'to' (see L. prefix '*ad–*') + *bassier* = 'lower' (Lit., it means a physical, forcible casting down or pressing down, but it is usually used in its figurative sense meaning to humble or degrade in position, dignity or rank.)] Thus, **abase** means 'the action of effectively making low'. Eg. Dan.4:37, "... those that walk in pride he is able to abase." (NOI. This is precisely what happened to King Nebuchadnezzar.) {abased 4x., abasing 1x., tot. = 9x.}

Abated – 6x., pp. [A.D. 1534, < E. **abate** (< OF. *abatre, a* = 'to' (see L. prefix '*ad–*') + *batre* = 'to beat' (i.e. 'to demolish or destroy with force' or 'to bring down or reduce in amount')) = 'to beat down' + **ed** = forms the pp. (see E. suffix '–ed'[3])] Thus, **abated** modifies its n. as 'having been knocked down or beaten down'. Eg. Gen.8:3, "... and after the end of the hundred and fifty days the waters were abated." Obviously, God did the 'abating' or the 'beating down' of the waters. This same power is seen in the life of Jesus Christ in Mk.4:39, "And he arose, and rebuked the wind, and said unto the sea, Peace, be still. And the wind ceased, and there was a great calm." (See also Ps.18:15.)

Abhor – 19x., v. [A.D. 1449, < L. *abhorrere, ab* = 'away from' (see L. prefix '*ab–*'[2]) + *horrere* = 'to shudder, bristle or shrink from'] Thus, **abhor** means 'the action of shrinking away from something (or someone) with a feeling of utter horror'; i.e. something repulsive. (The word involves a desperate feeling to get away from the source of the repugnance). Eg. Rom.12:9, "... Abhor that which is evil; cleave to that which is good." {abhorred 16x., abhorrest 2x., abhorreth 5x., abhorring 1x., tot. = 43x.}

Abide —82x., v. [A.D. 1000(LfG.), < OE. **abidan**, **a** = 'on' (see E. prefix 'a–'[1b]) + **bidan** = 'bide' (= 'to wait, remain, continue or dwell')] Thus, **abide** means 'the action of remaining and waiting for (even if it means enduring) until some means or an end'. There is a definite act of the will involved here. Eg. Ps.91:1, "He that dwelleth in the secret place of the most High shall abide under the shadow of the Almighty." {abideth 30x., abiding 9x., abode 69x., abodest 1x., tot. = 191x.}

Abjects —1x., n. pl. [A.D. 1430, < ME. **abject** (< L. *abjectus,* = 'something thrown away, as being no good' < *abjicere, ab* = 'away from' (see L. prefix '*ab–*'[2]) + *jacere* = 'to throw') + **s** = forms the pl.] Thus, **abjects** are 'two or more outcasts or degraded persons' (such as 'abject slaves'). Eg. Ps.35:15, "... yea, the abjects gathered themselves together against me." (NOI. Such people would be considered inferior, vile or unworthy, and so therefore expendable, or as we might say, "*garbage*".)

Abode — 69x., pp. and n. [A.D. 1250, < ME. **abide** (see 'Abide')] Thus, as a pp., **abode** modifies its n. as 'having stayed in or at someplace'. Eg. Jn.8:44, "Ye are of your father the devil, and the lusts of your father ye will do. He was a murderer from the beginning, and abode not in the truth, because there is no truth in him..." Furthermore, as a n., **abode** 'is the actual place where someone would stay'. Eg. Jn.14:23, "Jesus answered and said unto him, If a man love me, he will keep my words: and my Father will love him, and we will come unto him, and make our abode with him." (NOI. This appears to be the only time 'abode' is used as a n.) {abide 82x., abideth 30x., abiding 9x., abodest 1x., tot. = 191x.}

Abolish – 1x., v. [A.D. 1490, < F. *aboliss* < L. *abolere, ab* = 'away from' (see L. prefix '*ab–*'[2]) + *olere* = 'to grow or nourish'] Thus, **abolish** means 'the action of stopping the nourishing' (as in 'doing away with completely' or 'putting an end to something'). Eg. Isa.2:18, "And the idols he shall utterly abolish." {abolished 5x., tot. = 6x.}

Abominable – 23x., adj. [A.D. 1366, < F. *abominable* < L. *abominabilis* < *abominary, ab* = 'away from' (see L. prefix '*ab–*'[2]) + *ominari* = 'to forebode evil' (i.e. to sense something bad about to happen) (NOI. The L. *ominari* < *omen* = E. 'omen'. To the Greeks, 'omens' were signs of things to come and back then, like today, people tended to fear the future. An 'omen' was therefore something to be feared.)] Thus, **abominable** modifies its n. as being 'something that deserves intense aversion or abhorrence' (due to its evil nature). Eg. 2Chr.15:8, "... he took courage, and put away the abominable idols out of all the land of Judah and Benjamin..." {abominably 1x., abomination 76x., abominations 76x., tot. = 176x.}

Abomination – 76x., n. [A.D. 1325, < E. **abominable** (see 'Abominable') + **ation** = 'an action, process or state' (see E. suffix '–tion')] Thus, an **abomination** is 'the actual evil thing that is shunned' (such as a sinful practice, habit, person or thing). Eg. Deut.7:26, "Neither shalt thou bring an abomination into thine house, lest thou be a cursed thing like it: but thou shalt utterly detest it, and thou shalt utterly abhor it; for it is a cursed thing." (NOI. Whereas the adj. 'abominable' describes what a person, place or thing is like, the n. 'abomination' describes what he, she or it actually is. Consider also Pr.8:7.) {abominable 23x., abominably 1x., abominations 76x., tot. = 176x.}

Abound – 19x., v. [A.D. 1374, < OF. *abunder* < L. *abundare, ab* = 'away from' (see L. prefix '*ab–*'[2]) + *undare* = 'a rise of the waves to overflowing' (< *unda* = 'a wave')] Thus,

abound means 'the action of attaining a condition in which there is great plenty'. Eg. **Pr.28:20**, "A faithful man shall abound with blessings." (NOI. This word carries the similar idea as that found in **Ps.23:5**, "my cup runneth over.") {abounded 5x., aboundeth 3x., abounding 3x., abundance 68x., abundant 13x., abundantly 32x., tot. = 143x.}

About –632x., adv. and prep. [A.D. 880, < OE. **abutan** < **onbutan, on** = 'on' (see E. prefix 'a–'[1b]) + **butan** = 'outside or without'. (NOI. The original meaning of **onbutan** was 'around the outside of something', either all the way around, or part of the way around. Sometimes the KJV uses the words "round about" or "compassed about" in order to emphasize that the position was completely around (as in Josh.6:3). In other cases, it was understood by context that the completeness could be no other (as in Gen.41:42).)] Thus, as an adv., **about** modifies the action of the v. as 'happening on the outside' and qualifies this in one of two ways: **#1)** indicating an 'almost completion' of the v. Eg. Act.3:3, "Who seeing Peter and John about to go into the temple asked an alms."; or **#2)** indicating a 'full completion' of the v. Eg. Ecc.1:6, "The wind goeth toward the south, and turneth about unto the north; it whirleth about continually..." Furthermore, as a prep., **about** means 'on the outside' and qualifies the n. to which it is connected in one of two ways: **#1)** indicating an 'almost completion' of the n. Eg. Jud.8:10, "...about fifteen thousand men..." (Here, 'about' refers to an 'almost' nature of the word, rather than 'completely full' nature. So, in other words, there were a little less than 15,000 men.); **#2)** indicating a 'full completion' of the n. Eg. **Lk.2:49**, "... wist ye not that I must be about my Father's business? " Here, 'about' indicates that Christ was to encompass His Father's business completely.

Abroad – 80x., adv. [A.D. 1260, < OE. **a** = 'towards' (see E. prefix 'a–'[2]) + **broad** = 'wide'] Thus, **abroad** modifies its v. as 'happening on or over a wide area'. Eg. Neh.1:8,

"Remember, I beseech thee, the word that thou commandedst thy servant Moses, saying, If ye transgress, I will scatter you abroad among the nations." (NOI. The scattering of the Jews throughout the Middle East, and later throughout the world, gives ample meaning of 'abroad'.)

Abstain – 6x., v. [A.D. 1380, < OF. *abstenir* < L. *abstinere*, *abs* < *ab* = 'away from' (see L. prefix '*ab–*'[2]) + *tinere* = 'to hold'] Thus, **abstain** means 'the action of withholding or holding back from doing something'. (This NT. word refers chiefly to a persons own willpower to keep themselves from certain things or activities.) Eg. 1Ths.5:22, "Abstain from all appearance of evil," meaning that Christians are to hold themselves back from anything that has the appearance of evil. {abstinence 1x., tot. = 7x.}

Abuse – 3x., v. [A.D. 1413, < OF. *abuser* < L. *abuti*, *ab* = 'away from' (see L. prefix '*ab–*'[2]) + *uti* = 'use'] Thus, **abuse** means 'the action of using something in a manner which is 'away from' its proper usage' (i.e. 'to use improperly or misuse'). Eg. 1Cor.9:18, "What is my reward then? Verily that, when I preach the gospel, I may make the gospel of Christ without charge, that I abuse not my power in the gospel." {abused 1x., abusers 1x., abusing 1x., tot. = 6x.}

Accept – 25x., v. [A.D. 1360, < OF. *accepter* < L. *acceptare* < *accipere*, *ac* = 'to' (see L. prefix '*ad–*') + *cipere* < *capere* = 'to take'] Thus, **accept** means 'the action of taking or receiving something offered to one's self, with a consenting mind'. Eg. Pr.18:5, "It is not good to accept the person of the wicked, to overthrow the righteous in judgment." {acceptable 23x., acceptably 1x., acceptance 1x., acceptation 2x., accepted 29x., acceptest 1x., accepteth 4x., accepting 1x., tot. = 87x.}

Accomplish – 13x., v. [A.D. 1386, < OF. *acompliss* < LL. *accomplere*, *ac* = 'to' (see L. prefix '*ad–*') + *complere* = 'to fill up, or complete'] Thus, **accomplish** means 'the action of fully realizing or achieving an intended purpose'. Eg. Isa.55:11, "So shall my word be that goeth forth out of my mouth: it shall not return unto me void, but it shall accomplish that which I please, and it shall prosper in the thing whereto I sent it." {accomplished 26x., accomplishing 1x., accomplishment 1x., tot. = 41x.}

Accord –16x., v. [A.D. 1123, < OF. *acorder* < LL. *accordare*, *ac* = 'to' (see L. prefix '*ad–*') + *cordare* (< L. *cor*) = 'heart' (NOI. L. *cor* (heart) is found in many E. words such as 'cordial' = close to the heart; 'discord' = away from the heart; and 'record' = repeat by heart)] Thus, **accord** means 'the action of bringing heart-to-heart' (as in agreeing, reconciling or harmonizing. Hence, there is a mental and emotional bonding together.). Eg. Act.1:14, "These all continued with one accord in prayer and supplication, with the women, and Mary the mother of Jesus, and with his brethren." (See also 'Concord' and 'Discord'.) {according 793 x., accordingly 1x., tot. = 810x.}

Account [1] –2x., v. [A.D. 1303, < OF. *aconter* < L. *accomptare*, *ac* = 'to' (see L. prefix '*ad–*') + *comptare* (< L. *com* = 'together or with' (see L. prefix '*co–*') + *putare* = 'to reckon') = 'to calculate'] Thus, **account** means 'the action of a careful calculating in order to arrive at the correct answer or result'. Eg. 2Pt.3:15, "And account that the longsuffering of our Lord is salvation..." (NOI. **Account** is a different verb from 'count'. The first deals with an official financial reckoning, whereas the second is simply a process of 'counting up'. See 'Count'.) {accounted 12x., accounting 1x., tot. = 15x.}

Account [2] –15x., n. [A.D. 1260, < OF. *acont, a* = 'to' (< L. *ad*, see L. prefix '*ad–*') + *cont* (< L. *computum*) = 'a calculation'] Thus, an **account** is 'a thing which is calculated (such as a charge-account) in which purchases are made and paid for later'. Eg. Phi.1:18, "If he hath wronged thee, or oweth thee ought, put that on mine account." {accounts 1x., tot. = 16x.}

Accursed —20x., p. [A.D. 1220, < E. **accurse** (< OE. **acursian, a** = 'an intensity' (see E. prefix 'a–'[1b]) + **cursian** (< **curs** = 'a curse' + **ian** = 'the action of') = 'to curse') = 'an intensive curse' + **ed** = forms the p. (see E. suffix '–ed'[3]). Although this word's origins are obscure, one source suggests it has a root to L. *corruptus* = 'corrupt'] Thus, **accursed** modifies its n. as 'being in a state or condition of intense corruption'; i.e. the opposite of blessed. In other words, the presence and power of God (and His benefits) are taken away from a situation or person's life. Therefore, one might say that 'accursed' means the absence of God and His blessings, which will result in a state of corruption. Eg. Gal.1:8, "But though we, or an angel from heaven, preach any other gospel unto you than that which we have preached unto you, let him be accursed." {curse 101x., cursed 72x., cursedst 2x., curses 8x., cursest 1x., curseth 10x., cursing 12x., cursings 1x tot. = 227x.}

Accuse —16x., v. [A.D. 1297, < OF. *acuser* < L. *accausare, ac* = 'to' (see L. prefix '*ad*–') + *causare* = 'cause or reason'] Thus, **accuse** means 'the action of charging with sin, fault or blame'. Eg. Mk.3:2, "And they watched him, whether he would heal him on the sabbath day; that they might accuse him." (NOI. Rev.12:10 refers to Satan as the "accuser of our brethren" because he charges us with 'sin and blame' to the Heavenly Father.) {accusation 10x., accused 14x., accuser 1x., accusers 8x., accuseth 1x., accusing 1x., tot. = 51x.}

Aceldama —1x., pn. [A.D. 1382(WB.), trans. < Gk. ακελδαμα (*aceldama*) = 'field of blood'] Thus, **aceldama** is 'a name meaning field-of-blood'. Eg. Act.1:19, "And it was known unto all the dwellers at Jerusalem; insomuch as that field is called in their proper tongue, Aceldama, that is to say, The field of blood." (NOI. This was the name of a parcel of land, purchased with the 'blood-money' relinquished by Judas Iscariot after he betrayed Jesus.)

Acknowledge –16x., v. [A.D. 1481, < E. **ac** = 'to' (= L. *ac*, see L. prefix '*ad–*') + **knowledge** < obs. **aknow** = 'to admit or confess' (see also 'Know')] Thus, **acknowledge** means 'the action of a very intensive admission concerning something as being true'. Eg. **Ps.51:3**, "**For I acknowledge my transgressions: and my sin is ever before me.**" (Cp. Pr.3:6.) {acknowledged 3x., acknowledgement 1x., acknowledgeth 1x., acknowledging 3x., tot. = 24x.}

Acquaint – 1x., v. [A.D. 1297, < OF. *acointer* < L. *adcognitare*, *ad* = 'to' (see L. prefix '*ad–*') + *cognitare* = 'to make known'] Thus, **acquaint** means 'the action of making or becoming closely familiar with someone or something'. Eg. **Job.22:21**, "**Acquaint now thyself with him, and be at peace: thereby good shall come unto thee.**" (NOI. Although Job already knew the Lord, yet he was to come to know Him in a much greater way by the end of the story.) {acquaintance 11x., acquainted 2x., acquainting 1x., tot. = 15x.}

Acquit –2x., v. [A.D. 1230, < OF. *aquiter* < LL. *acquitare*, *ac* = 'to' (see L. prefix '*ad–*') + *quitare* = 'to settle or make quiet', *quies* = 'rest, quiet'] Thus, **acquit** means 'the action of appeasing or settling a creditor or claimant' (i.e. 'to discharge a debt or liability', or 'to free or clear from an accusation'). Eg. **Nah.1:3**, "**The LORD is slow to anger, and great in power, and will not at all acquit the wicked...**" (NOI. 'Acquit' is only used twice in the KJV, yet both times it deals with the debt-load of sin.)

Acre –1x., n. [A.D. 975, < ME. **aker** < OE. **ǽcer** < oo., (akin to ON. *akr*, OHG. *achar*, OS. *akkar*; all = 'a field, or pasture land'). (NOI. At the time of the Norman Conquest (A.D. 1066), an **acre** was a measure of land equal to what a yoke of oxen could plow in a day. Over the following centuries, because one man's oxen could plow more than another's, an acre was set at 4,840 square yards (or 160 square rods, where 1 rod = 16.5 ft., or 5.03 m.) by Kings Edward I, Edward III and Henry VIII, which is what it was in the 1611, and is still in use today.)] Thus, an **acre** is 'an area of field or pastureland equal to 4,840 square yards' (or 4,046.8 square m., or 43,560 square ft.). Eg. 1Sam.14:14, "And that first slaughter, which Jonathan and his armourbearer made, was about twenty men, within as it were an half acre of land, which a yoke of oxen might plow." {acres 1x., tot. = 2x.}

Adamant – 2x., adj. and n. [A.D. 885, < OF. *adamaunt* < L. *adamas* < Gk. αδαμας (*adamas*) = 'invincible', < αδαμαώ (*adamao*) = 'unconquerable', α (*a*) = 'not' (see Gk. prefix '*a*–') + δαμαώ (*damao*) = 'I conquer' or 'I tame'] Thus, as an adj., **adamant** modifies its n. as 'being unconquerable, invincible or indestructible'. Eg. Zec.7:12, "Yea, they made their hearts as an adamant stone..." (NOI. Figuratively, 'adamant' refers to someone being stubborn or inflexible to the demands or requests of another.) Furthermore, as a n., **adamant** is 'something hard, invincible or indestructible'. Eg. Eze.3:9, "As an adamant harder than flint have I made thy forehead..." (NOI. 'Adamant' came to be applied to the hardest of stones (such as a diamond) or metals.)

Adder – 4x., n. [A.D. 950, < ME. addre < OE. nǽdre < oo., (akin to ON. *nathr*, OHG. *natara*, OS. *nadra*; all = 'snake or serpent') (NOI. In OE., it was pronounced 'nadder', similar to the other languages, but as people would say, "*a nadder*", they would slur it to "*an adder*"; hence the 'n' was dropped off the word.)] Thus, an **adder** is 'a poisonous snake or serpent'. Eg. Gen.49:17, "Dan shall be a serpent by the way, an adder in the path..." (NOI. The 1611 marginal note says "*an arrow-snake*", and Ps.58:4 refers to the adder as being deaf.) {adders' 1x., tot. = 5x.}

Addicted – 1x., pp. [A.D. 1534, < E. **addict** (< L. *addictus*, *ad* = 'to' (see L. prefix '*ad–*') + *dictus* = 'to sign-over by decree' (< L. *dico* = 'to say')) = 'to intently sign over by decree' + **ed** = forms the pp. (see E. suffix '–ed'[3])] Thus, **addicted** modifies its n. (in this case, 'they') as 'having been given or delivered over, in an intense manner'. Eg. 1Cor.16:15, "I beseech you, brethren, (ye know the house of Stephanas, that it is the firstfruits of Achaia, and that they have addicted themselves to the ministry of the saints)." (NOI. The archaic usage means to be 'attached to something by ones own willpower'.)

Adjure –5x., v. [A.D. 1382(WB.), < Fr. *adjurer* < L. *adjurare*, *ad* = 'to' (see L. prefix '*ad–*') + *jurare* = 'to swear' (NOI. Our E. word 'jury' is also from L. *jurare*, and means 'a body of persons, summoned to serve on a judicial tribunal, sworn under oath to give a true verdict according to their understanding of the evidence'. An 'oath' is an appeal to bind someone before God, or something holy, that they bear witness to the truth, or promise to do something. See 'Oath'.)] Thus, **adjure** means 'the action of forcing an oath upon another person', in order to bring about a state of truth or justice. Eg. 2Chr.18:15, "And the king said to him, How many times shall I adjure thee that thou say nothing but the truth to me in the name of the LORD? " (NOI. A similar idea is also seen in 1Sam.14:28, "...Thy father straitly charged the people with an oath...") {adjured 2x., tot. = 7x.}

Administration – 1x., n. [A.D. 1315, < E. **administer** (< OF. *aministrer* < L. *administrare*, *ad* = 'to' (see L. prefix '*ad–*') + *ministrare* = 'to serve' (from which also we also get our E. word 'minister')) = 'an intensive service' (of the managing of affairs) + **ation** = 'an action, process or state' (see E. suffix '–tion')] Thus, an **administration** is 'the overall proper execution of the managing of affairs'. Eg. 2Cor.9:12, "For the administration of this service not only supplieth the want of the saints, but is abundant also by many thanksgivings unto

God." {administered 2x., and administrations 1x., tot. = 4x.}

Admiration –2x., n. [A.D. 1490, < E. **admire** (< L. *admirari*, *ad* = 'to' (see L. prefix '*ad–*') + *mirari* = 'wonder'; hence 'to wonder at' (NOI. Our E. word 'mirror' also comes from L. *mirari*.)) + **ation** = 'action, process or state' (see E. suffix '–tion')] Thus, **admiration** is 'the state of wondering at something or someone'. Eg. Rev.17:6, "And I saw the woman drunken with the blood of the saints, and with the blood of the martyrs of Jesus: and when I saw her, I wondered with great admiration." (NOI. When the Apostle John saw the Mother of Harlots sitting on the beast, his 'admiration' does not suggest approval, but rather the idea of, "What could this be??") {admired 1x., tot. = 3x.}

Admonish –3x., v. [A.D. 1325, < OF. *amonester* < L. *admonere*, *ad* = 'to' (see L. prefix '*ad–*') + *monere* = 'to remind or warn'] Thus, **admonish** means 'the action of calling to mind in an intensive way' (as in 'giving authoritative counsel against wrongdoing'). Eg. 1Ths.5:12, "And we beseech you, brethren, to know them which labour among you, and are over you in the Lord, and admonish you." {admonished 5x., admonishing 1x., admonition 3x., tot. = 12x.}

Ado – 1x., n. [A.D. 1280, (originally 2 words) < ME. **to do**, < ON. *at do* = 'doing activity, fuss or trouble'] Thus, **ado** is 'a state or condition of troublesome activity'. Eg. Mk.5:39, "And when he was come in, he saith unto them, Why make ye this ado, and weep? the damsel is not dead, but sleepeth."

Adoption –5x., n. [A.D. 1382(WB.), < E. **adopt** (< F. *adopter* < L. *adoptare*, *ad* = 'to' (see L. prefix '*ad–*') + *optare* = 'to choose') = 'to make a careful choice' (i.e. for oneself, especially a child, but it can also refer to adopting things, or even a new lifestyle. Personal preference over what is to be adopted is the governing factor here.) + **tion** = 'an action, process or state' (see E. suffix '–tion')] Thus, an **adoption** is 'the condition of being carefully chosen'. Eg. Eph.1:5, "Having predestinated us unto the adoption of children by Jesus Christ to himself, according to the good pleasure of his will."

Adorn –2x., v. [A.D. 1374, < OF. *adorner* < L. *adornare, ad* = 'to' (see L. prefix '*ad–*') + *ornare* = 'to equip or furnish' or 'to deck out' (NOI. We get our E. word 'ornate' from L. *ornare.*)] Thus, **adorn** means 'the action of making more beautiful by adding ornaments' (to embellish). Eg. Ti.2:10, "Not purloining, but shewing all good fidelity; that they may adorn the doctrine of God our Saviour in all things."

Adria – 1x pn. [A.D. 1525(TNT.), trans. < Gk. Αδριας (*Adrias*) < αδριατικ (*adriatic*) = 'without wood' (NOI. 'Adria' may have been named after the northern Italian city of Atria.)] Thus, **Adria** is 'the name (meaning 'without wood') of a body of sea water', where the apostle Paul's ship was lost at sea. Eg. Act.27:27, "But when the fourteenth night was come, as we were driven up and down in Adria, about midnight the shipmen deemed that they drew near to some country."

Adultery – 40x., n. [A.D. 1366, < L. *adulterium* < *adultery* (= 'mixed, impure'), *ad* = 'to' (see L. prefix '*ad–*') + *ulter* = 'other' (NOI. An 'adulterer' is one who goes and joins himself to a person other than his proper mate)] Thus, **adultery** is 'the finished act of an adulterer'; i.e. what the adulterer does (as in voluntary sexual relations involving a married person with someone other than their lawful spouse). Eg. Ex.20:14, "Thou shalt not commit adultery." (NOI. The word 'adultery' is sometimes used in the Bible to illustrate the spiritual act of 'idolatry', i.e. 'leaving God and joining one's heart with an idol'.) {adulterer 3x., adulterers 9x., adulteress 5x., adulteresses 3x., adulteries 5x., adulterous 4x., tot. = 69x.}

Advantage –4x., n. [A.D. 1330, (with intru. '**d** ') < OF. *avan-*

tage < OF. *avant* (= 'before or forward', i.e. 'ahead' (< LL. *abante*, *ab* = 'from' + *ante* = 'before')) + *age* = 'that which pertains to its root' (same as E. 'age', see E. suffix '–age')] Thus, **advantage** is 'the condition of being ahead of something or someone, and the things pertaining to it' (i.e. a position of superiority). Eg. 2Cor.2:11, "Lest Satan should get an advantage of us: for we are not ignorant of his devices." {advantaged 1x., advantageth 1x., tot. = 6x.}

Adventure —2x., v. [A.D. 1230, < OF. *aventure* < L. *advenire*, *ad* = 'to' (see L. prefix '*ad–*') + *venire* = 'to come' (NOI. E. 'advent' is also < L. *advenire*, which we use in reference to Christ's first and second coming or 'advent'.)] Thus, **adventure** means 'the action of exposing oneself to peril'; i.e. to run the risk or chance the loss (akin to the idea of 'to venture' oneself). Eg. Act.19:31, "And certain of the chief of Asia, which were his friends, sent unto him, desiring him that he would not adventure himself into the theatre." Here, Paul's disciples did not want him to run the risk of injury by entering the theatre. {adventured 1x., tot. = 3x.}

Adversary —22x., n. [A.D. 1330, < L. *adversarius* < L. *adversus* = 'turned towards or against' (< L. *advertere, ad* = 'to' (see L. prefix '*ad–*') + *vertere* = 'to turn')] Thus, an **adversary** is 'someone who has turned against you and has become an opponent or an antagonist'. Eg. Ex.23:22, "But if thou shalt indeed obey his voice, and do all that I speak; then I will be an enemy unto thine enemies, and an adversary unto thine adversaries." {adversaries 36x., tot. = 58x.}

Adversity —10x., n. [A.D. 1230, < OF. *aversite* < L. *adversitas* < L. *adversus* (= 'to turn against', or 'to be opposed to something or someone'.) < L. *advertere, ad* = 'to' (see L. prefix '*ad–*') + *vertere* = 'to turn' (NOI. From L. *advertere* we get our E. word 'advert' = to 'turn the attention' or to 'take notice'.)] Thus, **adversity** is 'the condition of being opposed, usually involving hardship or affliction'. Eg. Pr.17:17, "A friend loveth at all times, and a brother is born for adversity." {adversities 2x., tot. = 12x.}

Advertise – 2x., v. [A.D. 1430, < OF. *advertir* or *advertis* (= 'to inform or warn or give notice') < L. *advertere* (see 'Adversity') (NOI. Originally, 'advertise' was just another form of 'advert' (see 'Adversity'), (probably because of the OF. '*advertissement*') but over the years, 'advert' continued to follow the usual sense of L. *advertere* while 'advertise' followed more the sense of OF. *advertises.*)] Thus, **advertise** means 'the action of taking notice of something or giving heed to something'. Eg. Num.24:14, "And now, behold, I go unto my people: come therefore, and I will advertise thee what this people shall do to thy people in the latter days."

Advise – 3x., v. [A.D. 1297, < OF. *aviser* < L. *advisere, ad* = 'to' (see L. prefix '*ad–*') + *visere* = 'to look at' (< L. *videre* = 'to see')] Thus, **advise** means 'the action of looking at, viewing or instructing'. Eg. 2Sam.24:13, "So Gad came to David, and told him... now advise, and see what answer I shall return to him that sent me." (NOI. Notice the words, 'advise' and 'see' are put together, thereby strengthening the meaning of 'advise'.) {advised 2x., advisement 1x., tot. = 6x.}

Advocate – 1x., n. [A.D. 1340, < OF. *avocat* < L. *advocare, ad* = 'to' (see L. prefix '*ad–*') + *vocare* = 'to call' (NOI. Cp. also 'Convocation' and 'Provoke'.)] Thus, an **advocate** is 'a person who is called or summoned in to defend or speak on behalf of another person'. Eg. 1Jn.2:1, "My little children, these things write I unto you, that ye sin not. And if any man sin, we have an advocate with the Father, Jesus Christ the righteous." Here, Christ, the Advocate in heaven, speaks on behalf of Christians to the Father, and defends them as His property. (NOI. The now obs. E. word 'avowee' used to refer to a person whose job it was to defend the rights and properties of the church.)

Afar –51x., adv. [A.D. 1175, < E. **a** = 'motion onward' (see E. prefix 'a–'[1a]) + **far** < OE. **feor** (akin to Gk. περαν (*peran*) = 'beyond or further')] Thus, **afar** modifies its v. as 'happening far away or in a remote place'. Eg. Pr.31:14, "She is like the merchants' ships; she bringeth her food from afar." (NOI. In the KJV, this is most often expressed as 'afar off'.) {far 173x., tot. = 224x.}

Affect – 2x., v. [A.D. 1374, < Fr. *affecter* < L. *afficere, af* = 'to' (see L. prefix '*ad*–') + *facere* = 'to make or do' (NOI. Our E. word 'facility' (= 'ease or readiness in doing') comes from the L. root *facere*.)] Thus, **affect** means 'the action of aiming at, or aspiring to do something with the intent of having an influence upon'. Eg. Gal.4:17. "They zealously affect you, but not well; yea, they would exclude you, that ye might affect them." (NOI. This action word almost attacks, similar to how a disease attacks the body, or how a medicine attacks the disease. 'Affect' and 'effect' are not the same words, as the first is the action while the second is the result. See 'Effect'.) {affected 2x., affecteth 1x., tot. = 5x.}

Affection –6x., n. [A.D. 1230, < E. **affect** (see 'Affect') + **tion** = 'an action, process or state' (see E. suffix '–tion')] Thus, **affection** is 'the state or area in which one may be affected'. Eg. Col.3:2, "Set your affection on things above, not on things on the earth." (NOI. The KJV uses the word 'affection' in relation to a persons mind and emotions, which can be 'affected' by things of this world or the things of heaven.) {affectionately 1x., affectioned 1x., affections 2x., tot. = 10x.}

Affinity – 3x., n. [A.D. 1303, < Fr. *afinite* < L. *affinis, af* = 'to' (see L. prefix '*ad*–') + *finis* = 'end' (or lit., 'to the end')] Thus, an **affinity** is 'a social relationship of voluntary nature, involving a commitment to the end'. Eg. Ezr.9:14,

"Should we again break thy commandments, and join in affinity with the people of these abominations?..."

Affirm —3x., v. [A.D. 1330, < OF. *afermer* < L. *affirmare*, *af* = 'to' (see L. prefix '*ad–*') + *firmare* = 'to make firm' (< L. *firmus* = 'strong')] Thus, **affirm** means 'the action of an intense firming up and making strong'. Eg. Ti.3:8, "... these things I will that thou affirm constantly..." {affirmed 3x., tot. = 6x.}

Afflict —36x., v. [A.D. 1393, < L. *afflictus* < *affligere* (= 'to strike against' or 'to knock down') *af* = 'to' (see L. prefix '*ad–*') + *fligere* = 'strike or dash'] Thus, **afflict** means 'the action of overthrowing or striking down' (i.e. to cause pain either mentally or physically). Eg. Jud.16:19, "And she made him sleep upon her knees; and she called for a man, and she caused him to shave off the seven locks of his head; and she began to afflict him, and his strength went from him." {afflicted (incl. title of Ps.102) 55x., afflictest 1x., affliction 75x., afflictions 13x., tot. = 180x.}

Affliction —75x., n. [A.D. 1485, < E. **afflict** = 'to strike down mentally or physically' (see 'Afflict') + **ion** = 'an action, process or state' (see E. suffix '–tion')] Thus, an **affliction** is 'the condition of pain or discomfort', either physical or mental. Eg. Act.7:34, "I have seen, I have seen the affliction of my people which is in Egypt, and I have heard their groaning, and am come down to deliver them. And now come, I will send thee into Egypt." (NOI. 'Affliction' is also used to speak of a physical illness, from mild to severe, yet where the afflicted person is not confined to bed. See also 'Disease', Murrain', 'Sickness' and 'Weak'.) {afflict 36x., afflicted (incl. title of Ps.102) 55x., afflictest 1x., afflictions 13x., tot. = 180x.}

Affright —1x., v. [A.D. 1000(LfG.), < OE. **afyrhtan**, **a** = an intensity (see E. prefix 'a–'[1b]) + **fyrhtan** = 'frighten' (= 'to throw into terror')] Thus, **affright** means 'the intense action of affecting through sudden fear', usually for the purpose of gaining a mastery over. Eg. 2Chr.32:18, "Then they cried with a loud voice in the Jews' speech unto the people of Jerusalem that were on the wall, to affright them, and to trouble them; that they might take the city." {affrighted 9x., tot. = 10x.}

Afore —7x., adv., conj. and prep. [A.D. 898, < OE. **onforan, on** = 'a motion away from' (see E. prefix 'a–'[1a]) + **foran** = 'in front'] Thus, as an adv., **afore** modifies the action of the v. as 'being performed away out front of something in time or space'. Eg. Eph.3:3, "...as I wrote afore in few words." Furthermore, as a conj., **afore** joins words or phrases in a sentence, 'indicating a time-frame of well before'. Eg. 2Ki.20:4, "And it came to pass, afore Isaiah was gone out into the middle court..." Finally, as a prep. **afore** shows the relationship of a n., pn. or pro. to another word or phrase in the sentence as 'being away out front in terms of time and space'. Eg. Isa.18:5, "For afore the harvest, when the bud is perfect, and the sour grape is ripening in the flower, he shall both cut off the sprigs with pruning hooks, and take away and cut down the branches." (NOI. There is a difference between 'afore' and 'before', the latter being more 'directly in front of', i.e. 'right before'. These days, 'afore' has fallen into disuse, but it is still used in nautical terminology.) {aforehand 1x., aforetime 7x., tot. = 15x.}

Aforehand — 1x.adv. [A.D. 1430, < E. **afore** (see 'Afore') + **hand** (< OE. **hond**, akin to ON. *henda* = 'to catch' (the hand being the instrument of grasping))] Thus, **aforehand** modifies the action of the v. (in this case, 'is come') as 'being done well in advance'. Eg. Mk.14:8 , "... she is come aforehand to anoint my body to the burying." In this case, Christ's burying wasn't that same day (if it was, then 'beforehand' would have been used) but it was far enough away to say 'aforehand'. (NOI. 'Hand' became used in a variety of ways to convey the idea of something being 'close by' especially to one's body, although it is often used in a figurative sense. Eg. **Rom.13:12**, "**The night is far spent, the day is at hand...**") {afore 7x., aforetime 7x., tot. = 15x.}

Afraid – 193x. p. [A.D. 1330, < ME. **affray** < AF. *effrayer* < LL. *exfridare*, *ex* = 'out of' (see L. prefix '*ex*–') + *fridus* = 'peace'] Thus, **afraid** modifies its n., pro. or pn. as 'having no peace', or 'having run out of peace'. Eg. **Gen.3:10**, "**... I was afraid, because I was naked; and I hid myself.**" (NOI. Adam had no peace after he had sinned. See also 'Peace'. There is no peace saith my God to this wicked) {fear 400x., feared 74x., fearest 3x., feareth 20x., fearful 11x., fearfully 1x., fearfulness 3x., fearing 8x., fears 4x., tot. = 717x.}

Afresh – 1x adv. [A.D. 1509, < E. **a** = 'towards' (see E. prefix 'a–'[2]) + **fresh** (< OF. *freschir* < It. *fresco* = 'fresh, cool')] Thus, **afresh** modifies the action of the v. (in this case, 'crucify') as 'being like a new start or a new beginning'. Eg. **Heb.6:6**, "**... seeing they crucify to themselves the Son of God afresh, and put him to an open shame.**" (NOI. 'Afresh' is different from 'refresh'. The first speaks of something new, whereas the second speaks of 'freshening-up' an existing thing.)

Afterward – 66x., adv. [A.D. 1000(AT.), < E. **after** (< OE. **ǽftera** = 'hinder, rear, later or following') + **ward** = shows 'direction or tendency' (see E. suffix '–ward')] Thus, **afterward** modifies the action of the v. as 'being in the direction of after'; i.e. subsequent to. Eg. **Mt.4:2**, "**And when he had fasted forty days and forty nights, he was afterward an hungred.**" {after 1180x., (incl. title of Ps.51) afterwards 13x., hereafter 14x., tot. = 1,273x.}

Again – 672x., adv. [A.D. 894, < OE. **ongegn**, **on** = 'on or in' + **gegn** = 'towards or direct' (Therefore, **ongegn** = 'opposite' as in a direct line facing, but came to mean every idea of 'repetition, reversal or recurrence')] Thus, **again** modifies the action of the v. as 'coming at it once more'; i.e. happening a second time. Eg. Jn.3:7, "Marvel not that I said unto thee, Ye must be born again."

Against – 1667x., prep. [A.D. 1154, < OE. **agenes** (having the adverbial genitive ending **–es** and then later with an intru. **t**) = 'to stand in opposition to' (see 'Again') (NOI. 'Against' is an extended form of 'again'. It's easy to see the transition from 'again' to 'against'.)] Thus, **against** shows the relationship of a n., pro. or pn. to another word or phrase in the sentence as 'being in opposition to it, or in contradiction of it'. Eg. Gen.4:8, "... Cain rose up against Abel his brother, and slew him."

Agate – 3x., n. [A.D. 1570, < F. *agate* < L. *achates* < Gk. Αχατης (*Achates*) (= the name of a river in Sicily)] Thus, an **agate** is 'a precious quartz stone, with various stripes or bands of color through it, often in squiggly directions'. Eg. Ex.28:19, "And the third row a ligure, an agate, and an amethyst." (NOI. There are many different types of agate stones according to their colorful appearance. Hence, 'moss' agate, 'ribbon' agate, 'eye' agate, etc.) {agates 1x., tot. = 4x.}

Agone – 1x., pp [A.D. 1314, < E. **a** (see E. prefix 'a–'[1a]) + **gone** (pp. of the v. 'go') = 'lost or hopeless'] Thus, **agone** modifies its n. (in this case, 'three days') as 'being hopelessly lost over the shoulder of time, and never to be retrieved'. Eg. 1Sam.30:13, "And David said unto him, To whom belongest thou? and whence art thou? And he said, I am a young man of Egypt, servant to an Amalekite; and my master left me, because three days agone I fell sick." (NOI. Cp. 1Sam.9:20, "... three days ago... ," and 1Sam.30:13, "...three days agone..." 'Ago' implies the simple idea of time past, whereas 'agone' carries the idea of a sense of loss, as in 'lost and gone forever'. This seems to be the heart's cry of the young Egyptian servant who lamented the loss of three days.)

Agony – 1x., n. [A.D. 1382(WB.), < Gk. αγονια (*agonia*) < αγον (*agon*) = 'a contest'. (NOI. The Gk. word αγον (*agon*) originally meant 'an assembly of people', but soon became applied to the Greek Olympic games with its various competitions. Soon, αγον came to mean a 'contest'. A contestant in the games became known as an αγονια (our Gk. root word for 'agony'.) Each contestant would then struggle against an opponent, with all his might, for victory and to win the prize. The opponent of an αγονια became known as an αντιγονιστης (*antigonist*), using the prefix αντι (anti) = 'against'. This is where we get our E. word 'antagonist'. Therefore, αγονια came to mean 'a contestant under great stress and struggle'. The E. word 'agony' was an invention by Wycliffe.)] Thus, **agony** is 'the condition of a tremendous struggle'. Eg. Lk.22:44, "And being in an agony he prayed more earnestly: and his sweat was as it were great drops of blood falling down to the ground."

Agree – 7x., v. [A.D. 1366, < OF. *agreer* < It. *aggradare* < LL. *adgratare*, *ad* = 'to' (see L. prefix '*ad*–') + *gratare* = 'to make pleasing'] Thus, **agree** means 'the action of regarding with favor, or the action of pleasing'. Eg. Mt.18:19, "... if two of you shall agree on earth as touching any thing that they shall ask, it shall be done for them of my Father which is in heaven." {agreed 8x., agreement 6x., agreeth 2x., tot. = 23x.}

Agreement –6x., n. [A.D. 1398, < E. **agree** (see 'Agree') + **ment** = forms the n. (see E. suffix '–ment')] Thus, an **agreement** is 'a contract or state of mutual pleasing concerning the behavior and responsibilities of all involved'. Eg. Isa.36:16, "Hearken not to Hezekiah: for thus saith the king of Assyria, Make an agreement with me by a present, and come out to me: and eat ye every one of his vine, and every one of his fig tree, and drink ye every one the waters of his own cistern." (NOI. An 'agreement' and a 'covenant' are basically the same; however, a covenant tends to involve God and His plans, whereas an agreement is between people. See 'Covenant'.)

Ague – 1x., n. [A.D. 1377, < OF. *ague* < L. *acuta* = 'sharp' (used in Latin to refer to a 'sharp fever')] Thus, an **ague** is 'an acute, burning fever-sickness', similar to malaria with its burning-sweat/shivering-cold stages. Eg. Lev.26:16, "... I will even appoint over you terror, consumption, and the burning ague, that shall consume the eyes, and cause sorrow of heart..."

Ah – 18x., int. [A.D. 1280, < ME. **a** possibly < OF. *ah* = 'an expression of sorrow or false sorrow', usually followed by an expression mark (!)] Thus, **ah** is 'an emotional expression of sorrow'. Eg. Jer.22:18, "... They shall not lament for him, saying, Ah my brother! or, Ah sister! they shall not lament for him, saying, Ah lord! or, Ah his glory! " Furthermore, **ah** is also used as 'a means of mocking, expressing false sorrow'. Eg. Mk.15:29, "And they that passed by railed on him, wagging their heads, and saying, Ah, thou that destroyest the temple, and buildest it in three days."

Aha – 10x., int. [A.D. 1386, < E. **ah** (see 'Ah') = 'sorrow' + **ha** (see 'Ha') = 'joy'; meaning 'a joy over someone's sorrow', but never followed by an expression mark (!) (NOI. Originally written separately as 'a ha'.)] Thus, **aha** is 'an emotional expression of mockery or triumph over someone's sorrow or loss'. Eg. Ps.40:15, "Let them be desolate for a reward of their shame that say unto me, Aha, aha." (NOI. Eze.25:3,6 indicate the mockery of '**aha**' with clapping of hands and stamping of feet.)

Aileth – 7x., v. [A.D. 940, < E. **ail** (< OE. **eglan**) = 'to trouble or pain', either mental or physical + **eth** = forms the pres. ind. 3rd pers. sing. (see E. suffix '–eth')] Thus, **aileth** means 'the action of someone or something causing agony of heart and mind'. Eg. Gen.21:17 "... and the angel of God called to Hagar out of heaven, and said unto her, What aileth thee, Hagar?..." (NOI. All seven occurrences of 'aileth' in the KJV deal with mental/ emotional trauma.) {ailed 1x., tot. = 8x.}

Alabaster – 3x., n. [A.D. 1375, trans. < Gk. αλαβαστος (*alabastos*) = 'the name of a town in Egypt' and/or possibly 'the name of the Egyptian goddess Bast' (NOI. 'Bast' was the goddess of life and family and of the domestic cat and was often pictured as a cat in drawings and sculpture.)] Thus, **alabaster** is 'a pure white mineral, similar to marble', and is used to make vases or boxes. Eg. Mt.26:7, "There came unto him a woman having an alabaster box of very precious ointment, and poured it on his head, as he sat at meat." (NOI. The box itself was made of alabaster and inside the box was the precious ointment. Alabaster was very expensive, so this was not a 'cheap' box.)

Alarm –10x., n. [A.D. 1325, < OF. *alarme* < It. *allarme* = *all arme!* (= 'to arms!')] Thus, an **alarm** is 'a cry for people to take up arms for a battle or a fight'. Eg. Num.10:5, "When ye blow an alarm, then the camps that lie on the east parts shall go forward." (NOI. A careful reading of this passage will show that an 'alarm' was to be a certain sound of the trumpet. The modern meaning of 'alarm' now includes the emotional fright (eg. "She was alarmed at the news!"), which is felt when someone makes the call to arms, though this is not how the word is used in the KJV.)

Alas – 20x., int. [A.D. 1260, < OF. *alas*, *a* = 'ah!' + *las* = 'wretched' (< L. *lassus* = 'weary'), usually followed by an expression mark (!)] Thus, **alas** is 'an exclamation of sorrow, misery, disappointment or regret'. Eg. 2 Ki.6:5, "But as one was felling a beam, the axe head fell into the water: and he cried, and said, Alas, master! for it was borrowed."

Albeit – 2x., conj. [A.D. 1374, (originally 3 words) < ME. **all be it**] Thus, **albeit** means, 'although it be' or 'even though it be'. Eg. Eze.13:7, "Have ye not seen a vain vision, and have ye not spoken a lying divination, whereas ye say, The LORD saith it; albeit I have not spoken? "

Algum – 3x adj. [A.D. 1578(GB.), trans. < Hb. אלגומים (*algumeem*) < oo.] Thus, **algum** modifies its n. (in this case, 'tree') as 'being of an *algumeem* type, which is found in Lebanon'. Eg. 2Chr.2:8, "Send me also cedar trees, fir trees, and algum trees, out of Lebanon." (NOI. Winifred Walker ('All the Plants of the Bible', pg.8) suggests this was a 65 ft. (19.8 m.) high tree also known as the 'Grecian Juniper', found in the wooded mountain areas of Lebanon and Gilead. Some people say the 1611 made an error with 'algum' and 'almug' (see 'Almug'), claiming that one is a misprint of the other. Very little is known about these trees, however, they are two different words in Hb., and so the translators were correct in transliterating them as two different words in E.)

Alien – 5x., n. [A.D. 1330, < OF. *alien* < L. *alienus* < *alius* = 'other' (NOI. Our E. word 'alias' meaning 'otherwise called' also come from this L. root word.)] Thus, an **alien** is 'a person who belongs to another nation, race or family'. Eg. Job.19:15, "They that dwell in mine house, and my maids, count me for a stranger: I am an alien in their sight." (NOI. The idea of an 'alien-being' from another planet is a science-fiction invention of the 1940's.) {alienate 1x., alienated 7x., aliens 3x., tot. = 16x.}

Alienate – 1x., v. [A.D. 1430, < E. **alien** (see 'Alien') + **ate** = forms the v. (see E. suffix '–ate') (NOI. The L. *alienatus* was often used to mean the 'transferring of property from one person to another'.)] Thus, to **alienate** means 'the action of making foreign or strange'. Eg. Eze.48:14, "And they shall not sell of it, neither exchange, nor alienate the firstfruits of the land:

for it is holy unto the **LORD**." {alien 5x., alienated 7x., aliens 3x., tot. = 16x.}

Alleging – 1x., vbl.n. [A.D. 1450, < E. **allege** (< OF. *esligier* < L. *exlitigare* = 'to plead or declare before a court of law' or 'to declare as true') (< *ex* = 'out of' (see L. prefix '*ex*–') + *litigare* = 'to sue') + **ing** = forms the vbl.n. (see E. suffix '–ing'[1]) (NOI. Our E. word 'litigation' comes from the L. root *litigare.*)] Thus, **alleging** means 'the action of pleading and declaring something to be true'. Eg. Act.17:3, "Opening and alleging, that Christ must needs have suffered, and risen again from the dead; and that this Jesus, whom I preach unto you, is Christ."

Allegory – 1x., n. [A.D. 1382(WB.), < L. *allegoria* < Gk. αλληγορια (*allegoria*) = 'to speak otherwise' (< αλλος (*allos*) = 'something else' + αγορια (*agoria*) = 'a talk or discourse')] Thus, an **allegory** is 'a story in which the details speak of something else'. Eg. Gal.4:24, "Which things are an allegory: for these are the two covenants; the one from the mount Sinai, which gendereth to bondage, which is Agar." (NOI. Allegories were often used by people to teach. Bunyan's 'Pilgrim's Progress' is a prime example of an allegory about the Christian life. Also sometimes used to criticize a person, a business or the government, without actually coming out and saying so.)

Alleluia –4x., int. [A.D. 1382 (WB.), trans. < Gk. αλληλούια (*alleluia*), < Hb. הללויה (*halleluyah*), הלל (*halel*) = 'praise ye' + יה (*Yahh*) = 'the LORD' (Jehovah)] Thus, **alleluia** is 'the NT. way of saying "*Praise ye Jehovah*".' Eg. Rev.19:1, "And after these things I heard a great voice of much people in heaven, saying, Alleluia; Salvation, and glory, and honour, and power, unto the Lord our God." (NOI. Its meaning is also found in Ps.106:48, "Praise ye (Hb. הלל - *halal*) the **LORD** (Hb. יה - *Yahh*)".)

Allied – 1x., pp. [A.D. 1297, < E. **ally** = 'to fasten with intensity' (< OF. *alier* < L. *alligare, al* = 'to' (see L. prefix '*ad–*') + *ligare* = 'to fasten or bind') + **ed** = forms the pp. (see E. suffix '–ed'[3])] Thus, **allied** modifies its n. (in this case, 'Eliashib') as 'having been securely bound (united or joined), with force and intent, to someone else'. Eg. Neh.13:4, "And before this, Eliashib the priest, having the oversight of the chamber of the house of our God, was allied unto Tobiah."

Allow – 3x., v. [A.D. 1300, < OF. *alouer* < L. *allocare, al* = 'to' (see L. prefix '*ad–*') + *locare* = 'to stow or to place' (NOI. Our E. word 'allocate' comes from the L. root *allocare.*)] Thus, **allow** means 'the action of bestowing, granting or assigning with approval'. Eg. Lk.11:48, "Truly ye bear witness that ye allow the deeds of your fathers: for they indeed killed them, and ye build their sepulchres." {allowance 2x., allowed 1x., alloweth 1x., tot. = 7x.}

Allure –2x., v. [A.D. 1401, < OF. *alurer, a* = 'to' (= L. prefix '*ad–*') + *loire* = 'to attract or draw away' (NOI. The fishing tackle, known as the 'lure', comes from the OF. *alurer.*)] Thus, **allure** means 'the action of tempting, seducing and drawing away'. Eg. 2Pt.2:18, "For when they speak great swelling words of vanity, they allure through the lusts of the flesh, through much wantonness, those that were clean escaped from them who live in error."

Almighty –57x., pn. [A.D. 890, < E. **all** (< OE. **eall**, akin to OHG. *al*, ON. *allr*, Goth. *alls*) = 'inclusive' or 'the whole quantity of' + **might** (< OE. **miht**) = 'power to accomplish' (NOI. The Hb. שדי (*Shaddai*) = 'the all-sufficient one'. Many scholars believe its root word is the Hb. שד (*shad*) = 'breast'; and just as a mother's milk is all-sufficient for her newborn, so Almighty God is all-sufficient for His people.)] Thus, **Almighty** is 'a capitalized term (or name, meaning 'power to accomplish' or 'the all-sufficient one') reserved for God alone'. Eg. Rev.4:8, "... Holy, holy, holy, Lord God Almighty, which was, and is, and is to come." (NOI. 'Almighty' indicates His omnipotent ability to do anything He so chooses to do, and in precisely the method He chooses to do it. He is totally self-sufficient and not restrained or confined in the least way when it comes to doing whatsoever He wants to do. Moreover, God makes His all-sufficiency available for the needs of His people. The greatest use of this name is found in the book of Job with 32x., and next is the book of Revelation with 8x.)

Almond – 2x., n. [A.D. 1300, < OF. *almande* < L. *amygdala* < Gk. αμυγδάλη (*amugdale*) = 'almond'] Thus, an **almond** is 'the fruit (or nut) from a small tree known as the '*Prunis Amygdalus communis*''. Eg. Jer.1:11, "Moreover the word of the **LORD** came unto me, saying, Jeremiah, what seest thou? And I said, I see a rod of an almond tree." (NOI. The Israelites made the cups of the candlestick after the shape of the almond. See Ex.25:33-36.) {almonds 8x., tot. = 10x.}

Alms – 13x., n. [A.D. 1000(ASG.), < OE. **ǽlmysse** < LL. *eleemosyna* < Gk. ελεημοσύνη (*eleemosunay*) = 'compassion' (< Gk. ελεος (*eleos*) = 'pity') (NOI. 'Alms' are always pl., never sing.)] Thus, **alms** are 'a charitable-pity expressed as a relief of the poor from their poverty'. Eg. Mt.6:4, "That thine alms may be in secret: and thy Father which seeth in secret himself shall reward thee openly." {almsdeeds 1x., tot. = 14x.}

Almug – 3x., adj. [A.D. 1611(HB.), trans. < Hb. אלמגים (*almugeem*) < oo., but refers to a type of tree from Ophir] Thus, **almug** modifies its n. (in this case, 'tree') as 'being an *almugeem* type from the land of Ophir'. Eg. 1 Ki.10:11, "And the navy... brought in from Ophir great plenty of almug trees, and precious stones." (NOI. Winifred Walker ('All the Plants of the Bible', pg.12) suggests this is the 'red sandalwood tree', growing 20-ft. (6.09 m.) in height with a fine-grained, sweet smelling timber. See also 'Algum'.)

Aloes —5x., n. pl. [A.D. 950, < OE. **aluwan** (< L. *aloees* < Gk. αλόη (*aloay*)) = 'the name of a tree (of the genus 'aloe') found from Egypt to South Africa' whose pulp has a highly fragrant scent, which is used extensively in perfumes as well as in the 'embalming' of the dead, + **s** = forms the pl.] Thus, **aloes** are 'trees of the genus aloe', but the word soon became synonymous with their fragrant scent. Eg. Pr.7:17, "I have perfumed my bed with myrrh, aloes, and cinnamon." (NOI. Gilbert W. Reynolds has documented over 300 species of aloes. Both the leaves and the bitter tasting sap prevents animals and insects from eating it. See also 'Lign Aloes'.)

Aloof — 1x., adv. [A.D. 1532, < E. **a** (see E. prefix 'a–'[2]) + **loof** = 'a device for altering the course of a ship' (< Du. *loef* = a nautical term meaning to 'turn the ship into the wind and be clear of the shore')] Thus, **aloof** modifies its v. (in this case, 'stand') as being 'deliberately away from'. Eg. Ps.38:11, "My lovers and my friends stand aloof from my sore; and my kinsmen stand afar off." (NOI. 'Aloof' came to mean when a person 'steers clear' of their friends.)

Alpha —4x., pn. [A.D. 1382(WB.), trans. < Gk. αλφα (*alpha*) < Hb. א (*aleph*) = 'ox' or 'leader' (NOI. The Hb. letter א (*aleph*) was formed from the hieroglyph of an ox's head, indicating 'strength' and 'leadership'.)] Thus, **Alpha** is 'the first letter of the Greek alphabet and (when capitalized) refers to Christ as being before all creation, hence a reference to His deity'. Eg. Rev.22:13, "I am Alpha and Omega, the beginning and the end, the first and the last."

Already —31x., adv. [A.D. 1380, < ME. **al redi** (all ready), **al** = 'inclusive or entire' or 'the whole quantity of' (< OE. **eall**, akin to OHG. *al*, ON. *allr*, Goth. *alls*) + **redi** (< OE. **rǽde**) = 'to arrange or put in order'] Thus, **already** modifies the action of the v. as 'happening early', or 'before this time' or 'at this time'. Eg. Phil.3:12, "Not as though I had already attained, either were already perfect: but I follow after, if that I may apprehend that for which also I am apprehended of Christ Jesus." (NOI. Originally it meant that 'everything was arranged in order'; i. e. a state of complete preparation, however, over the years it came to include a sense of timing.)

Altar – 378x., n. [A.D. 1000(AT.), < L. *altare* < *altus* = 'high'] Thus, an **altar** is 'an elevated table-like structure made of wood or stone, on which sacrifices were offered to a deity'. Gen.8:20, "And Noah builded an altar unto the LORD..." (NOI. With the exception of 4 times, all the OT references to 'altar' are from the Hb. מזבח (*mizbeach*) < זבח (*zabach*) = 'to slaughter'. All those in the OT, who were close to God, were familiar with altars and the personal cost of doing sacrifice. Today, sacrifice to God is still an important aspect of a believer's life, as he or she sacrifices their time, talents and treasures up to God. Cp. Rom.12:1-2.) {altars 55x., tot. = 433x.}

Alter – 4x., v. [A.D. 1374, < LL. *alterare* < L. *alter* = 'other or another'] Thus, **alter** means 'the action of making a change in something, thereby making it different from what it originally was' (i.e. 'to change the appearance of something or to modify it'). Eg. Ps.89:34, "My covenant will I not break, nor alter the thing that is gone out of my lips." Here, God Himself used this word when describing how He would never make a change in His covenant relationship with His people. {altered 2x., altereth 2x., tot. = 8x.}

Although – 16x., conj. [A.D. 1325, (originally 2 words) < E. **all** (< OE. **eall**, akin to OHG. *al*, ON. *allr*, Goth. *alls*) = 'inclusive or entire' or 'the whole quantity of' (added to this word for emphasis) + **though** (see 'Though') = 'yet or however'] Thus, **although** is 'a very emphatic way of saying however'. Eg. Mk.14:29, "But Peter said unto him, Although all shall be offended, yet will not I." {though 233x., tot. = 249x.}

Altogether – 29x., adv. [A.D. 1140, < ME. **altogedere, al** = 'inclusive or entire' or 'the whole quantity of ' (< OE. **eall**, akin to OHG. *al*, ON. *allr*, Goth. *alls*) (added to this word for emphasis) + **togedere** = 'together' (see 'Together') = 'to be in company or in union'] Thus, **altogether** modifies the action of the v. as 'being emphatically gathered together', and having an emphasis on the 'togetherness' of it. Eg. Ps.19:9, "The fear of the LORD is clean, enduring for ever: the judgments of the LORD are true and righteous altogether." {together 484x., tot. = 513x.}

Alway – 23x., adv. [A.D. 885, (originally 2 words) < E. **all** (< OE' eall', akin to OHG. *al*, ON. *allr*, Goth. *alls*) = 'inclusive or entire' or 'the whole quantity of'. + **way** = 'a road or path' (note the sing. 'way')] Thus, **alway** 'denotes an accusative sense of 'all' and 'way', indicating the goal of the action with reference to space or distance'. Another way of expressing it might be 'all the way' or 'all along the way till the end'. Eg. Phil.4:4, "Rejoice in the Lord alway: and again I say, Rejoice." Here, 'alway' speaks not so much about 'time', but rather our pathway in life, so we are to rejoice in the Lord all along life's pathway. {always 62x., tot. = 85x.}

Always – 62x., adv. [A.D. 1230, (originally 2 words) < E. **all** (< OE. **eall**, akin to OHG. *al*, ON. *allr*, Goth. *alls*) = 'inclusive or entire' or 'the whole quantity of' + **ways** = 'roads or paths' (note the pl. 'ways')] Thus, **always** 'denotes a distributive sense of 'all' and 'ways', indicating each one of the ways'. Here, there is a greater emphasis on 'time' rather than space or distance. Another way of expressing it might be 'all the time' or 'at every moment'. Eg. 1Cor.15:58, "Therefore, my beloved brethren, be ye stedfast, unmoveable, always abounding in the work of the Lord, forasmuch as ye know that your labour is not in vain in the Lord." Hence, our "abounding in the work of the Lord" is to be done at every moment of our lives. {alway 23x., tot. = 85x.}

Amazed –21x., pp. [A.D. 1230, < E. **amaze, a** = 'intensity' (see E. prefix 'a–'[1b]) + **maze** (< OE. **masian** (< **mas** = **bewilder** + **ian** = 'the action of') = 'to bewilder or daze' or 'to wander in the mind') (**amaze** = 'an intensified bewilderment of the mind') + **ed** = forms the pp. (see E. suffix '–ed'[3])] Thus, **amazed** modifies its n. as 'having gone through the action of an intensified bewilderment of the mind', or 'an overwhelming astonishment' – often with great fear. Eg. Lk.5:26, "And they were all amazed, and they glorified God, and were filled with fear, saying, We have seen strange things to day." (NOI. This word is often close accompanied with words such as 'exceedingly', 'sore', 'greatly' 'trembled' and 'marvelled'.) {amazement 2x., tot. = 23x.}

Amazement –2x., n. [A.D. 1595, < E. **amaze** = 'an intensified bewilderment of the mind' (see 'Amazed') + **ment** = forms the n. and shows 'the means of the action' (see E. suffix '–ment')] Thus, **amazement** is 'the state or condition of having lost one's wits or presence of mind because of some dynamic happening'. Eg. 1 Pt.3:6, "Even as Sara obeyed Abraham, calling him lord: whose daughters ye are, as long as ye do well, and are not afraid with any amazement." {amazed 21x., tot. = 23x.}

Ambassador – 4x n. [A.D. 1374, < OF. *ambassadeur* < ML. *ambasciator* < *ambactus* = 'one who serves'] Thus, an **ambassador** is 'a person who represents the interests of their government to another country, and was sent to such'. Eg. Eph.6:20, "For which I am an ambassador in bonds: that therein I may speak boldly, as I ought to speak." Here, Paul considered himself God's ambassador to the people of earth. {ambassadors 8x., ambassage 1x., tot. = 13x.}

Ambassage – 1x., n. [A.D. 1548, < E. **ambassador** (see

'Ambassador') + **age** = that which pertains to the root word (see E. suffix '–age')] Thus, **ambassage** is 'the business or function of an ambassador' (i.e. his conveyance of matters on behalf of his government). Eg. Lk.14:32, "Or else, while the other is yet a great way off, he sendeth an ambassage, and desireth conditions of peace." (NOI. Though God could easily crush us because of our sin, we see Him sending Christ as an 'ambassage' to preach peace to us. See Eph.2:17.) {ambassador 4x., ambassadors 8x., tot. = 13x.}

Amber – 3x., adj. [A.D. 1398, < Fr. '*ambre jaune*', *ambre* < ML. *ambar* < Ar. *anbar* = 'a fossilized, semi-translucent resin' (NOI. Found chiefly by the shores of the Baltic sea, it's used in making jewelry and emits a fragrant odor when heated.) + *jaune* = 'yellow' (NOI. It is thought that the Crusaders brought this word, *ambre jaune*' to England and was later shortened to just *ambre.*)] Thus, **amber** modifies its n. as 'being a bright yellow color, which also allows some light to pass through it'. Eg. Eze.1:27, "And I saw as the colour of amber..."

Ambush –7x., n. and v. [A.D. 1300, < OF. *embuscher*, < LL. *inboscare, in* = 'in' + *boscus* = 'woods or bushes'] Thus, as a n., an **ambush** is 'a hiding of troops among the bushes in order to surprise the enemy'. Eg. Josh.8:2, "... lay thee an ambush for the city behind it." Furthermore, as a v., **ambush** means 'the action of hiding and surprising the enemy'. Eg. Josh.8:9, "... and they went to lie in ambush..." {ambushes 1x., ambushment 2x., ambushments 1x., tot. = 11x.}

Amen –78x., adj. and pn. [A.D. 950, < L. *amen* < Gk. αμήν (*amen*) < Hb. אמן (*amen*) = 'truth' or 'so be it' (< Hb. אמן (*aman*) = 'to confirm or strengthen')] Thus, as an adj., **amen** modifies its n. (such as a statement, lecture or an entire book) as 'truth' or 'so be it'. Eg. of a statement, Deut.27:16, "Cursed be he that setteth light by his father or his mother. And all the people shall say, Amen." Eg. of a lecture, Mt.6:13, "... For thine is the kingdom, and the power, and the glory, for ever. Amen." Eg. of a book, Jn.21:25, "And there are also many other things which Jesus did, the which, if they should be written every one, I suppose that even the world itself could not contain the books that should be written. Amen." Furthermore, as a pn., **Amen** is 'a title of, or reference to Christ as being Truth'. Eg. Rev.3:14, "... These things saith the Amen, the faithful and true witness..."

Amend – 6x., v. and p. [A.D. 1220, < ME. **amenden** < OF. *amender* < L. *emendare, e* = 'out' (see L. prefix '*ex–*') + *menda* = 'fault' (NOI. The fault can be either moral or physical.)] Thus, as a v., **amend** means 'the action of correcting by removing a fault or by getting rid of a mistake'. Eg. Jer.26:13, "Therefore now amend your ways and your doings..." Furthermore, as a p., **amend** means the actual 'process of amending or correcting a fault' (such as in 'a healing process'). Eg. Jn.4:52, "Then enquired he of them the hour when he began to amend..." {amends 1x., tot. = 7x.}

Amends – 1x., n. pl. [A.D. 1314, < E. **amend** (see 'Amend') < OF. *amendes* = 'reparation' (= 'the act of repairing') + **s** = forms the pl.] Thus, **amends** are 'compensations paid or reparations made for an injury'. Eg. Lev.5:16, "And he shall make amends for the harm that he hath done in the holy thing, and shall add the fifth part thereto, and give it unto the priest..." (NOI. When we cause injury or insult to a person, we have an obligation before God to right this wrong by going to the person and making amends. Cp. Lk.19:8-9.) {amend 6x., tot. = 7x.}

Amerce – 1x., v. [A.D. 1215, < AF. *amercier* < OF. *amerci, a* (= L. *ad*, see L. prefix '*ad–*') = 'to' + *merci* = 'payment or fee' (see 'Mercy') (NOI. Originally, this E. word was spelled **amercy** but, over the years, the **y** dropped off.)] Thus, **amerce**

means 'the action of levying a fine or penalty on someone'. Eg. Deut.22:19, "And they shall amerce him in an hundred shekels of silver, and give them unto the father of the damsel, because he hath brought up an evil name upon a virgin of Israel: and she shall be his wife; he may not put her away all his days." (NOI. 'Amerce' is not the same as 'immerse' (= 'to plunge under').)

Amethyst –3x., n. [A.D. 1290, < OF. *ametiste* < L. *amethystus* < Gk. αμεθυστος (*amethystos*), *a* = 'not' (see Gk. prefix '*a*–') + μεθυστο (*methysto*) = 'to get drunk' (NOI. Gk. μεθυσ (*methys*) = 'wine'. We get our E. word 'methyl' (as in methyl-alcohol, also known as 'wood alcohol') from this same root word.); but the word was given to a certain gemstone] Thus, **amethyst** is 'a precious gemstone of purple or blue-violet' (similar in color to the wine of grape juice). Eg. Ex.28:19, "And the third row a ligure, an agate, and an amethyst." (NOI. Because the original meaning of amethyst meant 'to not get drunk', the ancient Greeks used the gemstone as charm against getting drunk.)

Amiable – 1x., adj. [A.D. 1350, < OF. *amiable* < L. *amicabilem* < *amicus* = 'friend'] Thus, **amiable** modifies its n. (in this case, 'tabernacles') as 'being friendly in attitude, good natured or agreeable'. Eg. Ps.84:1, "... How amiable are thy tabernacles, O LORD of hosts! "

Amiss –4x., adv. [A.D.1250, < E. **a** = 'in' (see E. prefix 'a–'[2]) + **miss** < OE. **missan** = 'failure to hit the mark'] Thus, **amiss** modifies the action of the v. as 'being at fault' or 'having failed to achieve'. Eg. Lk.23:41, "And we indeed justly; for we receive the due reward of our deeds: but this man hath done nothing amiss." {miss 2x., missed 3x., missing 2x., tot. = 11x.}

Among –916x., prep. [A.D. 1000(ASG.), < OE. **ongemang**, **on** = 'in' + **gemang** = 'a mingling or a crowd of people' (NOI. By A.D. 1100, the OE. word had been shortened to **onmang** then later to **amang** and finally to **among**.)] Thus, **among** means 'to be in a crowd' or 'in the midst of'. Eg. 3Jn.1:9, "I wrote unto the church: but Diotrephes, who loveth to have the preeminence among them, receiveth us not." (NOI. Here we see that Diotrephes loved to be 'among' (in the midst of) a crowd of people who would look up to him.) {amongst 2x., tot. = 918x.}

Amongst —2x prep. [A.D. 1250, < E. **among** (see 'Among') + **st** = forms the adverbial genitive (indicating 'a dispersion or a changing of position')] Thus, **amongst** means the same as 'among' only with some extra 'moving around'. Eg. Gen.3:8, "... and Adam and his wife hid themselves from the presence of the LORD God amongst the trees of the garden." (NOI. Adam and Eve did not stand still in their attempts to avoid God, but instead moved around in the forest of trees to avoid detection.) {among 916x., tot. = 918x.}

Anathema — 1x., n. [A.D. 1526(TB.), trans. < L. *anathema* < Gk. αναθεμα (*anathema*) = 'to set aside', or 'something devoted' (in such a way that it cannot be taken back, either as a gift to God or something to be destroyed)] Thus, **anathema** is 'something separated for destruction', or simply, 'accursed'. Eg. 1Cor.16:2, "If any man love not the Lord Jesus Christ, let him be Anathema Maranatha." (NOI. The LXX used this word in Lev.27:28 in reference to things "devoted" to the LORD.) (See also 'Maranatha'.)

Ancestors —1x., n. pl. [A.D. 1297, < E. **ancestor** < OF. *ancestre* < L. *antecessor* < *antecedere, ante* = 'before' + *cedere* (< L. *cedo*) = 'go' + **s** = forms the pl.] Thus, **ancestors** are 'two or more people who have died and gone on before' (but more specifically refers to the people from whom a person is descended; i.e. 'parentage'). Eg. Lev.26:45, "But I will for their sakes remember the covenant of their ancestors, whom I brought forth out of the land of Egypt..."

Anchor —1x., n. [A.D. 880, < OE. **ancor** < L. *ancora* < Gk. αγκυρα (*agkura*) < αγκ (*agk*) = 'a hook or bend' (NOI. Our E. 'ankle' comes from this root.)] Thus, an **anchor** is 'a hooked or bent device used for holding or securing something'. Eg. Heb.6:19, "Which hope we have as an anchor of the soul, both sure and stedfast, and which entereth into that within the veil." (NOI. Ships use large, heavy iron anchors, equipped with two or more barb-like points to catch and grip the floor of an ocean or lake. Using rope or chain, they secure their position by lowering one or more anchors from the ship. Figuratively, the term 'anchor' is used to indicate a secure position.) {anchors 3x., tot. = 4x.}

Ancient — 26x., adj. and n. [A.D. 1340, < F. *ancien* < LL. *anteanus*, < L. *ante* = 'before'] Thus, as an adj., **ancient** modifies its n. as 'being before' (as in a long time ago); i.e. 'old'. Eg. Pr.22:28, "Remove not the ancient landmark, which thy fathers have set." Here, the 'landmark' is modified as being 'old'. Furthermore, as a n., an **ancient** is 'an older person'. Eg. Isa.3:2, "The mighty man, and the man of war, the judge, and the prophet, and the prudent, and the ancient." (NOI. Many scholars see 'Ancient' also as a reference to Christ. Eg. Dan.7:9, "I beheld till the thrones were cast down, and the Ancient of days did sit...") {ancients 10x., tot. = 36x.}

Ancients —10x., n. pl. [A.D. 1587, < E. **ancient** (see 'Ancient') + **s** = forms the pl.] Thus, **ancients** are 'two or more older people'. Eg. 1Sam.24:13, "As saith the proverb of the ancients, Wickedness proceedeth from the wicked: but mine hand shall not be upon thee." (NOI. This term usually implies their wisdom and stability.) {ancient 26x., tot. = 36x.}

Angel —201x., n. [A.D. 950, < OE. **engel** < LL. *angelus* < Gk. αγγελος (*angelos*) = 'a messenger'] Thus, an **angel** is 'a messenger'. Eg. Lk.1:19, "And the angel answering said unto him, I am Gabriel, that stand in the presence of God; and am sent to speak unto thee, and to shew thee these glad tidings." (NOI. The Bible indicates that most angels are the spiritual servants of God to deliver messages, execute judgment, war against evil spirits, minister to God's people, and generally do God's bidding. The word 'angel' is usually always connected with the name 'Lord' or 'LORD' or 'God', or a pronoun referring to God. It's interesting to compare this term with the references to angels in Revelation such as, "the angel of the church" (Rev.2:1) and an evil angel, "the angel of the bottomless pit" (Rev.9:11) and the "angel of the waters" (Rev.16:5).) {angel's 2x., angels 93x., angels' 1x., archangel 2x., tot. = 299x.}

Anger —234x., n. [A.D. 1200, < ON. *angr* = 'trouble, grief or affliction' (NOI. Of the several Hb. words translated 'anger', the most common, and interesting, one is אַף (*aph*) meaning 'the nostril', as in 'when the nostrils flare and hot air comes out of them!' Also of interest, is that of the 279 occurrences of 'anger' and its two variations, only 12 of them occur in the NT.)] Thus, **anger** is 'a powerful mental irritation that offends and inflames the emotions'. Eg. Col.3:21, "Fathers, provoke not your children to anger, lest they be discouraged." {angered 1x., angry 44x., tot. = 279 x.}

Angle —2x., n. [A.D. 880, < OE. **angul**< L. *angulus* = 'corner or bend'] Thus, an **angle** is 'a hook used to catch fish'. Eg. Isa.19:8, "The fishers also shall mourn, and all they that cast angle into the brooks shall lament, and they that spread nets upon the waters shall languish."

Angry — 44x., adj. [A.D. 1325, < E. **anger** (see 'Anger') + **y** = 'full of' or 'having the characteristics of' (see E. suffix '–y'[1])] Thus, **angry** modifies its n. as 'being full of anger', or 'to have the characteristics of anger'. Eg. Ps.7:11, "God judgeth the righteous, and God is angry with the wicked every day." (NOI. Only God can be full of anger with the wicked and still remain righteous, whereas we are told in Eph.4:26, "Be ye angry, and sin not: let not the sun go down upon your wrath." Therefore, God can do some things that man cannot.) {anger 234x., angered 1x., tot. = 279 x.}

Anguish – 17x., n. [A.D. 1220, < OF. *anguisse* = 'the awful feeling of choking' < L. *angustia* = 'tightness or distress' < L. *angu* = 'to strangle or squeeze'] Thus, **anguish** is 'a terrible suffering or crushing of the body or mind'. Eg. 2Cor.2:4, "For out of much affliction and anguish of heart I wrote unto you with many tears; not that ye should be grieved, but that ye might know the love which I have more abundantly unto you."

Anise – 1x., n. [A.D. 1300, < OF. *anis* < L. *anisum* < Gk. ανηθον (*anithon*) = 'the name of a wild dill-type of plant in Israel', whose spicy seeds were used to make pickles and to soothe infants (used as a weak tea for stomach troubles)] Thus, **anise** is 'a dill-type plant in Israel'. Eg. Mt.23:23, "Woe unto you, scribes and Pharisees, hypocrites! for ye pay tithe of mint and anise and cummin, and have omitted the weightier matters of the law, judgment, mercy, and faith: these ought ye to have done, and not to leave the other undone."

Anoint –35x., v. [A.D. 1303, < OF. *enoint* < *enoindre* < L. *inunguere*, *in* = 'in or on' (see L. prefix '*in–*'[2]) + *unguere* = 'smear or rub on'] Thus, **anoint** means 'the action of smearing something on'. Eg. Ex.30:26, "And thou shalt anoint the tabernacle of the congregation therewith, and the ark of the testimony." (NOI. Anointing with holy oil was a very sacred thing to the Israelite, as it signified that the person anointed was set apart for sacred duty and service to the Lord. The procedure involved a public ceremony of pouring holy-oil over the top of the candidate's head and the offering up of prayers. This is why Jesus is called the 'Christ', meaning the 'Anointed One'. See 'Christ' and 'Messiah'.) {anointed 98x., anointedst 1x., anointest 1x., anointing 28x., tot. = 163 x.}

Anon —2x., adv. [A.D. 1000, < OE. **on an** = 'in one' (i.e. 'in one moment' ('without delay' – meaning 'now') or 'in one line' ('without interruption' – meaning 'very soon')) (NOI. 'Anon' is a difficult word to comprehend etymologically. It doesn't simply mean 'forthwith' or 'straightway', else the translators would have used those words. But by a comparison of the Gk. words translated 'anon', and how the same Gk. words were translated differently in other passages, the explanation given seems to be the most logical understanding of the word 'anon'.)] Thus, **anon** modifies the action of the v. as 'being now or very soon'. Eg. Mt.13:20, "But he that received the seed into stony places, the same is he that heareth the word, and anon with joy receiveth it."

Another —448x., adj. [A.D. 1205, originally 2 words, '**an other**' = 'one other', or 'a second (or a third or fourth, etc.) of other similar or different things'] Thus, **another** modifies its n. as 'being one more of similar or different things'. Eg. Gen.4:25, "And Adam knew his wife again; and she bare a son, and called his name Seth: For God, said she, hath appointed me another seed instead of Abel, whom Cain slew." {another's 5x., tot. = 453x.}

Answer — 131x., n. and v. [A.D. 800, < OE. **andswaru** < **and** = 'again' or 'in reply' + **swaru** = 'a swearing' (NOI. **Andswaru** was a 'swearing in reply' and was a solemn statement made to refute an accusation.)] Thus, as a n., **answer** is 'a reply to an accusation or a question'. Eg. Jn.19:9, "... Whence art thou? But Jesus gave him no answer." Furthermore, as a v., **answer** means 'the actual process of the reply'. Eg. Mt.22:46, "And no man was able to answer him a word..." {answerable 1x., answered 492x., answeredst 2x., answerest 6x., answereth 13x., answering 31x answers 3x., tot. = 679x.}

Answerable — 1x., adj. [A.D. 1548, < E. **answer** (see 'Answer')

+ **able** = an ability to do or perform (see E. suffix '–able')] Thus, **answerable** modifies its n. (in this case, 'the hanging') as 'being able to render an answer with the idea of obligation-to-answer'. Ex.38:18, "And the hanging for the gate of the court was needlework, of blue, and purple, and scarlet, and fine twined linen: and twenty cubits was the length, and the height in the breadth was five cubits, answerable to the hangings of the court." {answer 131x., answered 492x., answeredst 2x., answerest 6x., answereth 13x., answering 31x answers 3x., tot. = 679x.}

Ant —1x., n. [A.D. 1000, < OE. **amete** (or **emete** in other E. dialects) akin to OHG. *ameiza*, *a* = 'from or away' + *meiza* = 'to cut or to bite off'] Thus, an **ant** is 'an insect (of the family *Formicidae*) which has the ability to cut or bite'. Pr.6:6, "Go to the ant, thou sluggard; consider her ways, and be wise." (NOI. Of the 10,000 species of ants, the 'harvester ant' best fits the context of Pr.6:6-8 and 30:25.) {ants 1x., tot. = 2x.}

Antichrist —4x., n. [A.D. 1300, < LL. *antichristus* < Gk. αντιχριστος (*antichristos*), αντι (*anti*) = 'against' or 'in the place of' + χριστος (*christos*) = 'Christ' (NOI. The Gk. αντι (*anti*) is used 22 x., in the NT. and is translated as "for", "because" and "in the room of ". Hence, 'antichrist' could mean both someone who is 'against Christ', as well as an imposter standing 'in the place of Christ'.)] Thus, an **antichrist** is 'someone who is against Christ' or 'has taken the place of Christ' and is applied to certain people who behave a certain way. Eg. 2Jn.1:7, "For many deceivers are entered into the world, who confess not that Jesus Christ is come in the flesh. This is a deceiver and an antichrist." Furthermore, **antichrist** is also 'a title, referring to a specific man (yet to come) who will control the world'. Eg. 1Jn.2:18, "Little children, it is the last time: and as ye have heard that antichrist shall come..." {Christ 555x., tot. = 559x.}

Antiquity — 1x., n. [A.D. 1380, < E. **antique** = (< F. *antique*

< L. *antiquus* = 'former, earlier or ancient' < *ante* = 'before') + **ity** = 'a state, condition or quality of' (see E. suffix '–ity')] Thus, **antiquity** is 'the quality or state of being old' (i.e. 'before'). Eg. Isa.23:7, "Is this your joyous city, whose antiquity is of ancient days? her own feet shall carry her afar off to sojourn."

Anvil – 1x., n. [A.D. 800, < OE. **anfilte, an** = 'on' + **filte** = 'to hit'] Thus, an **anvil** is 'a block of iron upon which metal is hit (to be shaped)'. Eg. Isa.41:7, "So the carpenter encouraged the goldsmith, and he that smootheth with the hammer him that smote the anvil, saying, It is ready for the sodering: and he fastened it with nails, that it should not be moved."

Apes – 2x., n. pl. [A.D. 700, < OE. **apa** < oo., but the word is often associated with the verb 'imitate' (possibly because of their ability to imitate what they see. "Monkey-see monkey-do"?) + **s** = forms the pl.] Thus, **apes** are 'two or more 4-footed animals, with human-like characteristics similar to large monkeys, only without tails'. Eg. 1 Ki.10:22, "For the king had at sea a navy of Tharshish with the navy of Hiram: once in three years came the navy of Tharshish, bringing gold, and silver, ivory, and apes, and peacocks." (NOI. Some commentaries suggest that 'ape' should really be 'monkey', but there is no etymological reason for this. Furthermore, the word 'monkey' was in English use since the 14th c., so the translators knew the difference between a monkey and an ape. In zoology, this family of animals is divided into: #1) those with long tails called 'monkeys'; #2) those with short tails called 'baboons'; and #3) those with no tails called 'apes'.)

Apiece – 8x., adv. [A.D. 1465, < ME. **a** (= 'one' (see E. prefix 'a–'[3])) + **piece** ('piece' n. < OF. *piece* = 'a thing which is part of a whole') and used in the sense of accounting] Thus, **apiece** modifies the action of the v. as 'acting on behalf of a part of the whole' (where the emphasis is on the thing(s) itself, rather than on the recipient of those things). Eg.

Num.17:6, "... and every one of their princes gave him a rod apiece, for each prince one, according to their fathers' houses, even twelve rods: and the rod of Aaron was among their rods." Here, 'apiece' modifies the pret. v. 'gave'. (NOI. Notice the use of 'apiece' and 'each', as they are not the same. 'Apiece' is the accounting part concerning the rods, while 'each' concerns the princes who gave the rods. 'Each' is OE. and means 'ever alike'.) {piece 43x., pieces 121x., tot. = 172x.}

Apostle – 19x., n. [A.D. 950(LfG.) < LL. *apostolus* < Gk. αποστολος (*apostolos*) = 'a messenger' (< Gk. αποστελλω (*apostello*), απο (*apo*) = 'away from' + στελλω (*stello*) = 'I send')] Thus, an **apostle** is 'one who is sent to perform an errand, some mission or service'. Eg. Rom.1:1, "Paul, a servant of Jesus Christ, called to be an apostle, separated unto the gospel of God." (NOI. Although this term is mostly applied to Paul and Peter, it is also applied to Christ in Heb.3:1, for He was also sent on a mission to earth by God the Father. He then said to the disciples in Jn.20:21, "... as my Father hath sent me, even so send I you.") {apostles 55x., apostles' 5x., apostleship 4x., tot. = 83x.}

Apothecary –4x., n. [A.D. 1366, < OF. *apotecaire* < LL. *apothecarius* < Gk. αποθεκη (*apothekay*) = 'a storehouse' (< αποτιθενη (*apotithenay*), απο (*apo*) = 'from' + τιθενη (*tithenay*) = 'to put or set')] Thus, an **apothecary** is 'someone who kept a store containing non-perishable goods such as spices, drugs, perfumes, preserves, etc.' Eg. Ex.30:35, "And thou shalt make it a perfume, a confection after the art of the apothecary, tempered together, pure and holy." (NOI. The modern idea of an apothecary being a drug-store came into being in the 1700's.) {apothecaries 1x., apothecaries' 1x., tot. = 6x.}

Apparel – 28x., n. [A.D. 1250, < ME. **aparail** < OF. *apareil* = 'the material provided to equip or prepare' (< OF. *apa-*

reillier = 'to prepare') (NOI. In E. literature, **apparel** has been used in reference to the rigging for ships, furniture for houses, guns for a fortress, decorations for a wall AND clothing for the body.)] Thus, **apparel** is 'clothing for the body that serves a special purpose, be it royalty, priesthood, mourning or whatever'. Eg. Est.5:1, "Now it came to pass on the third day, that Esther put on her royal apparel, and stood in the inner court of the king's house, over against the king's house..." (NOI. 'Apparel' is different from 'clothes' as it deals more with the function of the clothing. See 'Clothes'.) {apparelled 2x., tot. = 30x.}

Apparently –1x., adv. [A.D. 1400, < E. **apparent** < OF. *aparant* < L. *apparens* < *apparere, ap* = 'to' (see L. prefix '*ad–*') + *parere* = 'come forth into sight' or 'to be evident' (see 'Appear') + **ly** = 'very' or the idea of 'more' (see E. suffix '–y'[2])] Thus, **apparently** modifies the action of the v. (in this case, 'speak') as 'being very or more evidently'. Eg. Num.12:8, "With him will I speak mouth to mouth, even apparently, and not in dark speeches..."

Appeal –2x., v. [A.D. 1297, < OF. *apeler* (= 'to call') < L. *appellare, ap* = 'to' (see L. prefix '*ad–*') + *pellare* = 'to approach someone with a request' (as in 'intreat or implore') (NOI. A word related to *appellare* is *appellere* = 'to press or drive toward', as in 'driving a ship towards shore'.)] Thus, **appeal** means 'the action of approaching and imploring someone for an answer' (such as an opinion or a decision). Eg. Act.28:19, "But when the Jews spake against it, I was constrained to appeal unto Caesar..." {appealed 4x., tot. = 6x.}

Appear –54x., v. [A.D. 1250, < OF. *apareir* < L. *apparere, ap* = 'to' (see L. prefix '*ad–*') + *parere* = 'to come forth into sight' or 'to be evident'] Thus, **appear** means 'the action of being fully evident'; i.e. not hidden from sight. Eg. Mt.6:16, "Moreover when ye fast, be not, as the hypocrites, of a sad countenance: for they disfigure their faces, that they may appear unto men to fast. Verily I say unto you, They have their reward." {appearance 38x., appearances 2x., appeared 70x., appeareth 10x., appearing 6x., tot. = 180x.}

Appease – 1x., v. [A.D. 1330, < OF. *apaisier*, *a* = 'to' (= L. *ad*, see L. prefix '*ad*–') + *paisier* = 'peace' (< L. *pax* = 'peace or harmony')] Thus, **appease** means 'the action of making peaceful'; i.e. to soothe, pacify, or reduce to peace. Eg. Gen.32:20, "And say ye moreover, Behold, thy servant Jacob is behind us. For he said, I will appease him with the present that goeth before me..." {appeased 2x., appeaseth 1x., tot. = 4x.}

Appertain – 2x., v. [A.D. 1386, < OF. *apartenir* < LL. *appertinere*, *ap* = 'to' (see L. prefix '*ad*–') + *pertinere* = 'belong to or pertain' (see 'Pertain')] Thus, **appertain** means 'the action of belonging to something' (such as members of a family). Eg. Num.16:30, "But if the LORD make a new thing, and the earth open her mouth, and swallow them up, with all that appertain unto them, and they go down quick into the pit; then ye shall understand that these men have provoked the LORD." {appertained 3x., appertaineth 1x., tot. = 6x.}

Appetite – 4x., n. [A.D. 1303, < OF. *appetit* < L. *appetitus*, < *appetere*, *ap* = 'to' (see L. prefix '*ad*–') + *petere* = 'seek or search'] Thus, an **appetite** is 'an intense seeking or searching towards the pursuit of a goal' (but usually refers to hunger and food). Eg. Pr.23:2, "And put a knife to thy throat, if thou be a man given to appetite."

Apple – 8x., n. [A.D. 885, < ME. appel < OE. ppel = oo., but refers to the fruit of the *Malus pumila* (common apple) tree (NOI. 'Apple' is used 6x. as a figure of speech, as in Zec.2:8, "... the apple of his eye." Two of the Hb. words used are אישון (*iyshown*) and בבה (*babah*) and both refer to the middle of the eye, the black pupil, while the 3rd Hb. word used is בת (*bath*) and means 'a daughter'. This figure of speech refers to something very special and precious, as if it were one's own eye or one's own daughter. Some have suggested it refers to the tiny image of one's self that can be seen in the pupil of someone's eye.)] Thus, an **apple** is 'a fruit of the *Malus pumila* tree'. Eg. **SoS.2:3**, "As the apple tree among the trees of the wood, so is my beloved among the sons. I sat down under his shadow with great delight, and his fruit was sweet to my taste." (NOI. The term, 'Adam's Apple' (A.D. 1755) was coined to mean the piece of forbidden fruit that Adam ate, which then got stuck in his throat forming the large lump in a man's throat. In reality, that 'lump' is part of the 'larynx' or 'voice-box', which enlarges during adolescence, and makes the voice sound deeper. Because the larynx of a boy grows bigger than that of a girl, this explains why the boy has a deeper voice, and why his larynx protrudes out more than a girl's. Johnny Apple-seed (Jonathan Chapman, A.D. 1774 - 1845) became part of American folklore when, for 49 years of his life, he extensively planted apple trees throughout Ohio and Indiana. His favorite book was the Bible!) {apples 3x., tot. = 11x.}

Appoint —41x., v. [A.D. 1374, < OF. *apointier* < ML. *appunctare, ap* = 'to' (see L. prefix '*ad–*') + *punctare* = 'point' (as a definite place in time or space) < L. *pungere* = 'to prick' (NOI. Our E. words 'punctuate' and 'puncture' come from a similar L. root. See 'Point'.)] Thus, **appoint** means 'the action of deliberately establishing a definite time and/or place for something', either as part of a plan or a position (i.e. the action is definite and deliberate and not half-hearted or by chance). Eg. Act.6:3, "Wherefore, brethren, look ye out among you seven men of honest report, full of the Holy Ghost and wisdom, whom we may appoint over this business." {appointed 126 x., appointeth 1x., appointment 4x., tot. = 172x.}

Apprehend – 2x., v. [A.D. 1398, < L. *apprehendere, ap* = 'to' (see L. prefix '*ad–*') + *prehendere* = 'to grasp hold of' or 'to seize' (Cp. also 'Comprehend'.)] Thus, **apprehend** means 'the action of flying upon an opportunity and seizing it with the hands'. Eg. 2Cor.11:32, "In Damascus the governor under Aretas the king kept the city of the Damascenes with a garrison, desirous to apprehend me." Figuratively, **apprehend** means 'the action of seizing something with the mind'. Eg. Phil.3:12, "Not as though I had already attained, either were already perfect: but I follow after, if that I may apprehend that for which also I am apprehended of Christ Jesus." {apprehended 3x., tot. = 5x.}

Approach – 19x., v. [A.D. 1305, < OF. *aprochier* < LL. *appropiare*, *ap* = 'to' (see L. prefix '*ad–*') + *propiare* = 'to come nearer' < *prope* = 'near'] Thus, **approach** means 'the action of deliberately coming nearer'; i.e. not an accidental approach. Eg. Ps.65:4, "Blessed is the man whom thou choosest, and causest to approach unto thee, that he may dwell in thy courts: we shall be satisfied with the goodness of thy house, even of thy holy temple." {approached 2x., approacheth 1x., approaching 2x., tot. = 24x.}

Approve –3x., v. [A.D. 1340, < OF. *aprover* < L. *aprobare*, *ap* = 'to' (see L. prefix '*ad–*') + *probare* = 'to test the quality/goodness of something' or 'to approve by testing' (< L. *probus* = 'genuine or honest') (NOI. Our E. 'probate' (= 'the act of proving or putting to the test') < L. *probatum* < *probare*.)] Thus, **approve** means 'the action of a definite and intense probing and testing of something to reveal its quality'. Eg. Phil.1:10, "That ye may approve things that are excellent..." (See also Act.2:22 and 2Tim.2:15.) {approved 8x., approvest 1x., approveth 1x., approving 1x., tot. = 14x.}

Aprons – 2x., n. pl. [A.D. 1307, < E. **apron** < OF. *naperon* < OF. *nape* = 'cloth' (< L. *mappa* = 'cloth, tablecloth or napkin') (NOI. In ME. it was called a 'naperon', but as people would say "*a naperon*", they would slur it to "*an aperon*", hence the 'n' was dropped off the word, leaving 'aperon'.

Later, with more slurring, the 'e' was dropped, leaving 'apron'.) + **s** = forms the pl.] Thus, **aprons** are 'articles of clothing worn in front of the body as a covering, or worn to protect the clothes from dirt'. Eg. Gen.3:7, "And the eyes of them both were opened, and they knew that they were naked; and they sewed fig leaves together, and made themselves aprons."

Apt – 4x., adj. [A.D. 1398, < L. *aptus* = 'appropriate or fitted' (< L. *apere* = 'to attach')] Thus, **apt** modifies its n. as 'being fitted or suited for the occasion'. Eg. 2Tim.2:24, "And the servant of the Lord must not strive; but be gentle unto all men, apt to teach, patient." Here, "apt to teach" means the servant of the Lord must be a 'teacher at heart'.

Archangel – 2x., n. [A.D. 1000(AT.), < E. **arch** (< Gk. αρχη (*arche*) = 'first, foremost, beginning or leader' (not to be confused with the E. word 'arch' (see 'Arches'))) + **angel** (see 'Angel')] Thus, an **archangel** is 'the first and foremost angel' (the angel with the highest rank among all the other angels). Eg. Jude.1:9, "Yet Michael the archangel, when contending with the devil he disputed about the body of Moses, durst not bring against him a railing accusation, but said, The Lord rebuke thee." (NOI. An 'archenemy' is a person's first and foremost enemy, while 'archaeology' is the study of the 'first and foremost things' or 'beginnings', and a 'monarch' is one who 'leads alone'.)

Archer – 2x., n. [A.D. 1297, < F. *archer* < OF. *archier* < LL. *arcarius* < *arcus* = 'a curve or a bow' (same as OF. *arche* = 'bow' (see 'Arches')) (NOI. The F. suffix '–er' is the same as the E. suffix '–er', showing occupation.)] Thus, an **archer** is 'a person whose occupation it is to shoot with a bow'. Eg. Jer.51:3, "Against him that bendeth let the archer bend his bow..." {archers 12x., tot. = 14x.}

Arches – 15x., n. pl [A.D. 1297, < E. **arch** < OF. *arche* = 'an arc or a bow' (< L. *arcus* = 'a curve or a bow') + **s** = forms the pl.] Thus, **arches** are 'two or more things that are curved or bowed' (such as an archway of a bridge). Eg. Ezk.40:30, "And the arches round about were five and twenty cubits long, and five cubits broad." (NOI. This word is only used in Ezekiel 40, describing the future temple of the Lord.)

Arcturus – 2x., pn. [A.D. 1374, < L. *arcturus* < Gk. Αρκτουρος (*Arctouros*), αρκτος (*arctos*) = 'bear' + *ouros* = 'guardian or keeper'] Thus, **Arcturus** is 'a name, which means the great bear', and refers to a bright star of the first magnitude in the constellation 'Bootes'. Eg. Job.38:32, "Canst thou bring forth Mazzaroth in his season? or canst thou guide Arcturus with his sons? " (See also 'Mazzaroth'.)

Areopagus – 1x., pn. [A.D. 1611(HB.), trans. < Gk. Αρειος παγος (*Areios pagos*) = 'the hill of Ares' (the Gk. god of war, and several different myths offer explanations as to how the hill got its name.) (NOI. 'Mars' was the Roman god of war, hence "Mars hill " in Act.17:22. The blood-red planet of Mars is named after this Roman god.)] Thus, **Areopagus** is 'a name meaning the hill of Ares', which is located in Athens, Greece, and it was here that public speaking and debates took place. Eg. Act.17:19, "And they took him, and brought him unto Areopagus, saying, May we know what this new doctrine, whereof thou speakest, is? "

Aright – 5x., adv. [A.D. 970, < OE. **ariht**, **a** = 'on' or 'towards' (see E. prefix 'a–'[2]) + **riht** = 'straight, correct or proper' (see also 'Right')] Thus, **aright** modifies the action of the v. as 'being in the direction of straightness or correctness', especially in a moral sense (i.e. the standard of what is proper and acceptable in life). Eg. Ps.50:23, "Whoso offereth praise glorifieth me: and to him that ordereth his conversation aright will I shew the salvation of God." (NOI. 'Aright' is used once in a literal sense, meaning 'in a straight motion' or an 'even, equal, smooth motion'. Eg. Pr.23:31, "Look not thou upon the wine when it is red, when it giveth his colour in the cup, when it moveth itself aright.") {birthright 10x., right 359x righteous 238x., righteously 8x., righteousness 302x., righteousness' 4x., righteousnesses 3x., rightly 4x., unrighteous 9x., unrighteously 1x., unrighteousness 21x., tot. = 964x.}

Arise – 149 x., v. [A.D. 825(VP.), < OE. **arisan, a** = 'up' (see E. prefix 'a–'[1b]) + **risan** = 'to elevate' or 'get up'] Thus, **arise** means 'the action of a deliberate or intense rising motion' (i.e. not something accidental or by chance). Eg. Ps.44:26, "Arise for our help, and redeem us for thy mercies' sake." {ariseth 11x., arising 1x., arose 173x., rise 142x., risen 51x., risest 2x., riseth 14x., rising 39x., rose 131x., tot. = 713x.}

Ark – 230 x., n. [A.D. 825(VP.), < OE. **arc** or **earc** < L. *arca* < *arcere* = 'to keep or contain'] Thus, an **ark** is 'a box or a chest to act as storage'. Three 'arks' mentioned in the Bible are: **#1)** Noah's ark. Eg. Gen.6:14, "Make thee an ark of gopher wood..."; **#2)** the little basket-type ark made by the mother of Moses. Eg. Ex.2:3, "And when she could not longer hide him, she took for him an ark of bulrushes..."; and **#3)** the ark which housed the 10 commandments and served as a base for the mercy seat. Eg. Ex.25:21, "And thou shalt put the mercy seat above upon the ark; and in the ark thou shalt put the testimony that I shall give thee."

Armageddon – 1x., pn. [A.D. 1382(WB.), trans. < Gk. Αρμαγεδων (*Armageddon*) = 'the hill or city of Megiddo'] Thus, **Armageddon** is 'a name of a geographic territory in Israel, known as the hill or city of Megiddo'. Eg. Rev.16:16, "And he gathered them together into a place called in the Hebrew tongue Armageddon." (NOI. This area is also known as the 'Battle plain of Esdraelon', famous for two great victories: Barak over the Canaanites and Gideon over the Midianites. In Revelation, it is to be the place of the final battle and slaughter at the end of the Tribulation.)

Armour –24x., n. [A.D. 1297, < E. **arm** (< F.*armes* < L. *arma* = 'arms, gear or tackle' of a defensive type (NOI. Not to be confused with the body limb, which is < OS. '*arm*' < L. *armus* = 'the arm') hence, things used for fighting) + **ure** = 'an action or process' (see E. suffix '–ure')] Thus, **armour** is 'the defensive body covering worn by a soldier for protection during combat'. Eg. Eph.6:11, "Put on the whole armour of God, that ye may be able to stand against the wiles of the devil." (NOI. Armour breeds confidence in the one who wears it (see Lk.11:22). For the follower of God, the state of 'righteousness' is like wearing armour (see 2Cor.6:7).) {armies 43x., armourbearer 18x., armoury 3x., arms 29x., army 82. tot. = 199x.}

Array –34x., n. and v. [A.D. 1297, < OF. *areer, a* = 'to' (< L. *ad* (see L. prefix '*ad–*')) + *reer* = 'make ready or put in order'] Thus, as a n., an **array** is 'the orderly fashion in which people (usually soldiers) have been positioned for maximum effect'. Eg. Jud.20:20 "... and the men of Israel put themselves in array to fight against them at Gibeah." It's also used in reference to costly clothing fashions. Eg. 1Tim.2:9, "In like manner also, that women adorn themselves in modest apparel, with shamefacedness and sobriety; not with broided hair, or gold, or pearls, or costly array." (NOI. 'Apparel' is more functional clothing, as opposed to 'costly array', which tends to be more for show.) Furthermore, as a v., **array** means 'the action of setting in order for maximum effect'. Eg. Est.6:9, "And let this apparel and horse be delivered to the hand of one of the king's most noble princes, that they may array the man withal whom the king delighteth to honour..." Here, the function of royal apparel was for beauty and majesty, and it was to be arrayed (on Mordecai) for its maximum effect. {arrayed 11x., tot. = 45x.}

Arrogancy —4x., n. [A.D. 1529, < E. **arrogant** (< OF. *arrogant* < L. *arrogans* < L. *arrogare* = 'to ask, assume or claim for oneself') + **ancy** = 'a quality, condition or state of being' (see E. suffix '–ance')] Thus, **arrogancy** is 'the state or condition of being arrogant'. Eg. Pr.8:13, "The fear of the LORD is to hate evil: pride, and arrogancy, and the evil way, and the froward mouth, do I hate."

Arrow — 16x., n. [A.D. 835, < OE. **arwe** < Ger. root *arkhw* (= 'the thing that belongs to the bow') < L. *arcus* = 'bow' (NOI. OE. had two other words, which both meant 'arrow', these were **strǽl** and **flan**, but for some unknown reason, **arwe** was the more popular word.)] Thus, an **arrow** is 'the thing that belongs to the bow' (i.e. the long slender projectile, usually made of wood, often tipped at the front with a hard sharp point and feathered at the back for straight flight). Eg. Ps.91:5, "Thou shalt not be afraid for the terror by night; nor for the arrow that flieth by day." (See also 'Bow'[1].) {arrows 41x., tot. = 57x.}

Art[1]—3x., n. [A.D. 1225, < OF. *art* < L. *ars* = 'skill' (i.e. 'an ability that comes from learning and practice') or 'a skilled workmanship'] Thus, **art** is 'a skill or a skilled workmanship'. Eg. Ex.30:25, "And thou shalt make it an oil of holy ointment, an ointment compound after the art of the apothecary: it shall be an holy anointing oil." {arts 1x., tot. = 4x.}

Art[2]—492x., v. [A.D. 1000(ASG.), < OE. **eart** = 2nd pers. sing. pres. ind. of v. 'to be'] Thus, **art** means 'the 2nd pers. sing. pres. ind.'. Eg. Gen.3:9, "And the LORD God called unto Adam, and said unto him, Where art thou?" (NOI. 'Are' was only used with the pl. form of the 1st , 2nd and 3rd pers. pres. ind. (eg. 'we are', 'ye/you are' and 'they are'), however today, the word 'are' is also used for 2nd pers. sing. (eg. 'you (sing.) are').)

Artificer —2x., n. [A.D. 1393, < E. **artifice** (< F. *artifice* (skill, cunning) < L. *artificium*, *ars* = 'art' + *facere* = 'to make') + **er** = identifies a person according to their occupation (see E. suffix '–er')] Thus, an **artificer** is 'a craftsman or a person who makes things by art or skill'. Eg. Gen.4:22, "... she also bare Tubalcain, an instructer of every artificer in brass and iron..." {artificers 2x., tot. = 4x.}

Artillery – 1x., n. [A.D. 1386, < OF. *artillerie* = 'implements of war', < OF. *artillier* = 'a maker of bows and other war implements', < OF. *artil* = 'an implement of war', usually for discharging missiles (i.e. catapults, bows, slings, etc.), < ML. *articulum* = 'skillful or artful'] Thus, **artillery** is 'the implements of war that could be hurled at or used against an enemy'. Eg. 1Sam.20:40, "And Jonathan gave his artillery unto his lad, and said unto him, Go, carry them to the city." In this case, the artillery was a bow and arrows and, probably, a quiver for the arrows.

Ascend – 13x., v. [A.D. 1382(WB.), < L. *ascendere* < L. *adscandere*, *ad* = 'to' (see L. prefix '*ad*–') + *scandere* = 'to climb or rise'] Thus, **ascend** means 'the action of rising or climbing to a higher point'. Eg. Ps.139:8, "If I ascend up into heaven, thou art there..." {ascended 19x., ascendeth 2x., ascending 5x., ascent 4x., tot. = 43x.}

Ascribe – 3x., v. [A.D. 1382(WB.), < ME. **ascrive** < OF. *ascrivre* = 'to inscribe or attribute' < L. *ascribere*, *ad* = 'to' (see L. prefix '*ad*–') + *scribere* = 'to write'] Thus, **ascribe** means 'the action of adding by writing' (yet the way in which it is used in the Bible signifies more the idea of attributing either mentally or verbally). Eg. Deut.32:3, "Because I will publish the name of the LORD: ascribe ye greatness unto our God." {ascribed 2x., tot. = 5x.}

Ashamed – 122x., p. [A.D. 1000, < OE. **ascamian**, **a** = 'on' (see E. prefix 'a–'[1a]) + **scamian** (< **scamu** = 'shame' + **ian** = 'the action of') = 'to shame' (see 'Shame') + **ed** = forms the p. (see E. suffix '–ed'[4])] Thus, **ashamed** means 'to be intensely affected by shame so as to cause fear and disgrace'. Eg. 1Pt.4:16, "Yet if any man suffer as a Christian, let him not be ashamed; but let him glorify God on this behalf." {shame 100x., shamed 4x., shamefacedness 1x., shameful 2x., shamefully 4x., shamelessly 1x.tot. = 234x.}

Ashes —43x., n. pl. [A.D. 950, < OE. **asce** = 'the powdery incombustible matter that is left after burning' (< oo., but thought to be from an ancient Indo-European root word *as* = 'to burn')] Thus, **ashes** are 'the black powdery remains left after burning'. Eg. 2Pt.2:6, "And turning the cities of Sodom and Gomorrha into ashes condemned them with an overthrow, making them an ensample unto those that after should live ungodly."

Ashtaroth — 11x., n. and pn. [A.D. 1382(WB.), trans. < Hb. עשתרות (*Ashtarowth*) (which is pl. of) עשתרה (*ashteraw*) = 'a flock' or 'a ewe', and speaks of fertility (NOI. Some claim 'Ashtaroth' is a title similar to 'My lady' or 'My goddess', while others claim it means 'a star', but it was also the name of a town in Bashan.)] Thus, as a n., **Ashtaroth** was 'a town in Bashan, east of Jordan' (also spelled "Astaroth" in Deut.1:4). Eg. Josh.9:10, "And all that he did to the two kings of the Amorites, that were beyond Jordan, to Sihon king of Heshbon, and to Og king of Bashan, which was at Ashtaroth." Furthermore, as a pn., **Ashtaroth** was 'a pagan deity (a fertility goddess) worshipped by the Philistines'. Eg. 1Sam.31:10, "And they put his armour in the house of Ashtaroth: and they fastened his body to the wall of Bethshan."

Ashtoreth — 3x., pn. [A.D. 1611(HB.), trans. < Hb. עשתרת (*Ashtoreth*) (see "Ashtaroth' for a similar description)] Thus, **Ashtoreth** was 'a pagan deity (a fertility goddess, similar to Ashtaroth) worshipped by the Phoenicians'. Eg. 1Ki.11:5, "For Solomon went after Ashtoreth the goddess of the Zidonians, and after Milcom the abomination of the Ammonites."

Aside —72x., adv. [A.D. 1369, < ME. **a** = 'toward' (see E. prefix 'a–'[2]) + **side** = 'side'] Thus, **aside** modifies the action of the v. as 'happening on one side or the other, or away from the main direction'. Eg. Heb.12:1, "...let us lay aside every weight, and the sin which doth so easily beset us..." {backside 3x., side 444x., sides 48x., wayside 2x., tot. = 569x.}

Ask —109x., v. [A.D. 885, < OE. **ascian** (= 'to seek by words') < oo., but possibly from an Indo-European root word *ais* = 'to wish or desire'] Thus, **ask** means 'the action of seeking by words or question(s) so as to receive an answer'. Eg. Deut.13:14, "Then shalt thou enquire, and make search, and ask diligently..."

Asleep — 16x., adj.and adv. [A.D. 1154, < ME. **a** = 'toward' (see E. prefix 'a–'[2]) + **sleep** = 'sleep'] Thus, as an adj., **asleep** modifies its n. as 'being in or into a state of sleep'. Eg. Mt.8:24, "... the ship was covered with the waves: but he was asleep." Furthermore, as an adv., **asleep** modifies the action of the v. as 'happening in or into a state of sleep'. Eg. Act.7:60, "... And when he had said this, he fell asleep." (NOI. The use of the term 'asleep' to mean death was first used in A.D. 1297 by R. Gloucester when he wrote, "Kyng Edred nou aslepe in oure Louerd is." In modern spelling this would read, "King Edred now asleep in our Lord is.") {sleep 82x., tot= 98x.}

Asp – 1x., n. [A.D. 1340, < L. *aspis* < Gk. ασπις (*aspis*) < oo., but may possibly = 'shield', because it can inflate its neck into a 'hood' that resembles a 'shield'] Thus, an **asp** is 'a small venomous snake'. Eg. Isa.11:8, "And the sucking child shall play on the hole of the asp..." (NOI. Originating from Egypt, the 'asp' makes its home in the ground and has a bite that causes death unless treated right away. Asps were used to execute some criminals in the days of ancient Greece and Rome, and it is said that Cleopatra committed suicide by an asp, in 30 B.C., at the age of 39.) {asps 4x., tot. = 5x.}

Ass —86x., n. [A.D. 1000(AT.), < OE. **assa** < L. *asinus* < oo., however, it refers to a long-eared, 4-footed, usually ash colored beast of burden, somewhat smaller than a horse. (NOI. The ass and mule are two different animals. See 'Mule'. 'Donkey' is a modern name for the ass, first used in A.D. 1785. The ass eats grass, herbs and bark and lives up to about 8 years in the wild and up to about 20 years in captivity. They tend to be slow, sure-footed animals (although they have been clocked at speeds up to 43 miles (69.2 km.) per hour!) and were used to carry loads, and were eaten for their meat. Job had 500 she asses (Job.1:3). Their young are called 'colts'. See 'Colt'.)] Thus, an **ass** is 'a long-eared, 4-footed beast of burden, smaller than a horse and also known as a donkey'. Eg. Ex.20:17, "Thou shalt not covet thy neighbour's house, thou shalt not covet thy neighbour's wife, nor his manservant, nor his maidservant, nor his ox, nor his ass, nor any thing that is thy neighbour's." {ass's 4x., asses 64x., tot. = 154x.}

Assault —2x., n. and v. [A.D. 1230, < OF. *asaut* < ML. *assaltus* < L. *assilire* (= 'to leap upon, so as to overcome'), *ad* = 'to' (see L. prefix '*ad–*') + *salire* = 'to leap' (NOI. The E. 'assail' comes from L. *assilire*.)] Thus, as a n., **assault** is 'a forceful intentional leap upon someone or something'. Eg. Act.14:5, "And when there was an assault made both of the Gentiles, and also of the Jews..." Furthermore, as a v., **assault** means 'the action of a forceful leap'. Eg. Est.8:11, "... all the power of the people and province that would assault them..." {assaulted 1x., tot. = 3x.}

Assay — 1x., v. [A.D. 1330, < OF. *assaier* = 'to try' or 'put to the test', usually involving some type of pain or affliction] Thus, **assay** means 'the action of testing by force'. Eg.

Job.4:2, "If we assay to commune with thee, wilt thou be grieved? but who can withhold himself from speaking? " Here we see the torturous words put forth by Eliphaz the Temanite to Job. (NOI. 'Assay' is used in other E. literature as a n. in which it describes the refining fires for metals such as silver or gold.) {assayed 4x., assaying 1x., tot. = 6x.}

Assemble – 20x., v. [A.D. 1250, < OF. *assembler* < ML. *assimulare*, *as* = 'to' (see L. prefix '*ad*–') + *simul* = 'together'] Thus, **assemble** means 'the action of bringing together into one place to form an orderly rank and file'. Eg. 2Sam.20:4-5, "Then said the king to Amasa, Assemble me the men of Judah within three days, and be thou here present..." The context of this passage is military. (NOI. While 'assemble' has the idea of an orderly rank and file, 'gather' tends to mean a general coming together. See 'Gather'.) {assembled 37x., assemblies 6x., assembling 2x., assembly 49x., tot. = 114x.}

Assembly –49x n. [A.D. 1325, < OF. *assemblee* = 'an orderly gathering'] Thus, an **assembly** is 'the state of being assembled in an orderly fashion'. Eg. Jam.2:2, "For if there come unto your assembly a man with a gold ring, in goodly apparel, and there come in also a poor man in vile raiment." (See 'Assemble'.) (NOI. The Gk. συναγωγη (*sunagoge*) (E. 'synagogue') is here translated 'assembly'. James is thought to be the first of the NT. books, written perhaps in A.D. 45, to the early Jewish-Christians, who would have met in their local συναγωγη. See also 'Church' and 'Congregation'.) {assemble 20x., tot. = 69x.}

Assent – 1x., v. [A.D. 1297, < OF. *assenter* < L. *assentari*, *ad* = 'to' (see L. prefix '*ad*–') + *sentire* = 'to sense, feel or perceive'] Thus, **assent** means 'the action of complying with or agreeing' (with much feeling and heart). Eg. 2Chr.18:12, "And the messenger that went to call Micaiah spake to him, saying, Behold, the words of the prophets declare good to the king with one assent; let thy word therefore, I pray thee, be like one of theirs, and speak thou good." {assented 1x., tot. = 2x.}

Assure – 1x., v. [A.D. 1370, < OF. *aseurer* < ML. *assecurare*, *ad* = 'to' (see L. prefix '*ad–*') + *securus*= 'safe, sure or secure from danger'] Thus, **assure** means 'the action of making a big effort in order to make secure'. Eg. IJn.3:19, "And hereby we know that we are of the truth, and shall assure our hearts before him." {assurance 7x., tot. = 8x.}

Assurance – 7x., n. [A.D. 1374, < ME. **assure** (see 'Assure') + **ance** = a state of being (see E. suffix '–ance')] Thus, **assurance** is 'the state of being secure'. Eg. Heb.10:22, "Let us draw near with a true heart in full assurance of faith, having our hearts sprinkled from an evil conscience, and our bodies washed with pure water." {assure 1x., tot. = 8x.}

Asswage – 1x., v. [A.D. 1300, < OF. *asouagier* < L. *adsuaviare*, *ad* = 'to' (see L. prefix '*ad–*') + *suavis* = 'sweet or agreeable' (NOI. This word seems to have been spelled 'assuage' in the 1300's, then changed to 'asswage' in the 1400's until the 1700's, and then changed back to 'assuage'.)] Thus, **asswage** means 'the action of definitely making something milder and more agreeable'. Eg. Job.16:5, "But I would strengthen you with my mouth, and the moving of my lips should asswage your grief." {asswaged 2x., tot. = 3x.}

Astonied – 10x., pp. [A.D. 1350, < ME. **astony** < **astone** < OF. *estoner* (= 'to stun') < L. *extonare*, *ex* = 'out' + *tonare* = 'thunder' (lit., to be 'thunder struck') + **ed** = forms the pp. (see E. suffix '–ed'[3])] Thus, **astonied** modifies its n. as 'having received a severe personal devastation, and not being able to protect from it or even correct it'. (All 10 occurrences of the word in the Bible deal with some negative event.) Eg. Ezr.9:3, "And when I heard this thing, I rent my garment and my mantle, and plucked off the hair of my head and of my beard, and sat down astonied." (NOI. Some sources simply claim that 'astony' and 'astonish' are the same word, yet the 1611 translators used them differently (see Eze.4:16-17) because the meanings are somewhat different. A careful study of how the two words are used in the Bible reveals that one indicated a much deeper and personal devastation than the other. Also, Jer.14:9 indicates that someone 'astonied' does not have the power to protect or correct the situation.)

Astonished – 34x., p. [A.D. 1513, < E. **astonish** < ME. **astony** (see 'Astonied') < **astone** < OF. *estoner* (= 'to stun') < L. *extonare*, *ex* = 'out' + *tonare* = 'thunder' (lit., to be 'thunder struck') + **ed** = forms the p. (see E. suffix '–ed'[4])] Thus, **astonished** means 'to be stunned or amazed by some unexpected event' (but not a 'severe personal devastation' as in 'astonied'). The feeling of astonishment can be: **#1)** over a disaster such as the destruction of Solomon's Temple. Eg. 1 Ki.9:8, "And at this house, which is high, every one that passeth by it shall be astonished, and shall hiss; and they shall say, Why hath the LORD done thus unto this land, and to this house? "; **#2)** over a miracle, such as when Jesus raised a little girl from the dead. Eg. Lk.8:56, "And her parents were astonished: but he charged them that they should tell no man what was done."; or **#3)** simply the feeling of amazement, not quite knowing what to make of a situation, such as the people's reaction to Jesus' sermon on the mount. Eg. Mt.7:28, "And it came to pass, when Jesus had ended these sayings, the people were astonished at his doctrine." {astonishment 21x., tot. = 55x.}

Astray – 22x., adv. [A.D. 1300, < OF. *estraier* < L. *extravagare*, *extra* = 'out of bounds' + *vagare* = 'to wander'] Thus, **astray** modifies the action of the v. as 'taking place while it wanders out of bounds'. Eg. 1Pt.2:25, "For ye were as sheep going astray; but are now returned unto the Shepherd and Bishop of your souls."

Astrologer —1x.n. [A.D. 1374, < ME. **astrology** (< OF. *astrologie* < L. *astrologia* < Gk. αστρολογια (*astrologia*), αστρον (*astron*) = 'star' + λογια (*logia*) = 'to speak') + **er** = identifies a person according to their occupation (see E. suffix '–er')] Thus, an **astrologer** is 'one whose job it was to look to the stars for knowledge'. Eg. Dan.2:10, "The Chaldeans answered before the king, and said... there is no king, lord, nor ruler, that asked such things at any magician, or astrologer, or Chaldean." (NOI. The earliest astrologers simply looked to the stars for clues to the answers about life, while modern astrologers assume that the stars and planets have a direct influence upon human behavior.) {astrologers 8x., tot. = 9x.}

Asunder —21x., adv. [A.D. 1000(ASG.), < OE. **a** = 'in' (see E. prefix 'a–'[1b]) + **sunder** = 'to separate one from another'] Thus, **asunder** modifies the action of the v. to mean 'a forceful dividing of something into pieces'. Eg. Act.1:18, "Now this man purchased a field with the reward of iniquity; and falling headlong, he burst asunder in the midst, and all his bowels gushed out." (NOI. This adv. modifies verbs of an already forceful action (such as 'cut', 'sawn', 'burst', 'clave', 'broken' and 'drove') thereby strengthening the idea of 'forcefully divide'.)

Athirst — 5x., adj. [A.D. 1000, < OE. **a** = 'in' (see E. prefix 'a–'[1b]) + **thirst** (similar to Ger. *durst* and Goth. *thaurstei* < *thaursus* = 'dry or parched') (see also 'Thirst')] Thus, **athirst** modifies its n. to mean 'a condition of no-water-to-be-had, and thereby suffering a severe thirst'. Eg. Jud.15:18, "And he was sore athirst, and called on the LORD, and said, Thou hast given this great deliverance into the hand of thy servant: and now shall I die for thirst, and fall into the hand of the uncircumcised?" {thirst 31x., tot. = 36x.}

Atonement —81x., n. [A.D. 1513, < E. **atone** = 'at one' (NOI. In the 1300's when two people were in agreement, or united together, they were said to be 'brought into a state of unity', or more simply, they were 'at one'. (The word 'one' was pronounced similar to how we pronounce the word 'own'.) By the 1500's, the two words were joined together as one-word 'atone' and also carried the idea of making amends for injustices done, and settling differences.) + **ment** = forms the n. and shows 'the result or product of the action' (see E. suffix '–ment')] Thus, an **atonement** is 'the result or product of having been made one'. Eg. Rom.5:11, "And not only so, but we also joy in God through our Lord Jesus Christ, by whom we have now received the atonement." Here, the result of being made 'one with God' is available in this life through Christ. {atonements 1x., tot. = 82x.}

Attain –6x., v. [A.D. 1300, < OF. *ataindre* < L. *attingere*, *ad* = 'to' (see L. prefix '*ad–*') + *tangere* = 'touch' (NOI. Our E. 'tangent' (often used in geometry) comes from L. *tangere.*)] Thus, **attain** means 'the action of touching or reaching through effort'. Eg. Pr.1:5, "A wise man will hear, and will increase learning; and a man of understanding shall attain unto wise counsels." Here, we learn that it's only through some strenuous effort that we can reach right up to the point of understanding (and the giving of) wise counsels. {attained 10x., tot. = 16x.}

Attend –11x., v. [A.D. 1300, < OF. *atendre* < L. *attendere*, *ad* = 'to' (see L. prefix '*ad–*') + *tendere* = 'to stretch' (NOI. Our E. 'tend' comes from L. *tendere.*)] Thus, **attend** means 'the action of stretching toward something' (i.e. 'to give earnest heed to' or 'pay strict attention to'). Eg. Pr.4:20, "My son, attend to my words; incline thine ear unto my saings." {attendance 4x., attended 3x., attending, 1x., attent, 2x., attentive. 5x., attentively 1x., tot. = 27x.}

Attentive –5x., adj. [A.D. 1374, < F. *attentive* (= 'to give careful attention or consideration') < L. *attendere* (see 'Attend')]

Thus, **attentive** modifies its n. as 'being very earnest to stretch one's facilities in order to give careful heed or consideration'. Eg. Lk.19:48, "And could not find what they might do: for all the people were very attentive to hear him." {attend 11x., attendance 4x., attended 3x., attending, 1x., attent, 2x., attentively 1x., tot. = 27x.}

Attire – 3x., n. [A.D. 1250, < OF. *atirer* < L. *ad tire*, *ad* = 'to' (see L. prefix '*ad–*') + *tire* = 'orderly row'] Thus, **attire** are 'items of clothing that have been set out (or put on) in a proper orderly fashion'. Eg. Jer.2:32, "Can a maid forget her ornaments, or a bride her attire? yet my people have forgotten me days without number." Here, the bride's attire would be the beautiful items of clothing that she has carefully put together to wear on her wedding day. (NOI. In other E. literature, attire is used to speak of the equipment of men and horses for war. See also 'Tire'.) {attired 1x., tot. = 4x.}

Audience – 12x., n. [A.D. 1374, < OF. *audience* < L. *audientia* < *audire* = 'to hear or listen'] Thus, an **audience** is a 'formal hearing' (as in an interview), usually in connection with an assembly of listeners, but can also be before an individual. Eg. Neh.13:1, "On that day they read in the book of Moses in the audience of the people; and therein was found written, that the Ammonite and the Moabite should not come into the congregation of God for ever."

Augment – 1x., v. [A.D. 1400, < OF. *augmenter* < LL. augmentare < L. *augmentum* < *augere* = 'to increase' (NOI. From L. *augere* we get our E. 'auction' = 'to increase' (the price).)] Thus, **augment** means 'the action of making greater in size and especially power'. Eg. Num.32:14, "And, behold, ye are risen up in your fathers' stead, an increase of sinful men, to augment yet the fierce anger of the LORD toward Israel." (NOI. The word 'increase' refers to making greater in size, but not necessarily power. See 'Increase'.)

Augustus —3x., pn. [A.D. 1395(WB.), < L. *Augustus* = 'divine or majestic' (NOI. This title was first given to Gaius Octavius, the grandson of Julius Caesar's sister, and successor to the throne of the Roman Empire in 27 B.C. After the death of Julius Caesar, in 44 B.C., he formed a partnership, with Marc Antony that later included Marcus Lepidus. Octavius finally won control of the whole Roman Empire from 27 B.C. until A.D. 14. (It was Octavius who commanded all to be taxed.) The next man to receive this title was Tiberius, who ruled from A.D. 14 until A.D. 37, and was ruling when Christ was crucified. Next came Gaius from A.D. 37 until A.D. 41; then came his uncle Claudius from A.D. 41 until A.D. 54 (who was believed to have been poisoned by his wife, Agrippina, in order to help her mad-man son, Nero, become emperor). After Claudius came Nero from A.D. 54 until A.D. 68, when he was forced to commit suicide. Nero was ruling when the Apostle Paul appealed to him (Act.25:21) and was beheaded in A.D. 67. (Historians believe it was Nero who set Rome on fire in A.D. 64, but he did not play a 'violin' or 'fiddle' since that instrument was not invented until about A.D. 1520. Some believe he played a 'lyre'.) All of these men wore the title of 'Augustus'. Only once does the NT. use the Gk. Αυγουστος (*Augoustos*), but three times it uses σεβαστος (*sebastos*) (= 'the venerable one'), from which we get the E. name 'Sebastian'.)] Thus, **Augustus** is 'a title meaning divine or majestic'. Eg. **Lk.2:1**, "And it came to pass in those days, that there went out a decree from Caesar Augustus, that all the world should be taxed." (See also 'Caesar'.)

Aul —2x., n. [A.D. 885, < OE. **awel** < oo., but some sources say 'to pierce' (NOI. Other OE. spellings include: **al**, **ǽl**, **alle** and **aule**. The spelling 'awl' seems to have come in the 1700's.)] Thus, an **aul** is 'a slender pointed instrument for piercing holes in leather, wood, etc'. (and used by rotating it back and forth and while exerting pressure). Eg. **Ex.21:6**, "Then his master shall bring him unto the judges; he shall also bring him to the door, or unto the door post; and his master shall bore his ear through with an aul; and he shall serve him for ever."

Austere —2x., adj. [A.D. 1330, < OF. *austere* < L. *austerus* (= 'stern severe or gloomy') < Gk. αυστηρος (*austeros*) = 'something rough or harsh' (< αυειν (*auein*) = 'to dry'; i.e. to become rough or harsh)] Thus, **austere** modifies its n. as 'being harsh, strict or severe'. Eg. Lk.19:21, "For I feared thee, because thou art an austere man: thou takest up that thou layedst not down, and reapest that thou didst not sow."

Author —3x., n. [A.D. 1300, < OF. *autor* < L. *auctor* < *augere* = 'to increase' (see 'Augment')] Thus, an **author** is 'one who makes things grow, or who originates things'. Eg. Heb.5:9, "And being made perfect, he became the author of eternal salvation unto all them that obey him." (NOI. An 'author' is also considered the 'owner' of what he originated, and so possesses all the rights and privileges connected thereto. See also 'Authority'.)

Authority —37x., n. [A.D. 1230, < ME. **author** (< OF. *auctorite* < L. *auctoria* = 'the power, or the right, to command or act' (see 'Author')) + **ity** = the state or condition of (see E. suffix '–ity')] Thus, **authority** is 'the right to command'. Eg. Mt.8:9, "For I am a man under authority, having soldiers under me: and I say to this man, Go, and he goeth; and to another, Come, and he cometh; and to my servant, Do this, and he doeth it." (NOI. 'Authority' refers to the author's ownership, especially his rights and privileges, even if the rights have been conferred upon him by others, as in 'the crowning of a king'.) {authorities 1x., tot. = 38x.}

Availeth —4x., v. [A.D. 1300, < ME. **availen** < OF. *a valoir*, *a* = 'to' (same as L. prefix '*ad–*') + *valoir* < L. *valere* = 'to be strong', + **eth** = forms the 3rd pers. sing. (see E. suffix '–eth')] Thus, **availeth** means 'the action and ability of a 3rd party to be a valuable service'. Eg. Jam.5:16, "Confess your faults one to another, and pray one for another, that ye may be healed. The effectual fervent prayer of a righteous man availeth much." Here, the "effectual fervent prayer of a righteous man" is that 3rd party that renders valuable service.

Avenge —17x., v. [A.D. 1375(used by Wycliffe in an article on the Antichrist), < OF. *avengier*, *a* = 'to' (same as L. prefix '*ad–*') + *vengier* = 'to inflict retributive punishment on behalf of someone else'] Thus, **avenge** means 'the action of meeting out an intensive punishment, on behalf of someone else, as a means of paying back an injustice done'. Eg. Rom.12:19, "Dearly beloved, avenge not yourselves, but rather give place unto wrath: for it is written, Vengeance is mine; I will repay, saith the Lord." {vengeance 45x., tot. 62x.}

Averse — 1x., adj. [A.D. 1597, < L. *aversus* (which is pp. of) *avertere*, *a* = 'away from' (see L. prefix '*ab–*'2) + *vertere* = 'to turn'] Thus, **averse** modifies its n. (in this case, 'men') as 'having a mental or emotional turning away, due to disinterest or repugnance'. Eg. Mic.2:8, "Even of late my people is risen up as an enemy: ye pull off the robe with the garment from them that pass by securely as men averse from war."

Avoid —5x., v. [A.D. 1300, < OF. *esvuidier*, *es* = 'out' (see L. prefix '*ex–*') + *vuidier* = 'empty'] Thus, **avoid** means 'the action of clearing out and making empty'. Eg. 2Tim.2:23, "But foolish and unlearned questions avoid, knowing that they do gender strifes." (NOI. The modern concept of 'avoid' is to 'sidestep' or 'run from', but the Apostle is not suggesting that Timothy hide himself around the corner from those who ask foolish and unlearned questions. Instead, he is counseling Timothy to recognize that these questions generate nothing but strife, and clear them off his desk. Furthermore he instructs Timothy to help these people to recover themselves out of the snare of the devil (1Tim.2:24-26).) {avoided 1x., avoiding 2x., avouched

2x., tot. = 10x.}

Avouched –2x., prp. [A.D. 1393, < ME. **avouch** < OF. *avochier* (= 'to cite as proof or guarantee') < L. *advocare* (see 'Advocate') (NOI. As L. words became more popular in the courts of law, certain F. words sprung like branches from a tree, having different meanings, yet having the same trunk. '*Avochier*' is such a word.) + **ed** = forms the prp. (see E. suffix '–ed'[2])] Thus, **avouched** means 'to have cited someone or something as being a proof, or a guarantee, for some cause or reason'. Eg. Deut.26:17, "Thou hast avouched the LORD this day to be thy God, and to walk in his ways, and to keep his statutes, and his commandments, and his judgments, and to hearken unto his voice." (NOI. Today, we say, "*I will vouch for him,*" but 'vouch' is weaker than 'avouch' because the prefix 'a–' adds more intensity to the word.)

Aware – 5x.adj. [A.D. 1095, < OE. **gewǽr**, **ge** = 'together' (having intensity; an OE. prefix similar to E. prefix 'a–'[1b]) + **wǽr** = 'cautious'] Thus, **aware** modifies its n. as 'being extra cautious'. Eg. Jer.50:24, "I have laid a snare for thee, and thou art also taken, O Babylon, and thou wast not aware: thou art found, and also caught, because thou hast striven against the LORD." (NOI. This prophecy was fulfilled in Dan.5 when Darius the Median took over Babylon. Cp. 1Pt.5:8.) {ware 6x., tot. = 11x.}

Awe –3x., n. [A.D. 1200, < ON. *agi* = 'dread' (i.e. 'clutching oneself and trembling in fear')] Thus, **awe** is 'a trembling fear, enough to make someone clutch themselves'. Eg. Ps.33:8, "Let all the earth fear the LORD: let all the inhabitants of the world stand in awe of him." (NOI. The idea of awe being a 'majestic and reverential wonder' seems to have evolved in the 1700's.)

Axletrees –2x., n. pl. [A.D. 1300, (originally 2 words) < ME.

axle tre, **axle** = 'the center spindle upon which a wheel revolves' + **tre** = 'tree' (< Gk. δορυ (*doru*) = 'shaft, spear, tree') (NOI. **Axletree** was shortened to 'axle' in A.D. 1634.) + **s** = forms the pl.] Thus, **axletrees** are 'two or more long shafts upon which wheels turn, as used on a chariot or an ox cart'. Eg. 1 Ki.7:32, "And under the borders were four wheels; and the axletrees of the wheels were joined to the base: and the height of a wheel was a cubit and half a cubit." (NOI. Solomon had ten mobile bases made of brass that had four wheels and two axletrees each.)

B

Baal – 63x., pn. [A.D. 1382(WB.), trans. < Hb. בעל (*bahal*) = 'lord or master'] Thus, **Baal** is 'a name meaning lord or master, and is usually applied to the chief heathen deity of the Canaanites'. Eg. 1Ki.16:32, "And he reared up an altar for Baal in the house of Baal, which he had built in Samaria." (NOI. Besides child sacrifice, 'Baal' worship involved lustful behavior, such as prostitution, which made it very appealing to man's fallen nature (Num.25:1-9). Sadly, a couple of Israelite parents named their sons 'Baal' (1Chr.5:5; 8:30).) {Baal's 1x., Baal-berith 2x., Baalgad 3x., Baalhamon 1x., Baalhanan 5x., Baal-hazor 1x., Baalhermon 2x., Baalmeon 3x., Baalpeor 6x., Baalperazim 4x., Baalshalisha 1x., Baaltamar 1x., Baalzebub 4x., Baalzephon 3x., Baalim 18x., Bamothbaal 1x., Bethbaal-meon 1x., Gurbaal 1x., Jerubbaal 14x., Kirjathbaal 2x., Meribbaal 4x., tot. = 141x.}

Baalim – 18x., pn. [A.D. 1382(WB.), pl. form of Baal (see 'Baal') (NOI. Hb. בעל (*Bahal*) + ים (*im*) = בעלים (*Bahalim*). The pl. indicates there were many of these idols set up in Israel.)] Thus, **Baalim** is 'the pl. name of the heathen deity Baal'. Eg. Jud.2:11, "And the children of Israel did evil in the sight of the LORD, and served Baalim."

Baalzebub – 4x., pn. [A.D. 1395(WB.), trans. < Hb. בעל זבוב (*bahalzeboob*) = 'lord of flies' (NOI. This was a deity worshipped by the Philistines; their patron god 'Baal-Zebul' or 'Prince Baal'. The ancient Hebrews changed it in mockery to בעל זבוב (*Bahalzeboob*) = 'lord of flies' as in 'dirt or dung'.)] Thus, **Baalzebub** is 'a name given by the ancient Hebrews to the Philistine god 'Baal', and means lord-of-the-flies'. Eg. 2 Ki.1:2, "And Ahaziah fell down through a lattice in his upper chamber that was in Samaria, and was sick: and he sent messengers, and said unto them, Go, enquire of Baalzebub the god of Ekron whether I shall recover of this disease." (See also 'Beelzebub'.) {Beelzebub 7x., tot. = 11x.}

Babbling – 1x., vbl.n. [A.D. 1230, < E. **babble** (akin to LG. *babblen*, and Fr. *babiller*; all refer to 'the unintelligible sounds made by an infant while trying to talk') + **ing** = forms the vbl.n. (see E. suffix '–ing'[1])] Thus, **babbling** is 'the making of unintelligible sounds by a person'. Eg. Pr.23:29, "Who hath woe? who hath sorrow? who hath contentions? who hath babbling? who hath wounds without cause? who hath redness of eyes? " (NOI. Some believe that 'babble' comes from the 'Tower of Babel', but this is not so. 'Babbling' is from the Hb. שיח (*siyach*) and is translated elsewhere as 'complaint' (1Sam.1:16), 'talking' (1Ki.18:27) and 'communication' (2Ki.9:11), whereas 'Babel' is a trans. < Hb. בבל (*babel*) (= 'to mix or confuse').) {babbler 2x., babblings 2x.tot. = 5x.}

Babe –6x., n. [A.D. 1393, < ME. **babe** < oo., but probably derived from 'ba' or 'baban', imitating the noises a baby makes] Thus, lit., a **babe** is 'one still in the womb, or a newborn from one day to a few months of age'. Eg. Lk.1:44, "For, lo, as soon as the voice of thy salutation sounded in mine ears, the babe leaped in my womb for joy." (Here, John the Baptist was still in the womb.) Eg. Ex.2:6, "And when she had opened it, she saw the child: and, behold, the babe wept..." (Here, Moses was 3 months of age outside the womb. See Ex.2:2.) Figuratively, a **babe** is one who is innocent and has no experience, or has stunted their spiritual growth through willful immaturity. Eg. Mt.11:25, "At that time Jesus answered and said, I thank thee, O

Father, Lord of heaven and earth, because thou hast hid these things from the wise and prudent, and hast revealed them unto babes." Eg. 1Cor.3:1, "And I, brethren, could not speak unto you as unto spiritual, but as unto carnal, even as unto babes in Christ." (See also 'Child', 'Daughter', 'Lad' and 'Son'.) {babes 9x., tot. = 15x.}

Backbiting – 1x., prp. [A.D. 1175, < ME. **backbite** (used figuratively, 'to bite someone on their back', meaning to inflict sharp wounds to someone's reputation when they are not looking) + **ing** – forms the prp. (see E. suffix '–ing'[3])] Thus, **backbiting** modifies its n. (in this case, 'tongue') as 'speaking evil of someone when they're not around to hear'. Eg. Pr.25:23, "The north wind driveth away rain: so doth an angry countenance a backbiting tongue." (NOI. The difference between 'backbiting' and 'slander', is that backbiting is done when the person is not around, while slander may be done in the presence of the person. See 'Slander'. Also, 'biting' is a function of the front teeth, while 'chew, crush, gnash or grind' is a function of the back teeth. Cp. Ps.35:16) {backbiters 1x., backbiteth 1x., backbitings 1x., tot. = 4x.}

Backsliding – 12x., prp. and vbl.n. [A.D. 1552, < E. **backslide** (used figuratively, 'to slide backwards', meaning 'to fall away from a commitment or a standard of excellence') + **ing** = forms the prp. and the vbl.n. (see E. suffix '–ing'[1,3])] Thus, as a prp. **backsliding** modifies its n. as 'turning away from its commitment, or falling from its standard of excellence'. Eg. Hos.4:16, "For Israel slideth back as a backsliding heifer..." (NOI. A heifer must be broken in for labor in the field and, until then, will kick back at the plowman and try to pull away from his steering. See 'Heifer'.) Furthermore, as a vbl.n., **backsliding** means 'the condition of having turned aside or fallen back from an excellent standard'. Eg. Hos.14:4, "I will heal their backsliding, I will love them freely: for mine anger is turned away from him." {backslider 1x., backslidings 4x.,

tot. = 17x.}

Bade — 18x v. pret. [A.D. 1300, < ME. **bid** (See 'Bid')] Thus, **bade** means 'the past-tense action of earnestly pressing for an answer or compliance to a request'. Eg. Act.11:12, "And the Spirit bade me go with them, nothing doubting. Moreover these six brethren accompanied me, and we entered into the man's house." (NOI. 'Bade' is a much stronger and more emphatic word than 'asked'.) {bid 17x., badest 1x., bidden 14x., biddeth 1x., bidding 1x., tot. = 52x.}

Bag — 11x., n. [A.D. 1230, < ME. **bagge**, probably < ON. *baggi* = 'a pack or bundle'] Thus, a **bag** is 'a small sack used to hold small items, made from cloth or leather, and capable of being closed at the opening'. Eg. Pr.7:20, "He hath taken a bag of money with him, and will come home at the day appointed." (See also 'Sack'.) {bags 3x., tot. = 14x.}

Bake —9x., v. [A.D. 1000(AT.), < OE. **bacan** = 'to toast or roast using a dry heat' (NOI. Modern oven controls list 'bake' as heat from the bottom, and 'broil' as heat from the top.)] Thus, **bake** means 'the action of cooking using dry heat' (such as 'in an oven or over a fire'). Eg. Lev.26:26, "... ten women shall bake your bread in one oven..." (See also 'Baken', 'Broiled', 'Cook', 'Fried' and 'Roasted'.) {baked 4x., bakemeats 1x., baken 9x., baker 8x., bakers 2x., bakers' 1x., baketh 1x., tot. = 35x.}

Bakemeats — 1x., n. pl. [A.D. 1386, < ME. **bakemeat** (< **baken** = 'the quality of having been baked using dry heat' (i.e. in an oven or over a fire) + **meat** = 'food in general') = 'food which has been baked' (such as pies, pastries, bread, etc.) + **s** = forms the pl.] Thus, **bakemeats** are 'food items that are cooked using dry heat', such as pies, pastries, breads, buns, etc. Eg. Gen.40:17, "And in the uppermost basket there was of all manner of bakemeats for Pharaoh; and the birds did eat them out of the basket upon my head."

Baken –9x., p. [A.D. 1325, < ME. **bake** (< OE. **bacan** = 'to toast or roast using a dry heat' (see 'Bake')) + **en** = forms the p. (see E. suffix '–en'[1])] Thus, **baken** means 'the quality of having been cooked using dry heat' (such as 'in an oven or over a fire'). Eg. 1Ki.19:6, "And he looked, and, behold, there was a cake baken on the coals, and a cruse of water at his head. And he did eat and drink, and laid him down again." (NOI. Etymologically speaking, there is no difference between 'baken' and 'baked', however with one exception (1Chr.23:29) 'baken' is only used when it is in reference to something connected with God.) {bake 9x., baked 4x., bakemeats 1x., baker 8x., bakers 2x., bakers' 1x., baketh 1x., tot. = 35x.}

Balance – 8x., n. [A.D. 1275, < OF. *balance* < LL. *bilanx* (= 'having two scales, or flat pans') < *bi* = 'two' + *lanx* = 'scale or flat pan'] Thus, a **balance** is 'a device having two scales, or flat pans, which are suspended by chains or cords to opposite ends of a bar, which is held at its center most point by either above with a suspending cord, or beneath with a supporting bar'. Eg. Isa.46:6, "They lavish gold out of the bag, and weigh silver in the balance..." (NOI. A 'balance' is sing. and refers to something (or someone) being put into one scale and tested for weight against the other scale which has a known weight placed into it.) {balances 10x., balancings 1x., tot. = 19x.}

Balances – 10x., n. pl. [A.D. 1275, < ME. **balance** (see 'Balance') + **s** = forms the pl.] Thus, **balances** refer to 'both sides of a balance'. Eg. Rev.6:5, "And when he had opened the third seal, I heard the third beast say, Come and see. And I beheld, and lo a black horse; and he that sat on him had a pair of balances in his hand." (NOI. Belshazzar was weighed in BOTH sides of the scale, and was still found wanting! See Dan.5:27.) {balance 8x., balancings 1x., tot. = 19x.}

Ball – 1x., n. [A.D. 1205, < ME. **bal** < ON. *bollr* (possibly < L. *follis* = 'a thing inflated', such as a bellows or bag) = 'a round spherical object'] Thus, a **ball** is 'a round spherical object', referring to a child's play-toy. Eg. Isa.22:18, "He will surely violently turn and toss thee like a ball into a large country: there shalt thou die, and there the chariots of thy glory shall be the shame of thy lord's house." (NOI. Archeologists have found many such play-toys dating as far back as the ancient Pharaohs. The analogy in Isaiah is similar to how a child will toss away a ball (a once useful and valued play-toy), in disgust, when it no longer performs properly. The child was not attempting to see how far he could throw it, but rather to discard it off to one side as of no value.)

Balm – 6x n. [A.D. 1220, < ME. **basme** < OF. *basme* < L. *balsamum* (NOI. We get the E. 'balsam' from this word.) = 'the oily, fragrant resin taken from plants and trees of the balsameaceous genus *Balsamea*'] Thus, **balm** is 'the resin from certain trees, and used for medicinal purposes'. Eg. Jer.51:8, "Babylon is suddenly fallen and destroyed: howl for her; take balm for her pain, if so be she may be healed." (NOI. The 'balm of Gilead' (see Jer.8:22) refers to the resin extracted from the tree '*Balsamea opobalsamum*', found in the middle east and valued for its medicinal properties. Today, we speak of "balmy weather" meaning 'soothing or nice weather'.)

Band [1] – 3x n [A.D. 1200, < ON. *band* = 'a thin strip that contains', < an Indo-European root word *bendh* = 'to bind'] Thus, a **band** is 'a flat strip of cloth or metal used as a binding for holding something together'. Eg. Job.39:10 "Canst thou bind the unicorn with his band in the furrow? or will he harrow the valleys after thee? " {bands 24x., swaddlingband 1x., tot. = 28x.}

Band [2] – 1x n. [A.D. 1394, < OF. *bande* = It. *banda* = 'a thin flat strip used in decorating', < old Teut. *bindan* = 'to bind' (NOI. Our E. word 'bandage' comes from the OF. root *bande*.)] Thus, a **band** is 'a thin flat strip of cloth or metal used as decorative trim'. Eg. Ex.39:23 "And there was an hole in the midst of the robe, as the hole of an habergeon, with a band round about the hole, that it should not rend."

Band [3] – 15x n. [A.D. 1490, < OF. *bande* (= same as 'Band'[2]) (NOI. Although the etymology is the same as 'Band'[2], the difference may have come when 'Alphonso de Castille' had his soldiers identify themselves by wearing a red-colored sash, and called them a *bandu*.)] Thus, a **band** is 'a small group of people or animals joined together for a military or tactical purpose'. Eg. Act.10:1 "There was a certain man in Caesarea called Cornelius, a centurion of the band called the Italian band." (NOI. Here, the 'band' was a small group of 100. See 'Centurion'. Cp. also 'Troop'.) {bands 22 x., banded 1x., tot. = 38x.}

Banishment –2x., n. [A.D. 1507, < E. **banish** < OF. *banir* = 'to condemn and exile as an outlaw' (akin to E. '**ban**' = 'to curse or scold') + **ment** = forms the n. and shows 'the means of the action' (see E. suffix '–ment')] Thus, a **banishment** is 'a judicial act whereby the accused is condemned and exiled'. Eg. Ezr.7:26, "And whosoever will not do the law of thy God, and the law of the king, let judgment be executed speedily upon him, whether it be unto death, or to banishment, or to confiscation of goods, or to imprisonment." {banished 2x., tot. = 4x.}

Bank [1] – 13x., n. [A.D. 1200, < ME. **banke** < ON. *banke* = 'a long pile or heap of earth, like rising ground'] Thus, a **bank** is 'a rising heap of earth'. Eg. Isa.37:33, "Therefore thus saith the LORD concerning the king of Assyria, He shall not come into this city, nor shoot an arrow there, nor come before it with shields, nor cast a bank against it." {banks 5x., tot. = 18x.}

Bank [2] – 1x., n. [A.D. 1474, < F. *banque* < It. *banca* = 'bench' (referring to the table of a money lender or exchanger) (NOI. The Gk. is τραπεζα (*trapeze* – this has nothing to do with the piece of gymnastic apparatus often used in a circus) and it refers to the table at which a money-exchanger would sit and exchange different kinds of money for a fee. He then paid back loans he made with interest. 'Bankrupt' (< It. *banca rotta* = 'a broken bench') is what his creditors did to his bench, among other things, when he could not repay his loans. For an interesting study in finance, see Deut.28:1-14.)] Thus, a **bank** is 'the table of the money lender'. Eg. Lk.19:23, "Wherefore then gavest not thou my money into the bank, that at my coming I might have required mine own with usury? "

Banner – 3x., n. [A.D. 1230, < OF. *banere* < ML. *bandum* = 'standard' (referring to the emblematic flag of an army, which was raised high and carried into battle, and gave the soldiers a rallying-point for a sense of direction and good cheer) (NOI. A 'standard-bearer' was the one who carried the flag.)] Thus, a **banner** is 'a piece of cloth with a king's emblem on it, attached to a pole and held high for display'. Eg. Ps.60:4, "Thou hast given a banner to them that fear thee, that it may be displayed because of the truth. Selah." {banners 3x., tot. = 6x.}

Banquet – 14x., n. [A.D. 1483, < OF. *banquet* < It. *banchetto* < *banco* = 'table', in the sense of food and meals] Thus, a **banquet** is 'a feast of good food, wine and sometimes entertainment'. Eg. Dan.5:10, "Now the queen, by reason of the words of the king and his lords, came into the banquet house..." (NOI. Cp. the context of Dan.5:1-2. Esther invited the king and Haman to her "banquet of wine" (see Est.5:4-6) which featured exotic and expensive wines, but which, no doubt, would have also had sumptuous food.) {banqueting 1x., banquetings 1x., tot. = 16x.}

Baptize —9x., v. [A.D. 1297, < OF. *baptizier* < LL. *baptizare* < Gk. βαπτιζειν (*baptizein*) = 'to immerse in water or liquid' (NOI. The E. suffix **ize** emphasizes an 'end result', in this case a 'state of being a baptized one'. See E. suffix '–ise'.)] Thus, **baptize** means 'the religious action of immersing someone in water to produce a state of change'. Eg. Mt.3:11a, "I indeed baptize you with water unto repentance..." Here, John's baptism was to produce a state of repentance (see also Act.19:3-4). Furthermore, figuratively, **baptize** is used in various senses including 'the action of Christ immersing a believer into the Holy Ghost and (spiritual) fire to produce another state of change'. Eg. Mt.3:11b, "... but he that cometh after me is mightier than I, whose shoes I am not worthy to bear: he shall baptize you with the Holy Ghost, and with fire." (NOI. An ancient Gk. recipe for pickles calls for them to be 'baptized' in vinegar, thus producing a state of change. They go in as cucumbers and come out as pickles. It is the opinion of the author that salvation comes by grace through faith, thus producing what the Bible calls a 'believer' (see Act.5:14). Baptism is subsequent to salvation and makes the believer into a 'baptized believer', thus publicly identifying the believer with Christ. See Act.2:41; 8:12, 36-37.) {baptism 22x., baptisms 1x., baptist 14x., baptist's 1x., baptized 61x., baptizest 1x., baptizeth 2x., baptizing 4x., tot. = 115x.}

Barbarian —3x., n. [A.D. 1549, < OF. *barbarien* < L. *barbaria* = 'foreign country'] Thus, a **barbarian** is 'someone from a foreign country whose language and customs are different'. Eg. 1Cor.14:11, "Therefore if I know not the meaning of the voice, I shall be unto him that speaketh a barbarian, and he that speaketh shall be a barbarian unto me." (NOI. in Paul's day, a 'barbarian' was a person who was not part of the Roman or Greek culture. See Rom.1:14.) {barbarians 2x., barbarous 1x., tot. = 6x.}

Barbarous — 1x., adj. [A.D. 1526, < L. *barbarus* < Gk.

βαρβαρος (*barbaros*) = 'foreign', as in 'uncivilized of speech' (NOI. The ancient Greeks scorned all foreign languages, likening them to a "bar-bar" sound, which is how they devised βαρβαρος (*barbaros*). The Romans borrowed the word for their Latin language and gave it a similar meaning.)] Thus, **barbarous** modifies its n. (in this case, 'people') as 'not being able to speak the civilized languages of Greek or Latin'. Eg. Act.28:2, "And the barbarous people shewed us no little kindness: for they kindled a fire, and received us every one, because of the present rain, and because of the cold." (NOI. Luke was not trying to belittle these people when he called them 'barbarous'. These people may have been crude in their attempts to speak Latin or Greek, but were most gracious in their manners towards those 'washed ashore' on their island.) {barbarian 3x., barbarians 2x., tot. = 6x.}

Bare[1] – 13x., adj. [A.D. 885, < OE. **bǽr** = 'without covering'] Thus, **bare** modifies its n. as 'being without clothing or covering'; i.e. nude. Eg. Isa.47:2, "Take the millstones, and grind meal: uncover thy locks, make bare the leg, uncover the thigh, pass over the rivers." (NOI. While 'bare' signifies 'no clothes', 'naked' can be either 'no clothes' or 'having only an undergarment'. See also 'Naked'.)

Bare[2] – 173x., v. pret. [A.D. 1000(AT.), < OE. **barian** (pret. of 'bear'; see 'Bear'[1]) (NOI. 'Bare' was the commonly accepted pret. of 'bear' and it was not till after A.D. 1611 that 'bore' began to replace it.)] Thus, **bare** means 'the past-tense action of holding, carrying or bringing forth'. Eg. Gen.31:39, "That which was torn of beasts I brought not unto thee; I bare the loss of it; of my hand didst thou require it, whether stolen by day, or stolen by night." {bear[1] 205x., bearers 3x., bearest 5x., beareth 25x., bearing 22x., borne 31x., tot. = 464x.}

Barked – 1x., v. pret. [A.D. 1300, < ME. **bark** (< ON. *borkr* = 'tree skin') + **ed** = forms the pret. (see E. suffix '–ed'[1]).

Thus, **barked** means 'the past-tense action of stripping off the bark from a tree'. Eg. Joe.1:7, "He hath laid my vine waste, and barked my fig tree: he hath made it clean bare, and cast it away; the branches thereof are made white." (NOI. This 'bark' is a different word from the 'bark' that a dog makes (which is from OE. **beorcan** = 'an abrupt cry').)

Barley —37x., n. [A.D. 966, < OE. **bǽrlic** < oo., but from the genus *Hordeum* (which contains more than 30 species of plants)] Thus, **barley** is 'a coarse cereal plant, the grain of which was used for feeding animals (being cheaper than wheat), but was also eaten by the poor'. Eg. 1Ki.4:28, "Barley also and straw for the horses and dromedaries brought they unto the place where the officers were, every man according to his charge."

Barrel —3x., n. [A.D. 1300, < OF. *baril* < oo., but refers to 'a cylindrical wooden vessel'] Thus, a **barrel** is 'a cylindrical wooden vessel with bulging sides, and able to hold about 31.5 gal. of liquid (119 liters), or about 196 lb. (89 kilo.) of flour'. Eg. 1Ki.17:12, "And she said, As the LORD thy God liveth, I have not a cake, but an handful of meal in a barrel, and a little oil in a cruse..." (Cp. also 1Ki.18:32-35.) {barrels 1x., tot. = 4x.}

Barren —23x., adj. and n. [A.D. 1200, < OF. *baraine* < oo., but some have suggested < Hb. עקר (*aqar*) = 'male' (i.e. 'male-like' and unable to produce) (Cp. Deut.7:14, where 'male' and 'female barren' are both the same Hb. Word.)] Thus, as an adj. **barren** modifies its n. (usually a woman, but also the 'ground' and 'believers' (in a figurative sense) – see 2Pt.1:8) as 'being incapable of reproducing'. Eg. Gen.11:30, "But Sarai was barren; she had no child." Furthermore, as a n., **barren** is 'a name or title emphasizing someone's barrenness' (similar to calling them, "*The Sterile One*"). Eg. Isa.54:1, "Sing, O barren, thou that didst not bear; break forth into singing, and cry aloud, thou that didst not travail with child..." {barrenness 1x., tot. = 24x.}

Base[1] —8x., adj. [A.D. 1393, < OF. *bas* < LL. *bassus*) = 'short or low'] Thus, **base** modifies its n. as 'being short or low, but is used in the figurative sense of morals'. Eg. Job.30:8, "They were children of fools, yea, children of base men: they were viler than the earth." { baser 1x., basest 2x., tot. = 11x.}

Base[2] — 10x., n. [A.D. 1325, < OF. *base* < L. *basis* < Gk. βασις (*basis*) = 'a step or pedestal'] Thus, a **base** is 'the bottom of something that acts as a support'. Eg. 1Ki.7:27, "And he made ten bases of brass; four cubits was the length of one base, and four cubits the breadth thereof, and three cubits the height of it." {bases 16x., tot. = 26x.}

Bason —5x., n. [A.D. 1220, < ME. **bascin** < OF. *bacin* < ML. *bachinus* < *bacca* = 'water vessel' (NOI. The 1611 uses both spellings of 'bason' and 'basin', as both were acceptable then, but the KJV uses only 'bason'. Likewise also with 'basons'.)] Thus, a **bason** is 'a hollow, circular vessel, being greater in width at the top than the depth, and used for holding liquids such as blood or water'. Eg. Jn.13:5, "After that he poureth water into a bason, and began to wash the disciples' feet, and to wipe them with the towel wherewith he was girded." {basons 18x., tot= 23x.}

Bastard —2x., n. [A.D. 1297, < OF. *bastard* < *bast* (< LL. *bastum*) = 'pack-saddle' + *ard* (the OF. masculine suffix) = 'son of'; therefore a 'son of a pack-saddle' or 'pack-saddle child' (i.e. 'one born out of wedlock, not born in the home')] Thus, a **bastard** is 'someone who was born out of wedlock'. Eg. Zec.9:6, "And a bastard shall dwell in Ashdod, and I will cut off the pride of the Philistines." (NOI. English law required that the parents be married BEFORE they have a child, otherwise the child was considered a 'bastard' (illegitimate) and not a proper son, and therefore was not entitled to the rights of a son, such as heritage and inheritance.) {bastards 1x., tot. = 3x.}

Bat –2x., n. [A.D. 1300, < ME. **bakke** apparently < Ice. *blacka* = 'to flap or flutter with wings' (NOI. **Bakke** was changed (or corrupted?) to **bat**, **batt** and **batte** around A.D. 1575. The Ullans language (similar to Scottish, and spoken in North-East Ireland) still use the word 'backie-bird' to mean a bat.)] Thus, a **bat** is 'a small flying mammal, that comes out at night, having its forelimbs modified as wings, which have a membrane-skin as a covering and extend to its hind feet' (of the order of *Chiroptera*). Eg. Lev.11:19, "And the stork, the heron after her kind, and the lapwing, and the bat." (NOI. There are about 1,000 different types of bats in the world, ranging in length (head to foot) from 1.5 in. (3.8 cm.) to the 12 in. (30.5 cm.) 'fox bat' having a wingspan of 5 ft. (1.5 meter) (inhabiting Africa, Asia, and the East Indies). In Palestine there are about 20 different types of bats, which eat mainly insects, though some in Egypt will eat fruit.) {bats 1x., tot. = 3x.}

Bath – 6x., n. [A.D. 1398, trans. < Hb. בת (*bath*) = 'daughter' (meaning 'the amount of water a daughter could carry in a jug from the well')] Thus, **bath** is 'a liquid unit of measure containing about 9.3 gal. (about 35.2 liters)'. Eg. Eze.45:11, "The ephah and the bath shall be of one measure, that the bath may contain the tenth part of an homer, and the ephah the tenth part of an homer: the measure thereof shall be after the homer." (NOI. 'Bath' and 'baths' always refer to a unit of measure, and not to bathing.) {baths 9x., tot. = 15x.}

Bathe – 18x., v. [A.D. 1000, < OE. **baðian** (< OE. (n.) **bǽth** (= 'a large vessel filled with a liquid', usually water) + **ian** = 'the action of') = 'immersing or dipping the body into a liquid for cleansing or refreshment'] Thus, **bathe** means 'the action of dipping or immersing the body in some type of liquid for the purpose of cleansing or refreshment'. Eg. Lev.15:27, "And whosoever toucheth those things shall be unclean, and shall wash his clothes, and bathe himself in water, and be unclean until the even." (NOI. In every occurrence of 'bathe', the Bible is careful to specify 'with water'. This is because 'bathe' simply meant to 'immerse in a liquid', which could have been anything including blood, sweat or tears. Today, we never say "*bathe with water*" because the 'water' is understood.) {bathed 1x., tot. = 19x.}

Battle – 170x., n. and v. [A.D. 1297, < ME. **bataille** < OF. *bataille* < LL. *battalia* = 'fighting exercises' (< L. *battuere* = 'to beat')] Thus, as a n., a **battle** is 'a hostile engagement of opposing forces on land or sea'. Eg. 1Cor.14:8, "For if the trumpet give an uncertain sound, who shall prepare himself to the battle? " Furthermore, as a v., **battle** means 'the action of fighting or striving in combat'. Eg. 1Sam7:10, "And as Samuel was offering up the burnt offering, the Philistines drew near to battle against Israel..." {battlement 1x., battlements 1x., battles 6x., tot. = 178x.}

Battlement –1x., n. [A.D. 1325, < ME. **batelment** < OF. *bateillement* = 'a low wall built on top perimeter of a house or fortress, with openings originally meant for shooting through' (See E. suffix '–ment')] Thus, a **battlement** is 'a low safety-wall built on top of a flat-roof house and extending around its perimeter'. Eg. Deut.22:8, "When thou buildest a new house, then thou shalt make a battlement for thy roof, that thou bring not blood upon thine house, if any man fall from thence." (NOI. The roof-top of houses were used often for domestic work, social gatherings, refreshment and prayer. Cp. Act.10:9.) {battle 170x., battlements 1x., battles 6x., tot. = 178x.}

Bay[1] – 1x., n. [A.D. 1398, < OF. *baie* < L. *baca* = 'berry'] Thus, a **bay** is 'a small berry-fruit found on certain trees'. Eg.

Ps.37:35, "I have seen the wicked in great power, and spreading himself like a green bay tree." (NOI. This is the *Laurus nobilis*, a dark evergreen-tree that can grow as high as 60 ft. (18.28 m.). Its berries are black and its dark green leaves are used in cooking fish. The Greeks used the branches for making crowns or wreaths for their heroes. The Hb. אזרח (*ezrach*) refers to something which rises from the soil on its own (i.e. without requiring transplanting), and suggests the idea of 'native born'.)

Bay [2] –3x., n. [A.D. 1385, < OF. *baie* < LL. *baia* = 'an inlet of the sea'] Thus, a **bay** is 'an indentation of the land, where it meets the sea, having a wide-mouthed opening'. Eg. Josh.15:2, "And their south border was from the shore of the salt sea, from the bay that looketh southward."

Bay [3] –2x., adj. [A.D. 1374, < OF. *bai* < L. *badius* = 'reddish-brown color'] Thus, **bay** modifies its n. (both times in reference to horses) as 'being a reddish-brown in color'. Eg. Zec. 6:3, "And in the third chariot white horses; and in the fourth chariot grisled and bay horses."

Bdellium – 2x., n. [A.D. 1382(WB.), < L. *bdellium* < Gk. βδελλιον (*bdellion*) = 'the sticky fragrant gum-resin that comes from certain balsameaceous plants' (NOI. The Hb. בדלח (*bedolach*) = 'something that is stuck together'.)] Thus, **bdellium** is 'the tree that produces bdellium gum', a yellow to light-red resin, which was used for perfumes and as a medicine to reduce inflammation. Eg. Gen.2:12, "And the gold of that land is good: there is bdellium and the onyx stone." (NOI. The OT. Jews were well aware of plant leaves being used as medicine, as seen in Eze.47:12. See also 'Coriander'.)

Beacon – 1x., n. [A.D. 950, < OE. **beacn** = 'a sign'; i.e. such as a lighthouse] Thus, a **beacon** is 'a fire or a structure built to act as a warning'. Eg. Isa.30:17, "One thousand shall flee at the rebuke of one; at the rebuke of five shall ye flee: till ye be left as a beacon upon the top of a mountain, and as an ensign on an hill."

Beam – 15x., n. [A.D. 826, < OE. **beam** = 'tree' (same as Ger. *baum*), however used to refer to a long piece of timber which has been shaped for a purpose] Thus, a **beam** is 'a long piece of wood that has been shaped to perform a task', such as the beams in a roof of a house or in a weaving device. Eg. 1Sam.17:7, "And the staff of his spear was like a weaver's beam; and his spear's head weighed six hundred shekels of iron: and one bearing a shield went before him." {beams 12x., tot. = 27x.}

Bear[1] – 205x., v. [A.D. 893, < OE. **beran** = 'to hold, carry or bring forth'] Thus, **bear** means 'the action of holding, carrying or bringing forth'. Eg. Gen.4:13, "And Cain said unto the LORD, My punishment is greater than I can bear." {bare[2] 173x., bearers 3x., bearest 5x., beareth 25x., bearing 22x., borne 31x., tot. = 464x.}

Bear[2] – 10x., n. [A.D. 1000, < OE. **bera** < old Teut. *beron* = 'the brown one' (as in 'the brown bear of Europe')] Thus, a **bear** is 'a massive-bodied 4-footed animal, having shaggy hair and short limbs, typically weighing 700 lb. (317.5 kilogram), and will eat both plants and flesh'. Eg. 1Sam.17:34, "And David said unto Saul, Thy servant kept his father's sheep, and there came a lion, and a bear, and took a lamb out of the flock." {bears 2x., tot. = 12x.}

Beast – 180x., n. [A.D. 1210, < OF. *beste* < L. *bestia* < oo., (NOI. Originally, the OE. word **deer** meant 'all four-footed animals' (possibly < Sans. *dheu* = 'to breathe'). However, its use became restricted to the species *Cervidae* (what we know as modern 'deer') because of their abundance in England and their desirability for food. So, the word 'deer' was replaced by 'beast'. Today, the word 'beast' has now generally been replaced by ‘animal’, which, interestingly is never used in the Bible. Usually, but not always, ‘beast’ refers to animals with a wild-nature. See also ‘Cattle’. In Act.28:3-4 a viper is called a beast, perhaps for emphasis.)] Thus, a **beast** is ‘an animal (usually four-footed) of both the domestic and wild species’ (but the context usually indicates if it’s domestic or wild). Eg. Deut.14:6, “And every beast that parteth the hoof, and cleaveth the cleft into two claws, and cheweth the cud among the beasts, that ye shall eat.” (NOI. ‘Beast’ is sometimes used of a spiritual being (Rev.4:7), and in reference to the ‘Anti-Christ’ (Rev.13:1-4) and the ‘False Prophet’ (Rev.13:11-14).) {beast’s 1x., beasts 156x., tot. = 337x.}

Beautiful —23x adj. and pn. [A.D. 1526, < E. **beauty** (< OF. *bealte* < ML. *bellitas* < L. *bellus* = ‘fine or pretty’) + **ful** = ‘full of’ or ‘having the characteristics of’] Thus, as an adj., **beautiful** modifies its n. as ‘having the characteristics of fine or pretty’. Eg. Isa.52:7, “How beautiful upon the mountains are the feet of him that bringeth good tidings, that publisheth peace; that bringeth good tidings of good, that publisheth salvation; that saith unto Zion, Thy God reigneth! ” Furthermore, as a n., **Beautiful** is ‘the name of a certain gate of Herod’s Temple in Jerusalem’. Eg. Act.3:2, “And a certain man lame from his mother's womb was carried, whom they laid daily at the gate of the temple which is called Beautiful, to ask alms of them that entered into the temple.” {beauty 49x., tot. = 72x.}

Beckoned —6x., v. pret. [A.D. 950(LfG.), < OE. **beacnian** (= ‘to signal by use of the hand or head’) < **beacen** = (‘a sign’) + **ed** = forms the pret. (see E. suffix ‘–ed’[1])] Thus, **beckoned** means ‘the past-tense action of signaling for attention by using the hand or head’. Act.19:33, “And they drew Alexander out of the multitude, the Jews putting him forward. And Alexander beckoned with the hand, and would have made his defence unto the people.” beckoning 2x., tot. = 8x.}

Bed —90x., n. [A.D. 995, < OE. **bedd** < oo., but possibly from an early Germanic word *badjam* = 'place for sleeping dug in the ground', therefore, 'bed' refers to a place of comfort used primarily for sleep (NOI. A 'bed' could be beautifully constructed (Eze.23:41) or a portable pallet (Mt.9:2). A 'bed' and 'couch' were sometimes the same device, though wealthy people often had a couch separate from a bed. However, a 'bed' was primarily used for sleeping, while a 'couch' was primarily used for comfort or relaxing. The Hb. and Gk. words translated 'bed' are basically all the same as those translated 'couch', suggesting that the translators saw a difference between them in meaning. See also 'Couch'.)] Thus, a **bed** is 'a flat device used primarily for sleeping on'. Eg. Job.33:15, "In a dream, in a vision of the night, when deep sleep falleth upon men, in slumberings upon the bed." (NOI. Figuratively, a **bed** can be found in death and hell (Ps.139:8), as well as in a place of idolatry (Rev.2:22).) {bed's 1x., bedchamber 6x., beds 10x., bedstead 2x., tot. = 109x.}

Bedstead —2x., n. [A.D. 1440, < E. **bed** (see 'Bed') + **stead** = 'a place' (see 'Stead')] Thus, originally, a **bestead** is 'a place where a bed is located', but it came to mean the metal or wooden framework that supports a bed. Eg Deut.3:11, "For only Og king of Bashan remained of the remnant of giants; behold, his bedstead was a bedstead of iron; is it not in Rabbath of the children of Ammon? nine cubits was the length thereof, and four cubits the breadth of it, after the cubit of a man." {bed 90x., bed's 1x., bedchamber 6x., beds 2x., tot. = 109x.}

Beelzebub —7x., pn. [A.D. 950(LfG.), trans. < Gk. βεελζεβουβ (*Beelzeboub*) = 'lord of flies' (< Hb. בעל זבוב (*Bahal zeboob*) = (see 'Baalzebub'))] Thus, **Beelzebub** is 'the NT. equivalent of the OT. name Baalzebub (meaning 'lord-of-flies') and is used in reference to the devil'. Eg. Lk.11:15, "But some of them said, He casteth out devils through Beelzebub the chief of the devils." {Baalzebub 4x., tot. = 11x.}

Beetle – 1x., n. [A.D. 800, < OE. **bitela** < **bitan** = 'to bite' (NOI. There are many varieties of beetles, all of the order of *Coleoptera* < Gk. κοληοπτερος (*koleopteros*) = 'sheath winged'.)] Thus, a **beetle** is a biting insect with hard wing covers. Eg. Lev.11:22, "Even these of them ye may eat; the locust after his kind, and the bald locust after his kind, and the beetle after his kind, and the grasshopper after his kind." (NOI. Beetles were considered sacred in Egypt, especially the famous 'scarab' beetle, and were part of their religion.)

Beeves – 7x., n. pl. [A.D. 1300, < E. **beef** < OF. *boef* < L. *bos* (NOI. Our E. 'bovine' (ox, bull or cow) comes from this word.)] Thus, **beeves** are 'two or more beef-type of cattle', such as the ox, bull or cow. Eg. Lev.22:19, "Ye shall offer at your own will a male without blemish, of the beeves, of the sheep, or of the goats."

Befall – 9x., v. [A.D. 897, < OE. **befeallan, be** = 'intense thoroughness' (see E. prefix 'be–'[2]) + **feallan** = 'to descend from a high position to a low position'] Thus, figuratively, **befall** means 'the action of an intense falling', usually referring to some form of evil. Eg. Deut.31:17, "Then my anger shall be kindled against them in that day, and I will forsake them, and I will hide my face from them, and they shall be devoured, and many evils and troubles shall befall them; so that they will say in that day, Are not these evils come upon us, because our God is not among us? " {befallen 7x., befalleth 3x., befell 5x., tot. = 24x.}

Before – 1796x., adv., conj. and prep. [A.D. 971, < OE. **beforan, be** = 'near' (as in 'directly in front of') (see E. prefix 'be–'[1])+ **foran** (or fore) = 'the front position'] Thus, as an adv., **before** modifies its v. as 'happening in a front or first position'. Eg. 2Cor.8:10, "... who have begun before, not only to do, but also to be forward a year ago." Furthermore, as a conj., (subordinating conj. See section on Grammar – Conjunctions) **before** indicates that 'something took place first prior to the action of the clause'. Eg. Jn.1:48, "... Jesus answered and said unto him, Before that Philip called thee, when thou wast under the fig tree, I saw thee." Finally, as a prep., **before** 'shows the physical relationship of a n., pro. or pn. to the rest of the sentence'. Eg. Jn.12:37, "But though he had done so many miracles before them, yet they believed not on him." Here, the prep., 'before', indicates that Jesus was directly in front of the people. (See also 'Afore') {beforehand 5x., beforetime 11x., tot. = 1812x.}

Begat – 225x., v. pret. [A.D. 1000, < E. **beget** (see 'Beget')] Thus, **begat** means 'the past-tense action of beget' (i.e. having acquired through effort). Eg. Act.7:8, "And he gave him the covenant of circumcision: and so Abraham begat Isaac, and circumcised him the eighth day; and Isaac begat Jacob; and Jacob begat the twelve patriarchs." {beget 10x., begettest 2x., begetteth 3x., begotten 24x., firstbegotten 1x., tot. = 265x.}

Beget – 10x., v. [A.D. 1000, < OE. **begitan, be** = 'intense thoroughness' (see E. prefix 'be–'[2]) + **gitan** = 'to get'] Thus, **beget** means 'the action of acquiring through effort', and is always used in the sense of a physical or a spiritual birth. Eg. Ecc.6:3, "If a man beget an hundred children, and live many years, so that the days of his years be many..." {begat 225x., begettest 2x., begetteth 3x., begotten 24x., firstbegotten 1x., tot. = 265x.}

Beggarly – 1x., adj. [A.D. 1400, < E. **beggar** (= 'one who must ask for alms in order to sustain life') (< **beg** = 'to ask alms') + **ly** (= 'the manner of') (See E. suffix '–y'[1])] Thus, **beggarly** modifies its n. (in this case, 'elements') as 'being poor and unable to work and needing to beg in order to stay alive'. Eg. Gal.4:9, "But now, after that ye have known God, or rather are known of God, how turn ye again to the weak and beggarly elements, whereunto ye desire again to be in bondage? " (NOI. Paul wrote Galatians to combat the effect of legalistic teachers who desired to put the Galatian believers back under bondage, the bondage of trying to keep the OT. laws as a means of being spiritual. He used the term 'weak and beggarly elements' as a figure of speech in reference to this bondage.) {beg 3x., beggar 3x., begged 3x., begging 3x, tot. = 13x.}

Begotten – 24x., adj. and pp. [A.D. 1200, < E. **beget** (see 'Beget')] Thus, as an adj., **begotten** modifies a n. (a son) as 'being unique and one-of-a-kind', and is, in fact, further qualified with the word 'only'. Eg. Jn.3:16, "For God so loved the world, that he gave his only begotten Son, that whosoever believeth in him should not perish, but have everlasting life." (NOI. This term shows Christ's deity because all of God's other 'sons' are adopted, while Jesus Christ is 'only begotten'. This term was also used of Isaac in Heb.11:17. Although Abraham had other children (see Gen.16:15 and 25:1-4), Isaac was unique, being the promised son and the line through which Christ would come.) Furthermore, as a pp., **begotten** modifies its n., pro. or pn. as 'having been a result of the past-tense action of beget' (as in either a physical or spiritual birth). Eg. Gen.5:4, "And the days of Adam after he had begotten Seth were eight hundred years: and he begat sons and daughters." {begat 225x., beget 10x., begettest 2x., begetteth 3x., firstbegotten 1x., tot. = 265x.}

Beguile – 2x., v. [A.D. 1225, < E. **be** = 'intense thoroughness' (see E. prefix 'be–'[2]) + **guile** = 'crafty trickery like a decoy' (see 'Guile')] Thus, **beguile** means the action of 'an intense or thorough application of crafty trickery upon someone'. Eg. Col.2:4, "And this I say, lest any man should beguile you with enticing words." {beguiled 5x., beguiling 1x., tot. = 8x.}

Behalf – 13x., n. [A.D. 1303, < ME. **behalve** < OE. **be healfe** = ‘by his side’ (understood as ‘on his side’)] Thus, **behalf** is ‘something on the side of’, and was understood as standing next to someone or representing their interests. Eg. Job.36:2, “Suffer me a little, and I will shew thee that I have yet to speak on God's behalf.” (NOI. The phrases, “in this behalf” and “in the behalf” refer to the interests of a person or thing. Cp. 2Chr.16:9 and Phil.1:29.)

Behave – 6x., v. [A.D. 1440, < E. **be** = ‘intense thoroughness’ (see E. prefix ‘be–’[2]) + **have** = ‘to hold or possess’] Thus, **behave** means ‘the action of an intense or thorough holding of ones’ self in conformity with what is considered a proper standard of behavior’. Eg. 1Chr.19:13, “Be of good courage, and let us behave ourselves valiantly for our people...” {behaved 9x., behaveth 1x., behaviour 4x., (incl. title of Ps.34) tot. = 20x.}

Behemoth – 1x., n. [A.D. 1382(WB.), trans. < Hb. בהמות (*b'hemoth*) < oo., Some scholars believe it was a hippopotamus or an elephant, but this does not explain the tail moving like a cedar. Others believe it was an extinct type of dinosaur (which means ‘terrible lizard’ and was first used in A.D. 1841. See also ‘Dragon’.) such as a ‘brachiosaurus’. (NOI. The Hb. בהמה (*b'hemah*) (not בהמות (*b'hemoth*)) is always translated “cattle’ or ‘beast’.)] Thus, a **behemoth** is ‘a very large air-breathing, vegetation-eating animal’; possibly an extinct type of dinosaur. Eg. Job.40:15, “Behold now behemoth, which I made with thee; he eateth grass as an ox.” (See also Job.40:15-24.)

Behold – 1326x., int. and v. [A.D. 825(VP.), < OE. **behealdan**, **be** = ‘intense thoroughness’ (see E. prefix ‘be–’[2]) + **healdan** = ‘to keep or maintain a grasp on something’] Thus, as an int., **behold** is used in a figurative sense of ‘intently grasping something with one's mind’ (i.e. ‘look here and pay attention'). Eg. 1Cor.15:51, "Behold, I shew you a mystery; We shall not all sleep, but we shall all be changed." Furthermore, as a v., **behold** means 'the pres. tense action of intently looking on something'. Eg. Jn.20:27, "Then saith he to Thomas, Reach hither thy finger, and behold my hands; and reach hither thy hand, and thrust it into my side: and be not faithless, but believing." {beheld 53x., beholdest 4x., beholdeth 4x., beholding 15x., tot. = 1402x.}

Behoved –2x., v. pret. [A.D. 890, < E. **behove** (< OE. **behofian** < **behof** (< **be** = 'intense thoroughness' (see E. prefix 'be–'[2]) + **hof** = 'to heave' (see 'Heave') + **ian** = 'the action of') = 'an intense lifting up, requiring much effort, but done in order to give a useful or necessary advantage', hence the idea of 'ought' or 'necessary') + **ed** = forms the pret. (see E. suffix '–ed'[1])] Thus, **behoved** means 'the past-tense action of gaining a useful or necessary advantage through strenuous effort'. Eg. Lk.24:46, "And said unto them, Thus it is written, and thus it behoved Christ to suffer, and to rise from the dead the third day."

Bekah – 1x., n. [A.D. 1611(HB.), trans. < Hb. בקע (*behkah*) = 'a division' and used in reference to the shekel (see 'Shekel'), meaning 'a divided shekel'] Thus, a **bekah** is 'a half-shekel'. Eg. Ex.38:26, "A bekah for every man, that is, half a shekel, after the shekel of the sanctuary, for every one that went to be numbered, from twenty years old and upward, for six hundred thousand and three thousand and five hundred and fifty men." (NOI. Today, we 'count out' money, but in the OT, money was 'weighed out' in balances. A 'shekel' of money weighed about ½ oz. (8.78 drams), and therefore a 'bekah' weighed ¼ oz. (4.39 drams). There were at least 3 types of shekels (gold, silver and copper). To calculate the value of the 'bekah', one need only find the current price of the metal per oz., divide by 16 (there are 16 drams per oz.) and multiply it by 4.39. Eg. Silver (at this writing) sells for about $5.35 US per oz., which means a 'bekah' would be worth about $1.47

US. Jewish Synagogues still collect the half-shekel.)

Bel – 3x., pn. [A.D. 1382(WB.), trans. < Hb. בל (*Bel*) = Hb. בעל (*bahal*) = 'lord or master' (see 'Baal') (NOI. 'Bel' was the name of the Babylonian sun-god, 'Marduk', said to have created man. His festival was celebrated in the spring and was considered the chief god of Babylon.)] Thus, **Bel** is 'the name of the chief Babylonian deity, whose name means lord'. Eg. Jer.51:44, "And I will punish Bel in Babylon, and I will bring forth out of his mouth that which he hath swallowed up: and the nations shall not flow together any more unto him: yea, the wall of Babylon shall fall."

Belch – 1x., v. [A.D. 1000(ASP.), < OE. **bealcian** = 'to eject or throw out forcefully' (as in 'a shout', or 'to force wind from the stomach out through the mouth')] Thus, **belch** means 'the action of ejecting forcefully'. Eg. Ps.59:7 "Behold, they belch out with their mouth: swords are in their lips: for who, say they, doth hear? " (NOI. The 'belching' here may only refer to the shouting 'dog-like' sounds and cursing by the enemies of king David, according to the context of Ps.59.)

Belial – 17x., pn. [A.D. 1225, trans < Hb. בליעל (*Beleyahal*) = 'worthlessness or wickedness'] Thus, **Belial** is 'a name (meaning 'wickedness') used to personify evil' and is, no doubt, a reference to Satan. Eg. 2Cor.6:15 "And what concord hath Christ with Belial? or what part hath he that believeth with an infidel? " (NOI. The Hb. בליעל (*Beleyahal*) is also translated as 'wicked' (Deut.15:9), 'ungodly men' (2Sam.22:5), 'evil' (Ps.41:8) and 'naughty' (Pr.6:12).)

Belied – 1x pret. v. [A.D. 1000(AT.), < OE. **belie** (< OE. **beleogan**, **be** = 'intense thoroughness' (see E. prefix 'be–'[2]) + **leogan** = 'to lie or deceive') = 'to deceive by lying' + **ed** = forms the pret. (see E. suffix '–ed'[1])] Thus, **belied** means 'the past-tense action of having purposely caused deception by lying' (similar to counterfeiting). Eg. Jer.5:12 "They have belied the LORD, and said, It is not he; neither shall evil come upon us; neither shall we see sword nor famine."

Believe – 143x., v. [A.D. 1200, < ME. **bileven**, **bi** = 'intense thoroughness' (see E. prefix 'be–'[2]) + **leven** = 'to believe'] Thus, **believe** means 'the action of a very intense or thorough belief in something or someone' (i.e. more than just a head-knowledge). Eg. Act.16:31 "And they said, Believe on the Lord Jesus Christ, and thou shalt be saved, and thy house." (NOI. Some people claim to 'believe' in God, yet their lives are anything but 'godly'. A genuine 'belief' will show itself in a godly life. See Jam.2:18.) {belief 1x., believed 116x., believers 2x., believest 8x., believeth 45x., believing 8x., unbelief 16x., tot. = 339x.}

Bellow – 1x., v. [A.D. 800, < OE. **bylgean** = 'to roar' (especially of cows and bulls)] Thus, **bellow** means the action of 'making a roaring sound like a bull or cow'. Eg. Jer.50:11 "Because ye were glad, because ye rejoiced, O ye destroyers of mine heritage, because ye are grown fat as the heifer at grass, and bellow as bulls."

Bellows – 1x., n. sing. [A.D. 800, < OE. **blǽstbel** = 'blast bag'] Thus, a **bellows** is 'a device for producing a blast of air', used to make a fire hotter. Eg. Jer.6:29, "The bellows are burned, the lead is consumed of the fire; the founder melteth in vain: for the wicked are not plucked away."

Belly – 49x., n. [A.D. 950, < OE. **bǽlg** = 'bag' < Teut. *balgiz* = 'inflated or swollen thing' (NOI. In A.D. 1340, 'belly' began to mean 'the stomach area'.)] Thus, a **belly** is 'a bag', but usually refers to the stomach area of people and animals. Eg. Num.5:22, "And this water that causeth the curse shall go into thy bowels, to make thy belly to swell, and thy thigh to rot: And the woman shall say, Amen, amen." (NOI. Figuratively, a **belly** also refers to 'the decorative part of the two pillars of Solomon's Temple' (1Ki.7:20), 'the seat of carnal affections' (Job.15:35), 'the womb' (Jer.1:5), 'hell' (Jn.2:2) and 'the deepest parts of a man' (Pr.26:22).) {bellies 1x., tot. = 50x.}

Bemoan – 5x., v. [A.D. 1000(AT.), < OE. **bemǽman, be** = 'intense thoroughness' (see E. prefix 'be–'[2]) + **mǽnan** = 'to complain'] Thus, **bemoan** means 'the action of an intense complaint over some loss, often accompanied by a low groaning sound'. Eg. Jer.22:10, "Weep ye not for the dead, neither bemoan him: but weep sore for him that goeth away: for he shall return no more, nor see his native country." (NOI. 'Bemoan' is not the same as 'lament'. See 'Lament'.) {bemoaned 1x., bemoaning 1x., tot. = 7x.}

Benefactors – 1x., n. pl. [A.D. 1494, < E. **benefactor** (< L. *benefacere, bene* = 'well' + *facere* = 'to do or make') = 'a well-doer' + **s** = forms the pl.] Thus, **benefactors** are 'two or more people who do well' (as in bestowing benefits upon others). Eg. Lk.22:25, "And he said unto them, The kings of the Gentiles exercise lordship over them; and they that exercise authority upon them are called benefactors."

Benefit – 5x., n. and v. [A.D. 1377, < ME. **benfet** < OF. *bienfait* < L. *benefactum* = 'a good deed'] Thus, as a n., a **benefit** is 'a good deed or a helpful advantage'. Eg. 2Cor.1:15, "And in this confidence I was minded to come unto you before, that ye might have a second benefit." Furthermore, as a v., **benefit** means 'the action of bestowing some good deed or helpful advantage'. Eg. Jer.18:10, "If it do evil in my sight, that it obey not my voice, then I will repent of the good, wherewith I said I would benefit them." {benefits 3x., tot. = 8x.}

Benevolence – 1x., n. [A.D. 1384, < OF. *benivolence* < L. *benevolentia* = 'well-wishing'] Thus, **benevolence** is 'the condition of promoting the happiness of others'. Eg. 1Cor.7:3, "Let the husband render unto the wife due benevolence: and likewise also the wife unto the husband." (NOI. This 'benevolence' is 'due' (something owed) both husband and wife to each other.)

Bereave –6x., v. [A.D. 888, < OE. **bereafian, be** = 'intense thoroughness' (see E. prefix 'be–'[2]) + **reafian** (< **reaf** = 'spoil' + **ian** = 'the action of') = 'to rob, spoil or plunder'] Thus, **bereave** means 'the action of an intense or thorough spoiling or taking away, usually involving some aspect of violence'. Eg. Jer.15:7, "And I will fan them with a fan in the gates of the land; I will bereave them of children, I will destroy my people, since they return not from their ways." {bereaved 6x., bereaveth 1x., tot. = 13x.}

Beryl – 8x., n. [A.D. 1300, < OF. *beril* < L. *beryllus* < Gk. βηρυλλος (*berullos*) < oo., but possibly means 'crystal'] Thus, **beryl** is 'a transparent precious stone, a silicate of aluminum and beryllium, usually of aquamarine blue and green'. Eg. Eze.1:16, "The appearance of the wheels and their work was like unto the colour of a beryl..." (NOI. 'Beryl' was used as the first stone in the fourth row on the High Priest's breastplate (Ex.28:20), and used to garnish the eighth foundation of the wall of the New Jerusalem (Rev.21:20). The ancient Egyptians believed that 'beryl' possessed magical qualities that would make them fearless, intelligent and victorious in sports, war and legal matters.)

Beseech – 67x., v. [A.D. 1175, < ME. **bisechen** < **biseken, bi** = 'intense thoroughness' (see E. prefix 'be–'[2]) + **seken** = 'to seek' (see also 'Seek')] Thus, **beseech** means 'the action of begging earnestly after, or imploring with great urgency'. Eg. 2Sam.24:10, "And David's heart smote him after that he had numbered the people. And David said unto the LORD, I have sinned greatly in that I have done: and now, I beseech thee, O LORD, take away the iniquity of thy servant; for I have done very foolishly." {beseeching 3x., besought 44x., tot. = 114x.}

Besiege —11x., v. [A.D. 1297, < ME. **besege, be** = 'intense thoroughness' (see E. prefix 'be–'[2]) + **sege** (< ME. **assiege** < OF. *asegier* < LL. *assediare, as* = 'to' (see L. prefix '*ad–*') + *sedium* = 'sitting') = 'to sit down' (as in across from an enemy with the purpose of warring against him)] Thus, **besiege** means 'the action of a very intensive long-term attack against a city or an enemy'. Eg. Deut.20:19, "When thou shalt besiege a city a long time, in making war against it to take it..." (NOI. A siege could take a couple of years. The idea was to prevent people and supplies from entering the city, till the inhabitants finally gave up. During this time, the attacker usually also tried to break through the walls or gates using battering-rams, catapults and towers. The longest siege recorded in history was that of Ashdod by Psammatik II of Egypt, which lasted 29 years.) {besieged 23x., siege 17x., tot. = 51x.}

Besom — 1x., n. [A.D. 893, < OE. **besma** = 'a bunch of twigs' (NOI. It comes from a shrub-type toxic plant known as *Cytisus scoparius*, having long stems with small bushy leaves, making it ideal to be used as a sweeper. 'Broom' (not used in the KJV) was a general word used in the 1600's, but it was different from the specific 'besom'.)] Thus, a **besom** is 'a bunch of twigs from a certain plant', used for sweeping. Eg. Isa.14:23, "I will also make it a possession for the bittern, and pools of water: and I will sweep it with the besom of destruction, saith the LORD of hosts."

Besought — 44x., v. pret. [A.D. 1175(?), < E. **beseech** (see 'Beseech')] Thus, **besought** means 'the past-tense action of begging earnestly after, or imploring with great urgency'. Eg. Act.16:15, "And when she was baptized, and her household, she besought us, saying, If ye have judged me to be faithful to the Lord, come into my house, and abide there. And she constrained us." {beseech 67x., beseeching 3x., tot. = 114x.}

Bestead – 1x., adj. [A.D. 1225, < ME. **bistad, bi** = 'intense thoroughness' (see E. prefix 'be–'[2]) + **stad** = 'place'] Thus, **bestead** modifies its n. (in this case, the pro. 'they') as 'being forcibly put in place', but when coupled with 'hardly' (= 'in a hard manner' (See also 'Hardly'.)), it modifies the pro. as 'being hard pressed in an evil way'. Eg. Isa.8:21, "And they shall pass through it, hardly bestead and hungry: and it shall come to pass, that when they shall be hungry, they shall fret themselves, and curse their king and their God, and look upward."

Bestow – 9x., v. [A.D. 1315, < ME. **bistowen, bi** = 'intense thoroughness' (see E. prefix 'be–'[2]) + **stowen** = 'to place'] Thus, **bestow** means 'the action of making a placement of something of importance in or to someplace of worth' (similar to making a deposit of money in the bank). Eg. Lk.12:18, "And he said, This will I do: I will pull down my barns, and build greater; and there will I bestow all my fruits and my goods." {bestowed 14x., tot. = 23x.}

Bethink – 2x., v. [A.D. 1000(ASG.), < OE. **biðencan, bi** = 'intense thoroughness' (see E. prefix 'be–'[2]) + **ðencan** = 'to think'] Thus, **bethink** means 'the action of occupying oneself in deep thought'. Eg. 1Ki.8:47, "Yet if they shall bethink themselves in the land whither they were carried captives, and repent, and make supplication unto thee..." {think 65x., tot. = 67x.}

Betimes – 5x., adv. [A.D. 1314, < ME. **bitime, bi** = 'intense thoroughness' (see E. prefix 'be–'[2]) + **time** = 'time'] Thus, **betimes** modifies the action of the v. as 'being an important or urgent time', normally requiring people to go the extra mile by rising up early or staying up late. Eg. 2Chr.36:15, "And the

LORD God of their fathers sent to them by his messengers, rising up betimes, and sending; because he had compassion on his people, and on his dwelling place." (NOI. 'Betimes' does not just mean 'early', but has a great sense of urgency about it. See also 'Early'.)

Betray —18x., v. [A.D. 1250, < ME. **bitraien, bi** = 'intense thoroughness' (see E. prefix 'be–'[2]) + **traien** = 'to hand over' (< OF. *trair* < L. *tradere* = 'to give over')] Thus, **betray** means 'the action of giving over into enemy hands with a sense of intensity and disloyalty'. Eg. Mk.14:18, "And as they sat and did eat, Jesus said, Verily I say unto you, One of you which eateth with me shall betray me." {betrayed 19x., betrayers 1x., betrayest 1x., betrayeth 3x., tot. = 42x.}

Betroth — 4x., v. [A.D. 1303, < ME. **bitrouthen, bi** = 'intense thoroughness' (see E. prefix 'be–'[2]) + **trouthen** = 'truth'] Thus, **betroth** means 'the action of an intense thoroughness of truth'. Eg. Deut.28:30, "Thou shalt betroth a wife, and another man shall lie with her." (NOI. Betrothing was when a man publicly declared his intentions of marrying a woman by a 'thoroughness of his truth'. The modern 'engagement ring' on a woman's finger is likewise a public pledge of a man's truthful intentions to marry her. The betrothal period lasted at least a year and also proved that the woman was pure. Cp. Ex.21:8-9 and Deut.20:7. A similar truth concerning Christ and the church is found in 2Cor.11:2, where the Holy Spirit is like the engagement ring (Eph.1:13-14.) See also 'Espoused'.) {betrothed 9x., tot. = 13x.}

Between —232x., prep. and adv. [A.D. 890, < OE. **betweonum, be** = 'by' (see E. prefix 'be–'[1])+ **tweonum** < **twa** = 'two' (NOI. Contextual studies of 'between' and 'betwixt' in Scripture indicate that 'between' has a more general idea of the 'space' separating two points)] Thus, as a prep., **between** means 'the space that separates two people, groups or things, without belonging or being close to either one'. Eg. Gen.15:17, "And it came to pass, that, when the sun went down, and it was dark, behold a smoking furnace, and a burning lamp that passed between those pieces." Furthermore, as an adv., **between** modifies the action of the v. as 'happening within the space that separates two people, groups or things without belonging or being close to either one'. Eg. Num.16:48, "And he stood between the dead and the living; and the plague was stayed." (NOI. Shakespeare's writings were contemporary with the 1611, having used 'between' some 223x., and 'betwixt' 60x. By studying the context of Shakespeare's two words, we find similar results to that of Scripture; namely, 'betwixt' seems to have more a meaning of being intimate and close (almost touching), whereas 'between' is more general and not as close.)

Betwixt – 16x., prep. and adv. [A.D. 931, < OE. **betweox, be** = 'by' (see E. prefix 'be–'[1])+ **tweox** < **twa** = 'two' (see 'Between')] Thus, as a prep., **betwixt** means 'a very close physical, mental, emotional or spiritual proximity between two people, groups or things'. Eg. Phil.1:23, "For I am in a strait betwixt two, having a desire to depart, and to be with Christ; which is far better." Here, Paul was very close emotionally and spiritually with his Christian friends on earth, but at the same time, very close with his desire to be with Christ in heaven. (NOI. Another illustration is seen in Jer.39:4. Notice the gate was, "betwixt the two walls". The gate was close enough to 'touch' either wall.) Furthermore, as an adv., **betwixt** modifies the action of the v. as 'happening in a very close physical, mental, emotional or spiritual proximity between two people, groups or things'. Eg. Gen.31:51, "And Laban said to Jacob, Behold this heap, and behold this pillar, which I have cast betwixt me and thee."

Beulah – 1x pn. [A.D. 1535(CB.), trans. < Hb. בעל (*bawal*) = 'married'] Thus, **Beulah** (meaning 'married') is 'the name God will call His land, indicating His delight for it'. Eg.

Isa.62:4, "Thou shalt no more be termed Forsaken; neither shall thy land any more be termed Desolate: but thou shalt be called Hephzibah, and thy land Beulah: for the LORD delighteth in thee, and thy land shall be married."

Bewail – 6x., v. [A.D. 1300, < ME. **be** = 'intense thoroughness' (see E. prefix 'be–'[2]) + **wail** (< ON. *veila* = 'to lament'; similar to Nor. *voela* = 'to bleat') = 'to express with mournful cries, pain or sorrow' (see also 'Wail')] Thus, **bewail** means 'the action of an intense, pitiful crying, used to express a deep sorrow or pain'. Eg. Rev.18:9, "And the kings of the earth, who have committed fornication and lived deliciously with her, shall bewail her, and lament for her, when they shall see the smoke of her burning." {bewailed 3x., bewaileth 1x., tot. = 10x.}

Bewitched – 3x., v. pret. [A.D. 1205, < ME. **biwicchen, bi** = 'intense thoroughness' (see E. prefix 'be–'[2]) + **wicchen** (< OE. (v.) **wiccian** < oo., but refers to the practice of witchcraft or enchantment) = 'to enchant' (see also 'Witch') + **ed** = forms the pret. (see E. suffix '–ed'[1])] Thus, **bewitched** means 'the past-tense action of being thoroughly enchanted'. Eg. Act.8:11, "And to him they had regard, because that of long time he had bewitched them with sorceries."

Bewray – 1x., v. [A.D. 1300, < ME. **bewreien, be** = 'intense thoroughness' (see E. prefix 'be–'[2]) + **wreien** < OE. **wregan** = 'to expose for the purpose of accusing'] Thus, **bewray** means 'the action of a thorough exposing'. Eg. Isa.16:3, "Take counsel, execute judgment; make thy shadow as the night in the midst of the noonday; hide the outcasts; bewray not him that wandereth." (NOI. Consider also the accusation against Peter because of his Galilean speech, in Mt.26:73.) {bewrayeth 3x., tot. = 4x.}

Bid – 17x., v. [A.D. 893, < OE. **biddan** < Teut. *beudan* = 'to stretch out' or 'to reach out'] Thus, **bid** means 'the action of earnestly pressing for an answer or compliance to a request'. Eg. Lk.10:40, "But Martha was cumbered about much serving, and came to him, and said, Lord, dost thou not care that my sister hath left me to serve alone? bid her therefore that she help me." (NOI. 'Bid' is a much stronger and more emphatic word than 'ask'. See 'Ask'.) {bade 18x., badest 1x., bidden 14x., biddeth 1x., bidding 1x., tot. = 52x.}

Bier – 2x., n. [A.D. 890, < OE. **bǽr** = 'a framework used for carrying a load'] Thus, a **bier** is 'a framework for transporting something' (usually a dead body). Eg. Lk.7:14, "And he came and touched the bier: and they that bare him stood still. And he said, Young man, I say unto thee, Arise."

Bill – 7x., n. [A.D. 1321, < ME. **bille** < ML. *bulla* (< L. *bulla* = 'bubble or round object'; often referring to a round seal attached to official documents) = 'an official document having a seal'] Thus, a **bill** is 'an official document' (such as a legal document of divorce or a business transaction). Eg. Lk.16:7, "Then said he to another, And how much owest thou? And he said, An hundred measures of wheat. And he said unto him, Take thy bill, and write fourscore."

Billows – 2x., n. pl. [A.D. 1552, < E. **billow** < ON. *bilgja* < Teut. *belgan* = 'to swell up' + **s** = forms the pl.] Thus, **billows** are 'the swelling of the sea waters as they rise up like mountains'. Eg. Jon.2:3, "For thou hadst cast me into the deep, in the midst of the seas; and the floods compassed me about: all thy billows and thy waves passed over me." (NOI. 'Billows' are different from waves. See 'Wave'[2].)

Bind – 49x., v. [A.D. 971, < OE. **bindan** = 'to secure using a band, rope or bond'] Thus, **bind** means 'the action of tying or making secure by use of a band, rope or a bond'. Eg. Act.12:8,

"And the angel said unto him, Gird thyself, and bind on thy sandals. And so he did..." (NOI. 'Bind' is also used in a figurative sense, as in Isa.61:1, "... to bind up the brokenhearted...") {bindeth 9x., binding 5x., bound 104x., tot. = 167x.}

Bird —28x., n. [A.D. 800, < ME. **byrd** < OE. **bridd** (pl. **briddas**) = 'a young of the feathered, flying tribes' (i.e. 'a young bird')] Thus, a **bird** is 'a generic term referring to the young of the feathered vertebrates, which use their forearms to fly', such as an eaglet. Eg. Ecc.10:20, "Curse not the king, no not in thy thought; and curse not the rich in thy bedchamber: for a bird of the air shall carry the voice, and that which hath wings shall tell the matter." (See also 'Fowl'.) {bird's 1x., birds 24x., birds' 1x., tot. = 54x.}

Birthday — 3x., n. [A.D. 1382(WB.), < OE. **gebyrt d g** (as found in the ASG. Mt.14:6), **gebyrt** = 'birth' + **d g** = 'day'] Thus, a **birthday** is 'the day (or celebration) of one's birth'. Eg. Mk.6:21, "And when a convenient day was come, that Herod on his birthday made a supper to his lords, high captains, and chief estates of Galilee." (NOI. The Bible only records two birthday celebrations, namely Pharaoh's and Herod's. Obviously, everyone kept track of their birthday in order to know how old they were.)

Birthright —10x., n. [A.D. 1535(CB.), < E. **birth** = 'the bearing of offspring' + **right** = 'the standard of value' (see 'Right')] Thus, a **birthright** is 'the right by birth', and refers to the legal standing and possessions of the first born male of a family. Eg. Gen.43:33, "And they sat before him, the firstborn according to his birthright, and the youngest according to his youth: and the men marvelled one at another." (NOI. A 'birthright' could be sold to another, before it takes effect (see Gen.25:31-34), or it could be taken from the first born by the father, usually because of gross sin. See 1Chr.5:1-2.)

Bishop – 6x.*, n. [A.D. 893, < OE. **biscop** < LL. *episcopus* < Gk. επισκοπος (*episkopos*), (επι (*epi*) = 'on or over' + σκοπος (*skopos*) = 'see') = 'overseer' (NOI. The Episcopalian Church takes its name from this word.)] Thus, a **bishop** is 'one who oversees the actions of others within a local church' (i.e a pastor). Eg. 1Tim.3:2, "A bishop then must be blameless, the husband of one wife, vigilant, sober, of good behaviour, given to hospitality, apt to teach." (NOI. 'Bishop' is also applied to Christ. See 1Pt.2:25.) (*incl. ps. of 2Tim. and Ti.) {bishoprick 1x., bishops 1x., tot. = 8x.}

Bishoprick – 1x., n. [A.D. 890, < OE. **biscoprice**, **bisceop** = 'bishop' (see 'Bishop') + **rice** = 'realm'] Thus, a **bishoprick** is 'the realm or province over which a bishop has control'. Eg. Act.1:20, "For it is written in the book of Psalms, Let his habitation be desolate, and let no man dwell therein: and his bishoprick let another take." {bishop 6x., bishops 1x., tot. = 8x.}

Bit[1] – 1x., n. [A.D. 893, < OE. **bite** (as in 'a bite of something', or 'something bitten off') (NOI. In about A.D. 1340, the word was applied to the metal piece put in the mouths of horses and mules, from which reins are attached, for the purpose of controlling the animal. It's not certain, from the origin of the word, whether the animal grips the bit, or the bit grips the animal.)] Thus, a **bit** is 'a piece of metal put into the mouths of horses and mules in order to control them'. Eg. Ps.32:9, "Be ye not as the horse, or as the mule, which have no understanding: whose mouth must be held in with bit and bridle, lest they come near unto thee." {bits 1x. tot. = 2x.}

Bit[2] – 2x., v. pret. [A.D. 1300, < OE. **bat** < **bitan** = 'to bite' (see 'Bite')] Thus, **bit** means 'the past-tense action of the v. bite'. Eg. Num.21:6, "And the LORD sent fiery serpents among the people, and they bit the people; and much people of Israel died." {bite 7x., biteth 2x., bitten 2x., tot. = 13x.}

Bite —7x., v. [A.D. 1000, < OE. **bitan** = 'to cut or pierce with the teeth'] Thus, **bite** means 'the action of cutting or piercing with the teeth'. Eg. Ecc.10:8, "He that diggeth a pit shall fall into it; and whoso breaketh an hedge, a serpent shall bite him." (NOI. 'Bite' is also used figuratively to mean 'a mental / emotion cutting or piercing', as in Gal.5:15, "But if ye bite and devour one another...") {bit^2 2x., biteth 2x., bitten 2x., tot. = 13x.}

Bitter —38x., adj. [A.D. 971, < OE. **biter** = 'biting, sharp or cutting' (< OE. root **bitan**) (as in 'not gentle and easy')] Thus, **bitter** modifies its n. as 'having a very harsh or biting characteristic, or as being something grievous to the taste or emotions'. Eg. Pr.5:4, "But her end is bitter as wormwood, sharp as a twoedged sword." {bitterly 9x., bitterness 22x., tot. = 69x.}

Bittern —3x., n. [A.D. 1000, < OE. **botor** < OF. *butor* < oo., but refers to a 'heron-like' bird (NOI. the '**n**' in '**bittern**' is intru. since the 1500's. The modern L. name is *botaurus* = 'a bird that bellows like an ox'.)] Thus, a **bittern** is 'a bird, similar to a heron, which emits a 'booming-cry' during mating season'. Eg. Zep.2:14, "And flocks shall lie down in the midst of her, all the beasts of the nations: both the cormorant and the bittern shall lodge in the upper lintels of it; their voice shall sing in the windows; desolation shall be in the thresholds: for he shall uncover the cedar work."

Blains —2x., n. pl. [A.D. 1000, < OE. **blegen** = 'an inflamed, swollen sore' (such as a blister) + **s** = forms the pl.] Thus, **blains** are 'two or more inflamed swollen sores on the body'. Eg. Ex.9:9, "And it shall become small dust in all the land of Egypt, and shall be a boil breaking forth with blains upon man, and upon beast, throughout all the land of Egypt." (NOI. It has been suggested that blains were a black-leprosy, a kind of elephantiasis, which also produced burning ulcers.)

Blame —4x., n. and v. [A.D. 1200, < OF. *blasmer* = 'to speak evil or bad of' < LL. *blastemare* < *blasphemare* (see 'Blaspheme')] Thus, as a n., **blame** is 'a fault or something bad'. Eg. Gen.43:9, "I will be surety for him; of my hand shalt thou require him: if I bring him not unto thee, and set him before thee, then let me bear the blame for ever." Furthermore, as a v., **blame** means 'the action of speaking evil of someone or something, or finding fault'. Eg. 2Cor.8:20, "Avoiding this, that no man should blame us in this abundance which is administered by us." {blamed 2x., blameless 15x., unblameable 2x., tot. = 23x.}

Blaspheme —10x., v. [A.D. 1340, < ME. **blasfemen** < OF. *blasfemer* < L. *blasphemare* < Gk. βλασφημεω (*blasphemeo*), βλασ (*blas*) (< βλαπτω (*blapto*) = 'to hurt or harm') = 'evil or hurtful words' + φημεω (*phemeo*) = 'to speak'] Thus, **blaspheme** means 'the action of speaking evil against someone with the intent of hurting them'. Eg. Rev.13:6, "And he opened his mouth in blasphemy against God, to blaspheme his name, and his tabernacle, and them that dwell in heaven." {blasphemed 16x., blasphemer 1x., blasphemers 2x., blasphemest 1x., blasphemeth 5x., blasphemies 6x., blaspheming 1x., blasphemous 2x., blasphemously 1x., blasphemy 14x., tot. = 59x.}

Blasphemy —14x., n. [A.D. 1225, < ME. **blasfemie** < LL. *blasphemia* < Gk. βλασφημια (*blasphemia*) < βλασφημοσ (*blasphemos*) (= the n. version of the v. 'blaspheme'. See 'Blaspheme'.) + **y** = 'in the manner of' (see E. suffix '–y'[1])] Thus, **blasphemy** is 'a series of hurtful or injurious words spoken against someone'. Eg. Mt.12:31, "Wherefore I say unto you, All manner of sin and blasphemy shall be forgiven unto men: but the blasphemy against the Holy Ghost shall not be forgiven unto men." {blaspheme 10x., blasphemed 16x., blasphemer 1x., blasphemers 2x., blasphemest 1x., blasphemeth 5x., blasphemies 6x., blaspheming 1x., blasphemous 2x., blasphemously 1x., tot. = 59x.}

Blast – 8x., n. [A.D. 1000, < OE. **blǽst** = 'a strong blow of wind' (as in 'a puff through the nostrils')] Thus, a **blast** is 'a strong blow of wind'. Eg. Ex.15:8, "And with the blast of thy nostrils the waters were gathered together, the floods stood upright as an heap, and the depths were congealed in the heart of the sea." {blasted 5x., blasting 5x., tot. = 18x.}

Blasting –5x., vbl.n. [A.D. 1460, < E. **blast** (see 'Blast') + **ing** = forms the vbl.n. (see E. suffix '–ing'[1])] Thus, a **blasting** is 'a powerful blow of hot and dry air, with continuing action'. Eg. Hag.2:17, "I smote you with blasting and with mildew and with hail in all the labours of your hands; yet ye turned not to me, saith the LORD." (NOI. 'Blasting' is always mentioned in connection with 'mildew', a fungus that causes damage to vegetation and usually comes because of dampness. See 'Mildew'.)

Blaze –1x., v. [A.D. 1384, < ME. **blasen** = 'to blow and make a sound' (akin to ON. *blasa* = 'to blow', as in 'the wind, bellows, or a trumpet'), as in 'to proclaim'] Thus, **blaze** means 'the action of raising one's voice and proclaiming something'. Eg. Mk.1:45, "But he went out, and began to publish it much, and to blaze abroad the matter, insomuch that Jesus could no more openly enter into the city, but was without in desert places: and they came to him from every quarter."

Bleating – 1x., vbl.n. [A.D. 1380, < E. **bleat** (< OE. **blǽtan** = 'similar to the sound made by a sheep, goat or calf') + **ing** = forms the vbl.n. (see E. suffix '–ing'[1])] Thus, **bleating** means 'the crying noise of a sheep'. Eg. 1Sam.15:14, "And Samuel said, What meaneth then this bleating of the sheep in mine ears, and the lowing of the oxen which I hear? " {bleatings 1x., tot. = 2x.}

Blemish –62x., n. [A.D. 1325, < OF. *blemiss* = 'to be pale' (as in complexion and appearance) or 'to be injured'] Thus, a **blemish** is 'a paleness or injury'. Eg. Eph.5:27, "That he might present it to himself a glorious church, not having spot, or wrinkle, or any such thing; but that it should be holy and without blemish." {blemishes 2x., tot. = 64x.}

Bless – 127x., v. [A.D. 950(LfG.), < OE. **bledsian** (< **bled** = 'blood' + **ian** = 'the action of') = 'to make holy by sprinkling with blood', thus bringing divine favor and thereby happiness to the worshipper (NOI. 'Bledsian' was often used in connection with pagan rituals, but was chosen to represent the L. *benedicere* (= 'praise' or 'speak well of') which, in turn, was chosen to represent the Hb. ברך (*bawrak*) (= 'to kneel down with praise') and the Gk. ευλογεω (*eulogeo*) (= 'to celebrate with praise').)] Thus, lit., **bless** means 'the action of sanctifying with blood', but carries the idea of showing divine favor and speaking well of. Eg. Gen.12:3, "And I will bless them that bless thee, and curse him that curseth thee: and in thee shall all families of the earth be blessed." (NOI. In Scripture, we find that God can 'bless' people; people can 'bless' God and people can 'bless' each other. When used as the vbl.n. 'blessing', we find it involves prosperity. See Lev.25:21, Jud.1:15 and Pr.10:22.) {blessed 302x., blessedness 3x., blessest 3x., blesseth 8x., blessing 67x., blessings 12x., tot. = 522x.}

Blessed – 302x., v. pret. and p. [A.D. 1175, < E. **bless** (see 'Bless') + **ed** = forms the pret. and p. (see E. suffix '–ed'[1,4])] Thus, as a v. pret., **blessed** means 'the past-tense action of bless'. Eg. Heb.11:20, "By faith Isaac blessed Jacob and Esau concerning things to come." Furthermore, as a p., **blessed** modifies its n. as being 'consecrated by blood' and enjoying divine favor. Eg. Ti.2:13, "Looking for that blessed hope, and the glorious appearing of the great God and our Saviour Jesus Christ." {bless 127x., blessedness 3x., blessest 3x., blesseth 8x., blessing 67x., blessings 12x., tot. = 522x.}

Blind –82x., adj., n. and v. [A.D. 975(RG.), < OE. **blind** < oo., but possibly from an Indo-European root word *bhlendh* = 'dim or obscure'] Thus, as an adj., **blind** modifies its n. as 'having very dim sight, or no sight at all'. Eg. Jn.9:6, "When he had thus spoken, he spat on the ground, and made clay of the spittle, and he anointed the eyes of the blind man with the clay." Furthermore, as a n., **blind** is 'a title for something or someone whose eyesight is very dim or not at all'. Eg. Isa.35:5, "Then the eyes of the blind shall be opened, and the ears of the deaf shall be unstopped." Finally, as a v., **blind** means 'the action of making someone's eyesight to be dim or not at all'. Eg. 1Sam.12:3, "... or of whose hand have I received any bribe to blind mine eyes therewith? and I will restore it you." (NOI. Blindness can be physical, mental or spiritual.) {blinded 5x., blindeth 1x., blindfolded 1x., blindness 7x., tot. = 96x.}

Blood – 447x., n. [A.D. 1000(ASG.), < OE. **blod** < Ger. *blotham* < oo., but possibly from an Indo-European root word *bhloto* = 'gush or spurt' (NOI. Our E. word 'sanguine' comes from L. *sanguis* = blood. Our E. word 'hemorrhage' comes from Gk. άιμα (*haima*) = 'blood'.)] Thus, **blood** is 'the red life-giving fluid that circulates through the bodies of man and animal'. Eg. Gen.9:4, "But flesh with the life thereof, which is the blood thereof, shall ye not eat." {bloodguiltiness 1x., bloodthirsty 1x., bloody 16x., tot. = 465x.}

Bloodguiltiness – 1x., adj. [A.D. 1535(CB.), < E. **blood** (see 'Blood') + **guilty** = 'having incurred guilt, or guilty of' (see 'Guilt') + **ness** = expresses a state, quality or condition (see E. suffix '–ness')] Thus, **bloodguiltiness** modifies the pro. as 'being guilty of shedding another man's blood' (i.e. murder). Eg. Ps.51:14, "Deliver me from bloodguiltiness, O God, thou God of my salvation: and my tongue shall sing aloud of thy righteousness." {blood 447x., guilt 2x., tot. = 450x.}

Bloody – 16x., adj. [A.D. 1000, < OE. **blodig** < **blod** (see 'Blood') + **y** = in the manner of (see E. suffix '–y'[1])] Thus, lit., **bloody** modifies its n. as 'having much blood'. Eg. Act.28:8, "And it came to pass, that the father of Publius lay sick of a fever and of a bloody flux: to whom Paul entered in, and prayed, and laid his hands on him, and healed him." (NOI. A 'bloody flux' was an inflammation of the large intestine, also known as colitis, causing diarrhea and producing bloody stools. It is often accompanied by fatigue, weight loss and loss of appetite.) Furthermore, figuratively, **bloody** means 'given over to the shedding of much blood'. Eg. Eze.7:23, "Make a chain: for the land is full of bloody crimes, and the city is full of violence." {blood 447x., bloodguiltiness 1x., bloodthirsty 1x., tot. = 465x.}

Blot – 13x., n. and v. [A.D. 1325, < oo., (and not known outside the E. language) but possibly from OF. *bloche* = 'a clod of earth', however, **blot** was used to indicate 'a stain or spot' (as in 'a blob of ink')] Thus, as a n., a **blot** is 'a spot or stain of ink that marks or covers'. Eg. Pr.9:7, "He that reproveth a scorner getteth to himself shame: and he that rebuketh a wicked man getteth himself a blot." Furthermore, as a v., **blot** means 'the action of covering something with a spot or stain of ink'. Eg. Ex.32:33, 'And the LORD said unto Moses, Whosoever hath sinned against me, him will I blot out of my book." (NOI. A 'blot' is different from a mark. See 'Mark'.) {blotted 6x., blotteth 1x., blotting 1x., tot. = 21x.}

Blush – 3x., v. [A.D. 1325, < ME. **bluschen** < OE. **blyscan** = 'glow' or 'become red'] Thus, **blush** means 'the action of becoming red in the face, neck and ears', caused by a mental state of anxiety, usually shame (see 'Shame') or embarrassment. Eg. Ezr.9:6, "And said, O my God, I am ashamed and blush to lift up my face to thee, my God: for our iniquities are increased over our head, and our trespass is grown up unto the heavens." (NOI. Animals do not blush because they cannot think in concepts, like people can, which can cause shame or embarrassment.)

Boast — 20x., n. and v. [A.D. 1297, < ME. (n.) **bost** and (v.) **bosten**; both < oo., but has the idea of 'bragging', in either a good or bad sense] Thus, as a n., a **boast** is 'a great show of words (like a play or an actual event) in which bragging is made over abilities and accomplishments'. Eg. Ps.34:2, "My soul shall make her boast in the LORD: the humble shall hear thereof, and be glad." Furthermore, as a v., **boast** means 'the action of extolling or bragging someone's abilities and accomplishments'. Eg. Ps.44:8, "In God we boast all the day long, and praise thy name for ever. Selah." (NOI. 'Boast' is different from 'vaunt'. Boasting can be either morally right or wrong, whereas vaunting is always morally wrong. See 'Vaunt'.) {boasted 2x., boasters 2x., boastest 1x., boasteth 4x., boasting 9x., boastings 1x., tot. = 39x.}

Boat — 6x., n. [A.D. 891, < OE. **bat** < oo., but akin to It. *batto* (= 'small sea vessel') and OF. *bat* (= 'small boat'), also Du. and Ger. *boot*] Thus, a **boat** is 'a small open vessel for transportation upon the water, powered by oars or sails'. Eg. Act.27:30 And as the shipmen were about to flee out of the ship, when they had let down the boat into the sea, under colour as though they would have cast anchors out of the foreship" (NOI. A 'boat' is different from a 'ship' in that a ship is more closed in and designed for extended periods at sea. See 'Ship'.)

Boil[1] — 9x., n. [A.D. 1000, < ME. **bile** < OE. **byle** akin to Ger. *beule* = 'a bump or swelling'] Thus, a **boil** is 'a hard, swollen painful inflammation on the body'. Eg. Ex.9:9, "And it shall become small dust in all the land of Egypt, and shall be a boil breaking forth with blains upon man, and upon beast, throughout all the land of Egypt." (NOI. A boil is bacterial skin infection, which gains entry through a hair follicle. The body combats the bacteria by attacking it with white blood cells and trying to force it from the body back up through the skin. The result is a painful swelling on the skin as the infected area fills with pus (a yellowish or greenish liquid made from white blood cells, bacteria and cellular debris). A single boil is sometimes called a furuncle, and a group of boils is called 'a carbuncle' (< L. *carbunculus* = 'glowing ember' (see 'Carbuncle')). Treatment includes warm, wet compresses several times a day.) {boils 2x., tot. = 11x.}

Boil[2] – 7x., v. [A.D. 1225, < ME. **boille** < OF. *boillir* < L. *buillere* = 'to bubble' (as in 'a hot liquid')] Thus, **boil** means 'the bubbling action of a liquid by the application of heat energy'. Eg. Lev.8:31, "And Moses said unto Aaron and to his sons, Boil the flesh at the door of the tabernacle of the congregation..." (NOI. Scientifically, a liquid, such as water, begins to boil when the heat energy applied becomes enough to overcome the forces that hold the individual water molecules together. Then, when the water molecules break apart, they vaporize and rise in the form of steam.) { boiled 3x., boiling 1x., tot. = 11x.}

Boisterous – 1x adj. [A.D. 1474, < ME. **boistrous** < AF. *bustous* = 'a rough road'] Thus, **boisterous** modifies its n. (in this case, 'wind') as 'being turbulent or rough in quality'. Eg. Mt.14:30, "But when he saw the wind boisterous, he was afraid; and beginning to sink, he cried, saying, Lord, save me." (NOI. No one can actually see the wind, but a person can see and feel the effects of the wind and hear the sound it makes. Perhaps it was the turbulent sound of the wind that first caught Peter's attention and got his eyes off of Jesus, or perhaps Peter looked past Jesus and saw the effects of the wind upon the sea behind Him. Either way, he looked, he feared, he sank, he cried and Jesus saved him.)

Bold – 11x., adj. [A.D. 1000(ASG.), < OE. **bald** or **beald** < oo., but possibly from an Indo-European root word *bhel* = 'to swell or blow'] Thus, **bold** modifies its n. as 'being filled with courage or fearlessness'. Eg. Phil.1:14 ,"And many of the brethren in the Lord, waxing confident by my bonds, are much more bold to speak the word without fear." {boldly 13x., boldness 10x., emboldened 1x., emboldeneth 1x., tot. = 36x.}

Bolled —1x., pp. [A.D. 1535(CB.), < ME. **boll** = 'to swell' + **ed** = forms the pp. (see E. suffix '–ed'[3])] Thus, **bolled** modifies its n. (in this case, 'flax') as 'having being swollen or podded for seed' (and refers to plants being mature, fully grown at harvest time and ready to release their seed). Eg. Ex.9:31, "And the flax and the barley was smitten: for the barley was in the ear, and the flax was bolled." (NOI. The 'boll weevil' is an insect (*Anthonomus grandis*) that destroys the cotton boll or pod.)

Bolster — 6x., n. [A.D. 1000, < OE. **bolster** (= 'something stuffed and swollen', such as a rough, stuffed sack) < Teut. *bolstro* < *bul* = 'to swell'] Thus, a **bolster** is 'a rough sack that has been stuffed and used as an under-pillow for resting or sleeping'. Eg. 1Sam.26:7, "So David and Abishai came to the people by night: and, behold, Saul lay sleeping within the trench, and his spear stuck in the ground at his bolster..." (NOI. Over top of the bolster sometimes went a softer 'pillow'. See also 'Pillow'.)

Bond[1] —13x., n. [A.D. 1225, < E. **band** (see 'Band'[1]), but more the sense of 'something that binds a person either with or without their consent'] Thus, a **bond** is 'something that binds a person' (such as a chain, an oath, a disease, etc.). Eg. Lk.13:16, "And ought not this woman, being a daughter of Abraham, whom Satan hath bound, lo, these eighteen years, be loosed from this bond on the sabbath day? " {bondage 39x., bonds 26x., tot. = 78x.}

Bond[2] – 6x., adj. [A.D. 1025, < OE. **bonda** = 'householder', < ON. *bonde* = 'peasant, tiller of the soil' (NOI. In ancient Norway and Denmark, the *bonde* were looked down upon as 'low-lifes'. This connotation was carried over at the Norman Conquest of England (A.D. 1066) when the free 'bonda', tilling his soil, now became a tenant to a powerful landlord. Soon 'bonda' came to mean 'a slave'.)] Thus, as an adj., **bond** modifies its n. as 'being under involuntary servitude' (as in 'slavery'). Eg. Eph.6:8, "Knowing that whatsoever good thing any man doeth, the same shall he receive of the Lord, whether he be bond or free." {bondmaid 2x., bondmaids 2x., bondman 6x., bondmen 17x., bondservant 1x., bondservice 1x., bondwoman 8x., bondwomen 3x., tot. = 46x.}

Bondage – 39x., n. [A.D. 1300, < ME. **bondage** (< AF. *bondage)* < **bond** (see 'Bond'[2]) + **age** = 'that which pertains to the root word (see E. suffix '–age')] Thus, a **bondage** is 'the state or condition of being in bonds or chains' (i.e. in prison or slavery and owing one's services to a master). Eg. 2Pt.2:19, "... for of whom a man is overcome, of the same is he brought in bondage." (NOI. Besides actual physical bonds, there are also mental/emotional and spiritual bonds as well. Eg. Num.30:5.) {bond[2] 6x., bondmaid 2x., bondmaids 2x., bondman 6x., bondmen 17x., bonds 26x., bondservant 1x., bondservice 1x., bondwoman 8x., bondwomen 3x., tot. = 111x.}

Bonnets – 6x., n. pl. [A.D. 1375, < ME. **bonat** < OF. *bonet* = 'a cap or head covering' (of soft material but with no brim) + **s** = forms the pl.] Thus, **bonnets** are 'two or more brimless soft caps or head-coverings'. Eg. Eze.44:18, "They shall have linen bonnets upon their heads, and shall have linen breeches upon their loins; they shall not gird themselves with any thing that causeth sweat." (Cp. also 'Hats'.)

Book – 188x n. [A.D. 872, < OE. **boc** = 'a written document containing one or more volumes' (see 'Volume'); possibly from old Germanic *bokiz* = 'beech', referring to tablets for writing on made from Beachwood trees (NOI. The Gk. βιβλος (*biblos*), from which we get our E. 'Bible' (lit., 'Book'), is said to have come from the ancient Phoenician city of 'Byblos' (now 'Jubayl'), about 21 miles (33.6 km.) north of modern Beirut. This city was famous for its ships, known as 'Byblos ships', and on return visits to Egypt, often came back loaded with papyrus scrolls. It is said that the Greeks began referring to the scrolls as 'βιβλος'.)] Thus, a **book** is 'a written document containing one or more volumes'. Eg. Deut.28:58, "If thou wilt not observe to do all the words of this law that are written in this book, that thou mayest fear this glorious and fearful name, THE LORD THY GOD." {books 8x., tot. = 196x.}

Booth –2x., n. [A.D. 1200, < ME. **bothe** = 'a temporary dwelling', like a hut or a tent] Thus, a **booth** is 'a make-shift, temporary dwelling' (usually made from tree branches and covered with other leafy branches). Eg. Jon.4:5, "So Jonah went out of the city, and sat on the east side of the city, and there made him a booth, and sat under it in the shadow, till he might see what would become of the city." (Cp. also 'Tabernacles'.) {booths 9x., tot. = 11x.}

Booties – 1x., n. pl. [A.D. 1542, < E. **booty** (see 'Booty') + **s** = forms the pl.] Thus, **booties** are 'the spoils from several wars or battles', not just one. Eg. Hab.2:7, "Shall they not rise up suddenly that shall bite thee, and awake that shall vex thee, and thou shalt be for booties unto them? " {booty 3x., tot. = 4x.}

Booty – 3x., n. [A.D. 1474, < ME. **botye** = 'loot, plunder or profit' (akin to Ger. *beute* = 'loot or plunder') < middle LG. *bute* = 'a sharing' (as in 'something taken and shared amongst the thieves')] Thus, a **booty** is 'the spoil, loot or plunder taken in a single war or battle'. Eg. Num.31:32, "And the booty, being the rest of the prey which the men of war had caught, was six hundred thousand and seventy thousand and five thousand sheep." {booties 1x., tot. = 4x.}

Bore – 2x., v. [A.D. 1000, < OE. **borian** (< **bor** = 'auger or aul' (a device with a sharp point which cuts holes by using a rotating motion (see 'Aul')) + **ian** = 'the action of')] Thus, **bore** means 'the action of making a hole in something by rotating an auger through it'. Eg. Ex.21:6, "Then his master shall bring him unto the judges; he shall also bring him to the door, or unto the door post; and his master shall bore his ear through with an aul; and he shall serve him for ever." (NOI. It wasn't until after 1611 that 'bore' also began to replace 'bare' as a pret. of the v. 'bear'[1].) {bored 1x., tot. = 3x.}

Borne – 31x., pp. [A.D. 1600, < E. **bear** (see 'Bear'[1])] Thus, **borne** modifies its n. as 'having been carried'. Eg. Jud.16:29, "And Samson took hold of the two middle pillars upon which the house stood, and on which it was borne up, of the one with his right hand, and of the other with his left." {bear[1] 205x., bare[2] 173x., bearers 3x., bearest 5x., beareth 25x., bearing 22x., tot. = 464x.}

Borrow – 8x., v. [A.D. 1000(ASG.), < OE. **borgian** < **borg** = 'surety or pledge' + **ian** = 'the action of'] Thus, **borrow** means 'the action of taking something from someone in exchange for a pledge or security that it will be returned' (the pledge or security is forfeited in case it is not returned). Eg. Deut.28:12, "The LORD shall open unto thee his good treasure, the heaven to give the rain unto thy land in his season, and to bless all the work of thine hand: and thou shalt lend unto many nations, and thou shalt not borrow." (NOI. The emphasis of this word is on 'the pledge or security given', which was kept in the event the item borrowed was not returned. The pledge was usually an item of value, but was sometimes just the verbal promise of its safe return. When Israel left Egypt (Ex.12:35-36), they borrowed much from the Egyptians and would probably have given them some small pledge or security should they not return the items. Remember, the plagues did not fall on the Israelites, so they would have had much grain and livestock from which they could have given a pledge. Cp. Deut.24:10-13.) {borrowed 3x., borrower 2x., borroweth 1x., tot. = 14x.}

Bosom –41x., n. [A.D. 971, < OE. **bosm** (akin to Ger. *busen*) < oo., but possibly from an old Aryan word *bhaghu* = 'arm'] Thus, a **bosom** is 'the enclosure formed by folding the arms across the upper chest'. Eg. Rut.4:16, "And Naomi took the child, and laid it in her bosom, and became nurse unto it." (NOI. Figuratively, the bosom is 'the place of warm affection'. Eg. Lk.16:22, "And it came to pass, that the beggar died, and was carried by the angels into Abraham's bosom..." The chest is referred to in the Bible as the 'breast'. See 'Breast'.)

Bosses – 1x., n. pl [A.D. 1300, < ME. **bos** (< OF. *boce* = 'a knob-like swelling') + **es** = forms the pl.] Thus, **bosses** are 'two or more ornamental knob-like humps that were located on two or more bucklers'. Eg. Job.15:26, "He runneth upon him, even on his neck, upon the thick bosses of his bucklers." (See 'Buckler'.)

Botch –2x., n. [A.D. 1377, < ME. **boche** < OF. *boche* < *boce* = 'a knob-like swelling'] Thus, a **botch** is 'a diseased swelling in the body'. Eg. Deut.28:35, "The LORD shall smite thee in the knees, and in the legs, with a sore botch that cannot be healed, from the sole of thy foot unto the top of thy head."

Bottle –15x., n. [A.D. 1375, < ME. **botel** < OF. *botele* < ML. *buticula* < LL. *buttis* = 'a vase, wine-skin or cask' (possibly from Gk. βυτις (*butis*) = 'a flask') used for holding liquids, and usually made from pottery or animal skins, having a long neck opening (NOI. Today, we think of bottles as made of glass, yet glass bottles were not generally known until about the first century B.C., when the Romans perfected the art of glass blowing. No one knows exactly when glass was discovered, though some think it was as far back as 3,500 B.C. with glass beads. Glass is made by a heat-fusion of large amounts of silica sand with small amounts of potash and lime.)] Thus, a **bottle** is 'a container with a long neck for holding liquids' (and usually made of clay or leather). Eg. Jer.19:1, "Thus saith the LORD, Go and get a potter's earthen bottle, and take of the ancients of the people, and of the ancients of the priests." {bottles 19x., tot. = 34x.}

Bough – 7x., n. [A.D. 1000(ASG.), < OE. **bog** = 'shoulder or arm' (as applied to the limb of a tree)] Thus, a **bough** is 'a large limb of a tree' (as opposed to a small limb, which is called a 'branch'). Eg. Gen.49:22, "Joseph is a fruitful bough, even a fruitful bough by a well; whose branches run over the wall." (See also 'Branch'.) {boughs 18x., tot. = 25x.}

Bounty – 3x., n. [A.D. 1250, < OF. *bonte* < L. *bonitas* = 'goodness' (< *bonus* = 'good')] Thus, **bounty** refers to 'good things' (i.e. wealth that can be used for good causes). Eg. 2Cor.9:5, "Therefore I thought it necessary to exhort the brethren, that they would go before unto you, and make up beforehand your bounty, whereof ye had notice before, that the same might be ready, as a matter of bounty, and not as of covetousness." {bountiful 2x.bountifully 6x., bountifulness 1x., tot. = 12x.}

Bow [1] – 58x., n. [A.D. 1000(AT.), < OE. **boga** = 'something curved or bent in an arc'] Thus, a **bow** is 'a strip of wood or metal with a string fastened to either end and having sufficient pressure so as to cause the strip to bend in a curve, and is used for shooting arrows' (see also 'Arrow'). Eg. Ps.7:12, "If he turn not, he will whet his sword; he hath bent his bow, and made it ready." Furthermore, a **bow** refers to 'a rainbow seen in the sky' (see 'Rainbow'). Eg. Gen.9:13, "I do set my bow in the cloud, and it shall be for a token of a covenant between me and the earth." (NOI. The only three references to the rainbow in the OT. are in Gen.9. It may be that, because it's called a 'bow' and not a 'rainbow', there is a subtle reference to the flood waters being used like a weapon against the earth, and therefore the rainbow was referred to as a 'bow'. Also noteworthy is that whether or not man sees the bow, God always does and remembers His promise of Gen.9:16.) {bowmen 1x., bows 14x., bowshot 1x., rainbow 2x., tot. = 76x.}

Bow[2] – 41x., v. [A.D. 893, < OE. **bugan** = 'bend' (probably akin to L. *fugere* = 'to flee')] Thus, **bow** means 'the action of bending the head or body in submission, respect, worship or to humble oneself' (in a physical or figurative sense). Eg. Eph.3:14, "For this cause I bow my knees unto the Father of our Lord Jesus Christ." {bowed 78x., boweth 3x., bowing 4x., tot. = 126x.}

Bowels – 39x., n. pl. [A.D. 1300, < ME. **bouel** < OF. *boel* < LL. *botellus* = 'small sausage' (but often used to refer to the small intestine) + **s** = forms the pl.] Thus, **bowels** are 'two or more intestines in the body, including the reproductive organs'. Eg. 2Chr.21:18, "And after all this the LORD smote him in his bowels with an incurable disease." (NOI. Figuratively, **bowels** refer to 'the deepest part of a man and his deepest emotions'. Eg. Phi.1:12, "Whom I have sent again: thou therefore receive him, that is, mine own bowels." (Cp. also 1Jn.3:17.))

Bracelet – 1x., n. [A.D. 1438, < OF. *bracelet* < *bracel* < L. *bracchiale* = 'armlet' (< *bracchium* = 'arm')] Thus, a **bracelet** is 'an ornamental band worn on the arm or wrist'. Eg. 2Sam.1:10, "So I stood upon him, and slew him, because I was sure that he could not live after that he was fallen: and I took the crown that was upon his head, and the bracelet that was on his arm, and have brought them hither unto my lord." {bracelets 10x.,

tot. = 11x.}

Bramble – 4x., n. [A.D. 1000(AT.), < OE. **bremel** = 'a rough, prickley shrub'] Thus, a **bramble** is 'a rough, prickly shrub' (such as the Blackberry). Eg. Lk.6:44, "For every tree is known by his own fruit. For of thorns men do not gather figs, nor of a bramble bush gather they grapes." {brambles 1x., tot. = 5x.}

Branch – 37x n. [A.D. 1297, < OF. *branche* < L. *branca* = 'animal paw'] Thus, a **branch** is 'a small limb of a tree extending from its trunk or from a bough'. Eg. Mt.24:32, "Now learn a parable of the fig tree; When his branch is yet tender, and putteth forth leaves, ye know that summer is nigh." (See also 'Bough'.) Furthermore, a **branch** can also refer to 'a limb of the candlestick used in the Tabernacle'. Eg. Ex.25:33, "Three bowls made like unto almonds, with a knop and a flower in one branch; and three bowls made like almonds in the other branch, with a knop and a flower: so in the six branches that come out of the candlestick." Finally, **Branch** is 'a reference to the Messiah'. Eg. Jer.33:15, "In those days, and at that time, will I cause the Branch of righteousness to grow up unto David; and he shall execute judgment and righteousness in the land." {branches 75x., tot. = 112x.}

Brandish – 1x., v. [A.D. 1325, < OF. *brandiss* < *brandir* (= 'to wave a sword') < *brand* = 'a sword'] Thus, **brandish** means 'the action of waving a sword in a threatening manner'. Eg. Eze.32:10, "Yea, I will make many people amazed at thee, and their kings shall be horribly afraid for thee, when I shall brandish my sword before them; and they shall tremble at every moment, every man for his own life, in the day of thy fall."

Brasen – 29x., adj. [A.D. 1000(LP.), < OE. **bræ̈sen** < **brass** (= 'an alloy of copper and tin and sometimes zinc' (see 'Brass')) + **en** = 'the natureof' (see E. suffix '–en'[3])] Thus,

brasen modifies its n. as 'being made of brass'. Eg. Ex.27:4, "And thou shalt make for it a grate of network of brass; and upon the net shalt thou make four brasen rings in the four corners thereof." {brass 126x., tot. = 155x.}

Brass – 126x., n. [A.D. 1000, < oo., but refers to 'alloys of copper, tin and zinc' (NOI. Zinc, though never mentioned in the Bible, was used in a crude form for 2,500 years in the making of brass, but it was not isolated as a pure element until A.D. 1796. Interestingly, the word 'zinc' came from the Ger. *zin* meaning 'tin'. Zinc has a mass weight of 65.38, while tin has a mass weight of 118.710, which means that 'ancient brass' (what is now called 'bronze') would have been much harder than our 'modern brass'. Brass symbolizes the qualities of strength, hardness and firmness (Job.6:12). It was used in making musical instruments (1Cor.13:1) and as a form of money (Mt.10:9).)] Thus, **brass** is 'any combination of copper-tin, or copper-tin-zinc'. Eg. 1Sam.17:38, "And Saul armed David with his armour, and he put an helmet of brass upon his head..." {brasen 29x., tot. = 155x.}

Bravery – 1x., n. [A.D. 1548, < Fr. *braverie* (= 'the action of being brave') < *brave* < It. *bravo* = 'bold or courageous'] Thus, **bravery** is 'the condition of possessing the qualities of bold courage'. Eg. Isa.3:18, "In that day the Lord will take away the bravery of their tinkling ornaments about their feet, and their cauls, and their round tires like the moon."

Brawler – 1x., n. [A.D. 1377, < ME. **brall** (< oo., but means 'to quarrel in a noisy and indecent manner') + **er** = identifies a person according to their occupation (see E. suffix '–er')] Thus, a **brawler** is 'a person whose manner of life is to argue with others and complain in a noisy and indecent manner'. Eg. 1Tim.3:3, "Not given to wine, no striker, not greedy of filthy lucre; but patient, not a brawler, not covetous." (See also 'Quarrel'.) {brawlers 1x., brawling 2x., tot. = 4x.}

Bray[1] – 1x., v. [A.D. 1382, < ME. **brayen** < OF. *breier* = 'to break' (as into small pieces) (NOI. In northern England, the term 'bray' is still used to mean 'hit or knock', as in "*He brayed on my door*".)] Thus, **bray** means 'the action of breaking, crushing, beating and pounding into small pieces or into a fine dust'. Eg. Pr.27:22, "Though thou shouldest bray a fool in a mortar among wheat with a pestle, yet will not his foolishness depart from him."

Bray[2] – 1x., v. [A.D. 1300, < ME. **braie** < OF. *braire* = 'to cry out' (< oo., but probably 'an imitation of the noise made by an ass when in hunger or pain')] Thus, **bray** means 'the action of uttering a loud harsh cry', such as a hungry ass would make. Eg. Job.6:5, "Doth the wild ass bray when he hath grass? or loweth the ox over his fodder? " {brayed 1x., tot. = 2x.}

Breach – 22x., n. [A.D. 1000, < ME. **breche** < OE. **bryce** < **brecan** (= 'break') < OF. *breche* = 'break'] Thus, a **breach** is 'a break, gap or rupture in something'. Eg. Eze.26:10, "... thy walls shall shake at the noise of the horsemen, and of the wheels, and of the chariots, when he shall enter into thy gates, as men enter into a city wherein is made a breach." {breaches 15x., tot. = 37x.}

Bread – 361x., n. [A.D. 950(LfG.), < OE. **bread** (akin to Ger. *braud* and *brot*) = 'a little piece or a fragment' (NOI. It was only after A.D. 1200 that 'bread' came to mean 'a piece of bread' as we understand it today.)] Thus, **bread** is 'a portion of a baked food made from dough (consisting of flour or meal, with or without leaven (yeast)) and milk, oil or water'. Eg. Gen.19:3, "And he pressed upon them greatly; and they turned in unto him, and entered into his house; and he made them a feast, and did bake unleavened bread, and they did eat." (NOI. Figuratively, bread refers to such things as: 'an entire meal' (Gen.18:5-8); 'affliction' (Deut.16:3); 'tears' (Ps.80:5); 'sorrows' (Ps.127:2); 'wickedness and deceit' (Pr.4:17;

20:17); 'adversity' (Isa.30:20); 'Jesus Christ, the Bread of life' (Jn.6:38); and 'sincerity and truth' (1Cor.5:8). (See also 'Cake', 'Food' and 'Loaf'.)) {shewbread 18x., tot. = 442x.}

Breadth – 89x., n. [A.D. 1523, < ME. **brede** (< OE. **brad** = 'width' (see also 'Broad')); to which was added the suffix **th** = further showing a state or condition (see E. suffix '–th')] Thus, **breadth** is 'the condition of measurement from side to side'. Eg. Gen.6:15, "And this is the fashion which thou shalt make it of: The length of the ark shall be three hundred cubits, the breadth of it fifty cubits, and the height of it thirty cubits." (Cp. also 'Wide'.) {broad 36x., handbreadth 3x., tot. = 128x.}

Breast – 18x., n. [A.D. 1000, < OE. **breost** akin to GER. *brust* < MHG. *briustern* = 'to swell' (NOI. Our E. word 'brisket' (the breast of an animal) comes from this root.)] Thus, a **breast** is 'the area just below the neck of both humans and animals' (the area we know as the chest). Eg. Jn.21:20, "Then Peter, turning about, seeth the disciple whom Jesus loved following; which also leaned on his breast at supper, and said, Lord, which is he that betrayeth thee? " Furthermore, **breast** refers to 'the soft protuberance of a female, consisting of milk-secreting glands, from which she may nourish a baby'. Eg. Lam.4:3, "Even the sea monsters draw out the breast, they give suck to their young ones..." {breasts 27x., tot. = 45x.}

Breastplate – 28x., n. [A.D. 1386, < E. **breast** (see 'Breast') + **plate** (< OF. *plate* = 'flat piece')] Thus, a **breastplate** is 'any sort of flat covering made to fit over the breast (chest) area of the body'. Eg. Ex 28:4 And these are the garments which they shall make; a breastplate, and an ephod, and a robe, and a broidered coat, a mitre, and a girdle... that he may minister unto me in the priest's office." (NOI. Figuratively, a breastplate refers to 'righteousness' (Eph.6:4) and 'faith and love' (1Ths.5:8). We often think of a 'breastplate' being made from metal, whereas the High Priest's breastplate was made of linen.)

{breastplates 3x., tot. = 31x.}

Breath —42x., n. [A.D. 893, < OE. **brǽð** = 'exhalation, steam or vapor'] Thus, a **breath** is 'the air exhaled in respiration'. Eg. Gen.2:7, "And the LORD God formed man of the dust of the ground, and breathed into his nostrils the breath of life; and man became a living soul." {breathe 4x., tot. = 46x.}

Breathe —4x., v. [A.D. 1300, < ME. **brethen** = 'the action of respiration' (see 'Breath')] Thus, **breathe** means 'the action of inhaling and exhaling air in respiration'. Eg. Josh.11:11, "And they smote all the souls that were therein with the edge of the sword, utterly destroying them: there was not any left to breathe: and he burnt Hazor with fire." (NOI. Figuratively, breathe refers to 'part of one's lifestyle'. Eg. Ps.27:12, "Deliver me not over unto the will of mine enemies: for false witnesses are risen up against me, and such as breathe out cruelty.") {breath 42x., breathed 4x., breatheth 1x., breathing 2x., tot. = 53x.}

Breeches —5x., n. pl. [A.D. 1205, < ME. **breech** (< OE. **brec** (pl. of **broc**) = 'garment covering from the waist to the knees') + **es** = forms a double pl. (because **brec** is already pl. in OE.)] Thus, **breeches** are 'a garment covering from the waist down to the knees'. Eg. Ex.28:42, "And thou shalt make them linen breeches to cover their nakedness; from the loins even unto the thighs they shall reach." (NOI. 'Breeches' are not to be confused with 'breaches'. See 'Breach'. Did 'breeches' have leggings, similar to trousers, or were they more like a 'wrap-around'? This author suggests breeches had leggings for the following reasons: #1) the double plural suggests leggings (as in more than one leg); #2) the purpose of breeches were for modesty when the priest ascended a height above the eyes of the worshippers; #3) another term 'breeches cloth' was used in ME. to signify a wrap-around garment with no leggings; and #4) the LV. uses the word *feminalia* (Ex.28:42; 39:27; Eze.44:18) (= 'breeches', like those worn by Roman soldiers in cold climate), which had leggings.)

Bribe —2x., n. [A.D. 1386, < ME. **brybe** < OF. *bribe* = 'a piece of bread given to a beggar' (< *briber* = 'to beg'), which gave the idea of 'alms' or perhaps, 'living upon alms'; this gave rise to the idea of 'something stolen'; but from here, it's unclear as to how it came to mean 'something given to pervert justice' (cp. 1Sam.8:3) (NOI. The original E. meaning of 'bribe' in A.D. 1386 was 'something stolen', but the CB. was the first to record its current meaning.)] Thus, a **bribe** is 'something given in order to pervert justice'. Eg. Amo.5:12, "For I know your manifold transgressions and your mighty sins: they afflict the just, they take a bribe, and they turn aside the poor in the gate from their right." {bribery 1x., bribes 3x., tot. = 3x.}

Brickkiln —3x., n. [A.D. 1481, < E. **brick** (= 'a block of hardened clay') + **kiln** (A.D. 725, < OE. **cylene** < L. *culina* = 'kitchen or cooking stove' (NOI. We get our E. 'culinary' from this L. root.)) = 'an oven used for baking'] Thus, a **brickkiln** is 'an oven in which bricks are baked so as to harden them'. Eg. Jer.43:9, "Take great stones in thine hand, and hide them in the clay in the brickkiln, which is at the entry of Pharaoh's house in Tahpanhes, in the sight of the men of Judah." (NOI. Bricks were made by hand with mud and straw (the straw giving extra strength as it decomposed within the brick) using simple molds, then dried in the sun before being 'fired' in the kiln to seal them and make them hard. Such kilns were fairly large with arch-shaped ceilings, having a hole in the very top to let the air and gases escape.)

Bride — 14x., n. [A.D. 1000(ASG.), < OE. **bryd** < old Teut. root *bruthiz* = 'a woman being married'] Thus, a **bride** is 'a woman either about to be married, or a newly wed'. Eg. Isa.62:5, "For as a young man marrieth a virgin, so shall thy sons marry thee: and as the bridegroom rejoiceth over the bride, so shall thy God rejoice over thee." (Cp. also Rev.21:9.) {bridechamber 3x., bridegroom 23x., bridegroom's 1x., tot. = 41x.}

Bridechamber – 3x., n. [A.D. 1579, < E. **bride** (see 'Bride') + **chamber** = 'a room in a house' (see 'Chamber')] Thus, a **bridechamber** is 'a room of a house where the guests are assembled and the wedding ceremony takes place'. Eg. Mk.2:19, "And Jesus said unto them, Can the children of the bridechamber fast, while the bridegroom is with them? as long as they have the bridegroom with them, they cannot fast." (See also 'Chamber'.) {bride 14x., chamber 52x., tot. = 69x.}

Bridle – 9x., n. and v. [A.D. 1000, < OE. **bridel** < **bregdan** = 'to pull or move quickly'] Thus, as a n., a **bridle** is 'a harness-device used on a horse, mule or ass' (consisting of a head-strap, bit and reins (or parts thereof), and used to restrain and guide the animal). Eg. Ps.32:9, "Be ye not as the horse, or as the mule, which have no understanding: whose mouth must be held in with bit and bridle, lest they come near unto thee." Furthermore, as a v., **bridle** means the action of 'restraining and/or guiding'. Eg. Jam.3:2, "For in many things we offend all. If any man offend not in word, the same is a perfect man, and able also to bridle the whole body." {bridles 1x., bridleth 1x., tot. = 11x.}

Brier – 3x., n. [A.D. 1000, < OE. **br r** = 'prickly plant or thorny bush' (NOI. Three different Hb. words are used, but all translated 'brier'.)] Thus, a **brier** is 'any of the wild, thorny-type bushes' found in Israel. Eg. Eze.28:24, "And there shall be no more a pricking brier unto the house of Israel, nor any grieving thorn of all that are round about them, that despised them; and they shall know that I am the Lord GOD." {briers 12x., tot. = 15x.}

Brigandine – 1x., n. [A.D. 1456, < OF. *brigandine* = 'armor for a brigand', consisting of a metal reinforced leather coat for the upper body (NOI. A 'brigand' was a foot soldier with light armor.)] Thus, a **brigandine** is 'a defensive coat of body-armor' (made of leather with an outer reinforcement of small metal rings or plates). Eg. Jer.51:3, "Against him that bendeth let the archer bend his bow, and against him that lifteth himself up in his brigandine: and spare ye not her young men; destroy ye utterly all her host." {brigandines 1x., tot. = 2x.}

Brim – 10x., n. [A.D. 1205, < ME. **brimme** (possibly < OE. **brim** = 'the sea') = 'the edge or border'] Thus, a **brim** is 'the edge or border of something'. Eg. Jn.2:7, "Jesus saith unto them, Fill the waterpots with water. And they filled them up to the brim."

Brimstone –15x., n. [A.D. 1300, < ME. **brinston** < OE. **brynstan** < **bryn** = 'burning' + **stan** = 'stone' (NOI. the ON. *brenni-steinn* also means 'sulfur' or 'amber' (due to its yellow color), as does also the Ger. *bernstein*, which is also used as a name.)] Thus, **brimstone** is 'a yellowish burning stone', or 'a stone that could burn'. Eg. Gen.19:24, "Then the LORD rained upon Sodom and upon Gomorrah brimstone and fire from the LORD out of heaven." (NOI. Scholars agree that this was sulfur, a yellow, brittle substance that emits a pungent odor when heated (similar to rotten eggs). It is often found in great quantities around hot springs, volcanoes and in meteorites. Ancient pagan religions sometimes burned sulfur in their ceremonies, and believed it to represent the human soul. Commercially, sulfur is used in the manufacture of black gunpowder, vulcanizing rubber and making sulfuric acid. The Bible seems to associate brimstone with death, as in Rev.21:8 and the description of the lake of fire. Interestingly, the gas emitted from sulfur (brimstone), in high concentrations, can quickly cause death by respiratory paralysis. This may be why God rained brimstone down on Sodom and Gomorrah.)

Brink —6x., n. [A.D. 1300, < ME. **brenk** = 'the edge' (as in something that could be fallen over), and usually refers to where the land and water meet] Thus, a **brink** is 'the very edge of where the land meets the water'. Eg. Josh.3:8, "And thou shalt command the priests that bear the ark of the covenant, saying, When ye are come to the brink of the water of Jordan, ye shall stand still in Jordan."

Broad —36x., adj. [A.D. 971, < OE. **brad** = 'width' (< oo., but = D. *breed* and Ger. *breit*)] Thus, **broad** modifies its n. as 'being of a certain dimension in width'. Eg. Ex.27:1, "And thou shalt make an altar of shittim wood, five cubits long, and five cubits broad..." (NOI. 'Broad' is often given certain physical limitations (such as 'six cubits broad') whereas 'wide' never has limitations to it (such as 'open wide thy mouth'). 'Broad' is therefore used more in the context of dimensions, and 'wide' is used to suggest 'wide openness'. See also 'Wide'.) {breadth 89x., broader 1x., tot. = 126x.}

Broided — 1x., pp. [A.D. 1386, < ME. **broid** (= 'the action of very skillful weaving') + **ed** = forms the pp. (see E. suffix '–ed'[3])] Thus, **broided** modifies its n. (in this case, 'hair') as 'having been very skillfully woven'. Eg. 1Tim.2:9, "In like manner also, that women adorn themselves in modest apparel, with shamefacedness and sobriety; not with broided hair, or gold, or pearls, or costly array." (NOI. In the Roman/Greek culture of Paul's day, women often had their hair skillfully woven into braids and elaborate designs.)

Broidered —8x., pp. [A.D. 1450, < ME. **broider** = 'to stitch' (as in ornamental needlework) + **ed** = forms the pp. (see E. suffix '–ed'[3])] Thus, **broidered** modifies its n. as 'having been very skillfully ornamented with needlework'. Eg. Eze.16:13, "Thus wast thou decked with gold and silver; and thy raiment was of fine linen, and silk, and broidered work; thou didst eat fine flour, and honey, and oil: and thou wast exceeding beautiful, and thou didst prosper into a kingdom." (NOI. The ancient skill of broidery is still an honored profession in the Middle East and Asia. The author has seen the fantastic broidery skills of an Asian woman, who was taught from a child how to count the tiny threads of a cloth and stitch it with the most beautiful and colorful designs. To further illustrate the ability of the human eye, the author once watched another Asian woman write the Ten Commandments on a single grain of rice, without the help of any optical magnification!)

Broiled – 1x., pp. [A.D. 1440, < E. **broil** < OF. *bruiller* = 'to cook by exposure to an open fire' + **ed** = forms the pp. (see E. suffix '–ed'[3])] Thus, **broiled** modifies its n. (in this case, 'fish') as 'having been cooked by exposure to an open fire'. Eg. **Lk.24:42**, "And they gave him a piece of a broiled fish, and of an honeycomb."

Brood – 1x., n. [A.D. 1000, < OE. **brod** < early Teut. root *brod* = 'that which is hatched by warmth' < *bro* = 'warmth'] Thus, a **brood** is 'a group of young offspring, hatched through eggs by warmth'. Eg. **Lk.13:34**, "O Jerusalem, Jerusalem, which killest the prophets, and stonest them that are sent unto thee; how often would I have gathered thy children together, as a hen doth gather her brood under her wings, and ye would not! "

Broth – 3x., n. [A.D. 1000, < OE. **broð** < Teut. root *bru* = 'to prepare by boiling'] Thus, **broth** is 'the liquid in which something (usually flesh) has been boiled'. Eg. **Jud.6:19**, "And Gideon went in, and made ready a kid, and unleavened cakes of an ephah of flour: the flesh he put in a basket, and he put the broth in a pot, and brought it out unto him under the oak, and presented it."

Bruise – 8x., n. and v. [A.D. 890, < OE. **brysan** < OF. *bruisier* = 'to break or shatter' (as in 'to dent or wound by beating')] Thus, as a n., a **bruise** is 'a wound caused by beating or by a heavy blow'. Eg. Jer.30:12, "For thus saith the LORD, Thy bruise is incurable, and thy wound is grievous." Furthermore, as a v., **bruise** means 'the action of wounding by the process of beating or by delivering a heavy blow'. Eg. Gen.3:15, "And I will put enmity between thee and the woman, and between thy seed and her seed; it shall bruise thy head, and thou shalt bruise his heel." {bruised 9x., bruises 1x., bruising 2x., tot. = 20x.}

Bruit —2x., n. [A.D. 1450, < OF. *bruit* < *bruire* = 'make a noise' or 'roar' (as in 'the propagation of a rumor')] Thus, a **bruit** is 'a rumor being shouted aloud for all to hear'. Eg. Jer.10:22, "Behold, the noise of the bruit is come, and a great commotion out of the north country, to make the cities of Judah desolate, and a den of dragons."

Brute —2x., adj. [A.D. 1460, < L. *brutus* = 'heavy, dull, irrational and stupid', especially in regards to some animals] Thus, **brute** modifies its n. as 'being dull, irrational and stupid'. Eg. 2Pt.2:12, "But these, as natural brute beasts, made to be taken and destroyed, speak evil of the things that they understand not; and shall utterly perish in their own corruption." (NOI. Both 'brute' and 'brutish' are used in reference to certain people who behave as 'dull, irrational and stupid' beasts.) {brutish 11x., tot. = 13x.}

Buckler —11x., n. [A.D. 1300, < OF. *boucler* = 'a shield with a boss' (< *boucle* = 'boss' (a round hump or knob-like protuberance))] Thus, a **buckler** is 'a small round shield (perhaps 22 in. (55.8 cm.) diameter) having a round protuberance in the center' (and was worn on the left arm using two leather straps while used in hand-to-hand combat). Eg. 1Chr.5:18, "The sons of Reuben, and the Gadites, and half the tribe of Manasseh, of valiant men, men able to bear buckler and sword, and to shoot with bow, and skilful in war..." (NOI. The 'buckler' was not a 'body-shield', but was used to protect a soldier from the striking blow of an enemy's hand-held weapon, such as a sword. The 'boss' on the buckler acted like a cushion against a blow, but could also act like a 'fist' as the buckler was 'punched' at the enemy.) {bucklers 5x., tot. = 16x.}

Buffet —2x., v. [A.D. 1225, < OF. *buffet* = 'to strike with the fist' < *buffe* = 'a hit', usually by the fist (NOI. This word may have originally been an attempt to imitate the sound of a fist hitting something soft, as in "*boof!*"] Thus, **buffet** means 'the action of hitting something or someone with the fist'. Eg. Mk.14:65, "And some began to spit on him, and to cover his face, and to buffet him, and to say unto him, Prophesy: and the servants did strike him with the palms of their hands." {buffeted 3x., tot. = 5x.}

Bull —2x., n. [A.D. 1200, < ME. **bole** (possibly < OE. **bulla**) = 'the male of the bovine (ox-like) animal'] Thus, a **bull** is 'the generic term for the male of the bovine animals', weighing 800-1000 lb. (360-450 kilo.), and used for breeding and their meat. Eg. Job.21:10, "Their bull gendereth, and faileth not; their cow calveth, and casteth not her calf." (NOI. A 'bull' and a 'bullock' were the same animal, but the difference is in what they were used for. The bull was used for breeding and for its meat, whereas the bullock was reserved for sacrifice. Both are mentioned together in Isa.34:7. There are 3 passages in which 'bulls' are spoken of in terms of sacrifice, but they are used in a generic sense, similar to Mk.1:37, "... All men seek for thee." (Only certain men were actually seeking for Jesus, yet the generic "all men" is used.) A modern-day 'steer' is a castrated bull. See also 'Bullock', 'Cattle', 'Cow', 'Kine' and 'Ox'.) {bullock 104x., bullock's 3x., bullocks 45x., bulls 10x., tot. = 164x.}

Bullock — 104x., n. [A.D. 1000, < OE. **bulluc** (possibly < OE. **bulla**) = 'the young male of the bovine (ox-like) animals, used for sacrifice to a deity'] Thus, a **bullock** is 'the male of the bovine animals (weighing 800-1000 lb. or 360-450 kilo.) and used only for sacrifice'. Eg. Ex.29:11, "And thou shalt kill the bullock before the LORD, by the door of the tabernacle of the congregation." (NOI. A 'bullock' was not used for breeding (as was the bull), nor for plowing (see Jer.31:18, as was the ox) but was kept aside to be sacrificed at a young age. Interestingly, a bullock was considered by God to be 'young' even at 7 years of age (Jud.6:25). Notice also that the evil prophets of Baal used bullocks in their sacrifices (1Ki.18:25).) {bull 2x., bullock's 3x., bullocks 45x., bulls 10x., tot. = 164x.}

Bulrushes – 2x., n. pl. [A.D. 1440, < ME. **bulrysche** (< **bul** = oo. but possibly from ME. **bole** (= 'a tree trunk', i.e. 'a stem') + **rysche** = 'a rush' (a plant that grows in marshy swampland)) = 'a plant, of the genus *Juncus*, with tall slender stems (either hollow or pith-filled), found along marshy swamps', + **s** = forms the pl.] Thus, **bulrushes** are 'two or more of any of the tall, rush-like plants that grow on the marshy water's edge', especially in Egypt. Eg. Ex.2:3, "And when she could not longer hide him, she took for him an ark of bulrushes, and daubed it with slime and with pitch, and put the child therein; and she laid it in the flags by the river's brink." (NOI. The stems (or stalks) of 'bulrushes' were used in the making of papyri (a type of writing paper) as well as being woven into chair-bottoms, baskets, etc.) {bulrush 1x., rush 3x., tot. = 6x.}

Bulwarks – 5x., n. pl. [A.D. 1418, < ME. **bulwerk**, **bul** (< **bole** = 'a tree trunk') + **werk** = 'a work' + **s** = forms the pl.] Thus, **bulwarks** are '2 or more heavy constructions (or 'works') made from tree trunks, and used in a war against a city' (as in 'a siege-tower'). Eg. Deut.20:20, "Only the trees which thou knowest that they be not trees for meat, thou shalt destroy and cut them down; and thou shalt build bulwarks against the city that maketh war with thee, until it be subdued." (NOI. Ps.48:13 indicates that Jerusalem had 'bulwarks' incorporated into its walls as part of its defense system.)

Burden —69x., n. and v. [A.D. 971, < OE. **byrðen** < **beran** = 'to hold, carry or bring forth' (see 'Bear'[1])] Thus, as a n., a **burden** is 'that which is carried' (as in 'a load'). Eg. Ex.23:5, "If thou see the ass of him that hateth thee lying under his burden, and wouldest forbear to help him, thou shalt surely help with him." Furthermore, as a v., **burden** means 'the action of laying a load upon someone or something'. Eg. 2Cor.12:16, "But be it so, I did not burden you: nevertheless, being crafty, I caught you with guile." (NOI. As a v., 'burden' is only used once in the Bible, in 2Cor.12:16. Although it is from the same root as the n., it was not used in an E. writing until A.D. 1541. Earlier Bible versions used the word 'grieved'.) {burdened 2x., burdens 25x., burdensome 5x., tot. = 101x.}

Burnished — 1x., adj. [A.D. 1325, < OF. *burnir* = 'to make bright', normally by polishing] Thus, **burnished** modifies its n. (in this case, 'brass') as 'being made bright and shiny'. Eg. Eze.1:7, "And their feet were straight feet; and the sole of their feet was like the sole of a calf's foot: and they sparkled like the colour of burnished brass." (See also 'Brass'.)

Bushel — 3x., n. [A.D. 1300, < ME. **boyschel** < OF. *boissiel* < *boiste* = 'a box' (NOI. The Gk. word is μοδιος (*modios*) and came from the L. *modius* meaning a 'peck' (a Roman dry measure of about 8 quarts (8.8 liters), which was ¼ of a modern bushel) and was used to measure grain (see also 'Measure'). Since A.D. 1300, the E. 'bushel' has varied greatly in its volume and weight, but the modern, Imperial Bushel was legally established in Great Britain in A.D. 1826, and contains 4 pecks, or 8 gal. (35.2 liters).)] Thus, a **bushel** (in NT. times) was 'a small box, used to measure grain, and held (perhaps) 8 dry quarts (8.8 liters)'. Eg. Lk.11:33, "No man, when he hath lighted a candle, putteth it in a secret place, neither under a bushel, but on a candlestick, that they which come in may see the light."

Busybody — 1x., n. [A.D. 1525(TNT.), < E. **busy** (< OE. **bisig** = 'active engagement') + **body** (< OE. **bodig** = 'the main mass or bulk of a man or animal') (NOI. The term **busybody**, rather than 'busyperson', gives the idea of 'a mass of human flesh getting in the way'.)] Thus, a **busybody** is 'someone who meddles or interferes in the affairs of other people' (and causes people to think of them as a 'carcass in the way'). Eg. 1Pt.4:15, "But let none of you suffer as a murderer, or as a thief, or as an evildoer, or as a busybody in other men's matters." {busy 1x., body 174x., tot. = 176x.}

Butler — 8x., n. [A.D. 1250, < OF. *butiller* < ML. *buticularius* = 'a servant in charge of the wine cellar, who dispenses the wine' (< *buticula* = 'bottle' (see also 'Bottle')) (NOI. A 14th c. It. surname was Buticularo, similar to our E. surname Butler.)] Thus, a **butler** is 'a wine steward, in charge of dispensing wine in a royal household'. Eg. Gen.40:13, "Yet within three days shall Pharaoh lift up thine head, and restore thee unto thy place: and thou shalt deliver Pharaoh's cup into his hand, after the former manner when thou wast his butler." {butlers 9x., butlership 1x., tot. = 10x.}

Buttocks — 3x., n. pl. [A.D. 1300, < E. **butt** (< OF. *bout* = 'end, or extremity') + **ock** (= a n. suffix having a diminishing force on the size or effect of the word) (NOI. Other examples of this suffix are found in 'hassock' (a small footstool); 'mattock' (a hand-held farm implement used to loosen soil); and 'tussock' (a small clump of growing grass).) + **s** = forms the pl.] Thus, **buttocks** are 'the two protuberances that form the hind-end of mankind'. Eg. Isa.20:4, "So shall the king of Assyria lead away the Egyptians prisoners, and the Ethiopians captives, young and old, naked and barefoot, even with their buttocks uncovered, to the shame of Egypt."

Byways – 1x., n. pl. [A.D. 1330, < E. **by** (= 'something of secondary or minor importance' (►**Important Note:** This is only one of the many meanings of 'by'.)) + **way** (= 'a road or pathway' (NOI. Akin to L. *via*, which is properly pronounced as 'wee-ah'.)) + **s** = forms the pl.] Thus, **byways** are 'two or more roads of secondary or minor importance'. Eg. Jud.5:6, "In the days of Shamgar the son of Anath, in the days of Jael, the highways were unoccupied, and the travellers walked through byways." (Cp. also 'Highway'.) {way 664x., tot. = 665x.}

Byword – 6x., n. [A.D. 1050, < E. **by** (= 'something of secondary or minor importance' (►**Important Note:** This is only one of the many meanings of 'by'.)) + **word** (= 'speech or utterance')] Thus, a **byword** is 'a single word or phrase indicating something insignificant or of no importance'. Eg. Deut.28:37, "And thou shalt become an astonishment, a proverb, and a byword, among all nations whither the LORD shall lead thee." (NOI. 'Byword' has been used in various senses in Early Modern English. Sir John Cheke (a brilliant Gk. scholar, A.D. 1514 – A.D. 1557) for instance, used it in place of the word 'parables' in his translation of Mt.13:3. But in the 1611, it always seems to mean 'something insignificant'. In Job.17:6 the insignificant 'byword' is compared to the louder, important beat-noise of the 'tabret' (see also 'Tabret'). Cp. also 'Proverb'.)

C

Cab – 1x., n. [A.D. 1535(CB.), trans. < Hb. קָב (*qab*) = 'to hollow out' (as in 'a hollow vessel'), and equal to about 1.5 liters] Thus, a **cab** is 'a unit of measurement equaling about 1.5 liters' (1.36 US dry quart). Eg. 2 Ki.6:25, "And there was a great famine in Samaria: and, behold, they besieged it, until an ass's head was sold for fourscore pieces of silver, and the fourth part of a cab of dove's dung for five pieces of silver."

Caesar – 21x., n. [A.D. 1382(WB.), < L. *Caesar* < oo., but may have originally meant 'long haired'. Born July 13, 100 BC., Gaius Julius rose to political power and consolidated the Roman Empire under his control. He was assassinated by Brutus, Cassius and others in 44 B.C. The name 'Caesar' would later become a title synonymous with 'king' or 'ruler'. (NOI. 'Gaius Julius' was his first and last name, while 'Caesar' was added by his parents to distinguish their particular branch of the 'Julius' family name.) Gaius Octavius was Caesar's adopted heir and took the name 'Caesar' as a public way of showing his connection with Caesar. In 44 B.C., he joined forces with Marc Antony (Julius Caesar's right hand man) and by 27 B.C., had taken over as sole ruler of the Roman Empire. He was awarded the title 'Augustus' by the Roman Senate, thus making him a 'god' and setting in motion the worshipping of Caesar, which later cost many Christians their lives. Octavius was the 'Caesar' in power when Jesus was born, and Tiberius was the 'Caesar' when Jesus was crucified and rose again. (NOI. Ger. *Kaiser* and Rus. *Czar* are derivatives of the title 'Caesar'.)] Thus, **Caesar** was 'a family name, but became a title meaning 'king' or 'ruler''. Eg. Mk.12:17, "And Jesus answering said unto them, Render to Caesar the things that are Caesar's, and to God the things that are God's. And they marvelled at him." (See also 'Augustus'.) {Caesar's 9x., Caesarea 17x., tot. = 47x.}

Cake – 13x., n. [A.D. 1230, < ME. **kake** < oo., but probably from an Indo-European root word *gag* = 'a round lump of something', and referred to a round mass of baked dough] Thus, a **cake** is 'a round mass of baked dough'. Eg. Num.15:20, "Ye shall offer up a cake of the first of your dough for an heave offering..." (NOI. A 'cake' was different from a 'loaf' in that a cake was baked on both sides (cp. Hos.7:8) while a loaf was baked on one side only, but in an oven. It could be made of figs (1Sam.30:12), oiled bread (Ex.29:23), barley bread (Jud.7:13) or bread (2Sam.6:19). See also 'Bread', 'Food' and 'Loaf'.) {cakes 25x., tot. = 38x.}

Calamity –19x., n. [A.D. 1490, < L. *calamitas* = 'severe damage or terrible disaster'] Thus, a **calamity** is 'a terrible disaster'. Eg. Pr.6:15, "Therefore shall his calamity come suddenly; suddenly shall he be broken without remedy." (NOI. Such a disaster will result in total ruination, unless the Lord intervenes. Cp. Ps.18:18.) {calamities 3x., tot. = 22x.}

Calamus – 3x., n. [A.D. 1388(WB.), trans. < Gk. καλαμος (*kalamos*) = 'a reed or a cane', which grows to various lengths (akin to Hb. קנה (*qaneh*))] Thus, a **calamus** is 'a reed or a cane, some of which are sweet to smell'. Eg. Ex.30:23, "Take thou also unto thee principal spices, of pure myrrh five hundred shekels, and of sweet cinnamon half so much, even two hundred and fifty shekels, and of sweet calamus two hundred and fifty shekels." (NOI. 'Sweet calamus' was used in making the holy anointing oil. When dried out, calamus has a fragrant smell and was also used in making perfume. See also 'Cane'.)

Caldron –6x., n. [A.D. 1300, < ME. **cauderon** < OF. *caudron* < LL. *caldaria* (= 'cooking pot') < L. *caldarius* (= 'hot bath') < *calidus* = 'hot' (NOI. The 'L' in 'CALDRON' was inserted in the 1500's to imitate the Latin.)] Thus, a **caldron** is 'a large pot, filled with liquid (usually water-based) and used for boiling'. Eg. 1Sam.2:14, "And he struck it into the pan, or kettle, or caldron, or pot; all that the fleshhook brought up the priest took for himself..." {caldrons 3x., tot. = 9x.}

Calf – 29x., n. [A.D. 800, < OE. **cealf** = 'a young cow' (normally up to one year old)] Thus, a **calf** is 'a young cow, from new-born until one year old'. Eg. Gen.18:7, "And Abraham ran unto the herd, and fetcht a calf tender and good, and gave it unto a young man; and he hasted to dress it." (NOI. Calves were used in sacrifice as well as feasts. Their hide was prized for being soft and supple.) {calf's 1x., calve 2x., calved 1x., calves 18x., calveth 1x., tot. = 52x.}

Calkers –2x., n. pl. [A.D. 1495, < E. **calk** or **caulk** (< OF. *cauquer* = 'to squeeze in with force' < L. *calcare* = 'to press in' or 'to press under the heel' < *calx* = 'a heel', i.e. 'of the foot') + **er** = identifies a person according to their occupation (see E. suffix '–er') + '**s**' = forms the pl. (NOI. The Hb. חזק בדק (*behdek khawzak*) = 'a strengthener' or 'a stopper of cracks or leaks'. The term was used of making ships watertight.)] Thus, **calkers** are 'two or more persons whose job it was to make ships watertight by forcing a 'calking material' (such as coarse flax or old rope) between the wooden joints, and then afterward sealing the joints with a resin or melted pitch'. Eg. Eze.27:9, "The ancients of Gebal and the wise men thereof were in thee thy calkers: all the ships of the sea with their mariners were in thee to occupy thy merchandise."

Calvary – 1x., pn. [A.D. 1000(ASG.), < L. *Calvaria* = 'skull' (< *calvus* = 'bald') < Gk. Κρανιον (*kranion*) = 'skull' (NOI. We get our E. 'cranium' from this word.)]

Thus, **Calvary** is 'a name meaning 'skull'' (and refers to a hill outside the city of Jerusalem where Christ was crucified). Eg. Lk.23:33, "And when they were come to the place, which is called Calvary, there they crucified him, and the malefactors, one on the right hand, and the other on the left." (NOI. There have been several 'suggested sites' where Calvary might be, but there are only two that hold the majority of interest. The first site is under the Catholic Church of the Holy Sepulcher, the history of which dates back to the 4th c. under Constantine, whose mother Helena determined this site. Located within what is considered the walls of the old city of Jerusalem, it was wrecked, destroyed and finally rebuilt in A.D. 1144 and since renovated. The second site, known today as 'Gordon's Calvary', is 250 yards north east of the Damascus Gate and was first suggested by German Scholar Otto Thenius in A.D. 1849 after viewing what looked to be the face of a skull in the side of the hill. However, it wasn't until A.D. 1885, when the famous British General Charles Gordon (of 'Khartoum-Egypt' fame) declared it to be the true site, that it caught on in popularity. See also 'Golgotha'.)

Calve –2x., v. [A.D. 1000, < OE. **cealfian** < **cealf** (see 'Calf') + **ian** = 'the action of')] Thus, **calve** means 'the action of giving birth to a calf'. Eg. Job.39:1, "Knowest thou the time when the wild goats of the rock bring forth? or canst thou mark when the hinds do calve? " {calf 29x., tot. = 31x.}

Camel –9x., n. [A.D. 950(LfG.), < L. *camelus* < Gk. καμηλος (*kamelos*) < Hb. גָּמָל (*gamal*) < possibly Ar. *jamala* = 'to bear a load' and refers to the four-footed, load-carrying animal of the middle east (NOI. In general, camels with two humps on their backs (the Bactrian camel) are known in the Bible as just 'camels', while those with one hump (the Arabian camel) are known as 'dromedaries' – see 'Dromedary'.)] Thus, a **camel** is 'a two-hump-backed, four-footed beast of burden used in the Middle East for carrying people and cargo'. Eg. Mt.23:24, "Ye blind guides, which strain at a gnat, and swallow a camel." {camel's 3x., camels 47x., camels' 3x., tot. = 62x.}

Camp –136x., n. and v. [A.D. 1525 < It. *campo* < L. *campus* = 'a field or plain' (as in 'a field of battle') (NOI. A 'campus' was first used in reference to an institute of learning by Princeton University, New Jersey, in A.D. 1774.)] Thus, as a n., a **camp** is 'a field where tents are set up in military fashion'. Eg. Jud.7:18, "When I blow with a trumpet, I and all that are with me, then blow ye the trumpets also on every side of all the camp, and say, The sword of the LORD, and of Gideon." Furthermore, as a v., **camp** means 'the action of lodging or living in a camp-like setting, for military purpose'. Eg. Isa.29:3, "And I will camp against thee round about, and will lay siege against thee with a mount, and I will raise forts against thee." {camped 1x., camps 7x., encamp 11x., encamped 33x., encampeth 2x., encamping 1x., tot. = 191x.}

Camphire –2x., n. [A.D. 1313, < F. *camphre* < ML. *camphora* < Ar. *kafur* (as in 'the *kafur* plant'), and is now understood to be the *Lawsonia inermis*, or the 'henna plant'] Thus, **camphire** is 'a plant in Israel that grows 9 ft. tall (2.74 m.), having white or yellow blossoms that emit a fragrant scent'. Eg. SoS.1:14, "My beloved is unto me as a cluster of camphire in the vineyards of Engedi." (NOI. 'Camphire' (today also known as 'camphor') was used as far back as the time of Moses in Egypt. Its leaves were dried and made into a 'cosmetic-dye paste' that was used by some to color the palms of hands and soles of the feet, the fingernails and toenails, the beards of men and the tails of horses.)

Cane –2x., n. [A.D. 1398, < OF. *cane* < L. *canna* < Gk. καννα (*kanna*) = 'a reed' (akin to Hb. קנה (*qaneh*))] Thus, **cane** is 'a reed-type plant found in Egypt, the Middle East and India' (but this one is modified as 'sweet cane' and therefore refers to '*Acorus calamus*'). Eg. Isa.43:24, "Thou hast bought me no sweet cane with money..." (See also 'Calamus'.)

Canker – 1x., n. [A.D. 1000, < OF. *cancre* < L. *cancer* = 'a crab' (i.e. a crawling, eating, malignant tumor; like a gangrene) (NOI. The Gk. γαγγραινα (*gaggraina*) (translated 'canker') = 'gangrene' (< γραιν (*grain*) = 'to gnaw') and refers to 'the slow dying and rotting of flesh', which if not amputated, will eat through to the bone and spread throughout the body, finally killing the patient. Causes of gangrene include: injury, bacterial infection, frostbite and diabetes. The second 'c' in E. 'cancer' is soft, but in the L. '*cancer*', both 'c's' are hard, which is how we got our E. 'canker'.)] Thus, a **canker** is 'a slow dying and rotting of the flesh, similar to gangrene'. Eg. 2Tim.2:17, "And their word will eat as doth a canker: of whom is Hymenaeus and Philetus." {cankered 1x., tot. = 2x.}

Cankerworm –6x., n. [A.D. 1530, < E. **canker** (see 'Canker') + **worm** (a member of the genus *Lumbricus*, having a long soft body divided into many segments. See 'Worm'), and refers (probably) to the early stages of the locust] Thus, a **cankerworm** is 'an underdeveloped locust (also called a 'hopper') that crawls along and eats vegetation'. Eg. Joe.1:4 "That which the palmerworm hath left hath the locust eaten; and that which the locust hath left hath the cankerworm eaten; and that which the cankerworm hath left hath the caterpiller eaten." (NOI. Some have suggested that this vs. describes the four stages of the locust life cycle, and others suggest they are four different insects. (This author suggests there are three different insects, the 'cankerworm' being a young 'locust'.) Locusts lay their eggs shortly after Israel's two yearly periods of rain; the latter rain being around March. The cankerworms (or hoppers) are born about two to three weeks later, and soon swarm together (about 50 per square meter or yard) to eat and devour (Nah.3:15). After about 30 days, and several moltings, they finally grow proper wings (as adult locusts) and can fly away (Nah.3:16 – Cambridge Edition (see section in beginning, 'Are There Problems in the King James Bible?') in swarms of millions, and sometimes billions. See also 'Caterpillar', 'Locust' and 'Palmerworm'.) {worm 14x., tot. = 20x.}

Captain – 139x., n. [A.D. 1375, < OF. *capitaine* < ML. *capitaneus* < *caput* = 'head' (NOI. E. literature, before 1611, always used 'captain' in a military sense, having lesser authorities beneath (i.e. 'lieutenant') and greater authorities over (i.e. 'major'). Cp. also 2Sam.18:5.)] Thus, a **captain** is 'a person who has been commissioned by a higher authority to be in charge (or 'the head') over certain others', in a military sense. Eg. Jud.11:6, "And they said unto Jephthah, Come, and be our captain, that we may fight with the children of Ammon." (NOI. A 'captain' could be over any number of soldiers. Eg. fifty soldiers (2Ki.1:9); 1,000 soldiers (1Sam.18:13); an entire host (1Sam.17:55); all Israel (1Sam.9:16).) {captains 119x., tot. = 258x.}

Captive – 59x., adj. and n. [A.D. 1374, < L. *captivus* = 'a prisoner' (< *capere* = 'to take or seize')] Thus, as an adj., **captive** modifies its n. as 'having been taken against their will and held as a prisoner'. Eg. Gen.14:14, "And when Abram heard that his brother was taken captive, he armed his trained servants, born in his own house, three hundred and eighteen, and pursued them unto Dan." Furthermore, as a n., a **captive** is 'someone who has been taken against their will and held as a prisoner'. Eg. Ex.12:29, "And it came to pass, that at midnight the LORD smote all the firstborn in the land of Egypt, from the firstborn of Pharaoh that sat on his throne unto the firstborn of the captive that was in the dungeon; and all the firstborn of cattle." {captives 43x., captivity 127x., tot. = 229x.}

Captivity – 127x., n. [A.D. 1325, < E. **captive** (see 'Captive') + **ity** = 'a state or condition' (see E. suffix '–ity')] Thus,

captivity is 'a state of time or condition, of a person (or persons) being taken against his will, and being held as a prisoner'. Eg. Job.42:10, "And the LORD turned the captivity of Job, when he prayed for his friends..." {captive 59x., tot. = 186x.}

Carbuncle –3x., n. [A.D. 1230, < OF. *charboucle* < L. *carbunculus* = 'live coal', 'glowing ember' or a 'red gem' (< *carbo* = 'coal') and probably referred to one of the many varieties of the 'garnet' gemstones (NOI. Garnet is a name which refers to six similar mineral-species namely: almandine, pyrope, spessartine, grossular, andradite and uvarovite.)] Thus, a **carbuncle** is 'a beautiful red gemstone, probably of the garnet-variety'. Eg. Ex.39:10, "And they set in it four rows of stones: the first row was a sardius, a topaz, and a carbuncle: this was the first row." (See also 'Sapphire' and 'Rubies'.) {carbuncles 1x., tot. = 4x.}

Carcase – 34x., n. [A.D. 1340, < F. *carcasse* < It. *carcassa* < ML. *carcosium* = 'a dead body'] Thus, a **carcase** is 'a dead body of (usually) an animal'. Eg. Lev.11:39, "And if any beast, of which ye may eat, die; he that toucheth the carcase thereof shall be unclean until the even." (NOI. Normally, 'carcase' refers to the dead body of an animal, but it sometimes refers to the dead body of a human who, because of his wicked lifestyle, was rejected by God. This means that 'carcase' was used as almost a derogatory term. See Deut.28:26 and Josh.8:29). With the exception of 'corpse' (Mk.6:29), the physically-dead structure of a human is simply called a 'dead body'. See Num.19:11. See also 'Corpse'.) {carcases 22x., tot. = 56x.}

Care[1] – 11x., n. [A.D. 1000(ASG.), < OE. **caru** (< an early Indo-European root word *gar* = 'to cry out' or 'scream') = 'mental suffering caused by anxiety or grief' (NOI. Because of the idea of a 'mental concern', by A.D. 1400 the meaning of 'care' expanded to include 'a charge to watch over and protect'. Context helps explain what is meant by 'care'.)] Thus, **care** is 'a mental state of sorrow and anxiety'. Eg. Eze.4:16, "... I will break the staff of bread in Jerusalem: and they shall eat bread by weight, and with care..." Furthermore, **care** is also 'a charge or a job to watch over and protect something'. Eg. 2Cor.11:28, "Beside those things that are without, that which cometh upon me daily, the care of all the churches." {carefulness 4x., cares 3x., caring (vbl.n.) 1x., tot. = 19x.}

Care[2] – 9x., v. [A.D. 1000, < OE. **carian, caru** (see 'Care'[1]) + **ian** = 'the action of' (NOI. This can mean either a 'grievous sorrowing' or a 'thoughtful concern'. Context helps explain which one.)] Thus, **care** means 'the action of sorrowing and grieving of the mind'. Eg. 2Sam.18:3, "... for if we flee away, they will not care for us; neither if half of us die, will they care for us." Furthermore, **care** also means 'the action of taking thoughtful concern'. Eg. Phil.2:20, "For I have no man likeminded, who will naturally care for your state." {cared 3x., carefully (adv.) 4x., carelessly (adv.) 3x., carest 3x., careth 7x., tot. = 29x.}

Careless – 5x., adj. [A.D. 1000, < OE. **care** (see 'Care'[1]) + **less** = 'devoid of' or 'free from'] Thus, **careless** modifies its n. as 'being devoid from any type of anxiety, sorrow, worry or thoughtful concern'. Eg. Jud.18:7, "Then the five men departed, and came to Laish, and saw the people that were therein, how they dwelt careless, after the manner of the Zidonians, quiet and secure." {careful 7x., tot. = 12x.}

Carnal – 11x., adj. [A.D. 1400, < LL. *carnalis* = 'fleshly' (< L. *caro* = 'flesh'), or 'body' as opposed to 'spirit'] Thus, **carnal** modifies its n. as 'having a fleshly attribute'. Eg. 1Cor.3:4, "For while one saith, I am of Paul; and another, I am of Apollos; are ye not carnal? " (NOI. It is important to realize that 'carnal' is the adj., and not the n., and therefore ascribes a flesh-like quality only to the n. If it modifies the n. 'things' (as in 1Cor.9:11), then it describes the 'things' as pertaining to the flesh; i.e. food, shelter, etc. If it modifies the n. 'mind' (as in Rom.8:7), then it describes the 'mind' as being filled with concerns for the flesh, i.e. no faith in God.) {carnally 4x., tot. = 15x.}

Carpenter – 3x., n. [A.D. 1325, < OF. *carpentier* < LL. *carpentarius* = 'wagon-maker' (< *carpentum* = 'a two-wheeled wagon'), yet in E. 'carpenter' was the title of someone who mostly did the heavy wood framing of a house or a structure, as opposed to making fine furniture] Thus, a **carpenter** is 'one who mostly does heavy-wood type of construction' (such as house-framing, roof-making, window shutters, etc. and sometimes even idols.). Eg. Isa.44:13 The carpenter stretcheth out his rule; he marketh it out with a line; he fitteth it with planes, and he marketh it out with the compass, and maketh it after the figure of a man, according to the beauty of a man; that it may remain in the house." (NOI. Justin Martyr, in his 'Dialogue with Trypho', spoke of Jesus working as a carpenter, making plows and yokes.) {carpenter's 1x., carpenters 9x., tot. = 13x.}

Carriage – 3x., n. [A.D. 1375, < E. **carry** (= 'to convey from one place to another')+ **age** = that which pertains to the root (see E. suffix '–age') (NOI. The idea of a 'carriage' being a wagon with wheels was first introduced in A.D. 1560, but only became popular in the 1700's.)] Thus, **carriage** is 'that which is carried' (as in 'valuables or stuff', similar to how we might say "*baggage*" or "*luggage*"). Eg. 1Sam.17:22, "And David left his carriage in the hand of the keeper of the carriage, and ran into the army, and came and saluted his brethren." {carriages 3x., tot. = 6x.}

Cart – 15x., n. [A.D. 1200, < ON. *kartr* = 'a heavy, two-wheeled vehicle'] Thus, a **cart** is 'a heavy, two-wheeled vehicle, used for carrying heavy goods'. Eg. 2Sam.6:3, "And they set the ark of God upon a new cart, and brought it out of the house of Abinadab that was in Gibeah: and Uzzah and Ahio, the sons of Abinadab, drave the new cart." (NOI. See also Amo.2:13.)

Case —8x n. [A.D. 1225, < OF. *cas* (= 'an event') < L. *casus* (= 'a chance' or 'a falling') < *cadere* = 'to fall'] Thus, a **case** is 'an event which befalls or happens to a person'. Eg. Deut.19:4, "And this is the case of the slayer, which shall flee thither, that he may live..." {cases 1x., tot. = 9x.}

Casement —1x., n. [A.D. 1430, < OF. *enchassement* = 'a window frame' (< *en* = 'in' + *casse* = 'frame' (< L. *capsa* = 'box')) + *ment* = 'the product or result' (same as E. suffix '-ment')] Thus, a **casement** is 'a box-like frame, set in a window opening, to which is attached, by hinges, a wooden shutter or an iron screen'. Eg. Pr.7:6, "For at the window of my house I looked through my casement."

Cassia —3x., n. [A.D. 1000(ASG.), < L. *cassia* < Gk. κασια (*kasia*) < Hb. קְצִיעָה (*ketseeaw*) = 'the reddish-brown inner bark of a *Cinnamomum cassia*, or 'cassia tree', used as a spice' (< Hb. קָצַע (*katsaw*) = 'to scrape off', because that's how they obtained the cassia spice)] Thus, **cassia** is 'the aromatic spice scrapped from the inner bark of the cassia tree'. Eg. Ps.45:8, "All thy garments smell of myrrh, and aloes, and cassia, out of the ivory palaces, whereby they have made thee glad." (NOI. 'Cassia' has antibacterial properties and was used in the making of the holy oil. It is similar to cinnamon in smell, but more aromatic. See also 'Cinnamon'.)

Cast — 501x., v. [A.D. 1200, < ME. casten < ON. *kasta* = 'to fling or hurl into a heap or pile'] Thus, **cast** means 'the action of flinging something so that it lands in a heap or as a heap'. Eg. Gen.31:51, "And Laban said to Jacob, Behold this heap, and behold this pillar, which I have cast betwixt me and thee." (See also 'Throw', 'Thrust' and 'Toss'.) {castaway 1x., castedst 1x., castest 3x., casteth 16x., casting 21x., outcast 1x., outcasts 7x., tot. = 551x.}

Castaway – 1x., n. [A.D.1525(TNT.), < E. **cast** (see 'Cast') + **away** (lit., 'on way') = 'a motion of removal'] Thus, a **castaway** is 'something or someone flung aside in a heap as rejected or disqualified'. Eg. 1Cor.9:27, "But I keep under my body, and bring it into subjection: lest that by any means, when I have preached to others, I myself should be a castaway." {away 915x., cast 501x., tot. = 1416x.}

Castle –9x., n. [A.D. 1000(ASG.), < OF. *castel* (NOI. Modern F. is *chateau*) < L. *castellum* = 'a fortress' or 'fortified village' (< *castrum* = 'fortified camp', < *castra* = 'camp')] Thus, a **castle** is 'a heavily fortified building (or series of buildings joined) as a means of defense against enemy attack'. Eg. 1Chr.11:5, "... Nevertheless David took the castle of Zion, which is the city of David." (NOI. In the 1300's, the NT. Gk. κωμη (*komay*) (= 'town' or 'village') was also rendered as 'castle' (as is seen in the WB. (in modernized spelling) – Jn.11:1, "And there was a sick man, Lazarus of Bethany, of the castle of Mary and Martha, his sisters.") but by the 1500's, was causing confusion, and was changed in subsequent E. Bibles.) {castles 6x., tot. = 15x.}

Castor –1x., pn. [A.D. 1525(TNT.), (Both 'Castor and Pollux' come from the Gk. Διοσκουροι (*Dioskuroi*) = 'the hero twins', but who they are is now further explained.) < Gk. Καστορ (*Kastor*) = 'the horseman' (< Gk. mythology – a horse-tamer, and one of the twin sons of Zeus (or Jupiter in Roman mythology). Known, with his twin brother Pollux as the 'heavenly twins', they are associated with the constellation 'Gemini' (< L. *geminus* = twin), Castor being the 'alpha' or first star (dimmer – being the 23rd brightest star in the sky) and Pollux being the 'beta' or second star (brighter – being the 17th brightest star in the sky). (NOI. Ancient astronomers once listed Castor as the brighter, causing modern day astronomers to conclude that either Castor has dimmed over 300 years or that Pollux has brightened.) The twins became the 'patron saints' of sailors and voyages after they helped to still a storm at sea.)] Thus, **Castor** is 'a name of a Gk. mythological god (meaning 'the horse-man'), and was part of the name given to an Alexandrian ship.' Eg. Act.28:11, "And after three months we departed in a ship of Alexandria, which had wintered in the isle, whose sign was Castor and Pollux." (See also 'Pollux'.)

Caterpiller –5x., n. [A.D. 1440, < ME. **catyrpel** < oo., but possibly from OF. *chatepelose* = 'a hairy cat' (< LL. *catta* = 'cat' + *pilosus* = 'hairy') and refers to the larva-stage of a moth or butterfly (NOI. 'Catyrpel' was changed to 'caterpiller' possibly to associate it with ME. '**piller** = 'plunderer, spoiler'. 'Piller' and 'caterpiller' were used synonymously in other ME. literature. Referring to the 'caterpiller', English children sometimes use the term, 'woolly bear'.)] Thus, a **caterpiller** is 'a crawling, underdeveloped moth or butterfly, in its larva-stage, having a long segmented body and many feet, and feeds continually on nearby vegetation.'. Eg. Joe.1:4, "That which the palmerworm hath left hath the locust eaten; and that which the locust hath left hath the cankerworm eaten; and that which the cankerworm hath left hath the caterpiller eaten." (NOI. Female moths (of which there are about 14 species) and butterflies (about 350 species) lay their eggs on trees, flowering buds and developing fruit in Israel during June or July. In one or two weeks, the eggs hatch, producing tiny hairy caterpillars (larva). These tiny creatures devour vegetation (leaves, fruit, green stalks, etc.) and molt their skin many times over the summer, each time becoming larger. Finally, they undergo a marvelous transformation: the moth larva spins a silk cocoon while the butterfly larva molt one last time into a 'chrysalis cocoon'. They emerge in the spring time as a fully-grown moth or butterfly and do not grow any larger. Moths and butterflies cannot chew plants, but instead, eat through a tube-like tongue such things as nectar from flowers, sap from trees, animal droppings and rotten fruit. Adult moths do not eat wool or clothing, but will lay eggs in them, and the larvae will eat the fibers for the protein in them. Nowadays, mothballs are used to keep the adult moths away. See also 'Cankerworm', 'Locust' and 'Palmerworm'.)

Cattle – 153x., n. pl. [A.D. 1275, < ME. **catel** < OF. *catel* < ML. *capitale* = 'property or wealth' (< L. *capitalis* = 'principal or chief' < *caput* = 'head') (NOI. Ancient people used domestic herd-type farm animals (such as horses, asses, camels, cows, bulls, oxen, sheep and goats, as opposed to wild animals such as lions, bears, etc.) as a form of money. By having many such animals, a man was considered wealthy. The L. word was difficult for many to say, so it mutated in pronunciation to 'catel', then to 'cattle'. The Romans called their money, *pecunia* (< *pecus* = 'a domestic animal', such as a cow or sheep) and the earliest coins had a picture of a cow on it.)] Thus, **cattle** are 'domestic herd-type farm animals that were used as a form of money or wealth'. Eg. Gen.13:2, "And Abram was very rich in cattle, in silver, and in gold." (NOI. Gen.3:14 indicates the 'serpent' was listed among the 'cattle', so it would have originally been some type of 'four-footed, herd-type farm animal' before God cursed it. (See 'Serpent'.) Gen.30:32 lists sheep and goats as cattle. Ex.9:3-6 lists also horses, asses, camels and oxen as cattle. Ecc.2:7 indicates there are large and small cattle. Today, we think of cattle as just being cows and bulls. Interestingly, cows and bulls can live for 12-15 years, but they hardly ever get past 5-6 years because of attacks from wild animals, disease, accident, or most often, they are slaughtered for their meat. See also 'Beast'.)

Caul –12x., n. [A.D. 1327, < OF. *cale* = a 'small cap' (as in 'a woman's netted head-dress'). The Hb. word (used 11 of the 12 times) is יֹתֶרֶת (*yothereth*) = 'covering or overhang', and no doubt refers to the caudate-lobe (a tail-like, roundish projection) on top of the liver. (NOI. The word 'caul' was used in E. literature to speak of such things as: a net for wrapping things in; a spider's web; or a thin membrane.)] Thus, a **caul** is 'the fatty, caudate-lobe, attached to the top of the liver of animals'. Eg. Ex.29:13 "And thou shalt take all the fat that covereth the inwards, and the caul that is above the liver, and the two kidneys, and the fat that is upon them, and burn them upon the altar." (NOI. Some have suggested the 'caul' is the diaphragm membrane, located beneath the ribcage (to which the liver is attached), however, the caudate-lobe makes more sense, because it is loaded with fat and blood – two things that were always sacrificed to God. 'Caul' is also used in Hos.13:8 (Hb. סְגוֹר (*segone*) = 'enclosure') in reference to the heart, and means either the pericardium membrane surrounding the heart, or the chest cavity itself.) {cauls 1x., tot. = 13x.}

Cauls – 1x., n. pl. [A.D. 1327, < E. **caul** (see 'Caul') = 'a woman's netted head-dress' + **s** = forms the pl. (NOI. The Hb. שְׁבִיס (*shawbis*) = 'headband'.)] Thus, **cauls** are 'two or more women's head-bands', probably colorful and decorated. Eg. Isa.3:18, "In that day the Lord will take away the bravery of their tinkling ornaments about their feet, and their cauls, and their round tires like the moon." {caul 12x., tot. = 13x.}

Cause – 328x., n. [A.D. 1225, < F. *cause* < L. *causa* = 'that which produces an effect, action or a condition'] Thus, a **cause** is 'something which produces an effect'. Eg. 1Sam.17:29, "And David said, What have I now done? Is there not a cause? " (See also 'Effect'.) {caused 94x., causeless 2x., causes 7x., causest 2x., causeth 32x., causing 4x., tot. = 469x.}

Causeway – 2x., n. [A.D. 1440, < ME. **causey** (< OF. *caucie*

< ML. *calciata* = 'paved road' < LL. *calciare* = 'to stamp down hard with the heel', making a slightly mounded, hard area) + '**way**' (< L. *via* = 'road or street') (NOI. The 1611 has a marginal note next to Pr.15:19, "*But the way of the righteous is raised up as a causey*".)] Thus, a **causeway** is 'a roadway, stamped down hard and raised or mounded'. Eg. 1Chr.26:16, "To Shuppim and Hosah the lot came forth westward, with the gate Shallecheth, by the causeway of the going up, ward against ward." (NOI. The 'causeway' at the Shallecheth gate, at Jerusalem, was like a ramp on the outside of the city going up to it. In England, today, 'causeway' refers to a sidewalk (i.e. a raised area beside the road) or a raised ramp.)

Cave – 33x.*, n. [A.D. 1220, < OF. *cave* < L. *cavus* = 'a hollow place' (*incl. title of Ps. 57 and 142)] Thus, a **cave** is 'a hollow in the earth' (particularly one that is more or less horizontal in the side of a hill or mountain). Eg. Gen.19:30, "And Lot went up out of Zoar, and dwelt in the mountain, and his two daughters with him; for he feared to dwell in Zoar: and he dwelt in a cave, he and his two daughters." (NOI. Caves in Israel are usually formed by the action of an underground water-table (mixing with carbon dioxide, found in decaying humus, to form carbonic acid), which erodes the limestone rock near the earth's surface. Most of the caves and caverns thus formed are horizontal with, perhaps, a few vertical passageways. Caves were used to live in (Gen.19:30), to bury people in (Gen.23:9), and for refuge (Josh.10:16).) {cave's 1x., caves 6x., tot. = 38x.}

Cease – 70x., v. [A.D. 1300, < ME. cesse < OF. *cesser* < L. *cessare* = 'to stop, yield or give over a frequently repeating matter'] Thus, **cease** means 'the action of stopping something which is happening repeatedly'. Eg. Gen.8:22, "While the earth remaineth, seedtime and harvest, and cold and heat, and summer and winter, and day and night shall not cease." (NOI. Seedtime, harvest, etc. are all things that happen repeatedly, over and over. See also 'Stop'.) {ceased 33x., ceaseth 10x., ceasing 7x., tot. = 120x.}

Cedar —51x., n. [A.D. 1000(ASG.), < OF. *cedre* < L. *cedrus* < Gk. κεδρος (*kedros*) < oo., but some suggest an ancient Ar. word meaning 'a firmly-rooted, strong tree'] Thus, a **cedar** is 'an evergreen tree of the species *Cedrus libani* (cedar of Lebanon)'. Eg. Ps.92:12, "The righteous shall flourish like the palm tree: he shall grow like a cedar in Lebanon." (NOI. Called the 'Monarch of Evergreens', cedar trees are not attacked by insects, because of the fragrant smell they give off; their wood is long lasting, a warm red color, and free from knots. They grow as high as 120 ft. (36.5 m.) having branches and roots that spread out well, and they can live for hundreds of years – there are cedar trees in Israel today over 2,000 years old. The oldest tree in the world is a sequoia tree, in Sequoia National Park, in California (named 'General Sherman') and is estimated to be about 4,000 years old.) {cedars 24x., tot. = 75x.}

Celebrate —3x., v. [A.D. 1534, < L. *celebrare* = 'to frequent in great numbers of people' (< *celebro* = 'to crowd or throng')] Thus, **celebrate** means 'the action of gathering a large crowd of people together for the purpose of bestowing honor'. Eg. Lev.23:41, "And ye shall keep it a feast unto the LORD seven days in the year. It shall be a statute for ever in your generations: ye shall celebrate it in the seventh month."

Celestial —2x., adj. [A.D. 1384, < OF. *celestial* < L. *caelestis* < *caelum* = 'sky or heaven' (NOI. The Gk. επουρανιος (*epouranios*) was understood in Koine times to include the stars and planets. This appears to be the meaning of the word in light of the context of 1Cor.15:39-41.)] Thus, **celestial** modifies its n. as 'being of a heavenly, or outer-space-type nature'. Eg. 1Cor.15:40, "There are also celestial bodies, and bodies terrestrial: but the glory of the celestial is one, and the glory of the terrestrial is another."

Censer – 12x., n. [A.D. 1250, < OF. *censier* (shortened from *encensier*) < L. *incensarium* = 'a vessel for burning incense in' (< L. *incendo* = 'to set fire to and burn')] Thus, a **censer** is 'a vessel in which incense is burned'. Eg. Num.16:18, "And they took every man his censer, and put fire in them, and laid incense thereon, and stood in the door of the tabernacle of the congregation with Moses and Aaron." (NOI. A 'censer' was a common household item in ancient Israel. That's why there was never any instructions given concerning making them, and that's also why Korah and his 250 companions each had a censer. See Num.16. See also 'Incense'.) {censers 8x., tot. = 20x.}

Centurion –20x., n. [A.D. 1275, < F. *centurion* < L. *centurio* = 'one in charge of a hundred' (< *centum* = 'hundred') (NOI. Although, originally, a 'centurion' was a Roman soldier over 100 other soldiers, in actual practice the number often varied anywhere from 80 to as many as 500, according to the particular need at the time. There were 60 centurions to a legion, comprising of junior and more senior centurions in rank and command. The most senior centurion was known as the *Primus pilus*.)] Thus, a **centurion** is 'a military commander in charge of (about) 100 soldiers'. Eg. Act.10:1, "There was a certain man in Caesarea called Cornelius, a centurion of the band called the Italian band." (See also 'Band'[3].) {centurion's 1x., centurions 3x., tot. = 24x.}

Certain – 196x., adj., adv., and n. [A.D. 1297, < OF. *certain* < L. *certanus* < *certus* = 'fixed or settled' (a variation of *cernere* = 'to decide')] Thus, as an adj., **certain** modifies its n. as 'being a particular fixed and known type'. Eg. Act.27:26, "Howbeit we must be cast upon a certain island." Furthermore, as an adv., **certain** modifies its v. as 'being performed in a fixed and known way'. Eg. Heb.10:27, "But a certain fearful looking for of judgment and fiery indignation, which shall devour the adversaries." Finally, as a n., **certain** (used 5x., and always in a pl. sense) refers to 'a particular group of people, whose associations or beliefs are decidedly known and without question'. Eg. Lk.18:9, "And he spake this parable unto certain which trusted in themselves that they were righteous, and despised others." {certainly 31x., certainty 7x., uncertain 2x., tot. = 236x.}

Certify – 5x., v. [A.D. 1330, < OF. *certifier* < ML. *certificare* (< *certus* = 'fixed' (see 'Certain') + *facere* = 'to make') = 'to make something fixed' (NOI. Our E. word 'certificate' comes from *certificare*.)] Thus, **certify** means 'the action of making something fixed, settled or sure' (as in a legal settlement or guarantee). Eg. Gal.1:11, "But I certify you, brethren, that the gospel which was preached of me is not after man." {certified 2x., tot. = 7x.}

Chafed – 1x., v. pret. [A.D. 1330, < ME. **chaufe** < OF. *chaufer* = 'to heat' (< L. *calefacere* = 'to make hot'; i.e. 'to make hot by rubbing or friction') + **ed** = forms the pret. (NOI. 'Chafed' is often used in a figurative sense of 'anger caused by friction'.)] Thus, **chafed**, used figuratively, means 'having been made to fret and fume because of irritation'. Eg. 2Sam.17:8, "For, said Hushai, thou knowest thy father and his men, that they be mighty men, and they be chafed in their minds, as a bear robbed of her whelps in the field." (NOI. The WB. used this word in Isa.44:15, "... and is chafed " ("... and warm himself " – KJV). Around A.D. 1900, when automobiles were first produced, they were often steam-driven, and the French gave the name of *chauffer* ('to heat') to the person who 'stoked the fire' for the steam and drove the car!)

Chaff – 14x., n. [A.D. 1000(ASG.), < OE. **ceaf** < oo., but possibly related to OHG. *cheva* = 'a husk or pod' (possibly from a Teut. root *kef* = 'to gnaw') but always used in reference to the outer skin around a cereal grain] Thus, **chaff** is 'the outer skin, or husk, around a cereal grain' such as wheat. Eg. Lk.3:17, "Whose fan is in his hand, and he will throughly purge his floor, and will gather the wheat into his garner; but the chaff he will burn with fire unquenchable." (NOI. 'Chaff' represents about 20% of the total weight of a grain, which explains why the wind can drive it away (Ps.1:4). Though once considered useless by the ancients, the chaff (also as 'bran') of wheat, rye and other cereal grains has gained acceptance today as a dietary source of fiber, rich in B vitamins and minerals. See also 'Wheat' and 'Winnoweth'.)

Chalcedony – 1x., n. [A.D. 1305, < L. *calcedonius* < Gk. χαλκηδων (*khalkedon*) < oo., (NOI. Some claim that it got its name from a place called Chalcedon in Bithynia (Asia) where the stones were first found, but there is no way of verifying this. Pliny the Elder (A.D. 23-79) describes a stone like that of 'chalcedony' originating from North Africa.); 'a translucent variety of quartz rocks, often grayish in color with a waxy-luster'; found in lava and sedimentary rocks] Thus, **chalcedony** is 'a quartz-type of stone with a milky or grayish appearance'. Eg. Rev.21:19, "And the foundations of the wall of the city were garnished with all manner of precious stones. The first foundation was jasper; the second, sapphire; the third, a chalcedony..." (NOI. 'Chalcedony' was used extensively for carving small signature-seals featuring various scenes of everyday life. The ancient mystics believed 'chalcedony' helped restore poor eyesight, could drive away bad dreams and give success in courts of law. In the Middle Ages, 'chalcedony' was thought to represent the zeal for truth.)

Chalkstones – 1x., n. pl. [A.D. 1386, < E. **chalk** (< OE. **cealc** < L. *calx* = 'lime' (used as a marking stick)) + **stone** = 'a pebble or small piece of rock' (see 'Stone') + **s** = forms the pl.] Thus, **chalkstones** are 'very soft lime-type stones, composed of microscopic shells, and of a grayish color'. Eg. Isa.27:9,

"By this therefore shall the iniquity of Jacob be purged; and this is all the fruit to take away his sin; when he maketh all the stones of the altar as chalkstones that are beaten in sunder, the groves and images shall not stand up." (NOI. 'Chalkstones' are also known as 'sedimentary rocks' because they are formed when rainwater washes the sediment down from the hills to settle on the bottoms of lakes, rivers and oceans, and forms 'calcium carbonate'. In England, people used to make chalk sticks from the sedimentary rocks that make up the White Cliffs of Dover.)

Chamber –52x., n. [A.D. 1225, < OF. *chamber* < L. *camera* = 'a room with a vaulted or arched roof, used for living in' (NOI. Although the L. *camera* means 'a large room', the word was borrowed in E. to mean 'the box-like device in which a photographic plate or paper is exposed to light through a lens'.)] Thus, a **chamber** is 'a vaulted-ceiling room of smaller size'. Eg. 2Ki.4:10, "Let us make a little chamber, I pray thee, on the wall; and let us set for him there a bed, and a table, and a stool, and a candlestick: and it shall be, when he cometh to us, that he shall turn in thither." (NOI. A 'chamber' often (but not always) referred to a bedroom as seen also in the E. 'chamberlain' (= 'one who attends to a nobleman in his bedchamber' (see 'Chamberlain')); 'chambering' (= 'sexual sin within a bedroom' (see 'Chambering')) and 'chambermaid' ('a female servant who cleans and tidies a bedroom'). A chamber could also be used for other things, such as a 'guard chamber' (1Ki.14:28), a 'summer chamber' (Jud.3:24) or even the sky (Ps.104:13). 'Chamber' and 'room' are different. See 'Room'.) {bedchamber 6x., bridechamber 3x., chambering 1x., chamberlain 6x., chamberlains 9x., chambers 66x., guestchamber 2x., tot. = 145x.}

Chambering – 1x., vbl.n. [A.D. 1449, < E. **chamber** (see 'Chamber') + **ing** = forms the vbl.n. (see E. suffix '–ing'[1])] Thus, **chambering** means 'the action of sexual sin within a bedroom'. Eg. Rom.13:13, "Let us walk honestly, as in the day;

not in rioting and drunkenness, not in chambering and wantonness, not in strife and envying." (NOI. In Rom.13:13, the WB. used "beddis"; the LV. used *"cubilibus"* = 'in bedding' (< L. *cubile* = 'bed').) {chamber 52x., chamberlain 6x., tot. = 59x.}

Chamberlain –6x., n. [A.D. 1225, < OF. *chamberlenc* < OHG. *chamarlinc* = 'one who attends to the personal needs of his master' (< L. *camera* = 'chamber' or 'room' (as in a 'bedroom'; see 'Chamber'))] Thus, a **chamberlain** is 'a person concerned with the personal or intimate needs of, and protection of, his master, within his bedroom or living quarters'. Eg. Est.2:14, "In the evening she went, and on the morrow she returned into the second house of the women, to the custody of Shaashgaz, the king's chamberlain, which kept the concubines: she came in unto the king no more, except the king delighted in her, and that she were called by name." (NOI. A 'Chamberlain' was a very trusted man in a household and his boss would depend heavily on him. Therefore, the title was sometimes applied to an important officer with critical duties, as in Rom.16:23. Tyndale renders 'eunuch' as 'chamberlain' in Act.8:27.) {chamber 52x., tot. = 58x.}

Chameleon – 1x., n. [A.D. 1340, < L. *chamaeleon* < Gk. καμαιλιον (*kamaileon*) < καμαι (*kamai*) = 'on the ground' + λιον (*leon*) = 'lion' (NOI. The Hb. word כח (*koach*) (translated 'chameleon' in Lev.11:30) is used elsewhere 125x., and is mostly translated as 'strength', 'power' and 'might'. This virtue may reflect the powerful grip that the chameleon has when holding onto a branch, and perhaps why the Gk. used λιον (*leon*).)] Thus, a **chameleon** is 'a small lizard-like reptile, up to 6 in. (15.24 cm.) in length, having a very long, sticky tongue which it can 'shoot out' and snag flies and insects'. Eg. Lev.11:30, "And the ferret, and the chameleon, and the lizard, and the snail, and the mole." (NOI. While the chameleon is known for its ability to change its skin color, there are other types of lizard that can also do the same thing. This change is a result of the temperature in the air and the emotions of the chameleon.)

Champaign – 1x., n. [A.D. 1400, < OF. *champaigne* < ML. *campania* = 'open country' (as in 'suited for agriculture or military use')] Thus, a **champaign** is 'a large, clear and level field of land'. Eg. Deut.11:30, "Are they not on the other side Jordan, by the way where the sun goeth down, in the land of the Canaanites, which dwell in the champaign over against Gilgal, beside the plains of Moreh? "

Chance – 6x., n. and v. [A.D. 1297, < ME. **cheance** < OF. *cheance* < LL. *cadentia* = 'falling' (< *cadere* = 'to fall') (as in 'it could fall this way or that way')] Thus, as a n., a **chance** is 'a befalling or a happening of events'. Eg. 1Sam.6:9, "... it was a chance that happened to us." Furthermore, as a v., **chance** means 'the action of a happening of events'. Eg. 1Cor.15:37, "And that which thou sowest, thou sowest not that body that shall be, but bare grain, it may chance of wheat, or of some other grain." (NOI. The word 'luck' is never used in the Bible. It comes from middle Du. *gheluc* = 'happiness, good fortune' and was probably first used in E. as a gambling term. Both 'chance' and 'luck' speak of something happening, but the difference is that 'chance' is the simple statement of the happening, whereas 'luck' concentrates on the result of the happening, i.e. "*did we win, or did we lose?*") {chanceth 1x., tot. = 7x.}

Chancellor –3x., n. [A.D. 1066, < OE. **canceler** < OF. *chancelier* < LL. *cancellarius* = 'an officer stationed at the bars in a tribunal, to keep the public away from the judge' (< *cancelli* = 'bars') (NOI. Originally, a 'chancellor' was what we might call an usher or a security guard. However, the status and importance of the *cancellarius* continued to increase over the years until he became 'the official secretary to the king', in charge of important functions, legal documents, etc.)] Thus, a **chancellor** is 'an official secretary to a king', in charge of the king's business and legal affairs. Eg. Ezr.4:8, "Rehum the chancellor and Shimshai the scribe wrote a letter against Jerusalem to Artaxerxes the king in this sort." (NOI. Rehum was 'chancellor' to king Artaxerxes and was stationed in Samaria to represent the king's official business.)

Chant – 1x., v. [A.D. 1386, < OF. *chanter* < L. *cantare* < *canere* = 'to sing' (usually a happy song, or to celebrate in song)] Thus, **chant** means 'the action of singing a happy song'. Eg. Amo.6:5, "That chant to the sound of the viol, and invent to themselves instruments of musick, like David." (NOI. 'Chant' was not used as a n. to mean 'a song or melody' until A.D. 1671.)

Chapel – 1x., n. [A.D. 1225, < OF. *chapele* < ML. *capella* = 'a sanctuary for relics' (NOI. *Capella* in ML. originally meant 'a place to store a cape' (< *cappa* = 'cape or cloak') and referred to the cloak of St. Martin, now preserved in the oratory of the Frankish kings as a relic, according to Catholic history. Born in A.D. 316, Martin was a military man with a growing interest in God and stationed in Amiens of Gaul, when he apparently saw a half-naked man. He then divided his cloak into two parts, giving one part to the man and keeping the other part for himself. The part he kept became known as 'The Cloak of St. Martin'. He later left the military, and joined himself to the disciples of a pastor named Hilary in the town of Poitiers, France, later becoming the pastor of the church in Tours, France, in A.D. 372. He got sick and died in A.D. 397, aged 81. Above his grave was built a small 'chapel' in which was kept his cloak. Later, the Frankish kings (A.D. 496 – 751) would take this cloak into battle with them and also use it to sanctify oaths. The 'chaplain' was originally the custodian of the chapel, but later the term was applied to a clergyman.)] Thus, a **chapel** is 'a room or a building used for the storage of religious relics and religious worship'. Eg. Amo.7:13, "But prophesy not again any more at Bethel: for it is the king's chapel, and it is the king's court." (NOI. This 'chapel' was the shrine of Jeroboam, housing one of the golden calves that he made (1Ki.12:28-29), and was next door to the king's court, which was his residence. The writer of first Kings called it a 'chapel', thus distinguishing it from the Temple of God in Jerusalem.)

Chapiter –13x., n. [A.D. 1425, < OF. *chapitre* < L. *capitulum* = 'the small head of a column'] Thus, a **chapiter** is 'a small head, or decorative top, of a column'. Eg. 1 Ki.7:16, "And he made two chapiters of molten brass, to set upon the tops of the pillars: the height of the one chapiter was five cubits, and the height of the other chapiter was five cubits." (NOI. The WB. and BB. called it a 'pommel', while the CB. called it a 'knoppe'. Both terms meant 'knob-like ornaments'. The GB. and the 1611 both called it a 'chapiter'.) {chapiters 16x., tot. = 29x.}

Chapmen – 1x., n. pl. [A.D. 890, < OE. **ceapman** (sing.) < **ceap** = 'barter' + **man** = 'man' ('men' = forms the pl.) (NOI. 'Chapman' meant several things in early E. including 'a negotiator' and 'a retailer'. But the 'itinerant peddler' seems to best fit the context.)] Thus, **chapmen** are 'two or more men who make their livelihood by traveling from place to place buying and selling their goods'. Eg. 2Chr.9:14, "Beside that which chapmen and merchants brought. And all the kings of Arabia and governors of the country brought gold and silver to Solomon." (NOI. The E. word 'chap' or 'chaps' (as in "These poor chaps are from the city.") refers to an undignified young man. It has nothing to do with 'chap' as in the word 'chapt' (see 'Chapt'). See also 'Merchant'.)

Chapt –1x., prp. [A.D. 1325, (alternate spelling of 'chapped') < E. **chap** = 'to crack' + **t** = forms the prp. (see E. suffix '–ed'[2])] Thus, **chapt** modifies its n. (in this case, 'ground') as 'being cracked with openings'. Eg. Jer.14:4, "Because the ground is chapt, for there was no rain in the earth, the plowmen were ashamed, they covered their heads."

Charge[1] –85x., n. [A.D. 1225, < OF. *charge* < L. *carrica* (= 'a load or burden') < *carrus* (= 'a wagon') (NOI. In the Bible, a 'charge' is not used to speak of a 'physical cargo' per say, but of 'a mental or emotional load', such as 'a responsibility given' (involving stewardship, safeguarding, repayment and management) or 'a command, from a superior, to perform a task'.)] Thus, a **charge** is 'a mental or emotional load, involving a responsibility given'. Eg. Deut.31:23, "And he gave Joshua the son of Nun a charge, and said, Be strong and of a good courage: for thou shalt bring the children of Israel into the land which I sware unto them: and I will be with thee." {chargeable (adj.) 5x., charges 6x., tot. = 96x.}

Charge[2] – 17x., v. [A.D. 1225, < ME. **chargen** (= 'to load or impose a command') < OF. *chargier* < ML. *carricare* (= 'to load')] Thus **charge** means 'the action of imposing a command or a responsibility upon someone'. Eg. 1Tim.5:21, "I charge thee before God, and the Lord Jesus Christ, and the elect angels, that thou observe these things without preferring one before another, doing nothing by partiality." {charged 51x., chargedst 1x., chargest 1x., charging 2x., overcharge 1x., tot. = 73x.}

Charger –17x., n. [A.D. 1305, < OF. *chargeoir* < L. *carricatorium* = 'a device or utensil made for hand-carrying of loads' (< L. *carrus* = 'a wagon') (NOI. Our E. word 'car' (as in 'passenger-car' or 'freight-car') comes from L. *carrus*.)] Thus, a **charger** is 'a utensil that carries a load', such as a large platter. Eg. Mt.14:8, "And she, being before instructed of her mother, said, Give me here John Baptist's head in a charger." {chargers 3x., tot. = 20x.}

Chariot –64x., adj. and n. [A.D. 1325, < OF. *chariot* = 'a two-wheeled, horse-drawn vehicle' (< *char* = 'a wagon'

(< L. *carrus* = 'a wagon'))] Thus, as an adj., **chariot** modifies its n. as 'being part of or connected to a chariot'. Eg. 1 Ki.7:33, "And the work of the wheels was like the work of a chariot wheel..." Furthermore, as a n., a **chariot** is 'a two-wheeled, (usually; cp. Isa.21:7) horse-drawn vehicle used for carrying as many as three people in a war, a race or a royal procession'. Eg. Ps.76:6, "At thy rebuke, O God of Jacob, both the chariot and horse are cast into a dead sleep." {chariots 113x., tot. = 177x.}

Charity – 28x., n. [A.D. 1154, < OF. *charite* < L. *caritas* = 'a love or dearness for something because of placing a high value on it' (NOI. The Gk. αγαπή (*agape*) is used 114x., in the NT. and is translated as 'love' in all but 29x., (where it is translated as 'charity' or 'charitable'). Jerome, in the LV., usually translated the NT. Gk. αγαπή as *dilectio* ('caring affection') but then, in a number of instances, as *caritas* ('caring affection including a high value'). He did this to avoid the more worldly association of the word *amor*. The WB., in using the LV., followed suit and translated *dilectio* as "love" and then *caritas* as 'charity'. The translators of the 1611 recognized the validity of this and did likewise. Therefore, 'charity' stands in a 'love-class' of its own.)] Thus, **charity** is 'a very caring-affection because of a very high value placed upon the object of affection'. Eg. 1Cor.13:13, "And now abideth faith, hope, charity, these three; but the greatest of these is charity." (NOI. 'Charity' results in godly actions, such as edification (1Cor.8:1), Christ-likeness (1Cor.13:4-8), a kiss of charity (1Pt.5:14) and feasts of charity (Jude.1:12). See also 'Love'.) {charitably 1x., tot. = 29x.}

Charmer – 1x., n. [A.D. 1340(HP.), < E. **charm** (< OF. *charme* < L. *carmen* = 'a song of incantation' (I.E. 'a magical song')) + **er** = identifies a person according to their occupation (see E. suffix '–er')] Thus, a **charmer** is 'a person who chants a song of incantation in order to exert magical powers'. Eg.

Deut.18:11, "Or a charmer, or a consulter with familiar spirits, or a wizard, or a necromancer."

Chaste – 3x., adj. [A.D. 1200, < OF. *chaste* < L. *castus* = 'morally pure or unpolluted' (NOI. Tyndale uses 'chaste' in place of 'eunuchs', as in Mt.19:12.)] Thus, **chaste** modifies its n. as 'being morally pure or unpolluted'. Eg. 1Pt.3:2, "While they behold your chaste conversation coupled with fear." {chasten 6x., chastened 8x., chastenest 1x., chasteneth 5x., chastening 6x., chastise 10x., chastised 6x., chastisement 5x., chastiseth 1x., tot. = 51x.}

Chasten – 6x., v. [A.D. 1526, < OF. *chastier* < L. *castigare* = 'to punish in order to correct' (< *castus* = 'morally pure' + *agere* = 'to drive, make or do')] Thus, **chasten** means 'the action of inflicting suffering, discipline or corrective punishment, for the purpose of moral purification'. Eg. Pr.19:18, "Chasten thy son while there is hope, and let not thy soul spare for his crying." {chaste 3x., chastened 8x., chastenest 1x., chasteneth 5x., chastening 6x., chastise 10x., chastised 6x., chastisement 5x., chastiseth 1x., tot. = 51x.}

Chastise – 10x., v. [A.D. 1325, < E. **chaste** (see 'Chaste') + **ise** = 'to make or conform to' (see E. suffix '–ise')] Thus, **chastise** means 'the action of conforming someone to a condition of chastisement'. Eg. Lk.23:16, "I will therefore chastise him, and release him." (NOI. Pilate was trying to evoke public sympathy for Jesus by having him beaten. Jesus would have looked like a sorry, beaten site (and He did). While 'chasten' is more the process, 'chastise' is the process with an emphasis on the end result. See also 'Chasten'.) {chaste 3x., chasten 6x., chastened 8x., chastenest 1x., chasteneth 5x., chastening 6x., chastised 6x., chastisement 5x., chastiseth 1x., tot. = 51x.}

Chatter – 1x., v. [A.D. 1225, (not a word, but a sound imitating a bird)] Thus, **chatter** means 'the action of uttering a series of rapid, inarticulate speech-like sounds, similar to that made by a bird'. Eg. Isa.38:14, "Like a crane or a swallow, so did I chatter: I did mourn as a dove: mine eyes fail with looking upward: O LORD, I am oppressed; undertake for me."

Check – 1x., n. [A.D. 1314, < OF. *eschec* = 'a rebuke' (NOI. Although *eschec* is used various ways in E. (as an int., n., adj. and v.), it actually comes from the game of chess. It's root word comes from the Persian *shāh* = 'king'. Chess may have originated in northern India or Afghanistan in A.D. 600, and is thought to have made its way through Persia around A.D. 1000.)] Thus, a **check** is 'a rebuke or reprimand'. Eg. Job.20:3, "I have heard the check of my reproach, and the spirit of my understanding causeth me to answer."

Cheek –9x., n. [A.D. 825(VP.), < OE. ceace = 'a jaw or jawbone', referring to the side of the face] Thus, a **cheek** is 'the area on the side of a face, below the eye'. Eg. Mt.5:39, "But I say unto you, That ye resist not evil: but whosoever shall smite thee on thy right cheek, turn to him the other also." {cheeks 5x., tot. = 14x.}

Cheer – 10x., n. and v. [A.D. 1225, < OF. *chere* < LL. *cara* = 'the face' (as in 'the pleasant countenance of the face')] Thus, as a n., **cheer** is 'an expression of one's countenance'. Eg. Act.27:36, "Then were they all of good cheer, and they also took some meat." Furthermore, as a v., **cheer** means 'the action of making the countenance glad'. Eg. Ecc.11:9, "Rejoice, O young man, in thy youth; and let thy heart cheer thee in the days of thy youth, and walk in the ways of thine heart, and in the sight of thine eyes: but know thou, that for all these things God will bring thee into judgment." {cheereth 1x., cheerful 4x., cheerfully 1x., cheerfulness 1x., tot. = 17x.}

Chemosh – 8x., pn. [A.D. 1587(GB.), trans. < Hb. כמוש (*keemosh*) = 'a subduer' (NOI. From the WB. to the BB. they used the L. *Chamos* < LXX Gk. Χαμως (*Khamos*).)] Thus, **Chemosh** is 'the name of a deity, whose name means 'a subduer', and worshipped by the Moabites and Ammonites'. Eg. Jud.11:24, "Wilt not thou possess that which Chemosh thy god giveth thee to possess?..." (NOI. The worship of 'Chemosh' was brought to Jerusalem by King Solomon (1Ki.11:7) and later abolished by King Josiah (2Ki.23:13).)

Cherub –30x., n. [A.D. 825(VP.), < LL. *cherub* < Hb. כרוב (*kerub*) < oo., but possibly from Assyrian *kirubu* < *karâbu* = 'to be near' (as in 'a body guard' or 'a personal servant')] Thus, a **cherub** is 'a type of celestial being having wings and acts as a personal servant, or body guard, of God'. Eg. 2Chr.3:12, "And one wing of the other cherub was five cubits, reaching to the wall of the house: and the other wing was five cubits also, joining to the wing of the other cherub." (NOI. The Bible indicates that God rides on a cherub (Ps.18:10), and there was a man named Cherub (Ezr.2:59). The cherub had wings and a composite form of man and animal, and seems to have the job of guarding the Person of God.) {cherubims 64x., cherubim's 1x., tot.95x.}

Cherubims –64x., n. pl. [A.D. 825(VP.), Hb. masculine pl. of E. **cherub** (see 'Cherub') (NOI. The Hb. pl. is made by adding ים (*im*) to the end of the word (as in כהן (*kohen* = 'priest' sing.) becomes כהנים (*kohenim* = 'priests', pl.). (See 'Baalim' for another example.) Likewise, כרוב (*kerub* = 'cherub', sing.) becomes כרבים (*kerubim* = 'cherubim', pl.). The question is 'if 'cherubim' is already pl., then why the added 's'? The WB., for example, does not add the 's', nor does the Oxford edition (see 'Are There Problems With The King James Bible?' in front section), yet the 1611 HB. does. Why? The OED. indicates that the pl. form (cherubim) was more commonly used than the sing. (cherub), so the addition of the 's' avoided confusion. In fact, as far back as the 13th C., the spelling 'cherubims' has been used.)] Thus, **cherubims** are 'two or more cherubs'. Eg. Gen.3:24, "So he drove out the man; and he placed at the east of the garden of Eden Cherubims, and a flaming sword which turned every way, to keep the way of the tree of life." (NOI. Cherubims were used to guard the Garden of Eden (Gen.3:24) and surround the throne of God (Eze.10). Their images were made of gold and fastened to the top of the mercy seat (Ex.25:18) while pictures of them were sewn into the vail of the Tabernacle (Ex.36:35). Their images were also used in Solomon's Temple (1Ki.6:23) and will be used in Ezekiel's Temple (Eze.41:25) yet to come.)

Chesnut – 2x., n. [A.D. 1519, < ME. chasteine < OF. *chastaigne* < L. *castanea* < Gk. κασταέα (*kastanea*) = 'nut from Kastana', a city in Pontus (north east Asia Minor) where these trees grew in abundance] Thus, a **chesnut** is 'a large edible nut from the tree *Castanea*, which is thought to come from a city of the same name'. Eg. Eze.31:8, "The cedars in the garden of God could not hide him: the fir trees were not like his boughs, and the chesnut trees were not like his branches; nor any tree in the garden of God was like unto him in his beauty." (NOI. The chesnut tree can grow to a height of 100 ft. (30.5 m.) and has massive, wide-spreading branches.)

Chide –4x., v. [A.D. 1000(AT.), < OE. cidan = 'quarrel' (as in 'to scold noisily') (NOI. 'Chide' has no further etymological roots; it's only found in E.)] Thus, **chide** means 'the action of giving loud, scolding noises of anger'. Eg. Ex.17:2, "Wherefore the people did chide with Moses, and said, Give us water that we may drink. And Moses said unto them, Why chide ye with me? wherefore do ye tempt the LORD? " {chiding 1x., chode 2x., tot. = 7x.}

Chief – 283x., adj. and n. [A.D. 1297, < OF. *chief*

(= 'principal or capital') < L. *caput* = 'head' (NOI. 'Chief' emphasizes the idea of 'first' or 'first-in-line', whereas 'head' emphasizes more the idea of 'top' or 'top-of-the-heap'. See also 'Head'.)] Thus, as an adj., **chief** modifies its n. as 'being the first in rank and file above a group of similar nouns'. Eg. 1Pt.5:4, "And when the chief Shepherd shall appear, ye shall receive a crown of glory that fadeth not away." Furthermore, as a n., a **chief** is 'the first or principal of a group'. Eg. 1Tim.1:15, "This is a faithful saying, and worthy of all acceptation, that Christ Jesus came into the world to save sinners; of whom I am chief." {chiefest 8x., chiefly 3x., tot. = 294x.}

Child –201x., n. [A.D. 950(LfG.), < OE. **cild** < Gothic *kilpei* = 'womb' (i.e. 'offspring of the womb')] Thus, lit., a **child** is 'a male or female human offspring, from newborn up until adulthood'. Eg. 1Cor.13:11, "When I was a child, I spake as a child, I understood as a child, I thought as a child: but when I became a man, I put away childish things." Furthermore, **child** is used in a figurative sense to simply mean 'offspring'. Eg. Act.13:10, "And said, O full of all subtilty and all mischief, thou child of the devil, thou enemy of all righteousness, wilt thou not cease to pervert the right ways of the Lord? " (NOI. 'Child' is used in reference to unborns (Gen.38:24); to newborns (Gen.17:10-12); to three-month-olds (Ex.2:2); to weaned (about one-year-old Gen.21:8); to 12-year-olds (Lk.2:42-43); to 15-year-olds (cp. Gen.17:24-25 and 21:5,8,14-16). See also 'Babe', 'Daughter', 'Lad' and 'Son'.) {child's 4x., childbearing 1x., childhood 2x., childish 1x., childless 7x., children 1803x., children's 19x., tot. = 2038x.}

Chimney –1x., n. [A.D. 1330, < OF. *chiminee* (= 'fireplace') < ML. *caminata* < L. *caminus* (= 'a furnace for heating an apartment or smelting of metal' or 'an oven') < Gk. κάμινος (*kaminos*) = furnace (NOI. The Hb. ארבה (*arubbah*) is translated 8x., as 'windows', and 'chimney' in Hos.13:3 where it refers to 'a lattice where smoke escapes'.)] Thus, a **chimney**

is 'the part of a fireplace through which the smoke escapes'. Eg. Hos.13:3, "Therefore they shall be as the morning cloud, and as the early dew that passeth away, as the chaff that is driven with the whirlwind out of the floor, and as the smoke out of the chimney."

Chode –2x., v. pret. [A.D. 1535(CB.), < E **chide** (see 'Chide')] Thus, **chode** means 'the past-tense action of giving loud, scolding noises of anger' (as in 'having scolded'). Eg. Gen.31:36, "And Jacob was wroth, and chode with Laban: and Jacob answered and said to Laban, What is my trespass? what is my sin, that thou hast so hotly pursued after me? "

Choler –2x., n. [A.D. 1382(WB.), < ME. **colre** < OF. *colere* = 'bile' < F. *colère* = 'anger' < LL. *cholera* = 'bile' (NOI. Ancient physicians thought that bile (that bitter liquid secreted by the liver) was what caused anger. In fact, the E. word 'choleric' refers to an angry disposition. The disease 'cholera' comes from the L. *cholera*.)] Thus, **choler** is 'a very bitter-type of anger'. Eg. Dan.11:11, "And the king of the south shall be moved with choler, and shall come forth and fight with him, even with the king of the north: and he shall set forth a great multitude..." (NOI. It is worth pointing out that 'choler' doesn't happen overnight. It comes from a long standing state of anger and frustration.)

Chop –1x., v. [A.D. 1362, (akin to Swedish *kappa* = 'to cut') < oo., but possibly from OF. *coper* = 'to cut off'] Thus, **chop** means 'the action of cutting with a quick, heavy blow, or a series of such blows', using an axe or a heavy blade. Eg. Mic.3:3, "Who also eat the flesh of my people, and flay their skin from off them; and they break their bones, and chop them in pieces, as for the pot, and as flesh within the caldron."

Christ – 555x., n. and pn. [A.D. 950(LfG.), < OE. **Crist** < L. *Christus* < Gk. Χριστος (*Cristos*) = 'the Anointed One' (< χριειν (*crien*) = 'to anoint') < Hb. משיח (*Mashiyach*)

= 'the Anointed One'] Thus, as a n., **Christ** is 'the title of the Anointed One from God'. Eg. Mt.2:4, "And when he had gathered all the chief priests and scribes of the people together, he demanded of them where Christ should be born." Furthermore, as a pn., **Christ** is 'the name of the Anointed One sent from God'. Eg. Mt.1:16, "And Jacob begat Joseph the husband of Mary, of whom was born Jesus, who is called Christ." (NOI. Jesus Christ was anointed by God to come to earth for the purpose of dying a substitutionary death for the sins of the world. Cp. Jn.1:29; 1Tim.1:15. See also 'Anoint' and 'Messiah'.) {antichrist 4x., antichrists 1x., Christ's 16x., Christian 2x., Christians 1x., Christs 2x., tot. = 581x.}

Christian –2x., n. [A.D. 1285, < ME. **Crist** (see 'Christ') + **ian** = an E. suffix meaning 'belonging to'] Thus, a **Christian** is 'a person who belongs to Jesus Christ' (i.e. Christ has become the person's Lord, meaning owner and master (cp. 1Cor.6:20;7:23)). Eg. Act.26:28, "Then Agrippa said unto Paul, Almost thou persuadest me to be a Christian." (NOI. It was in the Asian city of Antioch where disciples of Jesus Christ were first called Christians (Act.11:26). The term 'Christian' was originally a derogatory term in the first-century Roman world, as an archeological discovery (dating back to first-century Rome) shows. It's a sketch of a young man with his hand raised in worship to a figure on a cross, which has the body of a man and the head of a donkey (a derogatory picture of Jesus Christ). Beneath it is the Gk. inscription, ΑΛΕΞΑΜΕΝΟΣ ΣΕΒΕΤΕ ΘΕΟΝ (*Alexamenos sebete theon*) = 'Alexander worships (his) God'. (NOI. The Gk. grammar is crude, but then again it was probably done by Roman children whose first language was Latin.) Obviously, this young man, Alexander, was ridiculed for being a Christian.) {christians 1x., tot. = 3x.}

Chronicles – 38x., n. pl. [A.D. 1303, < ME. **cronikle** < OF. *cronique* < L. *chronica* < Gk. χρονικά (*cronika*) = 'annal' ('a record of a single event or fact') + **s** = forms the pl.] Thus, **chronicles** are 'two or more records of events that happened'. Eg. 1 Ki.14:19, "And the rest of the acts of Jeroboam, how he warred, and how he reigned, behold, they are written in the book of the chronicles of the kings of Israel."

Chrysolite –1x., n. [A.D. 1300, < ME. **crisolite** < OF. *crisolite* < L. *chrysolithos* < Gk. χρυσολιθος (*chrusolithos*), (< χρυσος (*chrusos*) = 'gold' + λιθος (*lithos*) = 'stone') = 'a bright yellow colored stone'] Thus, a **chrysolite** is 'a bright yellow precious stone, of magnesium and iron', used in the foundation of the New Jerusalem. Eg. Rev.21:20, "The fifth, sardonyx; the sixth, sardius; the seventh, chrysolite..."

Chrysoprasus – 1x., n. [A.D. 1275, ME. **crisopase** < OF. *crisopase* < L. *chrysoprasus* < Gk. χρυσοπρασος (*chrusoprasos*) (< χρυσος (*chrusos*) = 'gold' + πρασον (*prason*) = 'leek' (i.e. the green vegetable) (see 'Leek')) = 'a golden-green colored stone'] Thus, a **chrysoprasus** is 'a golden-green precious stone', used in the foundation of the New Jerusalem. Eg. Rev.21:20, "... the tenth, a chrysoprasus..."

Church –77x., n. [A.D. 696, < ME. **chirche** < OE. **cirice** < Ger. *kirika* < early Byzantine Gk. κυριακον (*kuriakon*) = 'house of the Lord' (< κυριος (*kurios*) = 'Lord') (NOI. The northern English and Scottish use the word 'kirk' to mean 'a church', and also a man's name, 'Kirk'. The NT. Gk. word for 'church' is εκκλησια (*ecclesia*), and is commonly understood to mean 'a called out assembly'. In fact, some modern Bibles translate it simply as 'assembly'. However, etymologist (Bishop) Richard Trench explains the ancient Gk. usage of 'ecclesia' as being "the lawful assembly in a free Greek city of all those possessed of the right of citizenship, for the transaction of public affairs". This explains why εκκλησια is translated as 'assembly' in Act.19:32,39,41, and as 'church' everywhere else. Some words in Gk. are difficult to translate into another language without a keen understanding of the times and customs, εκκλησια being one of them, and it would seem the translators of the 1611 understood this.)] Thus, a **church** is 'the house of the Lord'. Eg. Col.4:16, "And when this epistle is read among you, cause that it be read also in the church of the Laodiceans; and that ye likewise read the epistle from Laodicea." (See also 'Assembly'and 'Congregation'.) {churches 37x., tot. = 114x.}

Churl – 2x., n. [A.D. 800, < OE. **ceorl** (akin to Ger. *kerl*) (NOI. In OE. **ceorl** meant 'a peasant or a freeman', but in early ME. it meant 'a common man, or a country man'. By A.D. 1611, it had degenerated to mean 'a rude man' or 'one of disgraceful manners'.)] Thus, a **churl** is 'a rude person with disgraceful manners'. Eg. Isa.32:5, "The vile person shall be no more called liberal, nor the churl said to be bountiful." {churlish 1x., tot. = 3x.}

Churlish – 1x., adj. [A.D. 1000, < OE. **churl** (see 'Churl') + **ish** = shows 'characteristic or nature of' (see E. suffix '–ish'[1])] Thus, **churlish** modifies its n. as 'having the nature or characteristics of a churl'. Eg. 1Sam.25:3, "Now the name of the man was Nabal... but the man was churlish and evil in his doings..." {churl 2x., tot. = 3x.}

Churning – 1x., vbl.n. [A.D. 1440, < E. **churn** (= 'to agitate milk so as to make butter') + **ing** = forms the vbl.n. (see E. suffix '–ing'[1])] Thus, **churning** means 'the act of one who churns milk so as to make butter'. Eg. Pr.30:33, "Surely the churning of milk bringeth forth butter, and the wringing of the nose bringeth forth blood: so the forcing of wrath bringeth forth strife."

Cieled – 4x., pp. and prp. [A.D. 1430, < E. **ciel** (< OF. *ciel* = 'sky, heaven or canopy' < L. *caelum* = 'sky or heaven') = 'to overlay the interior walls and upper surface with wood'

+ **ed** = forms the pp. and the prp. (NOI. Our E. word 'ceiling' (= 'the overhead interior surface of a room') comes from 'ciel'.)] Thus, as a pp., **cieled** modifies its n. as 'having been cieled, or having the interior walls and upper surface overlaid with wood'. Eg. 2Chr.3:5, "And the greater house he cieled with fir tree, which he overlaid with fine gold, and set thereon palm trees and chains." Furthermore, as a prp., **cieled** modifies its n. as 'having the interior walls and upper surface overlaid with wood'. Eg. Jer 22:14, "That saith, I will build me a wide house and large chambers, and cutteth him out windows; and it is cieled with cedar, and painted with vermilion." {cieling 1x., tot. = 5x.}

Cinnamon – 4x., n. [A.D. 1386, < L. *cinnamomum* < Gk. κινναμωμον (*kinnamomon*) < Hb. קִנָּמוֹן (*qinnamown*) = 'to erect' (i.e. 'the manner in which the dried bark forms itself into rolls') (NOI. Of the tree family *Cinnamomum zeylanicum*. Cinnamon is from a tropical evergreen tree of the laurel family growing up to 30 ft. (9.144 m.) in its wild state. It is similar to 'cassia' in smell, but less aromatic.)] Thus, **cinnamon** is 'the dried bark of cinnamon trees (the name meaning 'to erect'), and used for its flavor and aroma'. Eg. Pr.7:17, "I have perfumed my bed with myrrh, aloes, and cinnamon." (NOI. Cinnamon is mentioned in Chinese writings dating back to 2800 B.C. The Egyptians used it in cooking, various medicinal preparations and the embalming process. Always considered a precious commodity, by the 1st century A. D., Pliny the elder wrote that 12.34 oz. (350 grams) of cinnamon was equal in value to over 11 lb. (5 kilo.) of silver. Nero, who murdered his wife, showed his remorse by burning a year's supply of cinnamon at her funeral. It was also used in the making of holy anointing oil (Ex.30:23). See also 'Cassia'.)

Circle – 1x., n. [A.D. 1000, < OE. **circul** < OF. *cercle* < L. *circulus* = 'an orbit, ring or circumference' (NOI. The OED.

Defines it as '*a plane figure bounded by a single curved line, called the circumference, which is everywhere equally distant from a point within, called the center. But often applied to the circumference alone, without the included space.* Also, our E. word 'circus' comes from the L. *circulus* and refers to the large ring in which the artists and animals perform. The Roman circus was usually performed in an oval, roofless enclosure, so the *circulus* was not always perfectly round, and neither is the earth. In fact, many circles are not perfectly round.)] Thus, a **circle** is 'a round (or somewhat round) ring or circumference'. Eg. Isa.40:22, "It is he that sitteth upon the circle of the earth, and the inhabitants thereof are as grasshoppers; that stretcheth out the heavens as a curtain, and spreadeth them out as a tent to dwell in."

Circuit –3x., n. [A.D. 1382(WB.), < OF. *circuit* < L. *circuitus* < *circuire* = 'go around' (< *circum* = 'around' + *ire* = 'go')] Thus, a **circuit** is 'a circular or roundabout type of journey'. Eg. 1Sam.7:16, "And he went from year to year in circuit to Bethel, and Gilgal, and Mizpeh, and judged Israel in all those places." {circuits 1x., tot.4x.}

Circumcise – 10x., v. [A.D. 1250, < L. *circumcisus*, (which is pp. of) *circumcidere* = 'to cut around' (< *circum* = 'around' + *caedere* = 'to cut')] Thus, lit., **circumcise** means 'the action of circumcision'. Eg. Gen.17:11, "And ye shall circumcise the flesh of your foreskin; and it shall be a token of the covenant betwixt me and you." (NOI. Figuratively, circumcise means 'the action of cutting away the rebellion of the heart', as in Deut.10:16. (See 'Circumcision'.)) {circumcised 39x., circumcising 2x., circumcision 36x., uncircumcised 43x., tot. = 127x.}

Circumcision – 36x., n. [A.D. 1175, < OF. *circumcisiun* < L. *circumcisionem* (= 'the act of cutting away' (i.e. 'the religious act of cutting away the foreskin of a man or a boy')), *circum*

= 'round about on both sides' + *caedere* = 'to cut or chop'] Thus, a **circumcision** is 'the complete act of cutting away the foreskin of a man or boy', done as a covenant-sign between OT. Jews and God. Eg. Act.7:8, "And he gave him the covenant of circumcision: and so Abraham begat Isaac, and circumcised him the eighth day..." Furthermore, figuratively, **circumcision** is 'the spiritual act of cutting away sin and rebellion from the heart toward God'. Eg. Rom.2:29, "But he is a Jew, which is one inwardly; and circumcision is that of the heart, in the spirit, and not in the letter; whose praise is not of men, but of God." Finally, **circumcision** is also 'a title given to Jewish believers (in the first-century church) who had accepted Jesus Christ as their Messiah, yet held to the laws of Moses'. Eg. Act.10:45, "And they of the circumcision which believed were astonished, as many as came with Peter, because that on the Gentiles also was poured out the gift of the Holy Ghost." (NOI. See also 'Concision'.) {circumcise 10x., circumcised 39x., circumcising 2x., uncircumcised 43x., tot. = 130x.}

Circumspect – 1x., adj. [A.D. 1422, < L. *circumspectus* (which is pp. of) *circumspicere* = 'to look around' (< *circum* = 'around' + *spicere* = 'to look at')] Thus, **circumspect** modifies its n. as 'being very watchful on all sides and very cautious'. Eg. Ex.23:13, "And in all things that I have said unto you be circumspect: and make no mention of the name of other gods, neither let it be heard out of thy mouth." {circumspectly 1x., tot. = 2x.}

Cistern – 4x., n. [A.D. 1300, < OF. *cisterne* < L. *cisterna* = 'a subterranean reservoir for water' (< L. *cista* (= 'box') < Gk. κίστη (*kistay*) = 'box')] Thus, a **cistern** is 'an artificial storage tank for water, dug in the earth'. Eg. Pr.5:15, "Drink waters out of thine own cistern, and running waters out of thine own well." (NOI. A 'cistern' always had a lid, whereas a pool was left open. Cisterns were in common use in Israel due to the long, dry summers, and some were constructed 100 ft.

(30.5 m.) in depth with stairs leading down. The Temple area in Jerusalem had at least 37 large cisterns, one of which could hold 2-3 million gal. (7.6-11.4 million liters). {cisterns 2x., tot. = 6x.}

Citizen – 2x., n. [A.D. 1314, < ME. **citesein** < Anglo Fr. *citezein* < OF. *citeain* < L. *civitas* = 'citizenship' (as in 'the members of a city, community or nation having the rights, responsibilities and privileges thereof') < L. *civis* = 'a single member of a *civitas*' (NOI. Our E. word 'politics' ('the affairs of state and the citizens within it') comes from the Gk. πολιτης (*polites*) translated 'citizen'.)] Thus, a **citizen** is 'a member of a city, community or nation having all the rights, responsibilities and privileges that come with membership'. Eg. Lk.15:15, "And he went and joined himself to a citizen of that country; and he sent him into his fields to feed swine." {citizens 1x., fellowcitizens 1x., tot. = 4x.}

City – 868x., n. [A.D. 1225, < OF. *cite* < L. *civitatum* = 'community of citizens' (NOI. Originally, this E. word was used in reference to any settlement, but was later reserved for larger towns.)] Thus, a **city** is 'a large or important town, with many citizens, having a system of rule and officers'. Eg. Act.21:39, "But Paul said, I am a man which am a Jew of Tarsus, a city in Cilicia, a citizen of no mean city: and, I beseech thee, suffer me to speak unto the people." {cities 448x., tot. = 1316x.}

Clad – 2x., pp. and v. pret. [A.D. 1300, < OE. **clǽðan** = 'to provide with clothing' + **d** = forms the pp. and v. pret. (see E. suffix '–ed'[1, 3]) (NOI. The translators of the 1611 seem to make a distinction between 'clad' and 'clothed', depending on what is being put on. They used 'clad' for an outer, wrap-around garment, such as a cloak; and they used 'clothed' for all other articles.)] Thus, as a pp., **clad** modifies its n. (in this case, 'he') as 'having been in the condition of being covered with a cloak'. Eg. Isa.59:17, "For he put on righteousness as a breastplate, and an helmet of salvation upon his head; and he put on the garments of vengeance for clothing, and was clad with zeal as a cloke." Furthermore, as a v. pret., **clad** means 'the past-tense action of covering with a cloak'. Eg. 1 Ki.11:29, "... the prophet Ahijah the Shilonite found him in the way; and he had clad himself with a new garment..."

Clamour –1x., n. [A.D. 1382(WB.), < OF. *clamor* < L. *clamor* (= 'a noisy outcry') < *clamare* = 'to cry out, shout or call'] Thus, a **clamour** is 'a loud, noisy out crying of dissatisfaction'. Eg. Eph.4:31, "Let all bitterness, and wrath, and anger, and clamour, and evil speaking, be put away from you, with all malice." {clamorous 1x., tot. = 2x.}

Clave[1] –6x., v. pret. [A.D. 1300, < E **cleave** (see 'Cleave'[1])] Thus, **clave** means 'the past-tense action of splitting open'. Eg. Num.16:31, "And it came to pass, as he had made an end of speaking all these words, that the ground clave asunder that was under them." {cleave[1] 4x., cleaveth 4x., cloven 2x., tot. = 16x.}

Clave[2] –8x., v. pret. [A.D. 1300, < E. **cleave** (see 'Cleave'[2])] Thus, **clave** means 'the past-tense action of joining together'. Eg. 2Ki.18:6, "For he clave to the LORD, and departed not from following him, but kept his commandments, which the LORD commanded Moses." {cleave[2] 26x., cleaved 3x., cleaveth 9x., tot. = 46x.}

Cleave[1] – 4x., v. [A.D. 910, < OE. **cleofan** = 'to cut open'] Thus, **cleave** means 'the action of cutting something open'. Eg. Lev.1:17, "And he shall cleave it with the wings thereof, but shall not divide it asunder." {clave 6x., cleaveth 4x., cloven 2x., tot. = 16x.}

Cleave[2] –26x., v. [A.D. 888,< OE. **cleofian** (< **cleof** = 'stuck together' + **ian** = 'the action of') = 'to be joined together or stick together'] Thus, **cleave** means 'the action of joining together'. Eg. Gen.2:24, "Therefore shall a man leave his father and his mother, and shall cleave unto his wife: and they shall be one flesh." {clave[2] 8x., cleaved 3x., cleaveth 9x., tot. = 46x.}

Cleft –2x., n. and pp. [A.D. 1300 (as a n.) and A.D. 1393 (as a pp.), (originally < OE. **geclyft** (adj.) = 'split or cloven', and used for smaller things (cp. its usage in Amo.6:11))] Thus, as a n., a **cleft** is 'a small opening'. Eg. Deut.14:6, "And every beast that parteth the hoof, and cleaveth the cleft into two claws, and cheweth the cud among the beasts, that ye shall eat." Furthermore, as a pp., **cleft** is used with the words, 'shall be', to form the future-perfect-tense, meaning 'the coming state or future condition of having been cut open'. Eg. Mic.1:4, "And the mountains shall be molten under him, and the valleys shall be cleft, as wax before the fire, and as the waters that are poured down a steep place." (See also 'Clift'.) {clefts 5x., tot. = 7x.}

Clemency –1x., n. [A.D. 1553, < L. *clementia* (= 'a condition of mildness') < *clemens* = 'mild, lenient, merciful or compassionate' (NOI. The NT. name Clement (Gk. Κλημης (*Klemes*) – see Phil.4:3) means the same as the L. *clemens*.)] Thus, **clemency** is 'a condition of being mild or lenient'. Eg. Act.24:4, "Notwithstanding, that I be not further tedious unto thee, I pray thee that thou wouldest hear us of thy clemency a few words."

Cliff – 1x., n. [A.D. 854, < OE. **clif** < early Ger. *kliban* = 'a high, steep face of a rock mass'] Thus, a **cliff** is 'a high, steep face of a mountain or rock mass'. Eg. 2Chr.20:16, "To morrow go ye down against them: behold, they come up by the cliff of Ziz; and ye shall find them at the end of the brook, before the wilderness of Jeruel."

Clift –1x., n. [A.D. 1300, < OE. **clyft** = 'an opening' (NOI.

It's a question as to why the 1611 used 'clift' and not 'cleft', seeing as they both mean essentially the same thing. Upon comparing other Middle E. writings we find that the usage of 'clift' changed. Men like Geoffrey Chaucer (A.D. 1340-1400) used it in reference to parting of the legs, whereas almost 200 years later, men like Edmund Spenser (A.D. 1552-1599) used it in reference to the mountains or large rocks (eg. 'hewn out of rocky clift'). Hence, we conclude that by A.D. 1611 'clift' was used in reference to mountains and valleys while 'cleft' was used for other things.)] Thus, a **clift** is 'an opening, or hollow place, in a mountain or a cavern in a valley', at least large enough for a person to fit into. Eg. Ex.33:22, "And it shall come to pass, while my glory passeth by, that I will put thee in a clift of the rock, and will cover thee with my hand while I pass by." (See also 'Cleft'.) {clifts 2x., tot. = 3x.}

Clods – 6x., n. [A.D. 1398, < OE. **clott** (akin to MHG. *kloz* = 'lump' and Du. *klos* = 'block') = 'a lump or clump' (NOI. 'Clod' was especially used in reference to earth or clay) + **s** = forms the pl.] Thus, **clods** are 'two or more hard, lumps of earth'. Eg. Isa.28:24, "Doth the plowman plow all day to sow? doth he open and break the clods of his ground? "

Cloke – 7x., n. [A.D. 1275, < OF. *cloque* < ML. *clocca* = 'bell' (NOI. The 'cloke' resembled the shape of a bell.)] Thus, a **cloke** is 'a loose cape worn as an outer-garment over other clothing'. Eg. Lk.6:29, "And unto him that smiteth thee on the one cheek offer also the other; and him that taketh away thy cloke forbid not to take thy coat also." (NOI. A 'cloke' extended from the shoulders and down as far as mid-calf. The word is also used figuratively to mean 'a covering', as in 1Pt.2:16.)

Closet – 2x., n. [A.D. 1340, < OF. *closet* < L. *clausum* = 'an enclosed space'] Thus, a **closet** is 'a small, private room', used for sleeping, secret counsel, private study, devotions, etc. Eg. Joe.2:16, "... let the bridegroom go forth of his chamber, and the bride out of her closet." {closets 1x., tot. = 3x.}

Clothes – 101x., n. pl. [A.D. 800, < OE. **claðas** < **clað** = 'cloth' (= 'a woven fabric') + **es** = forms the pl. (i.e. a collective pl. referring to 'coverings for the body') (NOI. The pl. of 'cloth' later became 'cloths' to distinguish it from 'clothes'.)] Thus, **clothes** are 'the collective coverings for the body, usually made of a woven fabric'. Eg. Neh.4:23, "So neither I, nor my brethren, nor my servants, nor the men of the guard which followed me, none of us put off our clothes, saving that every one put them off for washing." (See also 'Apparel', 'Garment' and 'Raiment'.)

Clothed –73x., pp. and v. pret. [A.D. 1220, < E. **clothe** < OE. **cl ðian** (= 'the action of putting clothes on') + **ed** = forms the pp. and v. pret. (see E. suffix '–ed'[1, 3])] Thus, as a pp., **clothed** modifies its n. as 'having had clothes put on'. Eg. Pr.31:21, "She is not afraid of the snow for her household: for all her household are clothed with scarlet." Furthermore, as a v. pret., **clothed** means 'the past-tense action of covering with clothes'. Eg. Mt.25:36, "Naked, and ye clothed me..." (NOI. See also 'Clad'.)

Clouted – 1x., pp. [A.D. 1000, < E. **clout** (see 'Clouts')) + **ed** = forms the pp. (see E. suffix '–ed'[3])] Thus, **clouted** modifies its n. (in this case, 'old shoes') as 'having been mended with patches'. Eg. Josh.9:5, "And old shoes and clouted upon their feet, and old garments upon them; and all the bread of their provision was dry and mouldy." {clouts 2x., tot. = 3x.}

Clouts –2x., n. pl. [A.D. 700, < OE. **clut** = 'a piece of cloth or leather' (like a patch) + **s** = forms the pl.] Thus, **clouts**, are 'two or more pieces of cloth or leather', used as patches for mending. Eg. Jer.38:12, "And Ebedmelech the Ethiopian said unto Jeremiah, Put now these old cast clouts and rotten rags under thine armholes under the cords. And Jeremiah did so." (NOI. The word 'clout' is still used in some parts of northern England to mean 'a piece of clothing'. An old English saying, still used, says, "*Don't cast a clout till May is out*," meaning, "*wait until after May before shedding your winter clothing*".) {clouted 1x., tot. = 3x.}

Clovenfooted –3x., adj. [A.D. 1415, < E. **cloven** (pp. of **cleave** (see 'Cleave'[1])) + **footed** = forms the adj. (< **foot** + **ed** (see E. suffix '–ed'[5]))] Thus, **clovenfooted** modifies its n. as 'having its foot (or feet) divided or split into two separate toes'. Eg. Lev.11:3, "Whatsoever parteth the hoof, and is clovenfooted, and cheweth the cud, among the beasts, that shall ye eat." {cloven 2x., foot 95x., tot. = 100x.}

Cluster –5x., n. [A.D. 800, < OE. **clyster** < oo., but possibly from same root word as 'clod' (see 'Clods'); however, refers to 'a collected group of similar things'] Thus, a **cluster** is 'a collected group of similar things' (normally referring to grapes). Eg. Num.13:24, "The place was called the brook Eshcol, because of the cluster of grapes which the children of Israel cut down from thence." {clusters 7x., tot. = 12x.}

Coast –62x., n. [A.D. 1300, < OF. *coste* < L. *costa* = 'rib or side'] Thus, a **coast** is 'a side or border of a land'. Eg. Deut.2:18, "Thou art to pass over through Ar, the coast of Moab, this day." {coasts 51x., tot. = 113x.}

Coat – 25x., n. [A.D. 1300, < OF. *cote* < Frank. *kotta* = 'coarse cloth' < oo., but refers to 'an outer-garment with sleeves'] Thus, a **coat** is 'an outer-garment with sleeves, covering from at least the shoulders to the waist'. Eg. Gen.37:3, "Now Israel loved Joseph more than all his children, because he was the son of his old age: and he made him a coat of many colours." (See also 'Mail'.) {coats 14x., tot. = 39x.}

Cock – 12x., n. [A.D. 897, < OE. **coc** (= 'a male domestic fowl') < oo., but possibly named after the sound it makes (i.e. "cock-a-doodle-doo!")] Thus, a **cock** is 'a male domestic fowl'. Eg. Jn.18:27, "Peter then denied again: and immediately the cock crew." (NOI. A 'cock' is the same as a rooster, but the word 'rooster' was not in use until A.D. 1772. See also 'Hen'.) {cockcrowing 1x., tot. = 13x.}

Cockatrice – 1x., n. [A.D. 1382(WB.), < OF. *cocatris* < ML. *calcatrix* (= 'she who treads') < L. *calcare* (= 'to tramp down') < *calx* = 'heel' (NOI. The 'cockatrice' (also called a 'basilisk') was actually a mythological serpent, that was supposed to have been hatched from a cock's egg, and could kill by staring. Ancient E. heraldry represents it as having the head, feet and wings of a cock, and the body of a serpent. The Hb. צפע (*tsepha*) = 'to hiss', and is translated 'adder' in Pr.23:32, yet is called a "*cockatrice*" in the 1611 marginal note.)] Thus, a **cockatrice** is 'a mythological serpent, having a cock's head, feet and wings, and having the power to kill by just staring at its enemy'. Eg. Isa.14:29, "... for out of the serpent's root shall come forth a cockatrice, and his fruit shall be a fiery flying serpent." (NOI. The question is, why did the translators of the 1611 use 'cockatrice' and not 'adder'? Though some may believe that the cockatrice actually exists, it is the opinion of this author that the translators used this mythological creature as a hyperbole to better translate the teaching of the vs. This is further illustrated by them putting the word "*adder*" in the marginal note of Isa.14:29.) {cockatrice' 2x., cockatrices 1x., tot. = 4x.}

Cockle – 1x., n. [A.D.1000(ASG.), < OE. **coccel** = 'a flowering weed that grows amongst barley' (NOI. This weed grows 3-4 ft. (.9-1.2 m.) high among barley crops and, if harvested together, can cause a mild poison. The Hb. word is באשה

(*boshah*) = 'stink', i.e. 'a stink-weed')] Thus, a **cockle** is 'a flowering stink-weed that grows amongst barley'. Eg. Job.31:40, "Let thistles grow instead of wheat, and cockle instead of barley. The words of Job are ended."

Coffer – 3x., n. [A.D. 1300, < OF. *cofre* = 'chest' (used for valuables) < L. *cophinus* = 'a basket' < Gk. κοφινος (*kophinos*) = 'a basket'] Thus, a **coffer** is 'a box or chest used for storing of valuables'. Eg. 1Sam.6:8, "And take the ark of the LORD, and lay it upon the cart; and put the jewels of gold, which ye return him for a trespass offering, in a coffer by the side thereof; and send it away, that it may go."

Coffin – 1x., n. [A.D. 1330, < OF. *cofin* (= 'a box used for a dead body') < L. *cophinus* = 'a basket' < Gk. κοφινος (*kophinos*) = 'a basket' (NOI. 'Coffin' and 'coffer' are from the same root word, differing from the time of OF. onward. They both mean 'a basket or chest', but differ in how they are used. Some middle E. writers actually used the word 'coffer' in place of coffin. Other writers of the same time-period used 'coffin' in reference to a pie-crust!)] Thus, a **coffin** is 'a box in which a dead body is placed for burial'. Eg. Gen.50:26, "So Joseph died, being an hundred and ten years old: and they embalmed him, and he was put in a coffin in Egypt." (NOI. The use of a coffin for burial seems to have been more common to Egypt than to Israel. The body of Christ was hastily wrapped with linen and spices and placed in a tomb. In fact, it seems most bodies were simply wrapped in cloth, with perhaps spices also, and placed in a dug-out grave. Job.21:26 speaks of 'worms' because the body was not in a coffin.)

Cogitations – 1x., n. pl. [A.D. 1225, < E. **cogitate** < L. *cogitatus* (which is pp. of) *cogitare* (= 'to thoroughly consider'), < *co* = 'together or with' (see L. prefix '*co*–') + *agitare* = 'to stir or revolve' (NOI. We get our E. 'agitate' from *agitare*.) + **ation** = 'state or condition' (see E. suffix '–tion')

+ **s** = forms the pl.] Thus, **cogitations** are 'two or more times of having thought things over and over' (i.e. revolving them in the mind and having considered them from all angles). Eg. Dan.7:28, "Hitherto is the end of the matter. As for me Daniel, my cogitations much troubled me, and my countenance changed in me: but I kept the matter in my heart."

College – 2x., n. [A.D. 1378, < OF. *college* < L. *collegium* = 'an association, society, guild or brotherhood'; i.e. 'a body of colleagues' (< *col* = 'together or with' (see L. prefix '*co-*') + *lego* = 'choose'; i.e. 'one is chosen along with another') (NOI. The word 'college' was well used in England from A. D. 1378 – 1611 as a place of religious and secular learning for teenage boys. This can be seen in the histories of colleges like 'Exeter College' (founded in A.D. 1314), and 'Eton College' (founded in A.D. 1440). Colleges tended to be smaller and more specific in teaching, whereas a 'university', such as 'Oxford University' (founded in A.D. 1096?), was larger and encompassed more areas of learning, the granting of degrees, and even included one or more colleges under its wing, such as 'Corpus Christi College in Oxford' (founded in A.D. 1525). However, the problem with using the word 'college' in the Bible comes when we consider the Hb. word behind it, משנה (*mishneh*) = 'double, second or repetition'. Many therefore claim the 1611 to be in error and should have translated it as 'the second', referring to the second-quarter of the city of Jerusalem. The WB. followed the LV., translating it as "the second dwelling", as did the CB. with "the second part". But the BB. called it "the house of the doctrine" and the GB. "the college". The 1611 called it "the college" (indicating their first choice) but included a marginal note saying, "*or, in the second part*". Interestingly, the old Rabbis claimed משנה (*mishneh*) was a series of teachings. Rabbi Mainonides (A.D. 1135–1204) and Rabbi Caro (A.D. 1488–1575) popularized the 'Mishneh' (teachings on the 'Second Law', or 'Deuteronomy' as taught orally from the time of Moses, and finally written down in the 2nd c. A.D.) and may be of those who saw a definite connection between משנה (*mishneh*) and 'teaching'. Therefore, משנה (*mishneh*) could easily have referred to a place where the teachings of Deuteronomy were transmitted orally from teacher to student, and there could well have been such a school in Jerusalem during the reign of king Josiah, where Huldah the prophetess taught and lived.)] Thus, a **college** is 'a place of learning where the students are chosen'. Eg. 2Chr.34:22, "And Hilkiah, and they that the king had appointed, went to Huldah the prophetess, the wife of Shallum the son of Tikvath, the son of Hasrah, keeper of the wardrobe; (now she dwelt in Jerusalem in the college:) and they spake to her to that effect."

Collops – 1x., n. pl. [A.D. 1362, < ME. **colope** < oo., but in reference to 'a small slice of bacon or some meat' + **s** = forms the pl. (NOI. Used figuratively it refers to a roll of flesh on the body. The Hb. word is פימה (*piymah*) = 'excessive fat'.)] Thus, **collops** are 'two or more rolls of flesh on the body'. Eg. Job.15:27, "Because he covereth his face with his fatness, and maketh collops of fat on his flanks."

Colony – 1x., n. [A.D. 1382(WB.), < ME. **colonie** < L. *colonia* < *colonus* (= 'a farmer' or 'tenant-farmer') < *colere* = 'to cultivate' (NOI. Roman 'colonies' were often formed of Roman ex-soldiers who, retaining their Roman citizenship, received lands and became farmers in a hostile or newly conquered country, and helped to keep it under control. Octavius is said to have planted the Roman colony in Philippi. The NT. Gk. κολωνια (*kolonia*) is actually a trans. of the L. *colonia*.)] Thus, a **colony** is 'a group of people who leave their homeland to settle in a new land, which is subject to the parent state, and may assist in the control thereof'. Eg. Act.16:12, "And from thence to Philippi, which is the chief city of that part of Macedonia, and a colony: and we were in that city abiding certain days." (NOI. To many Romans, being granted the title of 'colony' was a status symbol. Some important Roman cities could be granted the status of a 'colony' if it were well organized and self-governing and had a large percentage of Roman citizens there.)

Colour – 14x., n. [A.D. 1290, < AF. *colour* < L. *color* = 'pigment' or 'shade' (< L. *colos* = 'a covering') (NOI. The US. State, Colorado, is from Spanish *Rio Colorado* = 'the colored river'.)] Thus, a **colour** is 'a pigment, hue or shade that covers a surface area'. Eg. Lev.13:55, "And the priest shall look on the plague, after that it is washed: and, behold, if the plague have not changed his colour..." (NOI. Figuratively, colour was used of 'a cloak or disguise', as in Act.27:30.)

Colt –15x., n. [A.D. 1000(AT.), < OE. **colt** < oo., but refers to 'child, offspring or young'] Thus, a **colt** is 'a young offspring'. Eg. Jn.12:15, "Fear not, daughter of Sion: behold, thy King cometh, sitting on an ass's colt." (NOI. 'Colt' only refers to the young ass in the Bible, except in Gen.32:15, where it refers to a young camel. See also 'Ass'.) {colts 3x., tot. = 18x.}

Comely – 16x., adj. [A.D. 1000(ASP.), < OE. **Cymlic** = 'beautifully constructed' < **cyme** = 'fine or beautiful'] Thus, **comely** modifies its n. as 'being beautifully constructed'. Eg. Jer.6:2, "I have likened the daughter of Zion to a comely and delicate woman." {comeliness 5x., tot. = 21x.}

Comfort –66x., n. and v. [A.D. 1225, < OF. *conforter* < L. *confortare*, *con* = 'together or with' (see L. prefix '*co–*') + *fortare* = 'strong'] Thus, as a n., a **comfort** is 'a strengthening aid or assistance'. Eg. 1Cor.14:3, "But he that prophesieth speaketh unto men to edification, and exhortation, and comfort." Furthermore, as a v., **comfort** means 'the action of intensifying strength'. Eg. 1Ths.5:14, "Now we exhort you, brethren, warn them that are unruly, comfort the feebleminded..." (NOI. There is, however, also the inherent idea of 'to solace and soothe' in this word as seen in Isa.66:13. See also 'Consolation'.) {comfortable 2x., comfortably 5x., comforted 36x., comfortedst 1x., comforter 8x., comforters 5x., comforteth 5x., comfortless 1x., comforts 2x., tot. = 131x.}

Command – 104x., v. [A.D. 1300, < OF. *comander* < ML. *commandare, com* = 'together or with', giving sternness or intensity (see L. prefix '*co–*') + *mandare* = 'to commit, enjoin, or entrust' (< L. *manus* = 'hand' + *dare* = 'to give' (i.e. 'to give into the hand') (NOI. Our E. word 'mandate' (= 'an order from a superior') comes from L. *mandare.* See also 'Commend'.)] Thus, **command** means 'the authoritative action of enjoining instructions to a person or people'. Eg. Gen.18:19, "For I know him, that he will command his children and his household after him, and they shall keep the way of the LORD, to do justice and judgment; that the LORD may bring upon Abraham that which he hath spoken of him." {commanded 443x., commandedst 4x., commander 1x., commandest 3x., commandeth 13x., commanding 4x., commandment 177x., commandments 171x., tot. = 920x.}

Commandment – 177x., n. [A.D. 1250, < E. **command** (see 'Command') + **ment** = 'the result or product of an action' (see E. suffix '–ment')] Thus, a **commandment** is 'an order or instruction, which is given by the authority of a superior'. Eg. 1Jn.3:23, "And this is his commandment, That we should believe on the name of his Son Jesus Christ, and love one another, as he gave us commandment." (NOI. A 'commandment' is usually short and to the point, giving specific instructions concerning what is to be done.) {command 104x., commanded 443x., commandedst 4x., commander 1x., commandest 3x., commandeth 13x., commanding 4x., commandments 171x., tot. = 920x.}

Commend – 7x., v. [A.D. 1325, < ME. **commenden** < L. *com-*

mendare, *com* = 'together or with', giving sternness or intensity (see L. prefix '*co*–') + *mandare* = 'to commit, enjoin, or entrust' (NOI. This is the same etymology as 'command' (See 'Command'), and may seem confusing, however 'command' followed ML. *commandare*, while 'commend' followed L. *commendare* (= 'to commit into the hand for safe keeping'). See also 'Recommended'.)] Thus, **commend** means 'the action of confidently delivering something into the hand of another'. Eg. Lk.23:46, "And when Jesus had cried with a loud voice, he said, Father, into thy hands I commend my spirit: and having said thus, he gave up the ghost." {commendation 2x., commended 6x., commendeth 4x., commending 1x., tot. = 20x.}

Commission –1x., n. [A.D. 1380, < OF. *commission* < L. *commissio* < *committere*, *com* = 'together or with', giving sternness or intensity (see L. prefix '*co*–') + *mittere* = 'to send forth' (See also 'Commit'.)] Thus, a **commission** is 'an act of enjoining instructions upon someone and sending them out to complete those instructions'. Eg. Act.26:12, "Whereupon as I went to Damascus with authority and commission from the chief priests." {commissions 1x., tot. = 2x.}

Commit –75x., v. [A.D. 1386, < ME. **committee** < L. *committere*, *com* = 'together or with', giving sternness or intensity (see L. prefix '*co*–') + *mittere* = 'to send forth' (NOI. 'Commit' is the v. or action, while 'commission' is the n. or thing. See also 'Commission'.)] Thus, **commit** means 'the action of joining something together with something or someone else'. Eg. 2Tim.2:2, "And the things that thou hast heard of me among many witnesses, the same commit thou to faithful men, who shall be able to teach others also." (NOI. Of the 75 times this word is used, 64 of them deal with committing a sin, meaning the person spoken of went and joined himself to a sin.) {committed 92x., committest 1x., committeth 19x., committing 2x., tot. = 189x.}

Commodious –1x., adj. [A.D. 1420, < ML. *commodiosus* < L. *commodum* (= 'in good measure', as in 'convenience, useful or advantageous'), *com* = 'together or with' (see L. prefix '*co–*') + *modus* = 'measure'] Thus, **commodious** modifies its n. as 'being convenient and useful'. Eg. Act.27:12, "And because the haven was not commodious to winter in, the more part advised to depart thence also, if by any means they might attain to Phenice, and there to winter; which is an haven of Crete, and lieth toward the south west and north west."

Common –21x., adj. [A.D. 1297, < OF. *comun* < L. *communis*, *com* = 'together or with' (see L. prefix '*co–*') + *munis* = 'bound' or 'binding by obligation' (NOI. Our E. word 'immune' (= 'not bound', as in 'not bound by a disease or an obligation') comes from the L. root *munis*. See also 'Commune'.)] Thus, **common** modifies its n. as 'being equally bound or owned by two or more people'. Eg. Act.2:44, "And all that believed were together, and had all things common." {commonly 2x., tot. = 23x.}

Commonwealth – 1x., n. [A.D. 1470, < E. **common** (here applied to a body of people such as a nation. See 'Common'.) + **wealth** = 'a state of being prosperous and happy' (See 'Wealth'.)] Thus, a **commonwealth** is 'a condition of happiness and prosperity amongst a body of people'. Eg. Eph.2:12, "That at that time ye were without Christ, being aliens from the commonwealth of Israel, and strangers from the covenants of promise, having no hope, and without God in the world."

Commotion –1x., n. [A.D. 1471, < OF. *commotion* < L. *commotio*, *com* = 'together or with' giving sternness or intensity (see L. prefix '*co–*') + *motio* = 'motion or removal' (NOI. *Commotio* is an emotional word, speaking of a great jumbled, agitating, 'going-in-every-direction' kind of disturbance.)] Thus, a **commotion** is 'a great agitation or disturbance'. Eg. Jer.10:22, "Behold, the noise of the bruit is come, and a great commotion out of the north country, to make the cities of Judah desolate, and a den of dragons." {commotions 1x., tot. = 2x.}

Commune —8x., v. [A.D. 1297, < OF. *comuner* < L. *communis*, *com* = 'together or with' (see L. prefix '*co–*') + *munis* = 'bound' or 'binding by obligation' (NOI. Originally, 'commune' and 'common' were used interchangeably, but gradually 'commune' was used to deal more with close relationships. See also 'Common'.)] Thus, **commune** means 'the action of making thoughts and feelings common with another, in a close personal way'. Eg. Gen.34:6, "And Hamor the father of Shechem went out unto Jacob to commune with him." {communed 18x., communing 2x., communion 4x., tot. = 32x.}

Communicate —4x., v. [A.D. 1526, < L. *communicare* (= 'to impart to others and share', especially with respect to material things) < *communis* = 'common property' (see 'Common') (NOI. Today, 'communicate' has to do with thoughts and feelings rather than material possessions.)] Thus, **communicate** means 'the action of sharing things (mental, material or spiritual) with others'. Eg. 1Tim.6:18, "That they do good, that they be rich in good works, ready to distribute, willing to communicate." {communicated 2x., communication 6x., communications 2x., tot. = 14x.}

Communion — 4x., n. [A.D. 1382(WB.), < L. *communio* (= 'common sharing') < *communis* = 'shared by many or all' (NOI. 'Communion' combines the attributes of 'sharing' and 'close relationships' and applies them to a spiritual dimension. See 'Common' and 'Commune'.)] Thus, a **communion** is 'a spiritual union and sharing together'. Eg. 1Cor.10:16, "The cup of blessing which we bless, is it not the communion of the blood of Christ? The bread which we break, is it not the communion of the body of Christ? " {commune 8x., tot. = 12x.}

Compact – 1x., adj. [A.D. 1398, < L. *compactus* (which is pp. of) *compingere* (= 'to join or bind together with skill', < *com* = 'together or with' (see L. prefix '*co–*') + *pangere* = 'to fasten, plant, set or fix') < Sans. *paca* = 'band or fetter'] Thus, **compact** modifies its n. (in this case, 'a city') as 'being carefully built closely together'. Eg. Ps.122:3, "Jerusalem is builded as a city that is compact together." {compacted 1x., tot. = 2x.}

Companion – 13x., n. [A.D. 1297, < OF. *compaignon* < LL. *companio* (= 'someone with whom you share bread'), *com* = 'together or with' (see L. prefix '*co–*') + *panis* = 'bread'] Thus, a **companion** is 'a bread-fellow', or in general terms, 'an associate or comrade'. Eg. 1Chr.27:33, "And Ahithophel was the king's counsellor: and Hushai the Archite was the king's companion." {companions 21x., companions' 1x., tot. = 35x.}

Company [1] – 81x., n. [A.D. 1250, < OF. *compaignie* < LL. *companio* = 'a group of companions' (see 'Companion')] Thus, a **company** is 'two or more associates having similar things in common'. Eg. Act.4:23, "And being let go, they went to their own company, and reported all that the chief priests and elders had said unto them." {companies 17x., tot. = 98x.}

Company [2] – 5x., v. [A.D. 1340, < OF. *compaignier* (which is the v. form of) *compaignie* (= 'to have associations or fellowship with')] Thus, **company** means 'the action of having associations or fellowship with an individual or a group'. Eg. 1Cor.5:9, "I wrote unto you in an epistle not to company with fornicators." {companied 1x., tot. = 6x.}

Compare –4x., v. [A.D. 1375, < L. *comparare*, < *compar*, com = 'together or with' (see L. prefix '*co–*') + *par* = 'equal'] Thus, **compare** means 'the action of bringing things together to see if they're equal, by looking for points of likeness or difference'. Eg. Isa.46:5, "To whom will ye liken me, and make me equal, and compare me, that we may be like?" {comparable 1x., compared 5x., comparing 2x., comparison 4x., tot. = 16x.}

Compass [1] –6x., n. [A.D. 1300, < OF. *compas* < ML. *compassus*, *com* = 'together or with' (see L. prefix '*co–*') + *passus* = 'step or pace' (NOI. The origin of the word 'compass' is obscure, but primarily the word refers to 'an outside perimeter', where one's steps come around and join together. The word was also sometimes applied to a device for making round circles.)] Thus, a **compass** is 'a joining together of the steps' (as in 'an outside perimeter'). Eg. Ex 27:5, "And thou shalt put it under the compass of the altar beneath, that the net may be even to the midst of the altar." And also, Isa.44:13, "The carpenter... marketh it out with the compass...."

Compass [2] – 33x., v. [A.D. 1297, < OF. *compasser* = the v. form of OF. *compass* (see 'Compass'[1].)] Thus, **compass** means 'the action of making a perimeter by joining the steps together'. Eg. Josh.6:4, "And seven priests shall bear before the ark seven trumpets of rams' horns: and the seventh day ye shall compass the city seven times, and the priests shall blow with the trumpets." (NOI. The term, "fetch a compass" (as seen in Num.34:5 and 2Sam.5:23) refers to 'finding a perimeter'. See also 'Fetch'.) {compassed 44x., compassest 1x., compasseth 5x., compassing 3x., tot. = 86x.}

Compassion – 41x., n. [A.D. 1340, < OF. *compassion* < LL. *compassio* (= 'fellow suffering or feeling') < *compati*, *com* = 'together or with' (see L. prefix '*co–*') + *pati* = 'suffer'] Thus, **compassion** is 'a suffering together with another person'. Eg. Lk.10:33, "But a certain Samaritan, as he journeyed, came where he was: and when he saw him, he had compassion on him." {compassions 2x., tot. = 43x.}

Compel – 5x., v. [A.D. 1380, < OF. *compeller* < L. *compellere*, *com* = 'together or with' having intensity (see L. prefix '*co–*') + *pellere* = 'to drive' or 'to force'] Thus, **compel**

means 'the action of driving, squeezing or forcing together' (as in forcing someone to do something). Eg. Mk.15:21, "And they compel one Simon a Cyrenian, who passed by, coming out of the country, the father of Alexander and Rufus, to bear his cross." (NOI. In human affairs, it is a wise thing to consider the motive behind the compelling. Is there some sense of urgency or even greed?) {compelled 6x., compellest 1x., tot. = 12x.}

Complain —4x., v. [A.D. 1374, < OF. *complaindre* < ML. *complangere, com* = 'together or with' having intensity (see L. prefix '*co–*') + *plangere* = 'to bewail or lament' (NOI. *Complangere* is a very emotional word in which the user would strike their head or chest in grief over some injustice or great loss. The L. *com* is added for intensity more than anything else.)] Thus, **complain** means 'the action of voicing deep, heart-felt lamentation over a sorrow'. Eg. Job.7:11, "Therefore I will not refrain my mouth; I will speak in the anguish of my spirit; I will complain in the bitterness of my soul." {complained 2x., complainers 1x., complaining 1x., complaint 9x., (incl. title of Ps.102), complaints 1x., tot. = 17x.}

Complete —3x., adj. [A.D. 1374, < L. *completus* (which is pp. of) *complere, com* = 'together or with' having intensity (see L. prefix '*co–*') + *plere* = 'to fill'] Thus, **complete** modifies its n. as 'being filled up full to the top'. Eg. Col.2:10, "And ye are complete in him, which is the head of all principality and power."

Comprehend —2x., v. [A.D. 1340, < L. *comprehendere, com* = 'together or with' (see L. prefix '*co–*') + *prehendere* = 'to catch or suddenly take hold of' (Cp. also 'Apprehend'.)] Thus, **comprehend** means 'the action of suddenly grasping with the mind'. Eg. Eph.3:18, "May be able to comprehend with all saints what is the breadth, and length, and depth, and height." {comprehended 3x., tot. = 5x.}

Conceit –5x., n. [A.D. 1374, < ME. **conceyte** = the n. form of 'conceive' (see 'Conceive') but appears to have no other etymological roots (NOI. This word relates to 'conceive' in the same way that 'deceit' (the n.) relates to 'deceive' (the v.). The idea of 'conceit' meaning 'vanity', did not begin until about A.D. 1605.)] Thus **conceit** is 'something that originates in the mind', such as a thought or an idea. Eg. Pr.26:12, "Seest thou a man wise in his own conceit? there is more hope of a fool than of him." Here, the man believes his own thoughts and ideas are better than the God's Word on a matter. {conceits 2x., tot. = 7x.}

Conceive – 14x., v. [A.D. 1300, < OF. *conceveir* < L. *concipere, con* = 'together or with' having intensity (see L. prefix '*co*–') + *capere* = 'to take' (NOI. Originally, this word meant 'to take into the mind and hold' as in 'formulating a plan', but it later came to mean 'taking seed into the womb and becoming pregnant', which is how it is used in the Bible. Twice it's used figuratively, as in Job.15:35 and Isa.33:11.)] Thus, **conceive** means 'the action of receiving seed and becoming pregnant'. Eg. Jud.13:3, "And the angel of the LORD appeared unto the woman, and said unto her, Behold now, thou art barren, and bearest not: but thou shalt conceive, and bear a son." {conceived 46x., conceiving 1x., conception 3x., tot. = 64x.}

Conception –3x., n. [A.D.1300, < E. **conceive** (see 'Conceive') + **tion** = 'a state or condition' (see E. suffix '–tion')] Thus, a **conception** is 'a state or condition of being conceived'. Eg. Rut.4:13, "So Boaz took Ruth, and she was his wife: and when he went in unto her, the LORD gave her conception, and she bare a son." {conceive 14x., conceived 46x., conceiving 1x., tot. = 64x.}

Concern –2x., v. [A.D. 1450, < ML. *concernere* (= 'to sift or mix together'), *con* = 'together or with' (see L. prefix '*co*–') + *cernere* = 'to separate, decide or sift' (NOI. The word picture here is to put things through a strainer, looking for common things that either go through the strainer or are stopped by the strainer.)] Thus, **concern** means 'the action of bringing together things that are of relevance and importance'. Eg. Act.28:31, "Preaching the kingdom of God, and teaching those things which concern the Lord Jesus Christ, with all confidence, no man forbidding him." {concerneth 2x., concerning 242x., (incl. title of Ps.7) tot. = 246x.}

Concision – 1x., n. [A.D. 1382(WB.), < L. *concisio* < *concidere* (= 'to chop up in fine pieces with precision'), *con* = 'together or with' (see L. prefix '*co*–') + *caedere* = 'to cut, chop, strike or slaughter'] Thus, a **concision** is 'a chopping into pieces' (however, it is used to represent a certain group of unsaved people in the NT., who claimed that circumcision was necessary for salvation). Eg. Phil.3:2, "Beware of dogs, beware of evil workers, beware of the concision." (NOI. The 1611 has in the marginal note of Joel 3:14 "*concision*" as their secondary choice for 'decision'.)

Conclude – 1x., v. [A.D. 1300, < L. *concludere* (= 'to confine together'), *con* = 'together or with' (see L. prefix '*co*–') + *cludere* = 'to close, confine or blockade'] Thus, **conclude** means 'the action of binding thoughts together for the purpose of reaching a decision or judgment'. Eg. Rom3:28, "Therefore we conclude that a man is justified by faith without the deeds of the law." {concluded 3x., conclusion 1x., tot. = 5x.}

Concord – 1x., n. [A.D. 1300, < OF. *concorde* < L. *concordia* (= 'a peaceful agreeing of minds'), < *concors* (= 'of a similar mind'), *con* = 'together or with' (see L. prefix '*co*–') + *cor* = 'heart'(NOI. Although *cor* = 'heart', it is understood to be in reference to the 'mind'.)] Thus, a **concord** is 'a peaceful agreement of minds'. Eg. 2Cor.6:15, "And what concord hath

Christ with Belial? or what part hath he that believeth with an infidel? "

Concourse —2x., n. [A.D. 1382(WB.), < OF. *concours* < L. *concursus* < *concurrere* (= 'a running together'), *con* = 'together or with' (see L. prefix '*co–*') + *currere* = 'to run' (NOI. A *concursus* always referred to a group of people flowing together, as in 'a market place' or 'some great attraction'.)] Thus, a **concourse** is 'a crowd of people running together for some event'. Eg. Act.19:40, "For we are in danger to be called in question for this day's uproar, there being no cause whereby we may give an account of this concourse."

Concubine —22x., n. [A.D. 1297, < F. *concubine* < L. *concubina* (= 'a woman who lies down carnally with a man'), *con* = 'together or with' (see L. prefix '*co–*') + *cubare* = 'to lie down'] Thus, a **concubine** is 'a woman who cohabits with a man, without the full legal status of being his wife'. Eg. Jud.20:5, "And the men of Gibeah rose against me, and beset the house round about upon me by night, and thought to have slain me: and my concubine have they forced, that she is dead." (NOI. Concubines seem to have been more common from the days of Abraham throughout the Judges. After that, they seemed to be more the choice of kings David and Solomon, and after that it seems the practice dropped off. The practice of having concubines never seemed to end in happiness for anyone, nor did it have the full blessing of God.) {concubines 17x., tot. = 39x.}

Concupiscence – 3x., n. [A.D. 1340, < LL. *concupiscentia* < *concupiscens* (which is pp. of) *concupiscere* (= 'to greatly desire after'), *con* ='together or with' with intensity (see L. prefix '*co–*') + *cupere* = 'to passionately wish for, or desire as a lover' (NOI. Our E. word 'Cupid' (the Roman god of love, son of Venus) comes from L. *cupido* = 'desire or passion'.)] Thus, a **concupiscence** is 'an eager, sensual appetite and lustful desire'. Eg. 1Ths.4:5, "Not in the lust of concupiscence, even as the Gentiles which know not God."

Condemn —24x., v. [A.D. 1300, < OF. *condemner* < L. *condemnare* (= 'to completely blame or find guilty'), *con* = 'together or with' with intensity (see L. prefix '*co–*') + *damnare* = 'to sentence or pass judgment upon'] Thus, **condemn** means 'the action of pronouncing someone to be completely guilty'. Eg. Jn.8:11, "She said, No man, Lord. And Jesus said unto her, Neither do I condemn thee: go, and sin no more." {condemnation 12x., condemned 21x., condemnest 1x., condemneth 4x., condemning 2x., uncondemned 2x., tot. = 66x.}

Condescend — 1x., v. [A.D. 1340, < OF. *condescendre* < LL. *condescendere* (= 'to make oneself go down to where others are'), *con* = 'together or with' (see L. prefix '*co–*') + *descendere* = 'to sink or go down' (see 'Descend')] Thus, **condescend** means 'the action of stooping down to be with others'. Eg. Rom.12:16, "Be of the same mind one toward another. Mind not high things, but condescend to men of low estate. Be not wise in your own conceits."

Conduct —3x., v. [A.D. 1400, < L. *conductus* (which is pp. of) *conducere* (= 'to unite and lead together'), *con* = 'together or with' (see L. prefix '*co–*') + *ducere* = 'to lead'] Thus, **conduct** means 'the action of uniting for the purpose of leading'. Eg. 2Sam.19:15, "So the king returned, and came to Jordan. And Judah came to Gilgal, to go to meet the king, to conduct the king over Jordan." {conducted 2x., tot. = 5x.}

Coney — 2x., n. [A.D. 1200, < OF. *conil* < L. *cuniculus* = 'rabbit' or 'underground tunnel' (NOI. In ME., the word 'rabbit' (first used in A.D. 1398) was applied only to the young bunnies, while the adult was called a 'coney'. Some have identified Lev.11:5 as an error in the Bible, stating that rabbits do not have a four-part stomach system, like a cow, and therefore do not chew the cud. However, studies have shown that rabbits have a fermentation chamber inside them, which allows them to bring back partly-digested food and chew on it. Some believe the 'coney' (Hb. שָׁפָן (*shaphan*)) to be a 'badger', but given the description "feeble folk" (Pr.30:26), this makes little sense. Others have identified it with the 'Syrian Rock Hyrax' (A.D. 1832, < Gk. ὕραξ (*hoorax*) = 'a shrew-mouse'), known to be in that area, and which lives among the rocks and also chews the cud. These creatures have rabbit-like features and look like giant, golden hamsters.] Thus, a **coney** is 'an adult rabbit, or rabbit-like animal'. Eg. Lev.11:5, "And the coney, because he cheweth the cud, but divideth not the hoof; he is unclean unto you." (See also 'Hare'.) {conies 2x., tot. = 4x.}

Confection – 1x., n. [A.D. 1387, < ME. **confect** < L. *confectus* (which is pp. of) *conficere* (= 'to thoroughly make or prepare'), *con* = 'together or with' (see L. prefix '*co–*') + *facere* = 'to make' + **tion** = 'a state or condition' (see E. suffix '–tion') (NOI. The modern sense of confections being candies, light pastries and tasty treats, seems to have begun in E. literature around A.D. 1400. The word 'confetti' (A.D. 1815) (= 'small pieces of colored paper, thrown at parties') also comes from the L. *confectus*.)] Thus, a **confection** is 'something that is made (usually an ointment or a perfume) by a process of compounding things together'. Eg. Ex.30:35, "And thou shalt make it a perfume, a confection after the art of the apothecary, tempered together, pure and holy." {confectionaries 1x., tot. = 2x.}

Confectionaries – 1x., n. pl. [A.D. 1599, < E. **confection** (see 'Confection') + **ary** (= 'connected with or pertaining to') + **ies** = forms the pl.] Thus, **confectionaries** are 'two or more people who practice the art of making confections'. Eg. 1Sam.8:13, "And he will take your daughters to be confectionaries, and to be cooks, and to be bakers." {confection 1x., tot. = 2x.}

Confederate –3x., pp. and prp. [A.D. 1387, < LL. *confoederatus* (which is pp. of) *confoederare* (= 'to unite'), *con* = 'together or with' (see L. prefix '*co–*') + *foederare* (= 'to seal or establish by treaty') < *foedus* = 'a treaty or league'] Thus, as a pp., **confederate** modifies its n. as 'having made a unity, league or alliance'. Eg. Gen.14:13, "And there came one that had escaped, and told Abram the Hebrew; for he dwelt in the plain of Mamre the Amorite, brother of Eshcol, and brother of Aner: and these were confederate with Abram." Furthermore, as a prp., **confederate** modifies its n. as 'being in a unity, league or alliance'. Eg. Ps.83:5, "For they have consulted together with one consent: they are confederate against thee." {confederacy 3x., tot. = 6x.}

Confess –28x., v. [A.D. 1340, < OF. *confesser* < L. *confessus* (which is pp. of) *confiteri* (= 'to admit or acknowledge') < L. *con* = 'together or with' having intensity (see L. prefix '*co–*') + *fateri* = 'to own up' (NOI. The idea of 'acceptance and ownership' can also been seen, by contrast, with the opposite word, 'deny', as seen in Lk.12:8-9. See 'Deny'.)] Thus, **confess** means 'the action of thoroughly admitting the ownership or relationship that one has in something'. Eg. Rom.10:9, "That if thou shalt confess with thy mouth the Lord Jesus, and shalt believe in thine heart that God hath raised him from the dead, thou shalt be saved." (NOI. Salvation is by (God's) grace through (our) faith (see Eph.2:8-9). Therefore, it is one's faith that prompts one to confess (or verbally acknowledge) Jesus to be the Lord of one's life (i.e. 'I claim Jesus to be my Lord'. A confession as such will also show itself in a changed life. See 'Lord' and 'Salvation'). Other types of confession include: to God over one's sin (1Jn.1:9); or to others concerning doctrine (Act.23:8) or to one another concerning one's faults (Jam.5:16).) {confessed 7x., confesseth 3x., confessing 3x., confession 6x., tot. = 47x.}

Confidence —38x., n. [A.D. 1430, < L. *confidentia* < *confidere* (= 'to have full trust in'), *con* = 'together or with' (see L. prefix '*co–*') + *fidere* = 'to trust'] Thus, a **confidence** is 'a state of full, unreserved trust in the reliability of someone or something'. Eg. Heb.10:35, "Cast not away therefore your confidence, which hath great recompence of reward." {confidences 1x., confident 8x., confidently 1x., tot. = 48x.}

Confirm —13x., v. [A.D. 1290, < ME. **confermen** < OF. *confermer* < L. *confirmare* (= 'to make altogether strong'), *con* = 'together or with' having intensity (see L. prefix '*co–*') + *firmare* = 'to strengthen, support or make fast'] Thus, **confirm** means 'the action of making altogether strong'. Eg. Ps.68:9, "Thou, O God, didst send a plentiful rain, whereby thou didst confirm thine inheritance, when it was weary."

Confiscation —1x., n. [A.D. 1543, < ME. **confiscate** < L. *confiscatus* (which is pp. of) *confiscare* (= 'to seize as forfeited to the public or state treasury'), *con* = 'together or with' (see L. prefix '*co–*') + *fiscus* = 'money bag or treasury' (NOI. In Scotland, the state prosecutor is called the 'Procurator Fiscal', < L, *procurator fiscalis* = 'an agent of the imperial treasury'.) + **tion** = 'a state or condition' (see E. suffix '–tion')] Thus, **confiscation** is 'the state or condition of having assets seized by the government and put into the treasury'. Eg. Ezr.7:26, "And whosoever will not do the law of thy God, and the law of the king, let judgment be executed speedily upon him, whether it be unto death, or to banishment, or to confiscation of goods, or to imprisonment."

Conflict —2x., n. [A.D. 1430, < L. *conflictus* (= 'a clash, impact or fight') (which is pp. of) *confligere*, *con* = 'together or with' (see L. prefix '*co–*') + *fligere* = 'to strike down'] Thus, a **conflict** is 'a clashing together in an effort for mastery'. Eg. Col.2:1, "For I would that ye knew what great conflict I have for you, and for them at Laodicea, and for as many as have not seen my face in the flesh."

Conformable —1x., adj. [A.D. 1511, < E. **conform** (< OF. *conformer* < L. *conformare*, *con* = 'together or with' (see L. prefix '*co*–') + *formare* = 'to form, shape or fashion') + **able** = shows 'capability of being' (see E. suffix '–able')] Thus, **conformable** modifies its n. (in this case, 'his death') as 'being capable of being formed or shaped like or similar in character'. Eg. **Phil.3:10**, "That I may know him, and the power of his resurrection, and the fellowship of his sufferings, being made conformable unto his death." Here, Paul is not saying that his life IS conformed to Christ's death, for then he would be physically dead, but rather his life is CAPEABLE of being conformed to Christ's death. {conformed 2x., tot. = 3x.}

Confound —5x., v. [A.D. 1290, < OF. *confondre* < L. *confundere* (= 'to pour together, mix or confuse'), *con* = 'together or with' (see L. prefix '*co*–') + *fundere* = 'to pour or scatter'] Thus, **confound** means 'the action of mixing so as the ingredients cannot be distinguished'. Eg. **Gen.11:7**, "Go to, let us go down, and there confound their language, that they may not understand one another's speech." {confounded 50x., tot. = 55x.}

Confusion —26x., n. [A.D. 1290, < OF. *confusion* < L. *confusio* (= 'a disorderly mess', which also causes disgrace) *con* = 'together or with' having intensity (see L. prefix '*co*–') + *fusio* = 'a pouring or scattering'] Thus, a **confusion** is 'the act or state of ghastly disorder causing embarrassment or a blushing disgrace'. Eg. **Lev.18:23**, "Neither shalt thou lie with any beast to defile thyself therewith: neither shall any woman stand before a beast to lie down thereto: it is confusion." {confused 2x., tot. = 28x.}

Congealed —1x., pp. [A.D. 1384, < ME. **congele** < OF. *congeler* < . *congelare* (= 'to become frozen', as in 'changing from a liquid state to a solid state'), *con* = 'together or with' having intensity (see L. prefix '*co–*') + *gelare* = 'to freeze') (< L. *gelum* = 'frost, cold') + **ed** = forms the pp. (see E. suffix '–ed'[3])] Thus, **congealed** modifies its n. (in this case, 'the depths') as 'having been frozen or solidified together'. Eg. Ex.15:8, "And with the blast of thy nostrils the waters were gathered together, the floods stood upright as an heap, and the depths were congealed in the heart of the sea."

Congratulate –1x., v. [A.D. 1548, < L. *congratulatus* (which is pp. of) *congratulari* (= 'to rejoice together'), *con* = 'together or with' (see L. prefix '*co–*') + *gratulari* = 'to express joy'] Thus, **congratulate** means 'the action of rejoicing together with someone', because of that person's good fortune. Eg. 1Chr.18:10, "He sent Hadoram his son to king David, to enquire of his welfare, and to congratulate him, because he had fought against Hadarezer, and smitten him..."

Congregation –364x., n. [A.D. 1340, < F. *congregation* < L. *congregatio* (= 'a group or brotherhood' or 'a flocking together') < L. *congregatus* (which is pp. of) *congregare, con* = 'together or with' (see L. prefix '*co–*') + *gregare* = 'to collect into a flock' (< L. *grex* = 'a flock')] Thus, a **congregation** is 'an assemblage of people together into a group'. Eg. Ex.35:1, "And Moses gathered all the congregation of the children of Israel together, and said unto them." (see also 'Assembly' and 'Church'.) {congregations 3x., tot. = 367x.}

Conquer – 1x., v. [A.D. 1230, < OF. *conquerre* < L. *conquaerere* (= 'to hunt, seek out or investigate'), *con* = 'together or with' having intensity (see L. prefix '*co–*') + *quaerere* = 'to hunt or seek'] Thus, **conquer** means 'the action of acquiring by force of arms'. Eg. Rev.6:2, "And I saw, and behold a white horse: and he that sat on him had a bow; and a crown was given unto him: and he went forth conquering, and to conquer." {conquering 1x., conquerors 1x., tot. = 3x.}

Conscience —31x., n. [A.D. 1225, < OF. *conscience* < L. *conscientia* (= 'moral knowledge within' or 'a sense of guilt') < *conscire, con* = 'together or with' (see L. prefix '*co–*') + *scire* = 'to know' (NOI. The OED. indicates that ME. **conscience** took the place of OE. **inwit**, which meant 'the mind within man'.)] Thus, a **conscience** 'is an inner sense of guilt, or right and wrong'. Eg. Act.24:16, "And herein do I exercise myself, to have always a conscience void of offence toward God, and toward men." (NOI. A 'conscience' may be weak and easily defiled (1Cor.8:7), or it may be seared and beyond feeling (1Tim.4:2) or it may be kept good, strong and pure (1Tim.1:5).) {consciences 1x., tot. = 32x.}

Consecrate — 14x., v. [A.D. 1387, < L. *consecratus* (which is pp. of) *consecrare, con* = 'together or with' having intensity (see L. prefix '*co–*') + *sacrare* = 'to make sacred'] Thus, **consecrate** means 'the action of making holy and setting apart for holy purposes'. Eg. Ex.30:30, "And thou shalt anoint Aaron and his sons, and consecrate them, that they may minister unto me in the priest's office." (NOI. 'Consecrate' and 'Dedicate' are different. See 'Dedicate'. {consecrated 14x., consecration 9x., consecrations 4x., tot. = 41x.}

Consecration — 9x., n. [A.D. 1382(WB.), < L. *consecratio* = 'the act of consecrating' (see 'Consecrate')] Thus, a **consecration** is 'the act of consecrating someone to the Lord'. Eg. Lev.8:33, "And ye shall not go out of the door of the tabernacle of the congregation in seven days, until the days of your consecration be at an end: for seven days shall he consecrate you." {consecrate 14x., consecrated 14x., consecrations 4x., tot. = 41x.}

Consent[1] — 6x., n. [A.D. 1300, ME. **consente** < OF. *consente* < *consentir* (see 'Consent'[2])] Thus, a **consent** is 'an agreement in feeling and opinion'. Eg. Lk.14:18, "And they all with one consent began to make excuse. The first said unto him, I have bought a piece of ground, and I must needs go and see it: I pray thee have me excused."

Consent[2] –9x., v. [A.D. 1225, < OF. *consentir* < L. *consentire* (= 'to agree in feeling or sentiment'), *con* = 'together or with' (see L. prefix '*co*–') + *sentire* = 'to feel'] Thus, **consent** means 'the action of agreeing with, or being in harmony with, someone and thereby granting one's permission'. Eg. 1Tim.6:3, "If any man teach otherwise, and consent not to wholesome words, even the words of our Lord Jesus Christ, and to the doctrine which is according to godliness." {consented 4x., consentedst 1x., consenting 2x., tot. = 16x.}

Consider –67x., v. [A.D. 1375, < OF. *considerer* < L. *considerare* (= 'to observe and contemplate' (possibly from 'observing the stars)), *con* = 'together or with' (see L. prefix '*co*–') + *sidus* = 'constellation' or 'star'] Thus, **consider** means 'the action of careful observation and deep contemplation'. Eg. Pr.6:6, "Go to the ant, thou sluggard; consider her ways, and be wise." {considered 16x., considerest 2x., considereth 9x., considering 4x., tot. = 98x.}

Consist –1x., v. [A.D. 1526, < L. *consistere* (= 'to stand still'), *con* = 'together or with' having intensity (see L. prefix '*co*–') + *sistere* = 'to stand'] Thus, **consist** means 'the action of standing together, firm and solid'. Eg. Col.1:17, "And he is before all things, and by him all things consist." {consisteth 1x., tot. = 2x.}

Consolation –15x., n. [A.D. 1374, < L. *consolatio* (= 'the act of consoling or comforting'), < *consolare* (= 'to alleviate sorrow or distress'), *con* = 'together or with' having intensity (see L. prefix '*co*–') + *solari* = 'to soothe or comfort' (NOI. *Solari* is the L. root for the E. 'solace'. By adding the L. prefix '*con*' it intensifies the idea of 'solace' to make the stronger word, 'consolation'. See also 'Solace'.)] Thus, a **consolation** is 'the act of greatly soothing or the state of being greatly comforted'. Eg. Lk.6:24, "But woe unto you that are rich! for ye have received your consolation." (see also 'Comfort') {consolations 3x., tot. = 18x.}

Conspiracy —10x., n. [A.D. 1386, < E. **conspire** (< F. *conspirer* < L. *conspirare* (= 'to breathe together', as in 'agree or unite in a plot'), *con* = 'together or with' having intensity (see L. prefix '*co*–') + *spirare* = 'to breathe') + **acy** = an E. suffix (after the L. '*–acia*' and '*–atia*') expressing 'a state or condition' (NOI. This '–acy' suffix is only used on one other word in the KJV, 'confederacy'.)] Thus, a **conspiracy** is 'the act of conspiring together (i.e. 'plotting together') for evil purposes'. Eg. 2Ki.12:20, "And his servants arose, and made a conspiracy, and slew Joash in the house of Millo, which goeth down to Silla." {conspirators 1x., conspired 19x., tot. = 30x.}

Constant —1x., adj. [A.D. 1386, < OF. *constant* < L. *constans* (which is prp. of) *constare* (= 'to stand together'), *con* = 'together or with' having intensity (see L. prefix '*co*–') + *stare* = 'to stand'] Thus, **constant** modifies its n. (in this case, the pro. 'he') as 'standing strong and resolute in mind'. Eg. 1Chr.28:7, "Moreover I will establish his kingdom for ever, if he be constant to do my commandments and my judgments, as at this day." {constantly 3x., tot. = 4x.}

Constrain —1x., v. [A.D. 1340(HP.), < OF. *constreindre* < L. *constringere* (= 'to tightly draw together' or 'to constrict'), *con* = 'together or with' having intensity (see L. prefix '*co*–') + *stringere* = 'to draw tight together'] Thus, **constrain** means 'the action of thoroughly drawing something tightly together' (but it is used in a figurative sense to mean 'to urge or compel someone to do something', i.e. 'to force, yet not against the will'). Eg. Gal.6:12, "As many as desire to make a fair shew in the flesh, they constrain you to be circumcised; only lest they should suffer persecution for the cross of Christ." {constrained 6x., constraineth 2x., constraint 1x.,

tot. = 10x.}

Consult – 1x., v. [A.D. 1540, < F. *consulter* < L. *consultare* (which is the frequently used form of *consulere* = 'to seek advice or information'), or perhaps < *consilium* (= 'a jury or a body of people brought together for deliberation and discussion in order to decide on a plan or offer advice') (See also 'Counsel'.)] Thus, **consult** means 'the action of gathering together for the purpose of discussion and advice'. Eg. Ps.62:4, "They only consult to cast him down from his excellency: they delight in lies: they bless with their mouth, but they curse inwardly. Selah." {consultation 1x., consulted 13x., consulter 1x., consulteth 1x., tot. = 17x.}

Consume – 56x., v. [A.D. 1382(WB.), < L. *consumere, con* = 'together or with' having intensity (see L. prefix '*co–*') + *sumere* = 'to select, take or obtain' (< *sub* = 'under' + *emere* = 'to buy or gain')] Thus, **consume** means 'the action of using something completely up'. Eg. 2Ki.1:10, "And Elijah answered and said to the captain of fifty, If I be a man of God, then let fire come down from heaven, and consume thee and thy fifty. And there came down fire from heaven, and consumed him and his fifty." (NOI. 'Consuming' could be material, as in locusts eating up the vegetation (see Deut.28:42) or it could be immaterial, as in the days of one's life (see Ps.78:33).) {consumed 96x., consumeth 4x., consuming 3x., consumption 5x., tot. = 164x.}

Consumption –5x., n. [A.D. 1398, < L. *consumptio* (= 'a wasting away') < *consumere* (see 'Consume') (NOI. 'Consumption', as a disease, was later called 'tuberculosis', and discovered by Robert Koch in A.D. 1882. The disease is caused by microscopic organisms, which appear like short, skinny rods, called 'tubercles'. Tubercles may affect various tissues of the body, including the lungs (called 'pulmonary tuberculosis'), and thereby cause the victim chest pain, coughing up blood, difficulty in breathing, night sweats and weight loss. Whether tuberculosis was the 'consumption disease' of the Bible is only a guess.)] Thus, a **consumption** is 'a wasting away, a decay or destruction of the body'. Eg. Deut.28:22, "The LORD shall smite thee with a consumption, ...and they shall pursue thee until thou perish." {consume 56x., consumed 96x., consumeth 4x., consuming 3x., tot. = 164x.}

Contain – 7x., v. [A.D. 1290, < OF. *contenir* (= 'to hold or keep in') < L. *continere* (= 'to hold tightly together, hold back or restrain'), < *con* = 'together' having intensity (see L. prefix '*co–*') + *tenere* = 'to hold'] Thus, **contain** means 'the action of holding tightly together within fixed limits, or restraining from action'. Eg. 1Cor.7:9, "But if they cannot contain, let them marry: for it is better to marry than to burn." {contained 5x., containeth 1x., containing 1x., tot. = 14x.}

Contemn – 2x., v. [A.D. 1450, < L. *contemnere, con* = 'together or with' having intensity (see L. prefix '*co–*') + *temnere* = 'to scorn or despise'] Thus, **contemn** means 'the action of treating someone or something in an altogether scornful or contemptuous manner'. Eg. Ps.10:13, "Wherefore doth the wicked contemn God? he hath said in his heart, Thou wilt not require it." {contemned 4x., contemneth 1x., tot. = 7x.}

Contempt – 10x., n. [A.D. 1393, < L. *contemptus* (the n. form of the v. *contemnere*, see 'Contemn')] Thus, **contempt** is 'the act of disgracing, scorning or despising someone or something'. Eg. Ps.123:4, "Our soul is exceedingly filled with the scorning of those that are at ease, and with the contempt of the proud." {contemptible 4x., contemptuously 1x., tot. = 15x.}

Contend – 14x., v. [A.D. 1514, < L. *contendere* (= 'an intensive stretching or striving'), *con* = 'together or with' having intensity (see L. prefix '*co–*') + *tendere* = 'to stretch or strive' (NOI. The E. word 'tendon' (a tough, elastic cord connecting a muscle with a bone) also comes from L. *tendere*.)] Thus, **contend** means 'the action of struggling vigorously together with someone for mastery or control'. Eg. Deut.2:9, "And the LORD said unto me, Distress not the Moabites, neither contend with them in battle: for I will not give thee of their land for a possession; because I have given Ar unto the children of Lot for a possession." {contended 6x., contendest 1x., contendeth 3x., contending 1x., contention 9x., contentions 6x., contentious 5x., tot. = 45x.}

Content[1] –15x., adj. [A.D. 1400, < OF. *content* < L. *contentus* (= 'satisfied', which is pp. of) *continere* = 'to hold tightly together, hold back or restrain') < *con* = 'together' having intensity (see L. prefix '*co–*') + *tenere* = 'to hold' (See also 'Contain'.)] Thus, **content** modifies its n. as 'having its desires satisfied, or limited, by what one already has'. Eg. 1Tim.6:8, "And having food and raiment let us be therewith content." {contentment 1x., tot. = 16x.}

Content[2] –1x., v. [A.D. 1418, < OF. *contenter* (= 'to satisfy the mind or appetite') < ML. *contentare* (= 'to bend so as to satisfy'), *con* = 'together or with' having intensity (see L. prefix '*co–*') + *tenare* = 'to handle'] Thus, **content** means 'the action of satisfying so as to stop a complaint'. Eg. Mk.15:15, "And so Pilate, willing to content the people, released Barabbas unto them, and delivered Jesus, when he had scourged him, to be crucified."

Contentious –5x., adj. [A.D. 1430, < L. *contentiosis* = 'given to or characterized by contention' (i.e. 'a struggling together in opposition', almost 'war-like') < *contentio* < *contendere* (see 'Contend')] Thus, **contentious** modifies its n. as 'being given over to, or characterized by contention'. Eg. Pr.26:21, "As coals are to burning coals, and wood to fire; so is a contentious man to kindle strife." {contend 14x., contended 6x., contendest 1x., contendeth 3x., contending 1x., contention

9x., contentions 6x., tot. = 45x.}

Continual —33x., adj. [A.D. 1340, < OF. *continuel* < L. *continuus*, *con* = 'together or with' having intensity (see L. prefix '*co–*') + *tenere* = 'to hold together' or 'to contain'] Thus, **continual** modifies its n. as 'being securely held together by the hands of time, without a pause or break'. Eg. Pr.27:15, "A continual dropping in a very rainy day and a contentious woman are alike." (NOI. Sometimes, 'continuous' modified a n. that was used in a repeated fashion, such as 'day by day' (cp. Ex.29:38-42).) {continue 38x., continually 81x., continuance 5x., continued 29x., continueth 5x., continuing 4x., tot. = 195x.}

Contrary —24x., adj., adv. and n. [A.D. 1250, < ME. contrarie < L. *contrarius* (= 'a person in opposition with someone or something'), < *contra* = 'in opposition to' or 'against' + *arius* (a L. suffix) = 'a person concerned with' (NOI. The L. prefix *contra* is also found in words such as 'contradict' (= 'to speak against'), and 'contrast' (= 'to stand things against each other').)] Thus, as an adj., **contrary** modifies its n. as 'being in opposition or striving against someone or something'. Eg. 1Tim.1:10, "For whoremongers, for them that defile themselves with mankind, for menstealers, for liars, for perjured persons, and if there be any other thing that is contrary to sound doctrine." Furthermore, as an adv., **contrary** modifies its v. so as to 'make its action happen in opposition to someone or something'. Eg. Lev.26:21, "And if ye walk contrary unto me, and will not hearken unto me; I will bring seven times more plagues upon you according to your sins." Finally, as a n., **contrary** is 'a thing that is in opposition to someone or something'. Eg. Eze.16:34, "And the contrary is in thee from other women in thy whoredoms, whereas none followeth thee to commit whoredoms..." {contrariwise 3x., tot. = 27x.}

Contribution — 1x., n. [A.D. 1387, < LL. *contributio* < *con-*

tributus, *con* = 'together or with' (see L. prefix '*co*–') + *tribuere* = 'to give or pay'] Thus, a **contribution** is 'something given, along with similar gifts from others, for a specific purpose'. Eg. Rom.15:26, "For it hath pleased them of Macedonia and Achaia to make a certain contribution for the poor saints which are at Jerusalem."

Contrite – 5x., adj. [A.D. 1340(HP.), < L. *contritus* (which is pp. of) *conterere* (= 'to grind to pieces'), *con* = 'together or with' having intensity (see L. prefix '*co*–') + *terere* = 'to rub'] Thus, **contrite** modifies its n. as 'being ground to pieces' (in a figurative sense). Eg. Isa.66:2, "For all those things hath mine hand made, and all those things have been, saith the LORD: but to this man will I look, even to him that is poor and of a contrite spirit, and trembleth at my word." (NOI. This word is worthy of careful study in its other passages: Ps.34:18; 51:17 and Isa.57:15.)

Controversy – 13x., n. [A.D. 1382(WB.), < L. *controversia* < *controversus*, *contro* (same as *contra*, see 'Contrary') = 'in opposition to' or 'against' + *versus* (which is pp. of) *vertere* = 'to turn'] Thus, a **controversy** is 'a mental-emotional turning of one person against another, or against a group, causing contention and dispute'. Eg. Deut.25:1, "If there be a controversy between men, and they come unto judgment, that the judges may judge them; then they shall justify the righteous, and condemn the wicked." {controversies 1x., tot. = 14x.}

Convenient – 9x., adj. [A.D. 1374, < L. *conveniens* (which is prp. of) *convenire* (= 'to agree' or 'to unite'), *con* = 'together or with' having intensity (see L. prefix '*co*–') + *venire* = 'to come'] Thus, **convenient** modifies its n. as 'being agreeable, suitable and proper'. Eg. 1Cor.16:12, "As touching our brother Apollos, I greatly desired him to come unto you with the brethren: but his will was not at all to come at this time; but he will come when he shall have convenient time." {conveniently 1x., tot. = 10x.}

Conversant —2x., adj. [A.D. 1340(HP.), < OF. *conversant* < L. *conversans* (which is prp. of) *conversari* (= 'to dwell or associate with'), *con* = 'together or with' having intensity (see L. prefix '*co–*') + *versari* = 'to dwell or busy one's self with'] Thus, **conversant** modifies its n. as 'living or spending much of its time in a certain place'. Eg. 1Sam.25:15, "But the men were very good unto us, and we were not hurt, neither missed we any thing, as long as we were conversant with them, when we were in the fields." {conversation 20x., tot. = 22x.}

Conversation —20x., n. [A.D. 1340(HP.), < OF. *conversation* (= 'commerce, great acquaintance or familiarity') < L. *conversatio* (= 'familiarity or way of life') < *conversari* (see 'Conversant')] Thus, a **conversation** is 'a familiar manner of living, a behavior or lifestyle'. Eg. Gal.1:13, "For ye have heard of my conversation in time past in the Jews' religion, how that beyond measure I persecuted the church of God, and wasted it." {conversant 2x., tot. = 22x.}

Conversion — 1x., n. [A.D. 1340(HP.), < L. *conversio* (= 'a rotation' or 'a partial turn') < *convertere* (see 'Convert') (NOI. 'Conversion' is the visible result of true repentance and faith. See Act.3:19 and Isa.6:10.)] Thus, a **conversion** is 'a state or condition of being, or having been, converted'. Eg. Act.15:3, "And being brought on their way by the church, they passed through Phenice and Samaria, declaring the conversion of the Gentiles: and they caused great joy unto all the brethren." {convert 2x., converted 9x., converteth 1x., converting 1x., converts 1x., tot. = 15x.}

Convert —2x., v. [A.D. 1300, < L. *convertere*, *con* = 'together or with' having intensity (see L. prefix '*co–*') + *vertere* = 'to turn' (NOI. Used in a religious sense, it meant to thoroughly change someone's nature, belief and outlook; from thoughts and desires towards the world, to thoughts and desires towards heaven.)] Thus, **convert** means 'the action of turning around, or changing, in character or nature'. Eg. Isa.6:10, "Make the heart of this people fat, and make their ears heavy, and shut their eyes; lest they see with their eyes, and hear with their ears, and understand with their heart, and convert, and be healed. " {conversion 1x., converted 9x., converteth 1x., converting 1x., converts 1x., tot. = 15x.}

Convicted – 1x., pp. [A.D. 1595, < E. **convict** (< L. *convictus*, which is pp. of *convincere*, see 'Convince') + **ed** = forms the pp. (see E. suffix '–ed'[3])] Thus, **convicted** modifies its n. (in this case, the pro. 'they') as 'having been persuaded and overcome by force of logical argument'. Eg. Jn.8:9, "And they which heard it, being convicted by their own conscience, went out one by one, beginning at the eldest, even unto the last: and Jesus was left alone, and the woman standing in the midst."

Convince –2x., v. [A.D. 1530, < L. *convincere*, *con* ='together or with' having intensity (see L. prefix '*co*–') + *vincere* = 'to conquer, outlast or succeed' (NOI. The E. name 'Victor' (= 'conqueror') comes from the L. *vincere*.)] Thus, **convince** means 'the action of persuading and overcoming by force of logical argument'. Eg. Ti.1:9, "Holding fast the faithful word as he hath been taught, that he may be able by sound doctrine both to exhort and to convince the gainsayers."

Convocation – 16x., n. [A.D. 1387, < L. *convocatio* (= 'an assembling'), *con* = 'together or with' having intensity (see L. prefix '*co*–') + *vocare* = 'to call' (Cp. also 'Advocate' and 'Provoke'.) (NOI. When the leaders of the Church of England gather to discuss church matters, they call this a 'Convocation'.)] Thus, a **convocation** is 'a calling and assembling of people together'. Eg. Ex.12:16, "And in the first day there shall be an holy convocation, and in the seventh day there shall be an holy convocation to you; no manner of work shall be done in them, save that which every man must eat, that only may be done of you." (NOI. In the Bible, 'convocation' is always prefaced by the word 'holy', in which the people were not to perform any regular, day-to-day type of work.) {convocations 3x., tot. = 19x.}

Coping – 1x., n. [A.D. 1601, < ME. (v.) **cope** (= 'to build or finish with a cope') < ML. *capa* = 'a cloak or canopy-like covering, which has a sloping-down appearance') + **ing** = forms the n. (see E. suffix '–ing'[2]) (NOI. The Hb. word טפח (*tephach*) (= 'the width of the hand' or 'a span') gives us some idea as to the size of the cope.)] Thus, a **coping** is 'the very top level of stonework, or brickwork on a wall, and being made with a slope so as to cause rainwater to run off '. Eg. 1Ki.7:9, "All these were of costly stones, according to the measures of hewed stones, sawed with saws, within and without, even from the foundation unto the coping, and so on the outside toward the great court."

Copulation –3x., n. [A.D. 1400, < L. *copulatio* = 'a joining together, or a union', (i.e. 'a sexual union'), < *copula* (= 'a band, bond or link'), *co* = 'together or with' (see L. prefix '*co*–') + *apere* = 'to join' (NOI. Our E. word 'couple' comes from L. *copula*.)] Thus, a **copulation** is 'the state or condition of being joined together in sexual union'. Eg. Lev.15:16, "And if any man's seed of copulation go out from him, then he shall wash all his flesh in water, and be unclean until the even."

Cor –1x., n. [A.D. 1388(WB.), trans. < Hb. כר (*kor*) = 'round vessel'] Thus, a **cor** is 'a measure of capacity equaling a 'homer' (see 'Homer') or about 6.25 bushels (dry measure) or 53 gal. (liquid measure) or 200.6 liters'. Eg. Eze.45:14, "Concerning the ordinance of oil, the bath of oil, ye shall offer the tenth part of a bath out of the cor, which is an homer of ten baths; for ten baths are an homer."

Corban – 1x., n. [A.D. 1300*, trans. < Gk. κορβαν (*korban*) trans. < Hb. קרבן (*qorban*) (= 'a gift or offering') < קרב (*qarab*) = 'to come near' or 'to approach' (*Used in a popular poem entitled, 'Cursor Mundi', or 'Runner of the World', which contains almost 30,000 lines and talks about the history of the world.)] Thus, a **corban** is 'a gift given to God by the worshipper'. Eg. Mk.7:11, "But ye say, If a man shall say to his father or mother, It is Corban, that is to say, a gift, by whatsoever thou mightest be profited by me; he shall be free."

Coriander –2x., n. [A.D. 1388(WB.), < OF. *coriandre* (= 'the herb or seed coriander') < L. *coriandrum* < Gk. κοριαννον (*koriannon*), < κορος (*koros*) = 'a bug' (in reference to the disagreeable smell of the leaves) (NOI. The coriander plant grows up to 3 ft. (.9 m.) high, having small and very round seeds. When picked and left to dry, the seeds lose their disagreeable smell and become fragrant. The botanical name of the plant is '*Coriandrum sativum*'.)] Thus, a **coriander** is 'a 3 ft. (.9 m.) high, bright green plant that grows in Egypt, the leaves and seeds (yellowish-brown) of which are used in cooking and medicine'. Eg. Ex.16:31, "And the house of Israel called the name thereof Manna: and it was like coriander seed, white; and the taste of it was like wafers made with honey." (NOI. The OT. Jews were well aware of plant leaves being used as medicine, as seen in Eze.47:12. See also 'Bdellium'.)

Cormorant –4x., n. [A.D. 1320, < OF. *cormaran* < ML. *corvus marinus* = 'a raven, or crow, of the sea' (of the genus *Phalacrocorax*, of which there are about 25 species), a large greedy, food-craving black bird that grows up to 3 ft. (.9 m.) long, feeding on fish and living up to 23 years] Thus, a **cormorant** is 'a large sea-raven'. Eg. Lev.11:17, "And the little owl, and the cormorant, and the great owl."

Corn – 102x., n. [A.D. 700, < oo., but possibly from pre-Gremanic *kurnam* = 'small seed'; akin to OHG. *korn* and L.

granum (= 'grain or seed'); used in reference to all types of grain including wheat, barley, spelt and millet] Thus, **corn** is 'a general term for grain, but especially for wheat'. Eg. Jn.12:24, "Verily, verily, I say unto you, Except a corn of wheat fall into the ground and die, it abideth alone: but if it die, it bringeth forth much fruit."

Cornet – 7x., n. [A.D. 1400, < OF. *cornet* (= 'a little horn') < L. *cornu* = 'a horn' (NOI. The Hb. word שופר (*showphar*) was a wind-instrument made of an animal's horn (which explains why it was called a 'horn'), but is also translated as a 'trumpet' (see 'Trumpet'). The difference between them has to do with function; the cornet for celebration and the trumpet for announcement. For example, the vs. usually says, "sound of the cornet " thereby emphasizing the sound. The 'cornet' made a quieter sound than a trumpet, as is true with the modern cornet and trumpet.)] Thus, a **cornet** is 'a musical wind-instrument, made from an animal's horn and similar to a trumpet, but making a quieter sound, and used more for joy, celebration and worship'. Eg. 1Chr.15:28, "Thus all Israel brought up the ark of the covenant of the LORD with shouting, and with sound of the cornet, and with trumpets, and with cymbals, making a noise with psalteries and harps." (NOI. A 'coronet' (= 'a small crown') is a similar sounding word to a 'cornet', but they are not the same.) {cornets 2x., tot. = 9x.}

Corpse – 1x., n. [A.D. 1315, < ME. **corps** < OF. *corps* (originally spelled *cors*, but was later changed to reflect the L. spelling) < L. *corpus* = 'a body' (NOI. The usage of the 'corpse' appears to be for when a person was killed or martyred (such as in combat) but not killed in a disdainful manner, such as hanging a criminal. Cp. Josh.8:29. See also 'Carcase'.)] Thus, a **corpse** is 'a dead body, human or animal, that was killed'. Eg. Mk.6:29, "And when his disciples heard of it, they came and took up his corpse, and laid it in a tomb." (NOI. They took down Christ's 'body' and not His 'corpse' because He was not killed, as was John the Baptist in the vs. above, but instead, Christ laid down His own life. (See Jn.10:18.) {corpses 4x. tot. = 5x.}

Correct –7x., v. [A.D. 1340, < L. *correctus* (which is pp. of) *corrigere*, *con* = 'together or with' having intensity (see L. prefix '*co–*') + *regere* = 'to straighten or set right' (< *re* = 'back' (see L. prefix '*re–*'[1]) + *gere* = 'to carry'; i.e. 'to put something back where it ought to be'), as in 'to manage' (NOI. Our E. words 'rule' and 'regulate' come from the L. *regere*.)] Thus, **correct** means 'the definite action of managing by putting things back in their correct and proper place'. Eg. Pr.29:17, "Correct thy son, and he shall give thee rest; yea, he shall give delight unto thy soul." {corrected 2x., correcteth 2x,. correction 12x., tot. = 23x.}

Corrupt[1] –21x., adj. [A.D. 1325, < LL. *corruptibilis* = 'that which may be destroyed or made putrid' (see 'Corrupt'[2])] Thus, **corrupt** modifies its n. as 'being completely destroyed from its state of purity'. Eg. Ps.38:5, "My wounds stink and are corrupt because of my foolishness." {corrupted (pp.) 14x., corrupters (prp.) 2x., corruptible 7x., tot. = 44x.}

Corrupt[2] –12x., v. [A.D. 1300, < L. *corruptus* (which is pp. of) *corrumpere* (= 'to cause total destruction or putrification'), *con* = 'together or with' having intensity (see L. prefix '*co–*') + *rumpere* = 'to break or destroy' (NOI. *Rumpere* is an interesting L. root word, found also in such E. words as 'rupture' (= 'to burst') and 'abrupt' (= 'to break off').)] Thus, **corrupt** means 'the action of completely destroying from a state of purity'. Eg. Mt.6:19, "Lay not up for yourselves treasures upon earth, where moth and rust doth corrupt, and where thieves break through and steal." {corrupteth 1x., corrupting (vbl.n.) 1x., corruptly (adv.) 2x., tot. = 16x}

Corruption –21x., n. [A.D. 1340(HP.), < OF. *corruption* < L.

corruptionem = 'diseased, putrid or depraved' (see also 'Corrupt' and E. suffix '–tion')] Thus, a **corruption** is 'a state or condition of being completely destroyed from a former state of purity'. Eg. Ps.16:10, "For thou wilt not leave my soul in hell; neither wilt thou suffer thine Holy One to see corruption." {corrupt 33x., corrupted 14x., corrupters 2x., corrupteth 1x., corruptible 7x.,corrupting 1x., corruptly 2x., tot. = 81x.}

Cottage – 2x., n. [A.D. 1386, < ME. **cotage** < ML. *cotagium* < *cota* = 'a small hut or humble dwelling place' (NOI. The E. 'cotter' describes a man who lives in a cottage and farms a small piece of land.)] Thus, a **cottage** is 'a small, humble little dwelling or shelter, used by poor laborers, which could be easily dismantled and taken down'. Eg. Isa.1:8, "And the daughter of Zion is left as a cottage in a vineyard, as a lodge in a garden of cucumbers, as a besieged city." {cottages 1x., tot. = 2x.}

Couch[1] – 6x., n. [A.D. 1340, < OF. *couche* (= 'a bed') < *coucher* (see 'Couch'[2])] Thus, a **couch** is 'a type of bed on which a person lies down for rest'. Eg. Gen.49:4, "Unstable as water, thou shalt not excel; because thou wentest up to thy father's bed; then defiledst thou it: he went up to my couch." (NOI. Typically, a 'couch' was a place of rest and a bed was a place of sleep. See also 'Bed'.)

Couch[2] – 1x., v. [A.D. 1330, < OF. *coucher* < L. *collocare* = 'to lay in place'] Thus, **couch** means 'the action of lying down in a horizontal position'. Eg. Job.38:40, "When they couch in their dens, and abide in the covert to lie in wait? " {couched 2x., coucheth 1x., couching 1x., tot. = 5x.}

Couchingplace – 1x., n. [A.D. 1611(HB.), < E. **couching** = 'the action of lying down' (< '*couch*' (see 'Couch'[2]) + **place** = 'open space or area'] Thus, a **couchingplace** is 'an area where animals lie down together'. Eg. Eze.25:5, "And I will make Rabbah a stable for camels, and the Ammonites a couching-place for flocks: and ye shall know that I am the LORD." (NOI. This word was used as two separate words in the 1611, however the meaning is exactly the same.)

Coulter – 1x., n. [A.D. 1000, < OE. **culter** < L. *culter* = 'a knife, pruner, edge or spear point' (NOI. The 'coulter' was a sharp knife attached to a plow-beam, and used to make the first cut in the ground before the plowshare slices it open. See also 'Plowshares' and 'Share'.)] Thus, a **coulter** is 'a sharp knife or blade, attached in front of a plowshare, to make the initial vertical cut in the ground'. Eg. 1Sam.13:20, "But all the Israelites went down to the Philistines, to sharpen every man his share, and his coulter, and his axe, and his mattock." {coulters 1x., tot. = 2x.}

Council –23x., n. [A.D. 1125, < OF. *concile* < L. *concilium* (= 'an assembly or union'), *con* = 'together or with' (see L. prefix '*co–*') + *calare* = 'to call or summon' (NOI. The most famous 'council' in the Bible was the Sanhedrin, the great council at Jerusalem, consisting of seventy one members (quite possibly because there were 70 elders with Moses – see Num.11:24-25; the 'Mishneh' was the first document to record that there were 71 members (see 'College' for more on the Mishneh.)). The NT. Gk. word for 'council' is συνεδριον (*sunedrion*) and originally meant 'a place of those who sit together', then later 'council' or 'governing body'. There were other Sanhedrin-type councils in other cities, and it was to these, no doubt, that Christ referred to in Mt.10:17.)] Thus, a **council** is 'an assembled group of people for the purpose of discussion, debate and decision'. Eg. Mk.15:1, "And straightway in the morning the chief priests held a consultation with the elders and scribes and the whole council, and bound Jesus, and carried him away, and delivered him to Pilate." {councils 2x., tot. = 25x.}

Counsel[1] – 139x., n. [A.D. 1225, < ME. **conseil** < OF. *conseil* < L. *consilium* (= 'advice or a plan that is decided upon after careful thought and discussion') (see also 'Consult')] Thus, a **counsel** is 'a plan or advice that has been carefully thought through and formulated in order to maximize benefits'. Eg. Pr.8:14, "Counsel is mine, and sound wisdom: I am understanding; I have strength." {counsellor 14x., counsellors 21x., counsels 12x. tot. = 186x.}

Counsel[2] – 4x., v. [A.D. 1290, < ME. **conseiller** < OF. *conseiller* < L. *consiliari* (= 'to give advice'), < *consulere* (= 'to gather for deliberation'), *con* = 'together or with' having intensity (see L. prefix '*co–*') + *censere* (= 'to give an opinion') (see also 'Counsel'[1])] Thus, **counsel** means 'the action of giving carefully thought-through advice'. Eg. Rev.3:18 ,"I counsel thee to buy of me gold tried in the fire, that thou mayest be rich; and white raiment, that thou mayest be clothed..." {counselled 4x. tot. = 8x.}

Countenance –53x., n. [A.D. 1290, < OF. *contenance* (= 'look, visage or behavior') < ML. *continentia* (= 'restraint', as in 'the way in which one restrains oneself', as shown or seen in one's face) < *continere* (= 'to hold together'), *con* = 'together or with' having intensity (see L. prefix '*co–*') + *tenere* = 'to hold' (see also 'Incontinent')] Thus, a **countenance** is 'a holding-together of the face, that expresses an attitude or state of mind'. Eg. Neh.2:2 ,"Wherefore the king said unto me, Why is thy countenance sad, seeing thou art not sick? this is nothing else but sorrow of heart. Then I was very sore afraid." {countenances 2x., tot. = 55x.}

Countervail –1x., v. [A.D. 1330, < ME. **contrevailen** < OF. *contrevaloir*, < L. *contra* (= 'against') *valere* (= 'to be strong' or 'to be worthy')] Thus, **countervail** means 'the action of being strong against an opponent, or being equal to the challenge'. Eg. Est.7:4, "For we are sold, I and my people, to be destroyed, to be slain, and to perish. But if we had been sold for bondmen and bondwomen, I had held my tongue, although the enemy could not countervail the king's damage."

Country —179x., adj. and n. [A.D. 1275, < ME. **contree** < OF. *contree* < ML. *contrata*, (= lit., 'that which lies opposite, or in front of one', as in 'a tract of land, of undefined extent, stretching out before one's view') < *contra* = 'against'] Thus, as an adj., **country** modifies its n. (in this case, 'villages') as 'being part of, or belonging to, a certain geographical tract of land'. Eg. 1Sam.6:18, "And the golden mice, according to the number of all the cities of the Philistines belonging to the five lords, both of fenced cities, and of country villages, even unto the great stone of Abel..." Furthermore, as a n., a **country** is 'a specific geographical tract of land, having a name, people, a language (s), customs, etc.'. Eg. Gen.24:4, "But thou shalt go unto my country, and to my kindred, and take a wife unto my son Isaac." (See also 'Nation') {countries 55x., countrymen 2x., tot. = 236x.}

Courage —20x., n. [A.D. 1300, < ME. **corage** < OF. *corage* < VL. *coraticum*, *cor* = 'heart', as in 'the seat of feelings, firmly fixed'] Thus, **courage** is lit. 'heart', but refers to 'a quality of mind and emotion that enables one to face danger and difficulties without fear or running away'. Eg. Act.28:15, "And from thence, when the brethren heard of us, they came to meet us as far as Appii forum, and The three taverns: whom when Paul saw, he thanked God, and took courage." (NOI. It seems that 'courage' comes when an individual understands that he/she is acting under the authority and assurance of a higher power and authority, such as God. Consider Pr.28:1.) {courageous 5x., courageously 1x., tot. = 26x.}

Cousin —1x., n. [A.D. 1290, < OF. *cosin* < L. *consobrinus*, *con* = 'together or with' (see L. prefix '*co*–') + *sobrinus* = 'mother's sister's child' (< *soror* = 'sister') (NOI. The term 'cousin' was often used to mean more than just the child of one's aunt or uncle. It was also used in reference to a distant relative. Tyndale translated Rom.15:7 as, "Salute Andronicus and Junia, my cousins".)] Thus, a **cousin** is 'a relative, either distant or close, in relation to one's immediate family'. Eg. Lk.1:36, "And, behold, thy cousin Elisabeth, she hath also conceived a son in her old age: and this is the sixth month with her, who was called barren." {cousins 1x., tot. = 2x.}

Covenant –292x., n. [A.D. 1297, < OF. *covenant* < L. *convenire* (= 'to come together in agreement'), *con* = 'together or with' (see L. prefix '*co–*') + *venire* = 'to come' (NOI. A 'covenant', in the Bible, seems to have been a 'religious agreement', involving the presence of God and His purposes; whereas a simple 'agreement' tended to leave off the religious aspect. See 'Agreement'.)] Thus, a **covenant** is usually 'a religious agreement involving God, and/or His ways, and His people to do, or not do, certain things'. Eg. Jer.34:13, "Thus saith the LORD, the God of Israel; I made a covenant with your fathers in the day that I brought them forth out of the land of Egypt..." {covenanted 4x., covenants 3x., tot. = 299x.}

Covert –9x., n. [A.D. 1303, < OF. *covert* (= 'a concealed or sheltered place') < *covrir* = 'to cover'] Thus, a **covert** is 'a place of concealment or strategic hiding'. Eg. Job.38:40, "When they couch in their dens, and abide in the covert to lie in wait?"

Covet –8x., v. [A.D. 1225, < OF. *coveiter* < L. *cupere* = 'to desire' (possibly < Sans. *kup* = 'to become excited') (NOI. The object of one's coveting is within reach, whereas the object of one's 'desire' may be out of reach. See 'Desire'.)] Thus, **covet** means 'the action of eagerly wanting something within one's reach'. Eg. Ex.20:17, "Thou shalt not covet thy neighbour's house, thou shalt not covet thy neighbour's wife, nor his manservant, nor his maidservant, nor his ox, nor his ass, nor any thing that is thy neighbour's." (NOI. 'Covet', as an E. word, does not appear to be strictly negative. For example, a common expression is, "I covet your prayers". No one would think evil of 'covet' in this context. 'Covet' was commonly used in other ME. writings (Shakespeare included) to convey the simple idea of 'an eager longing after'. The 1611 used 'covet' in 1Cor.12:31 and 14:39 in regards to "the best gifts" and "prophecy". Now, while it can be argued that the Gk. word Paul used here, ζηλοω (*zeloo*), can also be used in a negative sense (i.e. Paul is condemning or mocking the Corinthian believers in their hot pursuit after the gifts, rather than encouraging them), yet the predominant usage of ζηλοω in the NT. is more a positive, ethical 'striving after'. One must still consider why the 1611 translators chose the word 'covet' for 1Cor.12:31 and 14:39, and why they did not frame it in a clearly negative sense, as they did for the other 6 usages of the word, and the other 33 variant uses of the word.) {coveted 3x., coveteth 2x., covetous 9x., covetousness 19x., tot. = 41x.}

Covetous –9x., adj. [A.D. 1300, < OF. *coveitos* = 'being full of covet' (same as E. **covet** (see 'Covet')) + **ous** = forms the adj. and indicates 'a state of abounding in, or overflowing in' (see E. suffix '–ous')] Thus, **covetous** modifies its n. as 'being full of, or abounding in an eager longing-after something within its reach'. Eg. Eph.5:5, "For this ye know, that no whoremonger, nor unclean person, nor covetous man, who is an idolater, hath any inheritance in the kingdom of Christ and of God." (NOI. 'Covetous' is always used in a negative sense; i.e. something bad according to God's laws.) {covet 8x., coveted 3x., coveteth 2x., covetousness 19x., tot. = 41x.}

Cow –6x., n. [A.D. 800, < OE. **cu** (same as Du. *koe*) = 'the female of the bovine (ox-like) animals' (the bull or bullock being the male) (See also 'Bull', 'Bullock', 'Cattle', 'Kine' and 'Ox'.)] Thus, a **cow** is 'the female of the bovine animals', used for breeding, dairy products and meat. Eg. Job.21:10, "Their bull gendereth, and faileth not; their cow calveth, and casteth not her calf." (NOI. A cow has 4 stomach compartments (called the rumen, the reticulum, the omasum and the abomasum), which aid in digestion, and it will chew its cud up to 8 hours a day. It has 32 teeth and can drink 30-40 gal. (113-151 liters) of water each day. Cows generally weigh from 850-1,000 lb. (385-453 kilo.), but tend to weigh more when producing high volumes of milk.) {cow's 1x., tot. = 7x.}

Crackling – 1x., vbl.n. [A.D. 1549, < E. (v.) **crackle** = 'to make sudden, sharp little crack-noises' + **ing** = forms the vbl.n. (see E. suffix '–ing'[1])] Thus, **crackling** is 'the making of rapid, repeated little cracking-sounds'. Eg. Ecc.7:6, "For as the crackling of thorns under a pot, so is the laughter of the fool: this also is vanity."

Cracknels – 1x., n. pl. [A.D. 1440, < E. **cracknel** (= 'a hard or brittle thin cake or biscuit') + **s** = forms the pl.] Thus, **cracknels** are 'two or more brittle, thin cakes or biscuits'. Eg. 1Ki.14:3, "And take with thee ten loaves, and cracknels, and a cruse of honey, and go to him: he shall tell thee what shall become of the child." (NOI. 'Cracknels' are still made today. One medieval recipe calls for 1 cup (240 mil.) of fine flour, 1 cup (240 mil.) of sugar, 1 tablespoon (15 mil.) of crushed coriander-seed, $^{1}/_{4}$ cup (60 mil.) of butter, 2 eggs yokes, 1 teaspoon (5 mil.) of cream and 1 teaspoon (5 mil.) of white rose-water. This was then kneaded into a soft paste, rolled into very thin cakes on a buttered tray, then given a light brushing of a mixture of 1 teaspoon (5 mil.) of rose-water and 1 egg yoke. They were pricked all over then baked in an oven.)

Craft – 6x., n. [A.D. 888, < OE. **cr ft** = 'skill or ingenuity' (< pre Ger. *kraf* = 'strength or power') (NOI. The sense of 'skill' (perhaps the idea of 'mental strength') seems to be exclusive to E.)] Thus, a **craft** is 'a skill or an ability' (usually with the hands, and in reference to an occupation). Eg. Act.18:3, "And because he was of the same craft, he abode with them, and wrought: for by their occupation they were tentmakers." (Mk.14:1 uses 'craft' with the idea of 'mental skill or ability'.) {craftiness 5x., craftsman 2x., craftsmen 7x., crafty 4x., tot. = 24x.}

Crafty – 4x., adj. [A.D. 893, < E. **craft** (see 'Craft') + **y** = 'having the characteristics of' (see E. suffix '–y'[1]) (NOI. 'Crafty' originally meant someone who was skillful or clever, but it came to mean someone who uses deception in executing an evil plan.)] Thus, **crafty** modifies its n. as 'being skillful in devising and executing underhanded, evil schemes'. Eg. 2Cor.12:16, "But be it so, I did not burden you: nevertheless, being crafty, I caught you with guile." (NOI. Paul, here, is basically repeating what his opponents charged him with – that of secretly profiting off the Corinthian Christians. He goes on to refute the charge. This example is used only to illustrate the concept of 'crafty'.)

Crag –1x., n. [A.D. 1300, < ancient Celt., akin to Gaelic *carr* = 'a rocky shelf' (NOI. Partridge, in his book 'Origins', suggests it may have meant 'to hang suspended'.)] Thus, a **crag** is 'a rough, broken projecting part of a rock'. Eg. Job.39:28, "She dwelleth and abideth on the rock, upon the crag of the rock, and the strong place."

Crane –2x., n. [A.D. 1000, < OE. **cran** (akin to Ger. *kranich*) = 'any of a large group (14 species of the family '*Gruidae*') of wading birds' (NOI. A crane is similar to a stork (see 'Stork') but larger than a heron, having long legs and a long neck, feeding on plants, insects and worms. This is why, in E., we 'crane our necks' when we stretch to see something. The modern mechanical lifting-device, used in construction, is also called a 'crane' because of it resemblance to the long-necked bird.)] Thus, a **crane** is 'a flying-creature similar to a stork or heron'. Eg. Isa.38:14, "Like a crane or a swallow, so did I chatter: I did mourn as a dove: mine eyes fail with looking upward: O LORD, I am oppressed; undertake for me." (NOI. On the ground they emit a bellowing-sound, but during migration, cranes tend to chatter, like as in Isa.38:14.)

Craveth —1x., v. [A.D. 1000, < OE. **crafian** (= 'to ask earnestly' or 'to beg and plead for something') + **eth** = forms the pres. ind. 3rd pers. sing. (see E. suffix '–eth')] Thus, **craveth** means 'the 3rd pers. pres. ind. sing. action of earnestly begging or pleading'. Eg. Pr.16:26, "He that laboureth laboureth for himself; for his mouth craveth it of him." {craved 1x., tot. = 2x.}

Create — 8x., v. [A.D. 1386, < L. *creatus* (which is pp. of) *creare* = 'to bring into being' or 'to produce' (having the idea of 'coming into existence')] Thus, **create** means 'the action of bringing something into being'. Eg. Isa.65:17, "For, behold, I create new heavens and a new earth: and the former shall not be remembered, nor come into mind." (NOI. 'Create' is a word in the Bible ascribed to the abilities of God, who alone can create something out of nothing. Cp. also Eph.3:9 and Rev.4:11.) {created 45x., createth 1x., creation 6x., creator 5x., creature 29x., creatures 12x., tot. = 106x.}

Creature —29x., n. [A.D. 1290, < OF. *creature* < LL. *creatura* (= a general term meaning 'that which is brought into being by a creator') < *creare* (see 'Create')] Thus, a **creature** is 'something that has been made by a creator'. Eg. Gen.1:24, "And God said, Let the earth bring forth the living creature after his kind, cattle, and creeping thing, and beast of the earth after his kind: and it was so." (NOI. In the Bible, a 'creature' is always something made by God. The word is used in reference to all sorts of animals (Gen.9:10) and man (2Cor.5:17), as well as certain spiritual beings (Eze.1:13, 20).) {create 8x., created 45x., createth 1x., creation 6x., creator 5x., creatures 12x.,

tot. = 106x.}

Creditor – 3x., n. [A.D. 1400, < L. *creditor* (= 'a money-lender'), < *credo* = 'I believe, trust' (NOI. The money-lender 'believed' in the honesty of the borrower to repay the money, and so gave him a certain amount of 'credit' (= 'belief or trust') so he could borrow a certain amount of money. From L. *credo* we also get our E. 'creed', which is a statement of belief, as in the 'Apostles' Creed' (said to have originated in the 1st c. by the Apostles, the first word being *credo*) that begins by saying, "*I believe in God, the Father Almighty, Creator of heaven and earth...*")] Thus, a **creditor** is 'a person who is owed money by a borrower, with whom belief or trust has been established'. Eg. Lk.7:41, "There was a certain creditor which had two debtors: the one owed five hundred pence, and the other fifty." (NOI. It is the opinion of the author that God is always man's first Creditor.) {creditors 1x., tot. = 4x.}

Creep – 7x., v. [A.D. 888, < ME. **crepen** < OE. **creopan** = 'to crawl along, close to the ground'] Thus, **creep** means 'the action of crawling along close to the ground' (sometimes used for secrecy, as in Ps.104:20 and 2Tim.3:6). Eg. Lev.11:29, "These also shall be unclean unto you among the creeping things that creep upon the earth; the weasel, and the mouse, and the tortoise after his kind." {creepeth 14x., creeping 29x., crept 1x., tot. = 51x.}

Crew – 5x., v. pret. [A.D. 1388(WB.), < E. (v) **crow** (see 'Crow')] Thus, **crew** means 'the past-tense action of the cry of a rooster' (see 'Cock'). Eg. Mk.14:72, "And the second time the cock crew. And Peter called to mind the word that Jesus said unto him, Before the cock crow twice, thou shalt deny me thrice. And when he thought thereon, he wept." {crow 7x., tot. = 12x.}

Crib – 3x., n. [A.D. 1000, < OE. **cribbe** < oo., but possibly < Ger. *krebe* = 'a basket' (NOI. Though a 'crib' can refer to 'a barrel-like feeding-trough for farm animals', it was widely used to mean the stall or little building in which they would live. Even today, we speak of putting a baby or young child in a 'crib'. A 'manger', on the other hand, referred only to a small box into which was put animal food. See also 'Manger'.)] Thus, a **crib** is 'a place for farm animals to live in'. Eg. Pr.14:4, "Where no oxen are, the crib is clean: but much increase is by the strength of the ox."

Crimson –5x., n. [A.D. 1400, < ME. **cremesyn** < It. *cremesino* < Ar. *qirmizi* < *qirmiz* (an insect, spelled in E. 'kermes') (NOI. The 'kermes insect' is about the size of a pea, and is found on oak trees near the Mediterranean Sea. The female insect is harvested by hand, and when dried out in the sun, is then crushed to obtain the deep red dye in its body. Our E. 'carmine' also comes from the Ar. *qirmizi*, and means 'deep red'.)] Thus, **crimson** is 'a very deep red color'. Eg. Isa.1:18, "Come now, and let us reason together, saith the LORD: though your sins be as scarlet, they shall be as white as snow; though they be red like crimson, they shall be as wool."

Cripple – 1x., n. [A.D. 950(LfG.), < OE. **crypel** (akin to OE. **creopan**), i.e. 'someone who must grope or crawl along' (see 'Creep')] Thus, a **cripple** is 'a person who cannot use one or more of his limbs, and must crawl or grope'. Eg. Act.14:8, "And there sat a certain man at Lystra, impotent in his feet, being a cripple from his mother's womb, who never had walked."

Crisping (pins)– 1x., vbl.n. [A.D. 1400, < OE. **crisp** (< L. *crispus* = 'curled' or 'crimped') + **ing** = forms the vbl.n. (NOI. Some suggest the KJV ought to read 'hand bags' instead of 'crisping pins', because of the Hb. word חריט (*chariyt* = 'cut out' or 'a hollow' < חרט (*cheret*) = 'an engraving tool' or 'a stylus'), which is translated '**bags**' in 2Ki.5:23, but the translators may have chosen 'crisping pins' in keeping with v24, "well set hair ". Crisping pins were similar to old-fashioned curling irons, in which a slender round-bar of metal was heated up and the hair was wrapped tightly around it for a short period of time, thus making curls in the hair. Theodore Child, in his book 'Wimples and Crisping Pins', pg. 22, comments on the passage of Isa.3, "*From this enumeration of objects we see that the Jewesses frizzled their hair in front and let it hang down the back in long tresses interwoven with ribbons, or else they curled their hair and let it fall ringlets, with a diadem to keep the forehead free, or a fillet inlaid with jewels, or a net-work of gold, similar to the coiffure of sequins won by the Jewesses of the East at the present day.*")] Thus, **crisping** means 'the state or condition of curling or crimping' (done to long hair, so as to form a fashionable design). Eg. Isa.3:22, "The changeable suits of apparel, and the mantles, and the wimples, and the crisping pins." (NOI. The term 'crisping pins' is still used today. The Mt. Carmel Training Center (a type of religious academy north of Waco Texas) publishes its dress code and forbids the use of 'crisping-pins' (http://www.shepherds-rod-message.org/misctracts/mtc.html). However, the Bible does not condemn the use of crisping pins, or curling irons, but rather condemns the overindulgence of outward adorning, which takes ones eyes off God and onto the things of this world. The Bible does indicate the use of modesty and balance in ones adornment (1Tim.2:9). See also 'Plaiting'.)

Crookbackt –1x., adj. [A.D. 1494, < E. **crookback** = 'an abnormality of the spinal column resulting in a twisted back or having a hunchbacked appearance' + **t** = forms the adj. (see E. suffix '–ed'[5])] Thus, **crookbackt** modifies its n. (in this case, 'man' in vs. 19) as 'having a twisted back or a hunchback'. Eg. Lev.21:20, "Or crookbackt, or a dwarf, or that hath a blemish in his eye, or be scurvy, or scabbed, or hath his stones broken." (NOI. We might wonder at these physical standards for the OT. priesthood, yet we must remember that God is the 'Employer' and He is the one who set the standard. God also set up other standards for the NT. pastor and deacon that we must also abide by. See 1Tim.3:1-12.)

Crop –2x., n. and v. [A.D. 700 (as a n.) and A.D. 1225 (as a v.), < OE. **cropp** = 'the top of a plant' and also 'a bird's craw' (possibly because it was at the top of the bird) (NOI. In the Bible, 'crop', as a n., does not refer to the harvest of a farmer, but to the 'food-pouch' of a bird. The Hb. word is מֻרְאָה (*mur'ah*) and means 'a craw' or 'food-pouch in the neck', which, in the case of a sacrificial bird, was removed and discarded. This pouch allowed for partial digestion before the bird swallowed the food down to its stomach. As a v., the Hb. word is קָטַף (*qataph*) which means 'to cut off' and this is where the v. goes back to one of the meanings of the n., 'the top of a plant'. Because plants were harvested by cutting their tops off, this gave birth to the meaning of the v.)] Thus, as a n., a **crop** is 'a receptacle for food (also called a 'craw' or a 'pouch') in the neck of a turtledove or a young pigeon'. Eg. Lev.1:16, "And he shall pluck away his crop with his feathers, and cast it beside the altar on the east part, by the place of the ashes." Furthermore, as a v., **crop** means 'the action of cutting the top off'. Eg. Eze.17:22, "Thus saith the Lord GOD; I will also take of the highest branch of the high cedar, and will set it; I will crop off from the top of his young twigs a tender one, and will plant it upon an high mountain and eminent." {cropped (spelled 'cropt' in the 1611, probably shortened in order to balance a line of text) 1x., tot. = 3x.}

Cross –28x., n. [A.D. 963, < OE. **cros** < OIr. *cros*, possibly a shortened form of L. *crux immissa* (= 'a cross with an insertion, or crossbar', i.e. 'a wooden instrument upon which criminals were hung and executed, having the form of the letter 't' ') also known as the 'Latin cross' (NOI. Early Christian tradition affirms Christ died on a Latin cross (eg. Justin Martyr in 'Dialogue with Trypho', chapter 91; and Irenaeus in his book, 'Against Heresies', book 2, chapter 24, paragraph 4). Of the various types of crosses 2,000 years ago, only the Latin cross would allow room for the inscription above the head of Jesus (Mt.27:37). The OE. **cros** was firmly fixed in people's minds to mean 'a heavy, upright beam of wood, to which another smaller beam was fastened, transverse-wise like a crossbar, forming the letter 't', upon which condemned criminals were nailed or fastened'. The Gk. word is σταυρος (*stauros*) (= 'a stake') which comes from the Gk. v. ιστημι (*histemi*) = 'to stand upright', and originally meant an upright beam in the ground. However, the NT. Gk. writers used the word to represent the Roman practice of cross-building. The Romans used two beams when making a cross (an upright and a crossbar) and often forced the condemned criminal to carry the crossbar, as in the case of Jesus, Jn.19:17. See also 'Crucify'.)] Thus, a **cross** was 'an upright, heavy beam, having a crossbar transversing near the top, upon which condemned (non-Roman citizen) criminals were executed'. Eg. Mt.27:40, "And saying, Thou that destroyest the temple, and buildest it in three days, save thyself. If thou be the Son of God, come down from the cross." (NOI. Jesus used the word 'cross' figuratively to symbolize a living-death, as in 'ceasing to live for one's self ' (Mt.10:38; 16:24). Paul amplified this in Gal.2:20.)

Crossway —1x., n. [A.D. 1450, < E. (adj.) **cross** (= 'the formation made when two lines meet and cross-over each other') + **way** (= 'a road or path')] Thus, a **crossway** is 'the place where two or more roads intersect and cross-over each other'. Eg. Oba.1:14, "Neither shouldest thou have stood in the crossway, to cut off those of his that did escape; neither shouldest thou have delivered up those of his that did remain in the day of distress."

Crow —7x., v. [A.D. 1000(ASG.), < OE. **crawian** = 'to make a loud noise like a cock (rooster)'] Thus, **crow** means 'the action of a rooster making its characteristic cry' (see 'Cock'). Eg. Mk.14:30, "And Jesus saith unto him, Verily I say unto thee, That this day, even in this night, before the cock crow twice, thou shalt deny me thrice." {crew 5x., tot = 12x.}

Crown –66x., n. [A.D. 950(LfG.), < ME. **croun** < AF. *coroune* < OF. *curune* < L. *corona* = 'a garland, wreath or curved ornament that sits on top' (NOI. There are 5 Hb. words all translated 'crown' in the OT. These include: קדקד (*qodqod*) = 'the top, or crown, of the head'; זר (*zer*) = 'a top border moulding, or crown'; נזר (*nezer*) = 'a head ornament, or crown, signifying consecration'; עטרה (*atarah*) = 'an ornament of beauty, or crown or wreath, that encompasses the head'; and כתר (*kether*) = 'a royal crown'. The NT. Gk. has only one word, στεφανος (*stephanos*) = 'a head ornament signifying royalty or a wreath signifying a victor of an Olympic game'. The Roman soldiers made for Jesus a crown (στεφανος) of thorns, showing their scorn and mockery of Him being a 'king'.)] Thus, a **crown** is 'a curved ornament that sits on top of a person's head (signifying royalty, victory, beauty or consecration), or on top of an object (such as the altar of incense) giving it beauty'. Eg. Rev.14:14, "And I looked, and behold a white cloud, and upon the cloud one sat like unto the Son of man, having on his head a golden crown, and in his hand a sharp sickle." (NOI. 'Crown' is also used figuratively as in Isa.28:1, and spiritually as in 2Tim.4:8. Interestingly, as there are Hb. words in the OT. translated 'crown', so there are 5 'crowns' to be won in the NT. These can be found in 1Cor.9:25; 1Ths.2:19; 2Tim.4:8; Jam.1:12; and 1Pt.5:4.) {crowned 6x., crownedst 1x., crownest 1x., crowneth 1x., crowning 1x., crowns 9x., tot. = 85x.}

Crucify – 16x., n. [A.D. 1300, < OF. *crucifier* < LL. *crucificare* < L. *crucifigere* = 'to execute a person by nailing or attaching him to a cross', although there was much more action involved (NOI. The Romans perfected this ghastly method of execution after they borrowed the idea from the Phoenicians at Carthage (B.C. 146–122?), but crucifixion may have originated under the Persian Empire, and from there been brought to Carthage. A condemned Roman citizen would never be crucified (except in rare circumstance) as seen in Paul's beheading, yet Peter (not a Roman citizen) was crucified, as goes tradition. According to Josephus, Roman crucifixion was a common sight (Antiquities of the Jews 17.10.10; 20.5.2). Usually, the condemned was first flogged with a leather whip, having pieces of metal or bone attached to the ends. This flogging (known as 'the intermediate death') ripped much flesh off the body, soaking the condemned in his own blood, after which he was forced to carry the crossbar of his own cross to his execution site. Upon arrival, he was stripped naked and nailed (or nailed and tied) to the assembled cross, which was hoisted upright with ropes and secured in a hole in the ground. Death was agonizingly slow in coming, sometimes taking several days. Crucifixion was so awful, that the Roman orator Cicero (A.D. 106–43), said, "*Let the very name of the cross be far away not only from the body of a Roman citizen, but even from his thoughts, his eyes, his ears*." In fact, the Romans had a derogatory term they used on unpleasant people, *furcifer* (pronounced '*fir-kif-er*'), which lit. meant, 'a cross-bearer', and was, of course, the punishment reserved for only the worst scoundrels! The OT. pronounces a curse upon someone who was hanged on a tree (Deut.21:20-21) and Gal.3:13 connects this with Christ's crucifixion. Because Jesus quoted Ps.22:1 while on the cross, scholars now view this Psalm as 'Messianic', and, taking note of vs. 16, claim it was a prophecy of His coming crucifixion, given perhaps hundreds of years before the method was even devised by man! See also 'Cross'.)] Thus, **crucify** means 'the action of executing someone by (beating them and) nailing them to a cross till they die'. Eg. Mt.20:19, "And shall deliver him to the Gentiles to mock, and to scourge, and to crucify him: and the third day he shall rise again." (NOI. 'Crucify' is used in a figurative sense in Heb.6:6.) {crucified 37x., tot. = 53x.}

Cruel —19x., adj. and n. [A.D. 1225, < OF. *cruel* < L. *crudelis*

(= 'harsh, hard') < *crudus* = 'raw meat', as in 'still bloody', and was later used to mean 'fierce or grievous' (NOI. We get our E. word 'crude' (= 'raw or rough') from L. *crudus*.)] Thus, as an adj., **cruel** modifies its n. as 'being of a bloody, fierce or raw nature'. Eg. Heb.11:36, "And others had trial of cruel mockings and scourgings, yea, moreover of bonds and imprisonment." Furthermore, as a n., **cruel** is 'something or someone who is harsh or rough in heart and mind, and takes pleasure in inflicting fierce or rough treatment on others'. Eg. Pr.5:9, "Lest thou give thine honour unto others, and thy years unto the cruel." {cruelly 1x., cruelty 5x., tot. = 25x.}

Crumbs —3x., n. pl. [A.D. 975(RG.), < OE. **cruma** = 'a small particle of a bread or a cake that breaks and falls off' + **s** = forms the pl. (NOI. The silent 'b' was added in about A. D. 1500, possibly because of the derivative word 'crumble', and also to match words like 'dumb' and 'thumb'.)] Thus, **crumbs** are 'two or more (usually many) small particles of a bread or cake that break and fall off'. Eg. Mt.15:27, "And she said, Truth, Lord: yet the dogs eat of the crumbs which fall from their masters' table."

Cruse —9x., n. [A.D. 1420, < oo., but possibly from ON. *krus* = 'a pot' (of some sort) (NOI. Many early ME. writers used 'cruse' in reference to a small jar for holding liquids and drinking from them. In the Bible, a cruse was often taken on a journey, so it probably had a narrow neck so it could be easily sealed, similar to our modern canteen.)] Thus, a **cruse** is 'a small waterproof canteen-type of jar used, for holding small amounts of liquid (eg. oil, water or honey), particularly for transport'. Eg. 1Sam.26:12, "So David took the spear and the cruse of water from Saul's bolster; and they gat them away..."

Crush —4x., v. [A.D. 1398, < OF. *croissir* = 'crash, smash, gnash or break'] Thus, **crush** means 'the action of squeezing (with sufficient force) something between two hard surfaces and breaking it into bits'. Eg. Lam.1:15, "The Lord hath trodden under foot all my mighty men in the midst of me: he hath called an assembly against me to crush my young men: the Lord hath trodden the virgin, the daughter of Judah, as in a winepress." {crushed 7x., (spelled 'crusht' by the 1611 in Num.22:25 - probably shortened in order to balance a line of text) tot. = 11x.}

Cry – 181x., n. and v. [A.D. 1225, < OF. *crier* (= 'to howl, shriek, exclaim or complain') < L. *quiritare* = 'to wail and lament loudly' or 'complain excessively' (NOI. In the 13th c., 'cry' came to include the idea of 'weep'. In fact, 'cry' has come to represent many different meanings, including shades of meaning caused by adding adjectives, therefore our definition here must be scaled back to its most basic idea.)] Thus, as a n., a **cry** is 'a loud, emotional outburst' (which can be of words and/or noises, caused by sorrow, guilt, fear or anger; or even the noises made by animals, as in Ps.147:9). Eg. Ex.3:9, "Now therefore, behold, the cry of the children of Israel is come unto me: and I have also seen the oppression wherewith the Egyptians oppress them." Furthermore, as a v., **cry** means 'the action of performing a loud, emotional outburst' (which may be done for reasons of sorrow, guilt, fear or anger; or it may even be the noises made by animals). Eg. Ps.57:2, "I will cry unto God most high; unto God that performeth all things for me." {cried 199x., cries 1x., criest 5x., crieth 17x., crying 31x., tot. = 434x.}

Crystal – 5x., n. [A.D. 1000(ASP.), < OF. *cristal* < L. *crystallum* (= 'ice or crystal rock or crystal dinking cup') < Gk. κρυσταλλος (*krustallos*) = 'to freeze or congeal' (as in 'clear ice')] Thus, **crystal** is 'a rock-like, transparent substance, similar in appearance to that of ice, and having several flat sides'. Eg. Rev.4:6, "And before the throne there was a sea of glass like unto crystal: and in the midst of the throne, and round about the throne, were four beasts full of eyes before and behind." (NOI. Ancient crystals have been found dating back to Nineveh of

3800 B.C. and, while some were used as jewelry, others may have been used as lenses for magnifying objects or starting fires. The ancient Romans carved great blocks of crystal into bowls, goblets and drinking cups. Crystal was often thought to be somehow made from, or in, freezing water, and this was held even up until A.D. 1900 when great advances in crystallography revealed the atomic structure of crystals, which then made advances in many of the other sciences including electronics. Today, crystals are classed into 15 different 'Isometric' (cubic) types and 32 different (though some say 33) 'Non-Isometric' (non-cubic) types.)

Cubit – 45x., n. [A.D. 1325, < L. *cubitum* = 'the elbow' (i.e. 'the distance between the elbow and the end of the middle finger'.) (NOI. The Hb. word אמה (*amah*) and the Gk. word πηχυς (*pechus*) both mean 'the forearm'. There were several different 'cubits' used in Bible days, including the Egyptian 'common cubit', which was based on a measure of 6 handbreadths (i.e. the width of the four fingers of a hand, when tightly pressed together, almost 3 in., or 7.6 cm.) or about 17.72 in. (45 cm.). Archeologists have found royal measuring sticks in ancient tombs, which indicate the Egyptians also had a 'royal cubit', which was 7 handbreadths, making it about 20.67 in. (52.5 cm.). The Babylonians also had a 'common cubit' (about 17.82 in., or 45.26 cm.) and a 'royal cubit' (about 20.8 in., or 52.8 cm.), which was 7 handbreadths. The Hebrew 'common cubit' or 'older cubit' was about 17.5 in. (44.5 cm.). The 'Siloam Inscription' (6 lines of ancient Hebrew script) was discovered in A.D. 1880 by a boy bathing in the waters of the Gihon Spring (located in the Kidron Valley, east of Jerusalem, outside the city wall), which was where one end of Hezekiah's water tunnel was dug (see 2Chr.32:30). The inscription, presumably done by the ancient tunnelers, was chiseled in the rock and said that the tunnel was 1,200 cubits long. Since the tunnel measures 1,750 ft. (533.4 m.), dividing it by 1,200 cubits equals 17.5 in. (44.5 cm.) per cubit. There was also Hebrew 'long cubit', which added an extra handbreadth making about 20.4 in. (51.8 cm.) (see Eze.40:5; 43:13). However, in general reckoning today, we round off the cubit to be about 18 in. (45.7 cm.).)] Thus, a **cubit** was 'the distance from the elbow to the fingertips'. Eg. Deut.3:11, "For only Og king of Bashan remained of the remnant of giants; behold, his bedstead was a bedstead of iron; is it not in Rabbath of the children of Ammon? nine cubits was the length thereof, and four cubits the breadth of it, after the cubit of a man." (NOI. This would have been the 'common cubit', as it was "after the cubit of a man".) {cubits 213x., tot. = 258x.}

Cuckow – 2x., n. [A.D. 1240, < OF. *coucou* < L. *cuculus* (= 'an imitation of the noise made by this bird', especially by the male during mating season) (NOI. There are 4 varieties of the cuckoo (modern spelling) in Israel: the 'Common', the 'Dideric', the 'Great Spotted' (which resembles a small hawk) and the 'Oriental'. The cuckoo bird (modern spelling) is known for its nice 'cooing sounds', but it's a very deceptive animal. The mother cuckoo will deposit her eggs in the nests of sparrows, which, when hatched, are about three times larger than the sparrow chicks. The cuckoo chick will often force the other sparrow chicks from the nest or starve them out. Strangely, the mother sparrow won't recognize the cuckoo chick as a foreigner, even though it may soon grow bigger than herself. She will then exhaust herself trying to feed the cuckoo's enormous appetite.)] Thus, a **cuckow** is 'any bird of the genus *Cuculus* known for its 'coo – cooing' sounds'. Eg. Lev.11:16, "And the owl, and the night hawk, and the cuckow, and the hawk after his kind." (NOI. The cuckoo was not to be eaten as it was considered unclean.)

Cud – 11x., n. [A.D. 1000, < ME. **cude** < OE. **cwidu** < oo., but possibly from Sans. *jatu* = 'resin or gum' (i.e. something 'chewy') (NOI. An A.D. 1720 variation of the word 'cud' was 'quid', which meant 'something held in the mouth for chewing', such as chewing-tobacco.)] Thus, a **cud** is 'a portion of newly-eaten food, brought up, from the first stomach of a ruminating animal, to be chewed on and digested'. Eg. Lev.11:3, "Whatsoever parteth the hoof, and is clovenfooted, and cheweth the cud, among the beasts, that shall ye eat."

Cumbered –1x., pp. [A.D. 1430, < E. (v.) **cumber** (= 'to hinder, trouble or distress', as in 'to mentally and emotionally overthrow') + **ed** = forms the pp. (see E. suffix '–ed'[3])] Thus, **cumbered** modifies its n. (in this case, 'Martha') as 'having been troubled or distressed to the point of mental and emotional overthrow'. Eg. Lk.10:40, "But Martha was cumbered about much serving, and came to him, and said, Lord, dost thou not care that my sister hath left me to serve alone? bid her therefore that she help me."

Cumbereth – 1x., v. [A.D. 1300, < E. (v.) **cumber** (see 'Cumbered') + **eth** = forms the pres. ind. 3rd pers. sing. (see E. suffix '–eth')] Thus, **cumbereth** means 'the pres. ind. 3rd pers. sing. action of causing great trouble and distress'. Eg. Lk.13:7, "Then said he unto the dresser of his vineyard, Behold, these three years I come seeking fruit on this fig tree, and find none: cut it down; why cumbereth it the ground? " (NOI. Here, 'cumbereth' is used in a figure of speech, as if the fig tree were causing trouble for the earth beneath it.)

Cumbrance – 1x., n. [A.D. 1303, < E. (v.) **cumber** (see 'Cumbered') + **ance** = 'the condition or state of being' (see E. suffix '–ance')] Thus, a **cumbrance** is 'something that is so disturbing that it overthrows a person both mentally and emotionally'. Eg. Deut.1:12, "How can I myself alone bear your cumbrance, and your burden, and your strife? "

Cummin –4x., n. [A.D. 897, < L. *cuminum* < Gk. κυμινον (*kuminon*) < Hb. כמן (*kammon*) (NOI. 'Cummin' belongs to the 'parsley family' of plants, and is not found growing in the wilds, but must be cultivated. Winifred Walker ('All the Plants of the Bible', pg.60) describes them saying, "*This little plant, the cummin, rises to 12 in. (30.5 cm.) in height, has finely cut leaves, and dainty pink or white flowers forming umbels (similar to umbrellas) at the tops of very much branched stems*". The seeds contain aromatic oil, used in medicine and as a spice for cooking. The seeds are collected by beating the plant with a rod.)] Thus, **cummin** is 'a parsley-like plant, growing to a height of 12 in. (30.5 cm.), and having aromatic seeds that are used in medicine and cooking'. Eg. Isa.28:27, "For the fitches are not threshed with a threshing instrument, neither is a cart wheel turned about upon the cummin; but the fitches are beaten out with a staff, and the cummin with a rod." (NOI. Apparently, the Jews considered cummin important enough so as to tithe it. See Mt23:23.)

Cunning – 33x., prp. and vbl.n. [A.D. 1325, < ME. **cunnen** < OE. **cunnan** (= 'to know how' or 'to be able') < oo., but probably from Ice. *kunnandi* = 'knowledge' (see E. suffix '–ing'[1, 3])] Thus, as a prp., **cunning** modifies it's n. as 'being able to do because of knowledge'. Eg. Ex.26:31, "And thou shalt make a vail of blue, and purple, and scarlet, and fine twined linen of cunning work: with cherubims shall it be made." Furthermore, as a vbl.n., **cunning** means 'an ability characterized by knowledge and the ability to do'. Eg. Ps.137:5, "If I forget thee, O Jerusalem, let my right hand forget her cunning." {cunningly 1x., tot. = 34x.}

Cupbearer – 1x. n. [A.D. 1483, < E. **cup** (< OE. **cuppe** < ML. *cuppa* (= 'a drinking-vessel') < L. *cupa* = 'a barrel or cask') + **bearer** (< E. **bear** (see 'Bear'[1]) + **er** = identifies a person to their occupation (see E. suffix '–er'))] Thus, a **cupbearer** was 'a person who gave wine or beverages to the king'. Eg. Neh.1:11, "... For I was the king's cupbearer." (NOI. The ancient 'cupbearer' was a trusted individual, hired to help guard the king. He would either himself taste-test the wine for poison, or have a junior member do it.) {cupbearers 2x., tot. = 3x.}

Curdled – 1x., v. pret. [A.D. 1382(WB.), < E. **curdle** (= 'to form into a curd') < (v.) **curd** = 'to make into curd' (< (n.) **curd** = oo. but possibly Celt. *cruth*, and refers to 'cheese formed by the coagulation (= 'to change from a liquid into a thickened mass') of milk' (see also 'Milk')) + **ed** = forms the pret. (see E. suffix '–ed'[1]) (NOI. Cheese was made from the milk of cows, sheep, camels or goats. To this milk was added a souring-agent (such as vinegar), which caused the curdling action, and produced soft cheese. Hard cheese was pressed, dried and aged for several months. Modern, store-bought milk has undergone a process of 'pasteurizing and homogenizing', which changes the chemical composition of the milk and renders it almost useless as far as cheese-making. 'Curdled' was spelled 'cruddled' in the 1611.)] Thus, **curdled** means 'the past-tense action of coagulating milk into cheese'. Eg. Job.10:10, "Hast thou not poured me out as milk, and curdled me like cheese? "

Cure[1] – 1x., n. [A.D. 1300, < OF. *cure* (= 'care, heed, or respect') < L. *cura* = 'care, concern or a medical treatment'] Thus, a **cure** is 'a remedy or a medical treatment'. Eg. Jer 33:6a, "Behold, I will bring it health and cure..." {cures 1x., tot. = 2x.}

Cure[2] –4x., v. [A.D. 1377, < OF. *curer* (= 'to cleanse, purify or purge') < L. *curare* = 'to care for or treat medically'] Thus, **cure** means 'the action of applying a medical treatment for the purpose of restoring health'. Eg. Jer 33:6b, "... and I will cure them, and will reveal unto them the abundance of peace and truth." (See also 'Heal'.) {cured 4x., tot. = 8x.}

Curious –10x., adj. [A.D. 1325, < OF. *curios* (= 'more careful than need be') < L. *curiosus* (= 'careful, diligent or inquisitive') < *cura* (see 'Cure'[1]) (NOI. Something that was made with diligence and carefulness would, no doubt, have also been very expensive. Cp. Act.19:19.)] Thus, **curious** modifies its n. as 'being made with great care and diligence to fine detail and workmanship'. Eg. Ex.28:8, "And the curious girdle of the ephod, which is upon it, shall be of the same, according to the work thereof; even of gold, of blue, and purple, and scarlet, and fine twined linen." {curiously 1x., tot. = 11x.}

Current – 1x., adj. [A.D. 1300, < OF. *courant* (= 'running') < L. *currens* (which is pp. of) *currere* = 'to run' (NOI. With respect to money, it means 'passing from one to another', i.e. 'money that is in circulation'.)] Thus, **current** modifies its n. (in this case, 'money') as 'being that which was in use by the merchant at that time'. Eg. Gen.23:16, "And Abraham hearkened unto Ephron; and Abraham weighed to Ephron the silver, which he had named in the audience of the sons of Heth, four hundred shekels of silver, current money with the merchant."

Curse[1] –47x., inf., and v. [A.D. 1050(?), < OE. **cursian** < **curs** (see 'Curse'[2]) + **ian** (= 'the action of')] Thus, as an inf., a **curse** is 'the open-ended action of invoking destruction upon someone or something'. Eg. Num.23:11, "And Balak said unto Balaam, What hast thou done unto me? I took thee to curse mine enemies, and, behold, thou hast blessed them altogether." Furthermore, as a v., **curse** means 'the action of invoking destruction upon someone or something'. Eg. Gen.12:3, "And I will bless them that bless thee, and curse him that curseth thee: and in thee shall all families of the earth be blessed." {cursed 72x., cursedst 2x., cursest 1x., curseth 10x., tot. = 132x.}

Curse[2] – 54x., n. [A.D. 1050(?), < OE. **curs** < oo., (NOI. A 'curse' is the opposite of a blessing (see 'Bless') and carries the idea of 'invoking or calling down a destruction on someone or something'.)] Thus, a **curse** is 'an utterance which invokes damage or destruction upon someone or something'.

Eg. Act.23:14, "And they came to the chief priests and elders, and said, We have bound ourselves under a great curse, that we will eat nothing until we have slain Paul." (See also 'Evil'.) {accursed (adj.) 20x., curses 8x., cursing 12x., cursings 1x., tot. = 95x.}

Custody –5x., n. [A.D. 1483, < L. *custodia* (= 'guarding or keeping') < *custos* = 'keeper or guardian' (NOI. Our E. word 'custodian' (= 'one who has custody of something') comes from the L. *custodia*.)] Thus, **custody** is 'the state or condition of guarding something that has been entrusted for safe-keeping by an official'. Eg. Num.3:36, "And under the custody and charge of the sons of Merari shall be the boards of the tabernacle, and the bars thereof, and the pillars thereof, and the sockets thereof, and all the vessels thereof, and all that serveth thereto."

Custom –20x., n. [A.D. 1200, < OF. *costume* < L. *consuetude* < *consuescere* (= 'accustom'), *con* = 'together or with' having intensity (see L. prefix '*co–*') + *suescere* = 'become used to' (NOI. '*Consuescere*' had a sense of 'legal-strength or force' attached to it, and may account for why it was used in reference to 'taxes' in A.D. 1325. A 'customer' was originally a 'customs official' before it came to mean 'a buyer' in A.D. 1409.)] Thus, a **custom** is 'something that is done repeatedly and established, and has acquired a sense of legality to it'. Eg. Mt.9:9, "And as Jesus passed forth from thence, he saw a man, named Matthew, sitting at the receipt of custom: and he saith unto him, Follow me. And he arose, and followed him." {accustomed 1x., 7x., tot. = 28x.}

Cymbal –1x., n. [A.D. 825(VP.), < L. *cymbalum* < Gk. κυμβαλον (*kumbalon*) (= 'a cup-shaped metal plate used as a musical instrument') < κυμβη (*kumbe*) = 'a cup or bowl' (NOI. Normally used in pairs (called 'cymbals') they are struck together to make a loud ringing sound, but are sometimes used alone and struck with a stick, thus producing a quieter sound. They were probably originally designed to beat time for the

Levitical choir. Ps.150:5 indicates two kinds of cymbals – louder (larger) and high-sounding (smaller).)] Thus, a **cymbal** is 'a single (probably smaller) concave metal plate, which when struck with a stick, makes a gentle, musical sound'. Eg. 1Cor.13:1, "Though I speak with the tongues of men and of angels, and have not charity, I am become as sounding brass, or a tinkling cymbal." (See also 'Charity' and 'Tinkling'.) {cymbals 16x., tot. = 17x.}

Cypress – 1x., n. [A.D. 1300, < OF. *cipres* < LL. *cypressus* < Gk. κυπαρισσος (*kuparisos*) (NOI. The Hb. word used is תרזה (*tirzah*), perhaps meaning 'hardness'. It is used as a funeral tree throughout the Middle East.)] Thus, a **cypress** is 'a cone-bearing evergreen tree having dense green foliage and hard, fragrant wood'. Eg. Isa.44:14, "He heweth him down cedars, and taketh the cypress and the oak, which he strengtheneth for himself among the trees of the forest: he planteth an ash, and the rain doth nourish it."

D

Dagger —3x., n. [A.D. 1375, < ME. **dag** < oo., but means 'to pierce or stab'] Thus, a **dagger** is 'a short pointed weapon, like a small sword, that was easily concealed and used for stabbing'. Eg. Jud.3:16, "But Ehud made him a dagger which had two edges, of a cubit length; and he did gird it under his raiment upon his right thigh." (NOI. Of all the weapons and warfare mentioned in the Bible, it's amazing the 'dagger' is only mentioned 3x.)

Dagon — 12x., pn. [A.D. 1382(WB.), < L. *Dagon* < Gk. Δαγοων (*Dagon*) < Hb. דגון (*Dagown*), possibly < Hb. דג (*dag*) = 'a fish' (NOI. Since the Middle Ages, 'Dagon', the chief Philistine idol, was represented as a 'sea-monster' having the head, arms and torso of a man and the tail of a fish. Because the Philistines lived mainly by the sea, a 'fish god' seems to make sense. (Excavations at Khorsabad, in Iraq, have discovered an idol having the head and hands of a man, and the body and tail of a fish.) However, other evidence suggests the idol was for grain, or perhaps the weather, and not fish. They claim that evidence found in the Ugarit Tablets (from the city of Ugarit on the Syrian coast, modern day 'Ras Shamra') dating from about 1580 – 1350 B.C., indicate that Dagon was the god of grain and farming (and possibly fertility), and that this same Dagon was brought to Philistia through the trade routes. The Bible gives it a brief description in 1Sam.5:4.)] Thus, **Dagon** is 'a name given to the chief idol of the Philistines, which had a head, hands and a stump or torso'. Eg. 1Sam.5:4, "And when they arose early on the morrow morning, behold, Dagon was fallen upon his face to the ground before the ark of the LORD; and the head of Dagon and both the palms of his hands were cut off upon the threshold; only the stump of Dagon was left to him." {Dagon's 1x., tot. = 13x.}

Dainty —3x., adj. [A.D. 1225, < OF. *daintie* < . L. *dignitas* (= 'worthiness or beauty') < L. *dignus* = 'worthy'] Thus, **dainty** (because it is used to describe food) modifies its n. as 'being delicious and pleasing to the taste'. Pr.23:6, "Eat thou not the bread of him that hath an evil eye, neither desire thou his dainty meats." (See also 'Food') {dainties 3x., tot. = 6x.}

Dale —2x., n. [A.D. 800, < OE. **dǽl** (akin to 'dell') = 'a small low place in the ground' (NOI. 'Dale' is still a very much used word in Britain.)] Thus, a **dale** is 'a small valley'. Eg. Gen.14:17, "And the king of Sodom went out to meet him after his return from the slaughter of Chedorlaomer, and of the kings that were with him, at the valley of Shaveh, which is the king's dale." (NOI. Both occurrences of 'dale' are in reference to the same place, near to Salem (or Jerusalem); and the 'king' here would be 'Melchizedek'. It appears the valley was renamed to be a 'dale' of the king, and since great kings owned vast estates, this valley of Shaveh would now be just a 'dale' in the great king's holdings. Some have identified it with the 'Valley of Kidron' just to the east of Jerusalem, which has great significance to Christ, of whom Melchizedek is a picture.)

Dam —5x., n. [A.D. 1297, < E. **dame** = 'a female mother of animals'] Thus, a **dam** is 'a female mother of animals' (such as a mother ox, bullock, sheep, goat or bird). Eg. Deut.22:6, "If a bird's nest chance to be before thee in the way in any tree, or on the ground, whether they be young ones, or eggs, and the dam sitting upon the young, or upon the eggs, thou shalt not take the dam with the young."

Damnation – 11x., n. [A.D.1300, < ME. **damn** (< OF. *damner* < L. *damnare* (of which the pp. is) *damnatus* = 'to condemn' or 'to doom' < L. *damnum* = 'harm, loss, penalty or damage' (NOI. Our E. 'damage' comes from L. *damnum/*)) + **ation** = 'an action, process or state' (see E. suffix '–tion') (See also 'Endamage'.)] Thus, **damnation** is 'the process or condition of damage and punishment'. Eg. Jn.5:29, "And shall come forth; they that have done good, unto the resurrection of life; and they that have done evil, unto the resurrection of damnation." Here we learn that the future state of evildoers shall be a condition of damage and punishment. {damnable 1x., damned 3x., tot. = 15x.}

Damsel – 40x., n. [A.D. 1199, < ME. **dameisele** < OF. *dameisele* < ML. *domnicella* < L. *domina* = 'young lady' (NOI. Originally, the ME. **dameisele** referred to 'an unmarried young lady of noble birth', but since the 1300's, it came to mean any young girl of marriageable age.)] Thus, a **damsel** is 'a young girl of marriageable age'. Eg. Gen.24:16, "And the damsel was very fair to look upon, a virgin, neither had any man known her..." (NOI. Some references indicate that a newly-wed young girl was still referred to as a damsel (Eg. Deut.22:16). Mk.5:42 indicates a damsel was at least 12 years of age, and both Gen.24:61 and 1Sam.25:42 make reference to damsels as young servant-type girls.) {damsel's 8x., damsels 3x., tot. = 51x.}

Dance – 8x., n. and v. [A.D. 1300, < OF. *dance* (v. *dancer*) < oo., but refers to 'the leaping-skipping and/or shaking or moving of the body limbs rhythmically'] Thus, as a n., a **dance** is 'the act of dancing as a performance'. Eg. Ps.149:3, "Let them praise his name in the dance..." Furthermore, as a v., **dance** means 'the action of leaping or moving the body parts in some type of rhythmical fashion' (usually as an expression of happiness, and often to music). Eg. Job.21:11, "They send forth their little ones like a flock, and their children dance." (Cp.

also 2Sam.6:14-16.) (NOI. Dancing played a part in the religious life of the nation Israel as they expressed their joy to God. With the exception of Ex.32, their dancing would not have been sensual (Eg. Mk.6:22) nor would the men and women have danced together as they do in modern dance clubs.) {danced 6x., dances 6x., dancing 7x., tot. = 27x.}

Dandled –1x., pp. [A.D. 1530, < E. **dandle** (< oo., but similar to It. *dandolare*) = 'to swing or dangle' + **ed** = forms the pp. (see E. suffix '–ed'[3])] Thus, **dandled** modifies its n. (in this case, the pro. 'ye') as 'having been moved lightly up and down' (as a mother would to a child upon her knees). Eg. Isa.66:12, "For thus saith the LORD, Behold, I will extend peace to her like a river, and the glory of the Gentiles like a flowing stream: then shall ye suck, ye shall be borne upon her sides, and be dandled upon her knees."

Danger –7x. n. [A.D. 1225, < OF. *dangier* (= 'peril or hazard') < L. *dominium* = 'lordship' < *dominus* = 'master' or 'lord' (NOI. Two Gk. words in the NT. are both translated 'danger', these being ενοχος (*enochos*) (= 'guilty of' and 'subject to') and κινδυνευω (*kinduneuo*) (= 'to be in jeopardy or peril'). There is a sense of 'cause and effect' here, the person being in danger because of something he has done.)] Thus, **danger** is 'the power of a master to inflict harm on his subject' (due to some action by the subject). Eg. Act.19:40, "For we are in danger to be called in question for this day's uproar, there being no cause whereby we may give an account of this concourse." {dangerous 1x., tot. = 8x.}

Dare –5x., v. [A.D. 888, < OE. **durran** = 'to show bravery in taking on a venture or in the face of danger'] Thus, **dare** means 'the action of bold courage to take on a venture or something dangerous'. Eg. Rom.5:7, "For scarcely for a righteous man will one die: yet peradventure for a good man some would even dare to die." {durst 9x., tot. = 14x.}

Dart –3x., n. [A.D. 1314, < OF. *dart* < oo., (however, it describes a pointed missile-type of weapon designed to pierce its target. It is thrown by hand or projected from some implement such as a bow. Some darts were first dipped in a flammable substance and ignited on fire before hurling them at the enemy.)] Thus, a **dart** is 'a weapon (such as an arrow or a javelin) designed to pierce or kill its targeted object'. Eg. Heb.12:20, "For they could not endure that which was commanded, And if so much as a beast touch the mountain, it shall be stoned, or thrust through with a dart." {darts 4x., tot. = 7x.}

Dash –7x., v. [A.D. 1290, < ME. **daschen** < oo., but probably an imitation of a smashing or crashing sound (NOI. Another early sense of 'dash' had the idea of speed.)] Thus, **dash** means 'the action of striking violently so as to break in pieces'. Eg. Ps.2:9, "Thou shalt break them with a rod of iron; thou shalt dash them in pieces like a potter's vessel." {dashed 5x., dasheth 2x., tot. = 14x.}

Daub – 1x., v. [A.D. 1325, < OF. *dauber* < L. *dealbare*, *de* = 'completely' (see L. prefix '*de–*'[3]) + *albare* = 'to whiten' (i.e. 'whitewash or plaster') < *albus* = 'white'] Thus, **daub** means 'the action of completely plastering something' (as in 'to coat or cover it with plaster'). Eg. Eze.13:11, "Say unto them which daub it with untempered morter, that it shall fall: there shall be an overflowing shower; and ye, O great hailstones, shall fall; and a stormy wind shall rend it." {daubed 7x., daubing 1x., tot. = 9x.}

Daughter –324x. n. [A.D. 1000(ASG.), < OE. **dohtor** (akin to Du. *dochter*, and Ger. *tochter*, and Goth. *daughter*, and Sans. *duhitar*) = 'a female child or descendent in relation to her parents' (NOI. The. Hb. word was בת (*bath*) which was often used in combination with other words to form names, such as בת-שבע (*Bath-Sheba*) meaning 'daughter of abundance'.)] Thus, a **daughter** is 'a female person in relation to her parents', regardless of her age. Eg. Gen.24:24, "And she said unto him, I am the daughter of Bethuel the son of Milcah, which she bare unto Nahor." (NOI. 'Daughter' is sometimes used in a figurative sense, referring to members of a group such as in Lam.4:22, "The punishment of thine iniquity is accomplished, O daughter of Zion..." See also 'Babe', 'Child', 'Lad' and 'Son'.) {daughter's 3x., daughters 254x., tot. = 581x.}

Day —1730x., n. [A.D. 950, < OE. **dǽg** (akin to Du. *dag*, Ger. *tag*, ON. *dagr*) < Sans. *dah* = 'to burn' (in reference to the suns rays)] Thus, **a day** is 'the time between morning and night in which the sun shines'. Eg. Gen.1:5a, "And God called the light Day, and the darkness he called Night...". {daily 63x., day's 9x., days 855x., days' 13x., daytime 7x., midday 3x., noonday 9x., yesterday 9x., tot. = 2698x.}

Daysman — 1x., n. [A.D. 1489, < E. **day** (in the sense of an 'appointed day' as in 'a summons') + **man** (referring to the person who called for and set the appointed day) = 'a person who would act as a mediator between two parties'. (NOI. In A.D. 1573, an E. writer wrote, *"If neighbours were at variance, they ran not straight to law: Daysmen took up the matter, and cost them not a straw."* The Hb. יכח (*yawkach*), in Job.9:33, refers to one who can plead, reason and decide.)] Thus, a **daysman** is 'someone who could help reconcile two opposing parties by acting as a mediator'. Eg. Job.9:33, "Neither is there any daysman betwixt us, that might lay his hand upon us both."

Dayspring — 2x., n. [A.D. 1300, < E. **day** = 'the light of day' (see 'Day') + **spring** = 'to leap forth' (see 'Spring'.)] Thus, a **dayspring** is 'the time when daylight breaks forth'. (cp. Jud.19:25) Eg. Job.38:12, "Hast thou commanded the morning since thy days; and caused the dayspring to know his place." (NOI. This term, 'dayspring' is given almost human qualities in Job and in Lk.1:78, and therefore seems to mean more than just the break of day.)

Deacon –2x., n. [A.D. 900, < OE. **deacon** < LL. *diaconus* < Gk. διακονος (*diakonos*) = 'a servant or table-waiter' (i.e. 'one who fulfills the wishes of those being served')] Thus, a **deacon** 'is one who serves or waits on others'. Eg. 1Tim.3:10, "And let these also first be proved; then let them use the office of a deacon, being found blameless." (NOI. The Gk. διακονεω (*diakoneo*) is usually translated 'to serve' or minister', yet 2x., it is purposely trans. as 'deacon' (see 1Tim.3:10,13). This is because the word 'office' is mentioned, thereby designating the διακονεω (*diakoneo*) as 'a recognized officer of the church' (evidenced by the laying on of the Apostle's hands in Act.6:6), and hence, the special name, 'deacon'. The Gk. διακονος (*diakonos*) is usually translated as a 'minister' (see 'Minister') except in reference to Phoebe, where she is referred to as a 'servant' (Rom.16:1,27), yet 3x., it is purposely trans. as 'deacons' (Phil.1:1; 1Tim.3:8,12). Again, this is because of its contextual connection with the word 'bishop' thereby recognizing 'deacon' as an officer of the church. Deacons were first used to serve the church by distributing food to the needy (Act.6) but, no doubt, their job description later changed a little as each church ordained their own.) {deacons 3x., tot. = 5x.}

Deadly – 7x., adj. [A.D. 893, < OE. **deadlic** < **dead** (< Indo-European root word *dheu* = 'insensible', i.e. 'without the capability of sense-or-perception in this life') (NOI. We understand death to be when the soul leaves the body. See Gen.35:18.) + **ly** = 'having appearance or characteristics of' (see E. suffix '–ly'[1])] Thus, **deadly** modifies its n. as 'being subject to death or causing death'. Eg. Mk.16:18, "They shall take up serpents; and if they drink any deadly thing, it shall not hurt them; they shall lay hands on the sick, and they shall recover." {dead 364x., deadness 1x., death 372x., deaths 4x., die 321x., died 201x., diest 1x., dieth 30x., tot. = 1301x.}

Deaf –15x., adj. [A.D. 825(VP.), < OE. **deaf** (akin to Du. *doof*, ON. *daufr*) < early Teut. *dheubh* = 'to be dull of perception' (NOI. Early E. writings always used the word in connection with the sense of hearing.)] Thus, **deaf** modifies its n. as 'being partially or completely unable to hear'. Eg. Ps.38:13, "But I, as a deaf man, heard not..."

Dearth – 8x., n. [A.D. 1250, < ME. **derthe** < OE. **deore** = 'costly or precious'] Thus, a **dearth** is 'a time when essential commodities, such as food, are scarce and therefore become costly'. Eg. Neh.5:3, "Some also there were that said, We have mortgaged our lands, vineyards, and houses, that we might buy corn, because of the dearth."

Debase –1x., v. [A.D. 1565, < ME. **de** = 'to the bottom' (see E. prefix 'de–'[3]) + **base** = 'low' (see 'Base' adj.)] Thus, **debase** means 'the action of taking or driving something right to the bottom'. Eg. Isa.57:9, "And thou wentest to the king with ointment, and didst increase thy perfumes, and didst send thy messengers far off, and didst debase thyself even unto hell."

Debate – 4x., n. and v. [A.D. 1300, < ME. **de** = 'a putting down' (see E. prefix 'de–'[4]) + **bate** = 'to beat down' (cp. 'Abated') (NOI. As a n. (< OF. *debat*) = 'an argument of strife and contention'. As a v. (< OF. *debatre*) = 'the act of beating down'.)] Thus, as a n., a **debate** is 'an argument of strife and contention taking place'. Eg. Rom.1:29, "Being filled with all unrighteousness, fornication, wickedness, covetousness, maliciousness; full of envy, murder, debate, deceit, malignity; whisperers." Furthermore, as a v., **debate** means 'the action of strife and contention'. Eg. Pr.25:9, "Debate thy cause with thy neighbour himself; and discover not a secret to another." {debates 1x., tot. = 5x.}

Debt – 7x., n. [A.D. 1225, < OF. *dete* < ML. *debita* for L.

debitum = 'something that is owed' (NOI. ME. spelled it as both 'det' and 'debte'. Finally, 'debt' became the official spelling.)] Thus, a **debt** is 'something that is owed to another'. Eg. 2Ki.4:7, "Then she came and told the man of God. And he said, Go, sell the oil, and pay thy debt, and live thou and thy children of the rest." {debtor 4x., debtors 5x., debts 2x., indebted 1x., tot. = 19x.}

Debtor —4x., n. [A.D. 1225, < OF. *detor* < L. *debitor* < *debere* (< *de* = 'away from' (see L. prefix '*de–*'[3]) + *habere* = 'to have') = 'to keep something away from someone, and thereby to owe it'] Thus, a **debtor** is 'someone who is in debt or owes something to another'. Eg. Rom.1:14, "I am debtor both to the Greeks, and to the Barbarians; both to the wise, and to the unwise." {debt 7x., debtors 5x., debts 2x., indebted 1x., tot. = 19x.}

Decay — 1x., n. [A.D. 1460, < OF. *decair* < L. *decadere*, *de* = 'away from' (see L. prefix '*de–*'[3]) + *cadere* = 'to fall'] Thus, a **decay** is 'a state or condition of having fallen away from a state of excellence'. Eg. Lev.25:35, "And if thy brother be waxen poor, and fallen in decay with thee; then thou shalt relieve him: yea, though he be a stranger, or a sojourner; that he may live with thee."

Decease —2x., n. [A.D. 1330, < ME. **deces** < OF. *deces* < L. *decessus* (= 'departure, death') < *decedere* (= 'withdraw, depart or leave') (NOI. 'Decease' appears to have been a more gentle way of referring to death. It is interesting to examine the context of where the words are used, and try to understand the gentleness.)] Thus, a **decease** is 'a withdrawing or departure from life'. Eg. 2Pt.1:15, "Moreover I will endeavour that ye may be able after my decease to have these things always in remembrance." {deceased 2x., tot. = 4x.}

Deceit — 34x., n. [A.D. 1275, < OF. *deceite* < L. *decepta* (which is pp. of) *decipere* (see 'Deceive')] Thus, a **deceit** is 'something that is fraudulent, deceptive or purposely misleading'. Eg. Col.2:8, "Beware lest any man spoil you through philosophy and vain deceit, after the tradition of men, after the rudiments of the world, and not after Christ." {deceitful 21x., deceitfully 11x., deceitfulness 3x., deceits 2x., deceivableness 1x., deceive 27x., deceived 34x., deceiver 5x., deceivers 3x., deceiveth 6x., deceiving 2x., deceivings 1x., tot. = 150x.}

Deceive —27x., v. [A.D. 1300,< OF. *deceveir* < L. *decipere* (= 'to ensnare, trap or catch by guile') < *de* = 'down' (see L. prefix '*de–*'[1]) + *capere* = 'to take'] Thus, **deceive** means 'the action of trapping someone or something by getting them to believe what is false'. Eg. Eph.4:14, "That we henceforth be no more children, tossed to and fro, and carried about with every wind of doctrine, by the sleight of men, and cunning craftiness, whereby they lie in wait to deceive." {deceit 34x., deceitful 21x., deceitfully 11x., deceitfulness 3x., deceits 2x., deceivableness 1x., deceived 34x., deceiver 5x., deceivers 3x., deceiveth 6x., deceiving 2x., deceivings 1x., tot. = 150x.}

Decently —1x., adv. [A.D. 1552, < ME. **decent** = 'fitting or appropriate' (which is an adj. < F. *decent* < L. *decens* (which is prp. of *decere* = 'be fitting')) + **ly** = 'the manner of' (See E. suffix '–y'[1])] Thus, **decently** modifies its v. (in this case, 'done') as 'happening in the manner of decency' (i.e. 'in a manner appropriate to the occasion'). Eg. 1Cor.14:40, "Let all things be done decently and in order."

Decision —2x., n. [A.D. 1490, < L. *decisio* (= 'a cutting down' or 'a settlement') < *decidere*, *de* = 'away from' (see L. prefix '*de–*'[3]) + *caedere* = 'to cut' (NOI. Our E. 'incision' means to 'cut into', while 'decision' means 'to cut away and separate' - i.e. 'to determine or to settle a question'.)] Thus, a **decision** is 'the act of making a choice by cutting'. Eg. Joe.3:14, "Multitudes, multitudes in the valley of decision: for the day of the

LORD is near in the valley of decision." (NOI. A butcher, or a chef, will use a meat-cleaver to 'chop into' a portion of meat and push it to one side. This is a graphic illustration of a 'decision'.) {decided 1x., tot. = 3x.}

Deck – 2x., v. [A.D. 1513, < Du. *dekken* = 'to cover, usually with beautiful clothes'] Thus, **deck** means 'the action of covering with beautiful clothes'. Eg. Job.40:10, "Deck thyself now with majesty and excellency; and array thyself with glory and beauty." {decked 6x., deckedst 2x., deckest 1x., decketh 1x., tot. = 12x.}

Declare – 95x., v. [A.D. 1325, < OF. *declarer* < L. *declarare*, *de* = 'completely' (see L. prefix '*de–*'[3]) + *clarare* (< L. *clarus* = 'clear') = 'to make clear'] Thus, **declare** means 'the action of taking something obscure and make it very clear, plain or obvious'. Eg. Ps.19:1, "The heavens declare the glory of God; and the firmament sheweth his handywork." {declaration 4x., declared 41x., declareth 4x., declaring 4x., tot. = 148x.}

Decline – 5x., v. [A.D. 1325, < OF. *decliner* < L. *declinare*, *de* = 'down' or 'away from' (see L. prefix '*de–*'[1, 3]) + *clinare* = 'to bend'] Thus, **decline** means 'the action of diverting down from or away from something, or turning aside from something'. Eg. Pr.7:25, "Let not thine heart decline to her ways, go not astray in her paths." (See also 'Incline'.) {declined 4x., declineth 2x., tot. = 11x.}

Decree – 25x., n. and v. [A.D. 1303, < OF. *decree* < L. *decretum* < *decernere*, *de* = 'away from' (see L. prefix '*de–*'[3]) + *cernere* = 'to separate' (NOI. This word was used by official governing bodies in reference to their authoritative decisions.)] Thus, as a n., a **decree** is 'an official decision or edict such as a law'. Eg. Lk.2:1, "And it came to pass in those days, that there went out a decree from Caesar Augustus, that all the world should be taxed." Furthermore, as a v., **decree** means 'the action of deciding or pronouncing the official edict'. Eg. Pr.8:15, "By me kings reign, and princes decree justice." {decreed 5x., decrees 3x., tot. = 33x.}

Dedicate – 11x., v. [A.D. 1530, < L. *dedicatus* < L. *dedicare, de* = 'away from' (see L. prefix '*de–*'[3]) + *dicare* = 'to proclaim'] Thus, **dedicate** means 'the action of sending something away by proclamation' (i.e. 'to devote or to set apart', or 'to seriously give something up to a person or a cause'). Eg. 1Chr.26:27, "Out of the spoils won in battles did they dedicate to maintain the house of the LORD." (NOI. Dedicating usually involves 'things' whereas consecrating involves 'people'. (See also Consecration'.)) {dedicated 17x., dedicating 2x., dedication 11x., tot. = 41x.}

Deed – 19x., n. [A.D. 825(VP.), < ME. **dede** < OE. **dǽd** = 'done'] Thus, a **deed** is 'some act that is done, performed or accomplished'. Eg. Act.4:9, "If we this day be examined of the good deed done to the impotent man, by what means he is made whole." (See also 'Indeed'.) {deeds 33x., tot. = 52x.}

Deemed– 1x., pp. [A.D. 1300, < ME. (v.) **deem** (< OE. **deman**) = 'to judge' (i.e. 'an opinion') + **ed** = forms the pp. (see E. suffix '–ed'[3])] Thus, **deemed** modifies its n. (in this case, 'shipmen') as 'having formed an opinion'. Eg. Act.27:27, "But when the fourteenth night was come, as we were driven up and down in Adria, about midnight the shipmen deemed that they drew near to some country."

Defamed– 1x., pp. [A.D. 1474, < ME. **defame** (< OF. *deffamer* < L. *diffamare, dis* = 'asunder' (see L. prefix '*dis–*') + *fama* = 'a report or reputation') = 'to rip apart a reputation' + **ed** = forms the pp. (see E. suffix '–ed'[3])] Thus, **defamed** modifies its n. (in this case, 'we') as 'having had the reputation torn asunder'. Eg. 1Cor.4:13, "Being defamed, we intreat: we are made as the filth of the world, and are the offscouring of all things unto this day."

Defer– 3x., v. [A.D. 1375, < ME. **differre** < OF. *differer* < L. *differre, dis* = 'utterly apart' (see L. prefix '*dis–*') + *ferre* = 'to bear or carry' (NOI. Another E. meaning of 'defer' is 'to yield over', but it has a slightly different root word (< OF. *deferer*) and it is not used in the Bible.)] Thus, **defer** means 'the action of setting something aside' (with negative emotion). Eg. Ecc.5:4, "When thou vowest a vow unto God, defer not to pay it; for he hath no pleasure in fools: pay that which thou hast vowed." {deferred 3x., deferreth 1x., tot. = 7x.}

Defied– 6x., pp. [A.D. 1377, < E. **defy** = 'to renounce faith' (see 'Defy') + **ed** = forms the pp. (see E. suffix '–ed'[3])] Thus, **defied** modifies its n. as 'having renounced faith, trust or confidence in something or someone'. Eg. 1Chr.20:7, "But when he defied Israel, Jonathan the son of Shimea David's brother slew him." {defy 5x., tot. = 11x.}

Defile– 39x., v. [A.D.1325, < OF. *defouler* (*de* = 'down' + *fouler* = 'to trample or tread under foot') = 'to trample under foot and oppress as if in a rage' (NOI. *Defouler* became associated with E. 'foul' (see 'Foul') and so came to mean 'desecrate or pollute'.)] Thus, **defile** means 'the action of angrily polluting by trampling under foot'. Eg. 1Cor.3:17, "If any man defile the temple of God, him shall God destroy; for the temple of God is holy, which temple ye are." {defiled 71x., defiledst 1x., defileth 9x., undefiled 7x., tot. = 127x.}

Defraud – 5x., v. [A.D. 1362, < L. *defraudare, de* = 'away from' (see L. prefix '*de–*'[3]) + *fraudare* = 'to cheat'] Thus, **defraud** means 'the action of taking away by cheating'. Eg. 1Ths.4:6, "That no man go beyond and defraud his brother in any matter: because that the Lord is the avenger of all such, as we also have forewarned you and testified." {defrauded 4x., tot. = 9x.}

Defy – 5x., v. [A.D. 1300, < OF. *defier* < ML. *disfidare*, *dis* = 'utterly apart' (see L. prefix '*dis–*') + *fidare* < *fidis* = 'faith, trust or confidence'] Thus, **defy** means 'the action of renouncing faith, trust or confidence in someone or something'. (NOI. The word was often used as an insult to challenge someone to combat or war.) Eg. 1Sam.17:10, "And the Philistine said, I defy the armies of Israel this day; give me a man, that we may fight together." {defied 6x., tot. = 11x.}

Degree – 7x., n. [A.D. 1230, < OF. *degree* < L. *degradus*, *de* = 'down from' (see L. prefix '*de–*'[1]) + *gradus* = 'a grade or a step'] Thus, literally, a **degree** is 'a step of a stairway, or a rung of a ladder'. (NOI. However, 'degree' is used figuratively in the Bible to represent a person's social or spiritual standing in life.) Eg. Ps.62:9, "Surely men of low degree are vanity, and men of high degree are a lie: to be laid in the balance, they are altogether lighter than vanity." (NOI. The word 'degrees' refer only to the sun dial of Ahaz (Isa.38:8) and 15 of the Psalms (Ps.120-134 titles). The meaning of 'degrees', in relation to the Psalms, remains a topic of debate amongst Bible scholars.) {degrees 24x., tot. = 31x.}

Delay – 3x., n. and v. [A.D. 1275, n. < OF. *delai* (v.) < OF. *delaier*, *de* = 'away' + *laier* = 'leave or let' (both OF. words are oo., but probably < L. *laissier* < *laxare* = 'slacken or undo'.)] Thus, as a n., a **delay**, is 'the act or fact of delaying' (i.e. 'lingering, loitering or procrastination'). Eg. Act.25:17, "Therefore, when they were come hither, without any delay on the morrow I sat on the judgment seat, and commanded the man to be brought forth." Furthermore, as a v., **delay** means 'the action of postponing, or putting off till another time'. Ex.22:29, "Thou shalt not delay to offer the first of thy ripe fruits, and of thy liquors: the firstborn of thy sons shalt thou give unto me." {delayed 2x., delayeth 2x., tot. = 7x.}

Delectable – 1x., adj. [A.D. 1400, < OF. *delectable* < L. *delect-*

abilis < *delectare*, *de* = 'away from' (see L. prefix '*de–*'[3]) + *lacere* = 'to entice' (see also 'Delight') (NOI. Other variations of this word used in early modern E. (but not in the KJV) include, 'delect', 'delectability', 'delectableness', 'delectably', 'delectary' and 'delectation'. Their usage suggests a stronger quality than just delightful; in fact, something extremely alluring.)] Thus, **delectable** modifies its n. (in this case 'things') as 'being something so desirable that it entices people in its direction', similar to alluring bait. (NOI. The Hb. word חמד (*chamad*) (translated 'delectable') is translated elsewhere as 'desire', 'covet', 'delight', 'pleasant', 'beauty' and 'lust'.) Eg. Isa.44:9, "They that make a graven image are all of them vanity; and their delectable things shall not profit; and they are their own witnesses; they see not, nor know; that they may be ashamed." Here, God says that those who use allurements (i.e. "delectable things") – presumably to attract others to their idolatrous ways – shall not profit.

Delicacies – 1x., n. pl. [A.D. 1374, < E. **delicacy** (< **delicate** (< L. *delicatus* = 'something small and luxuriously delightful') = 'something small and luxurious' + **acy** (= 'the quality of being')) = 'something of a luxurious quality' + **ies** = forms the pl.] Thus, **delicacies** are 'two or more small, luxuriously-delightful items'. Eg. Rev.18:3, "For all nations have drunk of the wine of the wrath of her fornication, and the kings of the earth have committed fornication with her, and the merchants of the earth are waxed rich through the abundance of her delicacies." {delicate 5x., delicately 4x., delicateness 1x., delicates 1x., deliciously 2x., tot. = 14x.}

Delicate – 5x., adj. [A.D. 1377, < L. *delicatus* = 'something small and luxuriously delightful' (NOI. Our E. 'delicatessen' comes from this L. word.)] Thus, **delicate** modifies its n. as 'being something small and luxuriously delightful' (i.e. something that only the wealthy can afford). (NOI. The idea of 'gentle', 'frail' or 'sensitive' became associated with 'delicate' in about the 1700's. See also 'Tender') Eg. Jer.6:2, "I have likened the daughter of Zion to a comely and delicate woman." {delicacies 1x., delicately 4x., delicateness 1x., delicates 1x., deliciously 2x., tot. = 14x.}

Delicately – 4x., adv. [A.D. 1377, < E. **delicate** (see 'Delicate') (< L. *delicatus*) = 'something small and luxuriously delightful' (cp. also 'Delicacies') + **ly** = 'in the manner of' (See E. suffix '–y'[1])] Thus, **delicately** modifies its v. as 'being done in a luxuriously-delightful manner'. Eg. Lk.7:25, "But what went ye out for to see? A man clothed in soft raiment? Behold, they which are gorgeously apparelled, and live delicately, are in kings' courts." {delicacies 1x., delicate 5x., delicateness 1x., delicates 1x., deliciously 2x., tot. = 14x.}

Delicates – 1x., n. pl. [A.D. 1374, < E. **delicate** (see 'Delicate') (< L. *delicatus*) = 'something small and luxuriously delightful' + **s** = forms the pl. (NOI. The WB. translates the words of Isa.47:8, "... thou that art given to pleasures," as "thou delicate". Other early E. writers also used 'delicate' to describe people addicted to luxury.)] Thus, **delicates** are 'two or more people who are given over to a life of luxury' (such as kings, princes and nobles). Eg. Jer.51:34, "Nebuchadrezzar the king of Babylon hath devoured me, he hath crushed me, he hath made me an empty vessel, he hath swallowed me up like a dragon, he hath filled his belly with my delicates, he hath cast me out." (NOI. The context of Jer.51:34-35 deals with people, rather than things, and we know there were many people 'addicted to luxury' who went into captivity. If Jer.51:34 referred to things, then the translators would have used the word 'delicacies'.) {delicacies 1x., delicate 5x., delicately 4x., delicateness 1x., deliciously 2x., tot. = 14x.}

Deliciously–2x., adv. [A.D. 1303, < E. **delicious** (adj.) (< OF. *delicious* < LL. *deliciosus* < L. *deliciae* = 'delight') = 'pleasing in the highest degree' + **ly** = 'the manner of' (See

E. suffix '–y'[1])] Thus, **deliciously** modifies its v. as 'being pleasing in the highest degree'. Eg. Rev.18:7, "How much she hath glorified herself, and lived deliciously..." {delicacies 1x., delicate 5x., delicately 4x., delicateness 1x., delicates 1x., tot. = 14x.}

Delight–51x., n. and v. [A.D. 1225, n. < OF. *delit* (v.) < OF. *delitier* (both < L. *delectare*, *de* = 'away from' (see L. prefix '*de–*'[3]) + *lacere* = 'to entice' (cp. also 'Delectable')) = 'something pleasing and enticing' (NOI. The word was spelled 'delite' until the early 1600's when the spelling changed to follow words such as 'flight' and 'light'.)] Thus, as a n., a **delight** is 'something that gives much pleasure or joy'. Eg. Pr.15:8, "The sacrifice of the wicked is an abomination to the LORD: but the prayer of the upright is his delight." Furthermore, as a v., **delight** means 'the action of affecting in a very pleasing way'. Eg. Ps.37:4, "Delight thyself also in the LORD; and he shall give thee the desires of thine heart." {delighted 12x., delightest 1x., delighteth 14x., delights 6x., delightsome 1x., tot. = 85x.}

Deliver– 296x., v. [A.D. 1225, < OF. *delivrer* < ML. *deliberare*, *de* = 'away from' (see L. prefix '*de–*'[3]) + *liberare* = 'to set free' < L. *liber* = 'free' (NOI. From *liber*, we also get our E. 'liberty' (= 'the state of being free'), and 'liberate' (= 'the act of setting free').)] Thus, **deliver** means 'the action of setting free from restraint'. Eg. Mt.6:13, "And lead us not into temptation, but deliver us from evil: For thine is the kingdom, and the power, and the glory, for ever. Amen." {deliverance 16x., deliverances 1x., delivered (incl. title of Ps.18) 291x., deliveredst 3x., deliverer 10x., deliverest 2x., delivereth 13x., delivering 3x., delivery 1x., tot. = 635x.}

Delusion – 1x., n. [A.D. 1420, < E. **delude** (< L. *deludere*, *de* = 'down' (see L. prefix '*de–*'[1]) + *ludere* = 'to play') = 'to play with a person in a deceitful manner, while pretending to be honest' + **ion** = 'a n. of condition or action' (See E. suffix '-tion')] Thus, a **delusion** is 'the act or fact of deceiving someone while pretending to be honest with them'. Eg. 2Ths.2:11, "And for this cause God shall send them strong delusion, that they should believe a lie." {delusions 1x., tot. = 2x.}

Demand —4x., v. [A.D. 1290, < OF. *demander* < ML. *demandare*, *de* = 'away from' (see L. prefix '*de–*'[3]) + *mandare* = 'to order' or 'to entrust' (NOI. Our E. 'mandate' (= 'a command from a superior officer') comes from L. *mandare.*)] Thus, **demand** means 'the action of urgent asking, with proper authority'. Eg. Job.40:7, "Gird up thy loins now like a man: I will demand of thee, and declare thou unto me." (NOI. When Job used this word toward God, in Job.42:4, he was not being disrespectful, but God has given man the authority to 'come and ask'. See Jer.33:3.) {demanded 7x., tot. = 11x.}

Den —19x., n. [A.D. 1000, < OE. **denn** (< pre Ger. *danjan* = 'a small room') = 'a cave or home of a wild beast or a poisonous creature' (NOI. In a modern family dwelling we sometimes refer to one of the rooms as a 'den'. This came about in A.D. 1771, and meant a small room in a house used for work or leisure.)] Thus, a **den** is 'a place where wild beasts or poisonous creatures live'. Eg. Ps.10:9, "He lieth in wait secretly as a lion in his den: he lieth in wait to catch the poor: he doth catch the poor, when he draweth him into his net." (NOI. Figuratively, a 'den' is also used when referring to the home of thieves or evil persons. See Mt.21:13.) {dens 9x., tot. = 28x.}

Denounce —1x., v. [A.D. 1300, < OF. *denoncier* < L. *denuntiare*, *de* = 'down' (see L. prefix '*de–*'[1]) + *nuntiare* = 'to make known by announcement'] Thus, **denounce** means 'the action of publicly declaring something or someone as bad'. Eg. Deut.30:18, "I denounce unto you this day, that ye shall surely perish, and that ye shall not prolong your days upon the land, whither thou passest over Jordan to go to possess it."

Deny –24x., v. [A.D. 1300, < OF. *denier* < L. *denegare*, *de* = 'completely' (see L. prefix '*de*–'[3]) + *negare* = 'to refuse' or 'to say no' (NOI. Our E. 'negate' (= 'to nullify or deny') comes from L. *negare*)] Thus, **deny** means 'the action of refusing completely'. Eg. Mt.10:33, "But whosoever shall deny me before men, him will I also deny before my Father which is in heaven." {denied 19x., denieth 4x., denying 4x., tot. = 51x.}

Depart –125x., v. [A.D. 1225, < OF. *departir* < L. *departire*, *de* = 'away from' with intensity (see L. prefix '*de*–'[3]) + *partire* = 'to divide' or 'to part'] Thus, **depart** means 'the action of dividing from, or separating from, someone or something' (with an emphasis on the 'from'). Eg. Phil.1:23, "For I am in a strait betwixt two, having a desire to depart, and to be with Christ; which is far better." {departed (incl. title of Ps. 34) 217x., departeth 8x., departing 12x., departure 2x., tot. = 364x.}

Deposed –1x., v. pret. [A.D. 1300, < E. **depose** (< OF. *deposer*, *de* = 'down from' (similar to E. prefix 'de–'[1]) + *poser* = 'to put or place') = 'to put down' + **ed** = forms the pret. (see E. suffix '–ed'[1]) (NOI. Early E. writings show the word was used in almost a 'ceremonial' or 'official' type of way.)] Thus, **deposed** means 'the past-tense action of laying or putting something or someone down'. Eg. Dan.5:20, "But when his heart was lifted up, and his mind hardened in pride, he was deposed from his kingly throne, and they took his glory from him." (NOI. God officially 'deposed' King Nebuchadnezzar from his throne for 7 years. See Dan.4.)

Deprived –3x., v. pret. and pp. [A.D. 1325, < E. **deprive** (< OF. *depriver* < *deprivare*, *de* = 'completely' (see L. prefix '*de*–'[3]) + *privare* = 'to release from') = 'to completely release from' + **ed** = forms the pret. and pp. (see E. suffix '–ed'[1,3])] Thus, as a v. pret., **deprived** means 'the past-tense action of completely releasing someone from something'. Eg. Job.39:17,

"Because God hath deprived her of wisdom, neither hath he imparted to her understanding." Furthermore, as a pp., **deprived** modifies its n. as 'having been completely released from someone or something'. Eg. Gen.27:45, "... why should I be deprived also of you both in one day? "

Deputed – 1x., pp. [A.D. 1382(WB.), < E. (v.) **depute** (= 'to set apart for a particular purpose' < OF. (pp.) *deputer* < LL. *deputare* = 'to allot') + **ed** = forms the pp. (see E. suffix '–ed'[3])] Thus, **deputed** modifies its n. (in this case, 'man') as 'having been separated and set aside for a special purpose'. Eg. 2Sam.15:3, "And Absalom said unto him, See, thy matters are good and right; but there is no man deputed of the king to hear thee." (See also 'Deputy'.) {deputies 3x., deputy 5x., tot. = 9x.}

Deputy – 5x., n. [A.D. 1405, < OF. *depute* (which is the n. form of the pp. *deputer*) = 'a person set apart and authorized to act on behalf of a higher authority as a representative or agent' (NOI. A 'deputy' usually had the power of an office, but not the actual office itself. This is seen in 1Ki.22:47. Emperor Claudius used many deputies, of which Gallio would have been one. He died in A.D. 65, some say by suicide, and some say Nero put him to death.)] Thus, a **deputy** is 'a person nominated to act on the behalf of a higher authority in legal and financial affairs'. Eg. Act.18:12, "And when Gallio was the deputy of Achaia, the Jews made insurrection with one accord against Paul, and brought him to the judgment seat." (See also 'Deputed'.) {deputed 1x., deputies 3x., tot. = 9x.}

Deride – 1x., v. [A.D. 1530, < L. *deridere*, *de* = 'to put down' (see L. prefix '*de-*'[2]) + *ridere* = 'to laugh at' or 'scorn' (NOI. 'Derision' is actually the older word, from A.D. 1400, and means 'the action or state of deriding'.)] Thus, **deride** means 'the action of putting someone down by mocking them or laughing at them'. Eg. Hab.1:10, "And they shall scoff at the kings, and the princes shall be a scorn unto them: they shall deride every strong hold; for they shall heap dust, and take it." {derided 2x., derision 15x., tot. = 18x.}

Descend – 10x., v. [A.D. 1300, < OF. *descendre* < L. *descendere, de* = 'down from' (see L. prefix '*de–*'[1]) + *scandere* = 'to climb' or 'to rise' (cp. 'ascend')] Thus, **descend** means 'the action of climbing down from a higher point of elevation'. Eg. 1Ths.4:16, "For the Lord himself shall descend from heaven with a shout, with the voice of the archangel, and with the trump of God: and the dead in Christ shall rise first." {descended 19x., descendeth 1x., descending 8x., descent 3x., tot. = 41x.}

Describe—4x., v. [A.D. 1513, < L. *describere, de* = 'down' or 'away from' (see L. prefix '*de–*'[1, 3]) + *scribere* = 'to write' or 'to draw' (NOI. Today, we use 'describe' meaning 'to set forth in words', meaning a verbal description. Yet, if we want it in written form, then we will often modify it with the words like, 'on paper' or 'in a paragraph'.)] Thus, **describe** means 'the action of writing down words'. Eg. Josh.18:6, "Ye shall therefore describe the land into seven parts, and bring the description hither to me, that I may cast lots for you here before the LORD our God." (NOI. The 'description' was put in writing and brought to Joshua.) {described 2x., describeth 2x., description 1x., tot. = 9x.}

Descry – 1x., v. [A.D. 1300, < oo., but apparently during the ME. period, **descrive** (= 'to transcribe or write down') was reduced to **descrie** and soon became blurred with OF. *descrier* (= 'to cry out') and so **descry** came to mean 'spying out and revealing an enemies position'. (NOI. The Hb. word is תּוּר (*tuwr*) = 'to seek or search out'.)] Thus, **descry** means 'the action of discovering an enemies position by observing it and revealing it'. Eg. Jud.1:23, "And the house of Joseph sent to descry Bethel. (Now the name of the city before was Luz.) "

Desert[1] – 1x., n. [A.D. 1297, < OF. *deserte* (= 'merit') < *deservir* (= 'to earn, deserve or merit', whether it be good or bad) (see also 'Deserve')] Thus, a **desert** is 'something earned, whether good (as a reward) or bad (as a judgment)'. Eg. Ps.28:4, "Give them according to their deeds, and according to the wickedness of their endeavours: give them after the work of their hands; render to them their desert." (NOI. In the Bible, 'desert', both sing. and pl., speaks of a judgment for sin. 'Desert' is different from the sweet-food at the end of a meal (called a 'dessert'), which if from the F. *desservir* = 'to clear the table'.) {deserts (Eze.7:27) 1x., tot. = 2x.}

Desert[2] – 41x., n. [A.D. 1225, < OF. *desert* < L. *desertus* (which is pp. of) *deserere* (= 'to abandon, give up or utterly forsake'), *de* = 'away from' with intensity (see L. prefix '*de–*'[3]) + *serere* = 'to join or entwine'] Thus, a **desert** is 'a place of utter abandonment, uninhabited, barren and uncultivated'. Eg. Jer.17:6, "For he shall be like the heath in the desert, and shall not see when good cometh; but shall inhabit the parched places in the wilderness, in a salt land and not inhabited." (NOI. Jesus indicated that a desert place makes a good place for rest. See Mk.6:31.) {deserts 5x., tot. = 46x.}

Deserve – 1x., v. [A.D. 1292, < OF. *deservir* < ML. *deservire*, *de* = 'completely' (see L. prefix '*de–*'[3]) + *servire* = 'to serve' (NOI. From this definition came the idea of 'merit or worth'.)] Thus, **deserve** means 'the action of serving completely or zealously'. Eg. Ezr.9:13, "And after all that is come upon us for our evil deeds, and for our great trespass, seeing that thou our God hast punished us less than our iniquities deserve, and hast given us such deliverance as this." (Cp. also Job11:6.) {deserveth 1x., deserving 1x., tot. = 3x.}

Desire – 111x., n. and v. [A.D. 1230, (the n. < OF. *desir*, and the v. < OF. *desirer*) both are from < L. *desiderare*, *de* = 'completely' (see L. prefix '*de–*'[3]) + *siderare* = 'a constellation’ (*sidus* = ‘star’); i.e. ‘a longing after the stars’ or ‘wishing upon a star’ (as in ‘longing after something wonderful, that happens to be out of ones reach’) (Cp. also ‘Consider’ and ‘Covet’)] Thus, as a n., a **desire** is ‘the state or condition of craving, wishing or longing after’. Eg. Pr.19:22, “The desire of a man is his kindness: and a poor man is better than a liar.” Furthermore, as a v., **desire** means ‘the action of craving, wishing or longing after’. Eg. 1Pt.2:2, “As newborn babes, desire the sincere milk of the word, that ye may grow thereby.” {desirable 3x., desired 50x., desiredst 2x., desires 3x., desirest 2x., desireth 17x., desiring 12x., desirous 6x., tot. = 216x.}

Desolate – 148x., adj., pn. and v. [A.D. 1374, < L. *desolatus* < *desolare, de* = ‘completely’ (see L. prefix ‘*de–*’[3]) + *solare* = ‘to make lonely’ (< *solus* = ‘alone’)] Thus, as an adj., **desolate** modifies its n. as ‘being completely alone or forsaken’. Eg. Mt.23:38, “Behold, your house is left unto you desolate.” Furthermore, as a pn., **Desolate** is ‘a name given to the land of Israel’. Eg. Isa.62:4, “Thou shalt no more be termed Forsaken; neither shall thy land any more be termed Desolate: but thou shalt be called Hephzibah, and thy land Beulah: for the LORD delighteth in thee, and thy land shall be married.” Finally, as a v., **desolate** means ‘the action of forsaking completely’. Eg. Eze. 12:19, “... that her land may be desolate from all that is therein, because of the violence of all them that dwell therein.” {desolation 46x., desolations 11x., tot. = 205x.}

Despair –3x., n. and v. [A.D. 1325, < OF. *desperer* < L. *desperare, de* = ‘without’ (see L. prefix ‘*de–*’[3]) + *sperare* = ‘hope, trust or look forward to’] Thus, as a n., **despair** is ‘a state of mind in which there’s no hope, or anything to look forward to’. (NOI. Today we often say, “*There’s no light at the end of the tunnel*”.) Eg. 2Cor. 4:8, “We are troubled on every side, yet not distressed; we are perplexed, but not in despair.” Furthermore, as a v., **despair** means ‘the action of giving up or losing all hope of a successful or happy outcome’. Eg.

1Sam.27:1, "... and Saul shall despair of me, to seek me any more in any coast of Israel: so shall I escape out of his hand." {despaired 1x., tot. = 4x.}

Despise –37x., v. [A.D. 1297, < OF. *despire* < L. *despicere, de* = 'down' (in a very negative sense) (see L. prefix '*de–*'[2]) + *spicere* (or *specere*) = 'to look at' (NOI. We get our E. 'specimen' (= 'a part taken to represent the whole') from *spicere* (or *specere.*)] Thus, **despise** means 'the action of looking down upon with scorn or disdain'. Eg. Pr.1:7, "The fear of the LORD is the beginning of knowledge: but fools despise wisdom and instruction." {despised 60x., despisers 2x., despisest 1x., despiseth 19x., despising 1x., tot. = 120x.}

Despite –2x., n. [A.D. 1290, n. < OF. *despit* < L. *despectus* (= 'a looking down upon') < *despicere* (see 'Despise')] Thus, **despite** means 'the state of looking down on with scorn or disdain'. Eg. Eze.25:6, "For thus saith the Lord GOD; Because thou hast clapped thine hands, and stamped with the feet, and rejoiced in heart with all thy despite against the land of Israel." {despiteful 3x., despitefully 3x., tot. = 8x.}

Destitute –8x., adj. and n. [A.D. 1382(WB.), < L. *destituere, de* = 'away from' (see L. prefix '*de–*'[3]) + *statuere* = 'to set up, put or place' (NOI. Our E. 'statue' (= 'an image made in the likeness of a person or animal') and 'statute' (= 'an ordinance of law') are from L. *statuere.*)] Thus, as an adj., **destitute** modifies its n. as 'being abandoned, deserted or put away'. Eg. Pr.15:21, "Folly is joy to him that is destitute of wisdom: but a man of understanding walketh uprightly." Furthermore, as a n., **destitute** is 'a reference to someone who is in an abandoned condition, as if they have been put away from other people'. Eg. Ps.102:17, "He will regard the prayer of the destitute, and not despise their prayer." (NOI. A careful reading of the context of Ps.102 will show that the Psalmist himself felt all alone. 'Destitute' is also used to describe the abandonment between a Christian brother or sister and their daily food (Jam.2:15).)

Destroy —261x., v. [A.D. 1225, < OF. *destruire* < L. *destruere, de* = 'down' (see L. prefix '*de–*'[1]) + *struere* = 'to build' or 'to pile up'] Thus, **destroy** means 'the action of an intentional undoing of the building process (as in a pulling down or a demolition) and to render it useless'. Eg. Ps.28:5, "Because they regard not the works of the LORD, nor the operation of his hands, he shall destroy them, and not build them up." (NOI. Although 'destroy' is usually applied to living beings such as people and animals, it is sometimes also applied to inanimate objects such as heathen idols, pictures and houses.) {destroyed 167x., destroyer 7x., destroyers 4x., destroyest 4x., destroyeth 8x., destroying 14x., destruction 94x., destructions 3x., tot. = 562x.}

Detain —2x., n. [A.D. 1292, < OF. *detenir* < L. *detinere, de* = 'away from' (see L. prefix '*de–*'[3]) + *tenere* = 'to hold'] Thus, **detain** means 'the action of holding someone back from where they were intending to go'. Eg. Jud.13:15, "And Manoah said unto the angel of the LORD, I pray thee, let us detain thee, until we shall have made ready a kid for thee." {detained 1x., tot. = 3x.}

Determine — 1.x., v. [A.D. 1374, < L. *determinare* (< *de* = 'down' (see L. prefix '*de–*'[1]) + *terminare* = 'a boundary' or 'a limit') = 'down to the limits' (NOI. Our E. 'terminate' (= 'to direct towards a finish') comes from L. *terminare.*)] Thus, **determine** means 'the action of placing a boundary or putting a limit on something'. Eg. Ex.21:22, "If men strive, and hurt a woman with child, so that her fruit depart from her, and yet no mischief follow: he shall be surely punished, according as the woman's husband will lay upon him; and he shall pay as the judges determine." {determinate 1x., determination 1x., determined 30x., tot. = 33x.}

Detest – 1x., v. [A.D. 1533, < L. *detestari, de* = 'down' (in a very negative sense) (see L. prefix '*de–*'[2]) + *testari* = 'bear witness' or 'call to witness' (NOI. In other E. literature, 'detest' is used in context with a calling upon God as a witness against.)] Thus, **detest** means 'to call upon God as a witness against something'. Eg. Deut.7:26, "Neither shalt thou bring an abomination into thine house, lest thou be a cursed thing like it: but thou shalt utterly detest it, and thou shalt utterly abhor it; for it is a cursed thing." {detestable 6x., tot. = 7x.}

Device – 16x., n. [A.D. 1290, < OF. *devis* (= 'a division, difference or desire') < L. *divisus* (which is pp. of) *dividere* = 'a carefully made division' in the sense of 'a carefully prepared plan' (see 'Divide')] Thus, a **device** is 'a carefully prepared plan, purpose or intention'. Eg. Est.8:3, "And Esther spake yet again before the king, and fell down at his feet, and besought him with tears to put away the mischief of Haman the Agagite, and his device that he had devised against the Jews." (NOI. Although there are 2x when 'device' is used in a positive and constructive sense, there are 14x when it is used in a negative and destructive sense; i.e. 'a bad or evil plan', especially when coupled with 'devise'.) (See also 'Devise'.) {devices 16x., tot. = 26x.}

Devil –61x., n. and pn. [A.D. 800, < OE. **deofol** < LL. *diabolus* < Gk. διαβολος (*diabolos*) = 'one who slanders' (< Gk. διαβαλλω (*diaballo*), δια (*dia*) = 'across or through' + βαλλω (*ballo*) = 'to throw') (see 'Slander')] Thus, as a n., a **devil** is 'one who slanders someone'. Eg. Mt.9:32, "As they went out, behold, they brought to him a dumb man possessed with a devil." (NOI. The emphasis of 'devil' as a n. is the trait of character. Some claim the 1611 should have used the word 'demon' instead of 'devil' in certain places, as in Mt.11:18. However, 'demon' (Gk. δαιμον (*daimon*)) was used very little in early modern E. and, of the times it was used, it often meant a 'supernatural being' or 'an indwelling spirit' or a 'cruel animal or person', and only on rare occasions 'an evil spirit'. This last meaning only took hold in English literature starting in the 1700's. Until then, 'devil' was the common word for Satan himself and any of the fallen angels who joined in with him.) Furthermore, as a pn., **Devil** is 'a name given to Satan himself'. Eg. Rev.20:2, "And he laid hold on the dragon, that old serpent, which is the Devil, and Satan, and bound him a thousand years." {devilish 1x., devils 55x., tot. = 117x.}

Devise –16x., v. [A.D. 1300, < OF. *deviser* < L. *dividere* = 'to carefully divide' in the sense of 'careful planning' (see 'Divide')] Thus, **devise** means 'the action of carefully making plans concerning someone or something'. (See also 'Device') Eg. Pr.3:29, "Devise not evil against thy neighbour, seeing he dwelleth securely by thee." (NOI. Although there are 4x when 'devise' is used in a positive and constructive sense, there are 12x when it is used in a negative and destructive sense; i.e. 'bad or evil planning'.) {devised 12x., deviseth 8x., tot. = 36x.}

Devote – 1x., v. [A.D. 1586, < L. *devotus* < *devovere*, *de* = 'away from' (see L. prefix '*de–*'[3]) + *vovere* = 'to make a solemn promise to a deity' (see 'Vow')] Thus, **devote** means 'to set apart by a solemn promise to a deity'. Eg. Lev.27:28, "Notwithstanding no devoted thing, that a man shall devote unto the LORD of all that he hath, both of man and beast..." {devoted 7x., devotions 1x., tot. = 9x.}

Devotions –1x., n. pl. [A.D. 1225, < E. **devotion** < OF. *devocion* < L. *devotio* (= 'prayer, piety or zeal') < *devovere* = 'to devote' (see 'Devote') and refers to 'something which has been devoted to a deity'] Thus, **devotions** are 'two or more religious objects that have been devoted to a deity'. Eg. Act.17:23, "For as I passed by, and beheld your devotions, I found an altar with this inscription, TO THE UNKNOWN GOD. Whom therefore ye ignorantly worship, him declare I unto you." (NOI.

Today, we speak of 'devotions' as being time spent alone with God, but in Act.17, the altars themselves were the 'devotions', or 'devoted things'.) {devote 1x., devoted 7x., tot. = 9x.}

Devour —71x., v. [A.D. 1315, < OF. *devorer* < L. *devorare, de* = 'down to the bottom' (see L. prefix '*de*–'[1]) + *vorare* = 'to swallow'] Thus, **devour** means 'the action of eating up ravenously like a beast, in a reckless greedy fashion'. Eg. 1Pt.5:8, "Be sober, be vigilant; because your adversary the devil, as a roaring lion, walketh about, seeking whom he may devour." {devoured 53x., devourer 1x., devourest 1x., devoureth 10x., devouring 6x., tot. = 142x.}

Devout —9x., adj. [A.D. 1225, < OF. *devot* < L. *devotus* (see 'Devote')] Thus, **devout** modifies its n. as 'being devoted, or given over, to divine worship and service'. Eg. Act.10:2, "A devout man, and one that feared God with all his house, which gave much alms to the people, and prayed to God alway."

Dew —37x., n. [A.D. 800, < OE. **deaw** (akin to Du. *dauw*, and Ger. *tau*, and Ice. *dögg*) = 'moisture condensed from the atmosphere' (possibly from Sans. *dhāw* = 'to flow') (NOI. 'Dew' happens when water molecules in the air reach a maximum saturation-point (i.e. 'as much as the air can hold') at a given temperature, and then condense (i.e. 'turn into water droplets'). This normally happens in late summer or fall when the ground is still warm from the daytime sun and the air is filled with moisture. The drop in night-time temperature condenses the moist air on warm surfaces, which results in dew. See also 'Frost'.)] Thus, **dew** is 'moisture that has condensed out of the atmosphere'. Eg. Deut.32:2, "My doctrine shall drop as the rain, my speech shall distil as the dew, as the small rain upon the tender herb, and as the showers upon the grass."

Diadem —4x., n. [A.D. 1290, < L. *diadema* (= 'a headband') < Gk. διαδημα (*diadaema*) < διαδειν (*diadein*) (= 'to bind around'), δια (*dia*) = 'across' + δειν (*dein*) = 'to bind'] Thus, a **diadem** is 'a band or wreath bound across the forehead, worn as a sign of royalty or dignity'. Eg. Isa.28:5, "In that day shall the LORD of hosts be for a crown of glory, and for a diadem of beauty, unto the residue of his people." (NOI. The kings of Persia wore these, as did Alexander the Great and the kings that followed him.)

Diamond —4x., n. [A.D. 1310, < ME. **diamant** < OF. *diamant* (= 'hardest of metals') < L. *diamant* < *adamas* = 'invincible', < Gk. αδαμαω (*adamao*) = 'unconquerable' (see 'Adamant')] Thus, a **diamond** is 'the hardest and most valuable of all gemstones'. Eg. Jer.17:1, "The sin of Judah is written with a pen of iron, and with the point of a diamond: it is graven upon the table of their heart, and upon the horns of your altars." (NOI. In Bible times, the diamond was used as a cutting tool and an engraving instrument. In A.D. 1797, diamonds were burned and shown to produce CO_2, proving they are made of carbon. In the geological hardness scale, the diamond is a perfect '10', the top of the scale. A diamond is more transparent than any other gemstone; conducts heat better than anything; makes an excellent electrical insulator; its atoms are packed closer together than any other substance; and it has the highest melting temperature – 3820 degrees Kelvin! As hard as a diamond is, a skilled jeweler can split it with a sharp blow in any of four specific directions. A good jeweler will make sure that none of these directions are exposed when it is mounted in a jewelry piece. Modern science has found a way to make synthetic diamonds by using carbon, iron, a few catalyst minerals and extreme heat and pressure.)

Diddest —1x., v. pret. [A.D. 1000, < E. **did** = pret. of **do** (< OE. **don** = 'to put, place or make') + **est** = pret form of 2nd pers. sing. ind. (see E. suffix '–edst')] Thus, **diddest** means 'the past-tense action of the v. 'do', in the 2nd pers. sing. ind.' Eg. Act.7:28, "Wilt thou kill me, as thou diddest the Egyptian yesterday? " (NOI. 'Diddest' is only used once in the Bible, and there is no difference in meaning between it and 'didst', both being common spellings in the 1600's. So why was it used? A possible reason for this one-time-only occurrence in the 1611 may simply have been the typesetter's method of balancing a line of text. See section entitled, 'Variant Spellings'. Note also, some KJV Bibles today have replaced it with 'didst'. See 'Didst'.) {did 1006x., didst 122x., do 1368x., doer 8x., doers 7x., doest 45x., doeth 96x., doing 39x., doings 51x., done 565x., dost 56x., doth 206x., undo 2x., tot. = 3572x.}

Didst –122x., v. [A.D. 1000, < E. **did** = pret. of **do** (< OE. **don** = 'to put, place or make') + **est** = pret. form of 2nd pers. sing. ind.] Thus, **didst** means 'the past-tense action of the v. 'do', in the 2nd pers. sing. ind.' Eg. Mt.13:27, "So the servants of the householder came and said unto him, Sir, didst not thou sow good seed in thy field? from whence then hath it tares? " (NOI. 'Didst' normally precedes an infinitive v. (eg. "didst not thou sow..." Mt.13:27). See also 'Diddest'.) {did 1006x., diddest 1x., do 1368x., doer 8x., doers 7x., doest 45x., doeth 96x., doing 39x., doings 51x., done 565x., dost 56x., doth 206x., undo 2x., tot. = 3572x.}

Diet –2x., n. [A.D. 1225, < OF. *diete* < L. *diaeta* < Gk. *διαιτα* (*diaita*) = 'way of living'] Thus, a **diet** 'is a prescribed manner of living as it relates to food'. Eg. Jer.52:34, "And for his diet, there was a continual diet given him of the king of Babylon, every day a portion until the day of his death, all the days of his life." (NOI. 'Diet' can also mean 'a day set for a meeting' (because of L. *dies* = 'day'). One of the more famous meetings was known as the 'Imperial Diet of Worms' (pronounced 'vorms', with a long 'o' – a city in Germany) in April A.D. 1521, in which Martin Luther appeared before the Emperor on charges of heresy concerning his writings. When asked to retract his writings, Luther replied,

"*Unless I am convinced by Scripture and plain reason - I do not accept the authority of the popes and councils, for they have contradicted each other - my conscience is captive to the Word of God. I cannot and I will not recant anything for to go against conscience is neither right nor safe. God help me. Amen.*")

Difference –12x., n. [A.D. 1340, < E. (v.) **differ** (< OF. *differer* < L. *differre*, *dis* = 'utterly apart' (see L. prefix '*dis*–') + *ferre* = 'to bear' or 'carry'; i.e. 'to separate things so as to make a distinction between them') + **ence** = 'the state or condition of' (see E. suffix '–ance')] Thus, a **difference** is 'the condition of being set apart in order to make a distinction'. Eg. Lev.10:10, "And that ye may put difference between holy and unholy, and between unclean and clean." {differ 1x., differences 1x., differeth 2x., differing 1x., tot. = 17x.}

Dignities – 1x., n. pl. [A.D. 1225, < E. **dignity** (see 'Dignity')] Thus, **dignities** are 'two or more people of noble rank or position in life'. Eg. 2Pt.2:10, "But chiefly them that walk after the flesh in the lust of uncleanness, and despise government. Presumptuous are they, selfwilled, they are not afraid to speak evil of dignities." {dignity 2x., tot. = 4x.}

Dignity – 4x., n. [A.D. 1225, < OF. *dignite* < L. *dignitas* = 'worthiness, office or rank' (< L. *dignus* = 'worthy')] Thus, **dignity** is 'the quality of being worthy, noble or excellent'. Eg. Est.6:3, "And the king said, What honour and dignity hath been done to Mordecai for this? Then said the king's servants that ministered unto him, There is nothing done for him." {dignities 2x., tot. = 4x.}

Diligence – 10x., n. [A.D. 1340, < E. **diligent** (see 'Diligent') + **ence** = 'the state or condition of' (see E. suffix '–ance') (NOI. The L. word is *diligentia* = 'with carefulness'.)] Thus, **diligence** is 'the state or condition of giving careful attention to something or someone'. Eg. 2Pt.1:10, "Wherefore the rather, brethren, give diligence to make your calling and election sure: for if ye do these things, ye shall never fall." {diligent 15x., diligently 37x., tot. = 62x.}

Diligent – 15x., adj. [A.D. 1340, < OF. *diligent* < L. *diligens* (which is prp. of *diligere* (= 'to choose, love or value highly'), *dis* = 'utterly apart' (see L. prefix '*dis*–') + *legere* = 'to choose or gather together') = 'careful or strict attention'] Thus, **diligent** modifies its n. as 'being strict and careful attention to doing something right'. Eg. Pr.10:4, "He becometh poor that dealeth with a slack hand: but the hand of the diligent maketh rich." {diligence 10x., diligently 37x., tot. = 62x.}

Diligently – 37x., adv. [A.D. 1340, < E. **diligent** (see 'Diligent') + **ly** = 'the manner of' (See E. suffix '–y'[1])] Thus, **diligently** modifies its v. as 'being done in a very careful and attentive manner'. Eg. Heb.11:6, "But without faith it is impossible to please him: for he that cometh to God must believe that he is, and that he is a rewarder of them that diligently seek him." (NOI. Here the 'seeking' of God is to be done in a very careful and attentive manner through much prayer and Bible study.) {diligence 10x., diligent 15x., tot. = 62x.}

Dim – 9x., adj. [A.D. 888, < OE. **dim** = 'obscure or dark'] Thus, **dim** modifies its n. as 'being dark or obscure'. Eg. 1Sam.4:15, "Now Eli was ninety and eight years old; and his eyes were dim, that he could not see." (NOI. It is used mainly to describe a person's failing eyesight, and once to describe the tarnishing of gold.) {dimness 2x., tot. = 11x.}

Diminish –8x., v. [A.D. 1417, (formed by a joining of 2 verbs) E. **diminue** (< OF. *diminuer* < L. *diminuere* < *deminuere*, *de* = 'completely' (see L. prefix '*de*—'[3]) + *minuere* = 'to make smaller') + E. **minish** < OF. *menuiser* < L. *minutus* (which is pp. of) L. *minuere* = 'to make smaller'] Thus,

diminish means 'the action of thoroughly making something smaller'. Eg. Deut.4:2, "Ye shall not add unto the word which I command you, neither shall ye diminish ought from it, that ye may keep the commandments of the LORD your God which I command you." {diminished 5x., diminishing 1x., tot. = 14x.}

Dine —3x., v. [A.D. 1297, < OF. *disner* < LL. *disjejunare, dis* = 'utterly apart' (see L. prefix '*dis–*') + *jejunare* = 'to fast'] Thus, **dine** means 'the action of breaking one's fast and eating'. Eg. Gen.43:16, "... Bring these men home, and slay, and make ready; for these men shall dine with me at noon." {dined 1x., dinner 4x., tot. = 8x.}

Direct —10x., inf. and v. [A.D. 1374, < L. *directus* (which is pp. of) *dirigere* (= 'to send in a straight line' or 'to set in order'), *di* = 'apart' (see L. prefix '*dis–*') + *regere* = 'to keep straight' or 'to guide' (i.e. 'keeping apart from other places and going straight for the goal')] Thus, as an inf., **direct** means 'the open-ended action of aiming toward a particular place'. Eg. Jer.10:23, "O LORD, I know that the way of man is not in himself: it is not in man that walketh to direct his steps." Furthermore, as a v., **direct** means 'the action of aiming towards a particular place'. Eg. Pr.3:6, "In all thy ways acknowledge him, and he shall direct thy paths." {directed 3x., directeth 3x., direction 1x., directly 2x., tot. = 19x.}

Dirt — 3x., n. [A.D. 1300, < ME. **drit** < ON. *drit* = 'excrement' (akin to Ice. *dritr*) (NOI. 'Dirt' was a word applied to anything (or anyone) foul, vile or worthless. This included human or animal excrement as well as general filth.)] Thus, **dirt** is 'something foul and worthless', such as excrement. Eg. Jud.3:22, "And the haft also went in after the blade; and the fat closed upon the blade, so that he could not draw the dagger out of his belly; and the dirt came out."

Disannul —3x., v. [A.D. 1494, < E. **dis** (= L. *dis* (see L. prefix '*dis–*')) = 'utterly apart' + ME. **annul** (< OF. *anuller* < LL. *annullare*, *ad* = 'to' (see L. prefix '*ad-*') + *nullus* = 'none or nothing') = 'to purposely make into nothing'] Thus, **disannul** means 'the action of utterly reducing something into nothing' (as in 'to put out of existence'). Eg. Isa.14:27, "For the LORD of hosts hath purposed, and who shall disannul it? and his hand is stretched out, and who shall turn it back? " {disannulled 1x., disannulleth 1x., disannulling 1x., tot. = 6x.}

Discern –17x., v. [A.D. 1374, < OF. *discerner* < L. *discernere*, *dis* = 'utterly apart' (see L. prefix '*dis–*') + *cernere* = 'to separate, divide or distinguish' (< *cerno* = 'to pick out') (See also 'Certain'.)] Thus, **discern** means 'the action of utterly separating and distinguishing between things or people'. Eg. Heb.5:14, "But strong meat belongeth to them that are of full age, even those who by reason of use have their senses exercised to discern both good and evil." {discerned 4x., discerner 1x., discerneth 1x., discerning 2x., tot. = 25x.}

Discharge – 1x., v. [A.D. 1330, < OF. *deschargier* < LL. *discarricare*, *dis* = 'utterly apart' (see L. prefix '*dis–*') + *carricare* = 'to load' (< L. *carrus* = 'a cart' or 'a wagon')] Thus, **discharge** means 'the action of unloading' (as in 'unloading a wagon, ship or a pack animal'). Eg. Ecc.8:8, "There is no man that hath power over the spirit to retain the spirit; neither hath he power in the day of death: and there is no discharge in that war; neither shall wickedness deliver those that are given to it." (NOI. With people, it usually means 'to relieve of a duty, debt or a benefit'.) {discharged 1x., tot. = 2x.}

Disciple – 29x., n. [A.D. 900, < OF. *disciple* < L. *discipulus* < *discipere* (< *dis* = 'utterly apart' (see L. prefix '*dis–*') + *capere* = 'to take apart') = 'to thoroughly take apart and analyze'] Thus, a **disciple** is 'one who learns by thorough analysis and study'. Eg. Lk.14:26, "If any man come to me, and hate not his father, and mother, and wife, and children, and brethren, and sisters, yea, and his own life also, he cannot be my disciple." (NOI. This vs. appears to conflict with Christ's other teachings on love, until we understand the word 'disciple'. To be Christ's disciple, a man must strongly reject (see 'Hate') what he thinks is important in his life (according to his five senses) and thoroughly re-analyze and re-examine everything by using Christ's teachings. (This idea of 'analyzing' is illustrated by the two examples Christ gave of building a tower and waging a war). Hence, the disciple begins to learn that God's thoughts and ways are higher than man's thoughts and ways (cp. Isa.55:8-9). Man thinks 'creature-comforts' are important, yet God allows suffering. Man wants his castle here, but Jesus said, "In my Father's house are many mansions: if it were not so, I would have told you. I go to prepare a place for you." (Jn.14:2)) {disciples 243x., disciples' 1x., tot. = 273 x.}

Discomfited –9x., pp. [A.D. 1225, < E. **discomfit** (< OF. *desconfit* < ML. *disconficere*, *dis* = 'utterly apart' (see L. prefix '*dis–*') + *conficere* = 'to make' or 'to put together') = 'to completely undo or take apart' (i.e. 'destroy') + **ed** = forms the pp. (see E. suffix '–ed'[3])] Thus, **discomfited** modifies its n. as 'having been destroyed or ripped apart'. Eg. Ex.17:13, "And Joshua discomfited Amalek and his people with the edge of the sword." {discomfiture 1x., tot. = 10x.}

Discord –2x., n. [A.D. 1230, < OF. *discorder* < L. *discordare*, *dis* = 'utterly apart' (see L. prefix '*dis–*') + *cordare* (< L. *cor*) = 'heart'] Thus, **discord** is 'the state or condition of when two or more hearts (of people) are turned from each other in anger or misunderstanding'. Eg. Pr.6:19, "A false witness that speaketh lies, and he that soweth discord among brethren." (Cp. 'Accord')

Discover – 12x., v. [A.D. 1300, < OF. *descovrir* < LL. *discooperire*, *dis* = 'asunder' (see L. prefix '*dis–*') + *cooperire* (< L. *co* = 'together' (see L. prefix '*co-*') + *operire* = 'to cover') = 'to earnestly cover'] Thus, **discover** means 'the action of uncovering or revealing something that has been earnestly covered up'. Eg. Pr.25:9, "Debate thy cause with thy neighbour himself; and discover not a secret to another." {discovered 22x., discovereth 2x., tot. = 36x.}

Discreet —3x., adj. [A.D. 1340, < OF. *discret* < L. *discretus* (which is pp. of) L. *discernere, dis* = 'apart' (see L. prefix '*dis–*') + *cernere* = 'to separate' (NOI. The L. '*discretus*' means 'the quality of being separated or discerned'. See also 'Discern'.)] Thus, **discreet** modifies its n. as 'being able to show wise discernment in picking and choosing ones words and actions'. Eg. Ti.2:5 "To be discreet, chaste, keepers at home, good, obedient to their own husbands, that the word of God be not blasphemed." {discreetly 1x., discretion 9x., tot. = 13x.}

Discretion —9x., n. [A.D. 1303, < OF. *discretion* < L. *discretio* (the n. form of the v.) < *discernere* (see 'Discern' and 'Discreet')] Thus, **discretion** is 'the ability to make distinction between right and wrong and make good decisions in one's life'. Eg. Pr.11:22, "As a jewel of gold in a swine's snout, so is a fair woman which is without discretion." {discreet 3x., discreetly 1x., tot. = 13x.}

Disdained —2x., pp. [A.D. 1380, < OF. *desdeignier, des* (= L. *dis* (see L. prefix '*dis–*')) = 'utterly apart', + *deignier* = 'to treat as worthy or valuable'] Thus, **disdained** modifies its n. as 'having looked upon someone or something as unworthy'. Eg. 1Sam.17:42, "And when the Philistine looked about, and saw David, he disdained him: for he was but a youth, and ruddy, and of a fair countenance."

Disease —15x., n. [A.D. 1330, < OF. *desaise, des* (= L. *dis* (see L. prefix '*dis–*')) = 'utterly apart', + *aise* = 'ease' = 'a comfortable state of body and mind' (see 'Ease')] Thus, a **disease** is 'a state or condition of the absence of bodily and mental comfort and tranquility'. Eg. 2Chr.21:15, "And thou shalt have great sickness by disease of thy bowels, until thy bowels fall out by reason of the sickness day by day." (NOI. 'Disease' can be of a spiritual nature (Ecc.6:2), or one of many organic viruses (2Ch.16:12), or as a result of a serious fall (2Ki.1:2). See also 'Affliction', 'Murrain', Sickness' and 'Weak'.) {diseased 8x., diseases 13x., tot. = 36x.}

Disgrace —1x., v. [A.D. 1549, < F. *disgracier* < It. *disgrazier*, < L. *disgratia*, *dis* = 'utterly apart' (see L. prefix '*dis–*') + *gratia* (< *gratus*) = 'pleasing, agreeable or dear' (see 'Grace')] Thus, **disgrace** means 'the action of making unfavorable, marring or disfiguring'. Eg. Jer.14:21, "Do not abhor us, for thy name's sake, do not disgrace the throne of thy glory: remember, break not thy covenant with us."

Disguise —3x., v. [A.D. 1325, < OF. *desguiser*, *des* (= L. *dis* (see L. prefix '*dis–*')) = 'utterly apart' + *guise* = 'dress, attire or manner' (NOI. This is the same as the E. 'guise'.)] Thus, **disguise** means 'the action of dressing in a manner totally different from one's normal attire'. Eg. 1Ki.14:2, "And Jeroboam said to his wife, Arise, I pray thee, and disguise thyself, that thou be not known to be the wife of Jeroboam; and get thee to Shiloh..." {disguised 5x., disguiseth 1x., tot. = 9x.}

Dishonour —11x., n. and v. [A.D. 1300, < OF. *deshonor* < L. *dishonorare*, *dis* = 'utterly apart' (see L. prefix '*dis–*') + *honorare* < *honor* = 'official dignity or repute' (see 'Honour')] Thus, as a n., **dishonour** is 'the state or condition of having one's dignity destroyed'. Eg. Pr. 6:33, "A wound and dishonour shall he get; and his reproach shall not be wiped away." Furthermore, as a v., **dishonour** means 'the action of destroying one's dignity'. Eg. Rom.1:24, "Wherefore God also gave them up to uncleanness through the lusts of their own hearts, to dishonour their own bodies between themselves." {dishonourest 1x., dishonoureth 3x., tot. = 15x.}

Disinherit –1x., v. [A.D. 1450, < E. **dis** (= L. *dis* (see L. prefix '*dis–*')) = 'utterly apart', + **inherit** = 'to make someone an heir' (see 'Inherit')] Thus, **disinherit** means 'the action of reversing the process of making someone an heir'. Eg. Num.14:12, "I will smite them with the pestilence, and disinherit them, and will make of thee a greater nation and mightier than they."

Dismayed –31x., pp. [A.D. 1297, < E. **dismay** (< ME. **desmaien** < OF. *desmaier, des* (= L. *dis* (see L. prefix '*dis–*')) = 'utterly apart' + OF. *maier* = 'be able') = 'the breaking down of someone's ability to perform' (as well as their courage) + **ed** = the pp. form (see E. suffix '–ed'[2])] Thus, **dismayed** modifies its n. as 'having had its ability to perform broken down or destroyed'. Eg. Josh.1:9, "Have not I commanded thee? Be strong and of a good courage; be not afraid, neither be thou dismayed..." {dismaying 1x., tot. = 32x.}

Disobedience –6x., n. [A.D. 1400, < OF. *desobedience* < L. *inobedientia, in* = 'not' (see L. prefix '*in-*'[1]) + *obedientia* < L. *obedire, ob* = 'toward' (see L. prefix '*o-*') + *audire* = 'to listen with the idea of complying with requests or instructions' (see 'Obedient')] Thus, **disobedience** is 'the state or condition of not listening nor submitting to instructions'. Eg. Col.3:6, "For which things' sake the wrath of God cometh on the children of disobedience." {disobedient 13x., disobeyed 1x., tot. = 20x.}

Dispatch –1x., v. [A.D. 1517, < Sp. *despachar* (or It. *Dispacciare)* < L. *dispactus, dis* = 'utterly apart' (see L. prefix '*dis–*') + *pactus* (which is pp. of) *pangere* = 'to fasten' or 'fix in place')] Thus, **dispatch** means 'the action of cutting loose and sending off' (as in 'to kill with speed'). Eg. Eze.23:47, "And the company shall stone them with stones, and dispatch them with their swords; they shall slay their sons and their daughters, and burn up their houses with fire." (NOI. 'Dispatch' was also used to describe several things, including: to send off troops and packages with speed, to escape quickly, to sell off, to stow away, as well as 'to kill with speed' (first recorded in A.D. 1530).)

Dispensation —4x., n. [A.D. 1374, < OF. *dispensation* < L. *dispensatio*, < (v.) *dispensare* (< *dispendere*, *dis* = 'utterly apart' (see L. prefix '*dis*–') + *pendere* = 'to weigh' (NOI. Our E. 'ponder' (= 'to weigh carefully in the mind') comes from this root.)) = 'to weigh out and distribute'] Thus, a **dispensation** is 'the state or condition of managing and distributing a person's affairs'. Eg. **Eph.1:10**, "That in the dispensation of the fulness of times he might gather together in one all things in Christ, both which are in heaven, and which are on earth; even in him." (NOI. In the Bible, 'dispensation' always deals with God's affairs towards man.)

Disperse —8x., v. [A.D. 1450, < L. *disperses* (which is pp. of) *dispergere*, *dis* = 'utterly apart' (see L. prefix '*dis*–') + *spargere* = 'to scatter') = 'to scatter abroad'] Thus, **disperse** means 'the action of scattering all around in different directions'. Eg. **Pr.15:7**, "The lips of the wise disperse knowledge: but the heart of the foolish doeth not so." {dispersed 10x., dispersions 1x., tot. = 19x.}

Displease —5x., v. [A.D. 1350, < OF. *desplaisir* < L. *displicere*, *dis* = 'utterly apart' (see L. prefix '*dis*–') + *placere* = 'be agreeable or pleasing' (< L. *placidus* = 'gentle or mild'), something displeasing would appear or behave as the opposite of gentle or mild] Thus, **displease** means 'the action of acting in a rough or disagreeable manner' (which would certainly not please someone). Eg. **Pr.24:18**, "Lest the LORD see it, and it displease him, and he turn away his wrath from him." {displeased 25x., displeasure 5x., tot. = 35x.}

Disposing —1x., prp. [A.D. 1380, < E. **dispose** (< OF. *disposer*,

< L. *disponere*, *dis* = 'utterly apart' (see L. prefix '*dis*–') + *ponere* = 'to place' or 'to lay down') = 'to put in their proper places' + **ing** = forms the prp. (see E. suffix '–ing'[3]) (NOI. Today, we think of 'disposing' something as 'getting rid of it'.)] Thus, **disposing** modifies its n. (in this case, 'lot') as 'being put where it belongs'. Eg. Pr.16:33, "The lot is cast into the lap; but the whole disposing thereof is of the LORD." {disposed 4x., disposition 1x., dispossess 2x., dispossessed 2x., tot. = 10x.}

Disposition – 1x., n. [A.D. 1374, < E. **dispose** (< L. *disposer*, *dis*, = 'utterly apart' (see L. prefix '*dis*–') + *poser* = 'to place' or 'to lay down') = 'to put in their proper places' + **tion** = 'action, process, state or condition'] Thus, a **disposition** is 'the condition of things having been put where they belong'. Eg. Act.7:53, "Who have received the law by the disposition of angels, and have not kept it." {disposed 4x., disposing 1x., dispossess 2x., dispossessed 2x.}

Dispossess – 2x., v. [A.D. 1494, < OF. *despossesser* < L. *dispossidere*, *dis* = 'asunder' (see L. prefix '*dis*–') + *possidere* = 'to sit in front of something' (see 'Possess')] Thus, **dispossess** means 'the action of removing someone from their property' (i.e. 'to take away their ownership'). Eg. Deut.7:17, "If thou shalt say in thine heart, These nations are more than I; how can I dispossess them? " {disposed 4x., disposing 1x., disposition 1x., dispossessed 2x., tot. = 10x.}

Dispute – 1x., v. [A.D. 1225, < OF. *desputer* < L. *disputare*, *dis* = 'utterly apart' (see L. prefix '*dis*–') + *putare* = 'to count or consider'] Thus, **dispute** means 'the action of pulling something into pieces and considering all the parts'. Eg. Job23:7, "There the righteous might dispute with him; so should I be delivered for ever from my judge."

Disquiet – 1x., v. [A.D. 1530, < E. **dis** (= L. *dis* (see L. prefix '*dis–*')) = 'asunder' + (v.) **quiet** (< LL. *quietare* = 'to make tranquil' < *quies* = 'tranquility') = 'to make tranquil'] Thus, **disquiet** means 'the action of tearing apart the tranquility'. Eg. Jer.50:34, "Their Redeemer is strong; the LORD of hosts is his name: he shall throughly plead their cause, that he may give rest to the land, and disquiet the inhabitants of Babylon." {disquieted 6x., disquietness 1x., tot. = 8x.}

Dissembleth – 1x., v. [A.D. 1513, < E. **dissemble** (< ME. '*dissimule*' < OF. *dissimuler* < L. *dissimulare*, *dis* = 'utterly apart' (see L. prefix '*dis–*') + *simulare* = 'to make like or imitate' (< L. *similes* = 'like')) + **eth** = pres. ind. 3rd pers. sing. (see E. suffix '–eth')] Thus, **dissembleth** means 'the pres. ind. 3rd pers. action of someone trying to hide their true likeness' (i.e. 'disguising their opinions and intentions'). Eg. Pr.26:24, "He that hateth dissembleth with his lips, and layeth up deceit within him." {dissembled 3x., dissemblers 1x., tot. = 5x.}

Dissension –3x., n. [A.D. 1300, < OF. *dissension* < L. *dissensio* < *dissentire* (< *dis* = 'utterly apart' (see L. prefix '*dis–*') + *sentire* = 'to think or feel') = 'to think or feel completely different' (NOI. The ending 'sion' in 'dissension' = E. **tion** and shows an action, process, state or condition.)] Thus, a **dissension** is 'the state or condition of thinking and feeling different in a very emotional way'. Eg. Act.15:2, "When therefore Paul and Barnabas had no small dissension and disputation with them, they determined that Paul and Barnabas, and certain other of them, should go up to Jerusalem unto the apostles and elders about this question." (NOI. Here, the early church struggled over whether a Gentile could be saved if he was not living by the laws of the OT.)

Dissimulation –2x., n. [A.D. 1384, < OF. *dissimulation* < L. *dissimulatio* (< *dissimulare*, *dis* = 'utterly apart' (see L. prefix '*dis–*') + *simulare* = 'to make like' or 'to imitate' (< L. *similes*

= 'like') + *tio* (= E. **tion** and shows an action, process, state or condition.)] Thus, a **dissimulation** is 'the state or condition of concealing true thoughts and intentions by falsehood and hypocrisy' (see also 'Dissembleth'). Eg. Gal.2:13, "And the other Jews dissembled likewise with him; insomuch that Barnabas also was carried away with their dissimulation." (NOI. The entire context of Gal.2 should be carefully studied so as to grasp the full weight of the word 'dissimulation'.)

Distaff —1x., n. [A.D. 1000, < OE. **distǽf**, **dis** (akin to LG. *di-esse* = 'strips of flax wrapped around a staff') + **stǽf** = 'a staff' (= 'a stick or rod used for walking, self defense or some other purpose')] Thus, a **distaff** is 'a 3-foot (.9m.) long stick used for holding the unprocessed bulk wool or flax'. Eg. Pr.31:19, "She layeth her hands to the spindle, and her hands hold the distaff." (NOI. Threads of wool were pulled from the distaff, using the fingers of the left hand, twisted between the thumb and index finger and onto a spindle of a spinning wheel, thereby resulting in a spool of thread.)

Distil —2x., v. [A.D. 1374, < L. *distillare* (more correctly *des-tillare*, *de* = 'away from' (see L. prefix '*de–*'[3]) + *stillare* = 'to drip' or 'to drop'] Thus, **distil** means 'the action of dripping away from'. Eg. Job.36:27-28, "For he maketh small the drops of water: they pour down rain according to the vapour thereof: Which the clouds do drop and distil upon man abundantly." (See also 'Dew'.)

Distress —33x., n. and v. [A.D. 1290, (n. < OF. *destrece*; and v. < OF. *destrecier*) both < L. *districtus* ((which is pp. of) *dis-tringere*, *dis* = 'utterly apart' (see L. prefix '*dis-*') + *stringere* = 'to draw up tight' or 'to press together tightly') = 'severely strict'] Thus, as a n., **distress** is 'the state of extreme affliction, sorrow and trouble'. Eg. Ps.118:5, "I called upon the LORD in distress: the LORD answered me, and set me in a large place." Furthermore, as a v., **distress** means 'the action of causing someone great sorrow, affliction and trouble'. Eg. Deut.2:9, "And the **LORD** said unto me, Distress not the Moabites, neither contend with them in battle..." {distressed 11x., distresses 8x., tot. = 52x.}

Distribute —5x., inf., prp. and pp. [A.D. 1434, < L. *distributus* (which is pp. of) *distribuere* (< *dis* = 'utterly apart' (see L. prefix '*dis–*') + *tribuere* = 'to grant, pay or give') = 'to deal out' as in 'shares of something'] Thus, as an inf., **distribute** means 'the open-ended action of dividing and giving out' Eg. 1Tim.6:18, "That they do good, that they be rich in good works, ready to distribute, willing to communicate." Furthermore, as a prp., **distribute** modifies its n. as 'being divided and given out'. Eg. Josh.13:32, "These are the countries which Moses did distribute for inheritance in the plains of Moab, on the other side Jordan, by Jericho, eastward." (NOI. Josh.13:32 is constructed for emphasis, using the past-tense 'did' with the prp. 'distribute'.) Finally, as a pp., **distribute** modifies its n. as 'performing a continuing action of dividing and giving out'. Eg. Lk.18:22, "Now when Jesus heard these things, he said unto him, Yet lackest thou one thing: sell all that thou hast, and distribute unto the poor, and thou shalt have treasure in heaven: and come, follow me." {distributed 6., distributeth 1x., distributing 1x., distribution 2x., tot. = 15x.}

Ditch —6x., n. [A.D. 1045, < ME. **dich** < OE. **dic** = 'a hole dug in the ground' (NOI. 'Ditches' were usually long and narrow, like a trench, and used for irrigation, drainage or protection, as in 'a moat'. However, they could also simply be a deep hole.)] Thus, a **ditch** is 'a hole dug in the earth, usually long and narrow, and normally used for irrigation'. Eg. Ps.7:15, "He made a pit, and digged it, and is fallen into the ditch which he made." (NOI. The 'ditch' in this vs. is the Hb. word שחת (*shachath*), which was also meant 'a grave' or 'a pit in which to trap lions'. 'Ditch' is also used figuratively in Pr.23:27 in reference to a whore and the danger connected with her.)

{ditches 1x., tot. = 7x.}

Divers —37x., adj. and n. pl [A.D. 1250, < ME. **divers** < OF. *divers* < L. *diversus* = 'to be turned in different ways' (which is pp. of) *divertere*, *di* = 'utterly apart' (see L. prefix *dis*-) + *vertere* = 'to turn')] Thus, as an adj., **divers** modifies its n. (always pl.) as 'being different in character or quality in comparison to other things or to each other'. Eg. Lk.4:40, "Now when the sun was setting, all they that had any sick with divers diseases brought them unto him; and he laid his hands on every one of them, and healed them." Furthermore, as a n. pl., **divers** are 'two or more persons that are different in character or quality from other people'. Eg. 2Chr.30:11, "Nevertheless divers of Asher and Manasseh and of Zebulun humbled themselves, and came to Jerusalem." {diverse 8x., diversities 3x., tot. = 48x.}

Diverse — 8x., adj. [A.D. 1297, < ME. **divers** (see 'Divers') (NOI. The 1611 used 'divers' and 'diverse' according to what would fit in a line of type. Eg. The 1611, in Est.1:7, uses 'divers' whereas the KJV uses 'diverse'; and in Mt.4:24 the 1611 uses 'diverse' whereas the KJV uses 'divers'. Hence, in 1611, there was no difference between the words. However, in the 1700's, 'diverse' became more directly associated with L. *diversus*.)] Thus, **diverse** means the same as 'divers'. Eg. Dan.7:7, "... it was diverse from all the beasts that were before it; and it had ten horns." {divers 37x., diversities 3x., tot. = 48x.}

Divide — 49x., v. [A.D. 1494, < ME. **dividen** < L. *dividere* (= 'to force assunder' or 'to separate'), *di* = 'apart' (see L. prefix '*dis*–') + *videre* = 'to see' or 'to separate' (possibly from Sans. *vidh* = 'to bore through') (NOI. Our E. 'individual' comes from ML. *individualis*, meaning 'something that is not divisible'.)] Thus, **divide** means 'the action of forcing something apart into two or more parts'. Eg. 1Ki.3:25, "And the king said, Divide the living child in two, and give half to the one, and half to the other." {divided 69x., divider 1x., divideth 10x., dividing 7x., division 6x., divisions 17x., tot. = 159x.}

Divination —12x., n. [A.D. 1374, < E. **divine** (< OF. *devin* < L. *divinare* = 'to predict or foretell' (< *divinus* = 'divine or divinely inspired')) + **ation**' = 'action, process, state or condition' (see E. suffix '–tion')] Thus, a **divination** is 'the condition of being able to foretell or predict the future'. Eg. Act.16:16, "And it came to pass, as we went to prayer, a certain damsel possessed with a spirit of divination met us, which brought her masters much gain by soothsaying." (See also 'Soothsayer'.)

Diviners —7x., n. pl. [A.D. 1340, < E. **divine** (see 'Divination') + **er** = 'identifies a person according to their occupation' (see E. suffix '–er') + **s** = forms the pl.] Thus, **diviners** are 'two or more people whose occupation it was to predict or foretell future events'. Eg. Zec.10:2, "For the idols have spoken vanity, and the diviners have seen a lie, and have told false dreams; they comfort in vain: therefore they went their way as a flock, they were troubled, because there was no shepherd."

Division —6x., n. [A.D. 1374, < E. **divide** (see 'Divide') + **ion** = 'action, process, state or condition' (see E. suffix '–tion')] Thus, a **division** is 'the state or condition of forcing things apart'. Eg. Ex.8:23, "And I will put a division between my people and thy people: to morrow shall this sign be." {divide 49x., divided 69x., divider 1x., divideth 10x., dividing 7x., divisions 17x., tot. = 159x.}

Divorce —1x., n. [A.D. 1377, < OF. *divorce* (= 'a dissolution of marriage') < L. *divortium* < *divertere* (< *di* = 'utterly apart' (see L. prefix *dis-*) + *vertere* = 'to turn') = 'utter separation' (NOI. 'Divorce' refers to the marital separation of a husband and wife and, interestingly, was always directed at the wife and not the husband.)] Thus, a **divorce** is 'an utter separation of a husband and wife'. Eg. Jer.3:8, "And I saw, when for all the causes whereby backsliding Israel committed adultery I had put her away, and given her a bill of divorce; yet her treacherous sister Judah feared not, but went and played the harlot also." (NOI. The 'bill' of divorce was the legal document that was placed in the hands of the rejected wife. See also 'Bill'.)

Divorcement –6x., n. [A.D. 1526, < E. **divorce** (se 'Divorce') + **ment** = forms the n. and shows 'the means of the action' (see E. suffix '–ment')] Thus, a **divorcement** is 'the instrument which causes the divorce between a husband and wife' (i.e. the 'bill of divorcement'). Eg. Mk.10:4, "And they said, Moses suffered to write a bill of divorcement, and to put her away."

Doctor – 1x., n. [A.D. 1303, < OF. *doctor* < L. *doctor* = 'teacher' (< L. *docere* = 'to teach') (NOI. In A.D. 1375, 'doctor' was applied to one who 'held the highest degree in a university'. It was often applied to religious teachers, but was not generally applied to medical teachers until the 1500's.)] Thus, a **doctor** is 'a well-studied teacher who gives instruction in some area of knowledge'. Eg. Act.5:34, "Then stood there up one in the council, a Pharisee, named Gamaliel, a doctor of the law, had in reputation among all the people, and commanded to put the apostles forth a little space."

Doctrine –51x., n. [A.D. 1382(WB.), < OF. *doctrine* < L. *doctrina* = 'teaching or learning'] Thus, **doctrine** is 'the state of teaching or that which is taught (i.e. 'lesson or group of lessons'). Eg 2Tim.3:16, "All scripture is given by inspiration of God, and is profitable for doctrine, for reproof, for correction, for instruction in righteousness."

Doest –45x., v. [A.D. 825(?), 2nd pers. sing. pres. ind. of v. 'do' (used predicatively, which seems to make the most sense. See section on 'KJV Pronouns' and E. suffix '–est'.)] Thus, **doest** means 'the pres. tense 2nd pers. ind. action of 'do', which makes a strong statement'. Eg. Gen.4:7, "If thou doest well, shalt thou not be accepted? and if thou doest not well, sin lieth at the door. And unto thee shall be his desire, and thou shalt rule over him." {did 1006x., didst 122x., do 1368x., doer 8x., doers 7x., doeth 96x., doing 39x., doings 51x., done 565x., dost 56x., doth 207x. (incl. title of Ps.54), tot. = 3570x.}

Doeth – 96x., v. [A.D. 825(?), 3rd pers. sing. pres. ind. of v. 'do' (used attributively, which seems to make the most sense. See section on 'KJV Pronouns' and E. suffix '–eth'.)] Thus, **doeth** means 'the pres. tense 3rd pers. ind. action of 'do', which makes a simple statement'. Eg. Gen.31:12, "... for I have seen all that Laban doeth unto thee." {did 1006x., didst 122x., do 1368x., doer 8x., doers 7x., doest 45x., doing 39x., doings 51x., done 565x., dost 56x., doth 207x. (incl. title of Ps.54), tot. = 3570x.}

Dog – 15x., n. [A.D. 1050, < OE. **docga** < oo., (NOI. No one knows where the word 'dog' came from, but it replaced the E. word 'hound', which was from A.D. 888, and referred to the powerful breeds of the animal used in hunting and guarding. They were not considered cute home pets as they are today. The Hb. word is כלב (*keleb*) which comes from a root word meaning 'to yelp' or 'to attack'. (The OT. name 'Caleb' also comes from כלב (*Kaleb*).) Nevertheless, it refers to a four-legged carnivorous (flesh-eating) animal, probably a descendent of the wolf, and may have been the earliest of all domesticated animals after Noah's flood. In the Bible, dogs are never pictured as enjoying tender-loving relations with humans, but instead, are pictured as rough, and sometimes wild scavengers. Dogs were even pictured on Egyptian pyramid walls as fierce hunters. In fact, some people were referred to as 'dogs' as a form of contempt and scorn. See 1Sam.17:43.)] Thus, a **dog** is 'a four-legged carnivore, similar to a wolf'. Eg. Ps.59:14, "And at evening let them return; and let them make a noise like a dog, and go round about the city." (NOI. Figuratively, a 'dog' referred to a male prostitute (Deut.23:18) and wicked people (Ps.22:16), among other things.) {dog's 2x., dogs 24x., tot. = 41x.}

Doleful – 2x., adj. [A.D. 1275, < E. **dole** (< OF. *dol* < LL. *dolium* < LL. *dolere* = 'to suffer' or 'to grieve') = 'grief or suffering' + **ful** = forms the adj., indicating 'the characteristic of'] Thus, **doleful** modifies its n. as 'being characterized by grief or sorrow'. Eg. Mic.2:4, "In that day shall one take up a parable against you, and lament with a doleful lamentation, and say, We be utterly spoiled…"

Dominion – 62x., n. [A.D. 1430, < OF. *dominion* < L. *dominium* = 'ownership or property' (< *dominus* = 'lord or master')] Thus, a **dominion** is 'the state or condition of governing control'. Eg. Ps.8:6, "Thou madest him to have dominion over the works of thy hands; thou hast put all things under his feet." {dominions 2x., tot. = 64x.}

Doorkeeper – 1x., n. [A.D. 1535, < E. **door** (< OE. **duru** (or **dor**) akin to ON. *dyrr* and Du. *deur* and Ger. *thur* = 'gate' or 'door') + **keeper** (< **keep** = 'observe, heed, regard' (see 'Keep') + **er** = identifies occupation (see E. suffix '–er')] Thus, a **doorkeeper** is 'one whose occupation it was to stand guard at the door of a building'. Eg. Ps.84:10, "For a day in thy courts is better than a thousand. I had rather be a doorkeeper in the house of my God, than to dwell in the tents of wickedness."

Dost – 56x., v. [A.D. 825(?) 2nd pers. sing. pres. ind. of v. 'do' (used predicatively, which seems to make the most sense. See section on 'KJV Pronouns' and E. suffix '–est'. See also 'Doth'.)] Thus, **dost** means 'the pres. tense 2nd pers. ind. action of 'do', which makes a strong statement'. Eg. Rom.14:10, "But why dost thou judge thy brother? or why dost thou set at nought thy brother? for we shall all stand before the judgment seat of Christ." {did 1006x., didst 122x., do 1368x., doer 8x., doers 7x., doest 45x., doeth 96x., doing 39x., doings 51x., done 565x., doth 207x. (incl. title of Ps.54), tot. = 3570x.}

Dote – 1x., v. [A.D. 1205, < ME. **doten** (akin to D. *dutten* (= 'to doze') and Ice. *dotta* (= 'to nod from sleep')) = 'to act silly, playful and weak-minded'] Thus, **dote** means 'the action of talking and acting foolishly')(as if one had not enough sleep). Eg. Jer.50:36, "A sword is upon the liars; and they shall dote: a sword is upon her mighty men; and they shall be dismayed." {doted 6x., tot. = 7x.}

Doth – 207x., v. [A.D. 825(?), 3rd per. sing. pres. ind. of v. 'do' (used attributively, which seems to make the most sense. See section on 'KJV Pronouns' and E. suffix '–eth'. See also 'Dost'.)] Thus, **doth** means 'the pres. tense 3rd pers. ind. action of 'do', which makes a simple statement'. Eg. Gen.45:3, "And Joseph said unto his brethren, I am Joseph; doth my father yet live? And his brethren could not answer him; for they were troubled at his presence." {did 1006x., didst 122x., do 1368x., doer 8x., doers 7x., doest 45x., doeth 96x., doing 39x., doings 51x., done 565x., dost 56x., tot. = 3570x.}

Double[1] –24x., adj. and n. [A.D. 1225, < OF. *double* (< L. *duplus*, *duo* = 'two' + *plus* = 'much, more') = 'twice as much'] Thus, as an adj., **double** modifies its n. as 'being twice as big or twice as much as before'. Eg. Deut.21:17, "But he shall acknowledge the son of the hated for the firstborn, by giving him a double portion of all that he hath: for he is the beginning of his strength; the right of the firstborn is his." Furthermore, as a n., a **double** is 'something that is twice as big, or twice as much'. Eg. Ex.22:7, "If a man shall deliver unto his neighbour money or stuff to keep, and it be stolen out of the man's house; if the thief be found, let him pay double." {doubletongued 1x., tot. = 25x.}

Double[2] – 2x., v. [A.D. 1290, < OF. *doubler* (< L. *duplare* < *duplus* (see 'Double'[1])) = 'to make twice as much'] Thus, **double** means 'the action of making something twice as big, or twice as great as before'. Eg. Ex.26:9, "And thou shalt couple five curtains by themselves, and six curtains by themselves, and shalt double the sixth curtain in the forefront of the tabernacle." {doubled (pp.) 4x., tot. = 6x.}

Doubletongued – 1x., adj. [A.D. 1382(WB.), < E. **double** (see 'Double'[1]) + **tongued** (< E. **tongue** (= 'voice, speech' – see 'Tongue') + **ed** = forms the adj. (see E. suffix '–ed'[5])) = 'saying two things that are not consistent'] Thus, **doubletongued** modifies its n. (in this case, 'deacons') as 'speaking inconsistent things' (as in 'deceitful or insincere speech'). Eg. 1Tim.3:8, "Likewise must the deacons be grave, not doubletongued, not given to much wine, not greedy of filthy lucre." {double[1] 24x., double[2] 2x., doubled 4x., tot. = 31x.}

Doubt[1] – 10x., n. [A.D. 1225, < ME. **dout** < OF. *doute* = 'condition of uncertainty' (see 'Doubt'[2]) (NOI. The L. spelling influenced the E. change of spelling from 'dout' to 'doubt'.)] Thus, a **doubt** is 'a state or condition of being uncertain'. Eg. Gal.4:20, "I desire to be present with you now, and to change my voice; for I stand in doubt of you." {doubtful (adj.) 2x., doubtless (adj. in Num.14:30; Isa.63:16; 1Cor.9:2; and Phil.3:8) 4x., doubts 2x., tot. = 18x.}

Doubt[2] – 3x., v. [A.D. 1225, < ME. **douten** < OF. *douter* < L. *dubitare* = 'to waver in opinion' or 'to be uncertain' (NOI. Our E. words 'dubitable' (= 'can be doubted') and 'indubitable (= 'cannot be doubted') come from this L. root *dubitare*.)] Thus, **doubt** means 'the action of hesitation and wavering in opinion'. Eg. Mk.11:23, "For verily I say unto you, That whosoever shall say unto this mountain, Be thou removed, and be thou cast into the sea; and shall not doubt in his heart, but shall believe that those things which he saith shall come to pass; he shall have whatsoever he saith." {doubted 4., doubteth 1x., doubting (prp.) 4x., doubtless (adv. in 2Sam.5:19; Ps.126:6; and 2Cor.12:1) 3x., tot. = 15x.}

Dowry —4x., n. [A.D.1330, < E. **dower** (< OF. *douaire* < ML. *dotarium* < L. *dotare* = 'to endow' or 'to provide some gift') + **ry** = 'a collection of things' (see E. suffix '–ery' [4]) (NOI. The basic idea of a 'dowry' was the 'price of a bride'. It was sometimes paid to a father-in-law for the economic loss of his daughter, and privilege of marrying her. In the case of Jacob, he paid Laban by giving him 14 years of service. A dowry often came with a bride and was used as an incentive for some man to marry her. Leah considered her children to be a good dowry. A dowry was also understood to be the estate a widow receives at the death of her husband. See Gen.30:20.)] Thus, a **dowry** is 'a collection of some form of wealth brought to a marriage either by the bride (for her husband) or by the groom (for his father-in-law)'. Eg. Gen.34:12, "Ask me never so much dowry and gift, and I will give according as ye shall say unto me: but give me the damsel to wife."

Drag - 2x., n. [A.D. 1388, < OE. (v.) **dragan** = 'to draw or pull slowly with force' (NOI. Although a 'drag' was a word describing a few different devices, in the Bible, the only type of drag mentioned was for fishing.)] Thus, a **drag** is 'a net-like device attached to ropes, which is pulled along the bottom of a lake or ocean by a boat, in hopes of catching fish, oysters, etc.'. Eg. Hab.1:15, "They take up all of them with the angle, they catch them in their net, and gather them in their drag: therefore they rejoice and are glad." (See also 'Draught'.) {dragging 1x., tot. = 3x.}

Dragon — 19x., n. [A.D. 1220, < OF. *dragon* < L. *draco* (= 'dragon, snake') < Gk. δρακων (*drakon*) (probably from Gk. δερκομαι (*derkomai*) = 'to see clearly', similar to how a reptile can stare at its prey without blinking), which is the NT. equal to the OT. Hb. תנין (*tanniyn*) = 'serpent, whale or dragon' (NOI. Today, many scoff at the word 'dragon', but dragons could well have been a variety of extinct dinosaur-lizards. Today, living on the Komodo island of Indonesia, is the world's largest lizard, called the Komodo Dragon (*Varanus komodoensis*). This 'dragon' reaches a length of 3 meters, or about 10 ft., however, scientists say it was not the largest, as the now extinct Australian *Varanus priscus* was perhaps 30 ft. (9.14 m.) long. The adult Komodo Dragons are cannibals and are fully capable of killing and eating a human. They have powerful claws, and long, forked tongues (to detect odor and taste). They can run as fast as a dog in pursuit of a prey, and are also excellent swimmers. They are not venomous, but their saliva is so full of bacteria, that their bite will result in sickness and death. Some suggest that the 'fiery flying serpent' (Isa.14:29; 30:6) was such a beast. The Bible describes dragons as deadly to man (Deut.32:3; Ps.44:19), and of various sizes ranging from very large (Eze.29:3) (and able to swallow up things whole (Jer.51:34)), to somewhat smaller (Isa.43:20). Rev.12:4 suggests they have a large, powerful tail. Dragons dwell in dens of the earth(Jer.10:22), in ruinous places (Isa.34:13; Jer.49:33; 51:37) and in the depths of the seas (Ps.74:13; Isa.27:1) and make a wailing noise (Mic.1:8). It is possible that the dragon may be somehow related with the 'serpent' of Gen.3:1. The largest, fiercest spiritual foe is Satan, whom the Bible refers to as a 'dragon' (Rev.20:2). See also 'Behemoth' and 'Leviathan'.)] Thus, a **dragon** was 'a dangerous wild beast, of varying size; some dwelling in wastelands and others in the sea; all of which now appear extinct'. Eg. Isa.27:1, "In that day the LORD with his sore and great and strong sword shall punish leviathan the piercing serpent, even leviathan that crooked serpent; and he shall slay the dragon that is in the sea." {dragons 16x., tot. = 35x.}

Drams –6x., n. pl. [A.D. 1440, < OF. *drame* (= 'the eighth part of an oz., or 60 grains') < L. *drachma* (= 'Greek weight' or 'a Greek silver coin') < Gk. δραχμή (*drachme*) = 'a handful' or 'as much as one can hold in the hand' (NOI. A δραχμή was the foremost silver coin used in the ancient Greek economy.) + s = forms the pl.] Thus, **drams** are 'two or more measures of weight, each one equal to an eighth of an oz., or 60 grains'. Eg. Ezr.2:69, "They gave after their ability unto the treasure of the work threescore and one thousand drams of gold, and five thousand pound of silver, and one hundred priests' garments."

Drank – 19x., v. pret. [A.D. 1000(AT.), < OE. **drincan** = 'to consume a liquid or beverage' (NOI. 'Drank' and the v. pret. 'drunk' are similar in meaning but differ in volume. See 'Drunk' for comments and note on word-count.)] Thus, **drank** means 'the past-tense action of consuming a liquid or beverage'. Eg. 1Ki.17:6, "And the ravens brought him bread and flesh in the morning, and bread and flesh in the evening; and he drank of the brook." (NOI. It is the author's opinion that Noah was not a man in the habit of drinking alcoholic beverages, and may never have tasted it prior to his experience in Gen.9:21. This would explain why a small amount would make him intoxicated.) {drink 369x., drinkers 1x., drinketh 17x., drinking 21x. drinks 1x., drunk 30x., drunkard 5x., drunkards 6x., drunken 33x., drunkenness 7x., tot. = 509x.}

Draught – 5x., n. [A.D. 1200, (pronounced, 'draft') < OE. **dragan** = 'to draw' (see 'Drag') and had a variety of meanings, but in the Bible its primary meaning is 'something which catches' (NOI. A 'draught house' (2Ki.10:27) was a public toilet or latrine, considered to be one of the most filthy of places, and the greatest insult to Baal.)] Thus, a **draught** is 'a hole in the ground which receives human waste', (cp. Deut.23:13). Eg. Mt.15:17, "Do not ye yet understand, that whatsoever entereth in at the mouth goeth into the belly, and is cast out into the draught? " Furthermore, a **draught** is 'a catch of prey' (such as a net full of fishes.). Eg. Lk.5:9, "For he was astonished, and all that were with him, at the draught of the fishes which they had taken."

Drave –13x., v. pret. [A.D. 1300, < E. **drive** < OE. **drifan** = 'to send with impelling force'] Thus, **drave** is 'the past-tense action of sending with a reasonable, impelling force'. Eg. 1Chr.13:7, "And they carried the ark of God in a new cart out of the house of Abinadab: and Uzza and Ahio drave the cart." (NOI. 'Drave' and 'drove'[2] are similar words in meaning but different in emphasis, or intensity. A study of the five Hb. words and two Gk. words (all translated 'drave') including their contexts, indicates that 'drave' is the stronger, or more emphatic word. Shakespeare also uses 'drove' 8x and 'drave' 4x, and by comparison, one can see that his use of 'drave' is the stronger word. See also 'Drove'[2].) {drive 57x., driven 49x., driver 2x., driveth 4x., driving 4x., drove[2] 9x., overdrive 1x., tot. = 139x.}

Dread – 9x., n. and v. [A.D. 1175, < ME. **dreden** < oo., but probably from OE. **ondrǽdan** = 'to fear greatly, with terror and awe'] Thus, as a n., **dread** is 'the state or condition of great fear and terror, with awe'. Eg. Gen.9:2, "And the fear of you and the dread of you shall be upon every beast of the earth, and upon every fowl of the air, upon all that moveth upon the earth, and upon all the fishes of the sea; into your hand are they delivered." Furthermore, as a v., **dread** means 'the action of fearing greatly coupled with terror and awe.' Eg. Deut.1:29, "Then I said unto you, Dread not, neither be afraid of them." {dreadful 9x., tot. = 18x.}

Dream – 74x., n. and v. [A.D. 1250, < ME. **drem** (possibly from OE. **dreman**) = 'the involuntary images, ideas or thoughts which are present during sleep'] Thus, as a n., a **dream** is 'a series of involuntary images, ideas or thoughts which are present in the mind during sleep'. Eg. 1Ki.3:5, "In Gibeon the LORD appeared to Solomon in a dream by night: and God said, Ask what I shall give thee." (NOI. Most dreams in the Bible are found in Gen. and Dan. and have divine intervention.) Furthermore, as a v., **dream** means 'the action of experiencing images, ideas or thoughts during sleep'. Eg. Joe.2:28, "And it shall come to pass afterward, that I will pour out my spirit upon all flesh; and your sons and your daughters shall prophesy, your old men shall dream dreams, your young men shall see visions." (See also 'Trance' and 'Vision'.) {dreamed 20x., dreamer 4x., dreamers 2x., dreameth 2x., dreams 21x. tot. = 123x.}

Dress —9x., v. [A.D. 1300(?), < OF. *dresser* (= 'to arrange' or 'set in order') < L. *directus* = 'straight, direct' (see 'Direct') (NOI. 'Dress' seems to be only used in the Bible in reference to a food-product or a sacrifice.)] Thus, **dress** means 'the action of arranging and setting in order a food or sacrifice'. Eg. 2Sam.12:4, "And there came a traveller unto the rich man, and he spared to take of his own flock and of his own herd, to dress for the wayfaring man that was come unto him; but took the poor man's lamb, and dressed it for the man that was come to him." {dressed 7x., dresser 1x., dresseth 1x., undressed 2x., tot. = 20x.}

Dromedary —1x., n. [A.D. 1280, < OF. *dromadaire* (= 'a great beast of burden, like a camel') < LL. *dromedarius* < L. *dromas* < Gk. δρομας (*dromas*) = 'running' (referring to the swiftness of the one-humped Arabian breed of camel) (See also 'Camel'.)] Thus, a **dromedary** is 'a one-humped, swift running camel from Arabia'. Eg. Jer.2:23, "How canst thou say, I am not polluted, I have not gone after Baalim? see thy way in the valley, know what thou hast done: thou art a swift dromedary traversing her ways." {dromedaries 3x., tot. = 4x.}

Dropsy — 1x., n. [A.D. 1290, < ME. **dropesie** (for **ydropesie**) < OF. *hydropisie* < L. *hydropisis* < Gk. ὑδρωψ (*hudrops*) (NOI. 'Dropsy' is a massive build up of fluid in certain parts of the body, including around the heart, liver, kidneys or brain'. The arms, legs, stomach and face may become bloated with fluid, and there may be much coughing and shortness of breath (caused by pressure against the diaphragm). Death often comes from heart failure. In 1998, a serious epidemic outbreak of dropsy happened in New Delhi, India resulting in thousands of cases, many deaths and much suffering. Health officials claim it was caused by consuming a mixture of mustard-seed oil and Satyanashi-seed oil.)] Thus, **dropsy** is 'a disease that causes a massive build up of fluids within the body, and bloats the face, arms, legs and stomach, resulting in much suffering and death by, usually, heart failure'. Eg. Lk.14:2, "And, behold, there was a certain man before him which had the dropsy."

Drought – 10x., n. [A.D. 1000, < OE. **drūgath** (= 'dryness of weather') < **dryge** = 'dry'] Thus, a **drought** is 'a dryness in the weather' (i.e. 'no rain'). Eg. Deut.8:15, "Who led thee through that great and terrible wilderness, wherein were fiery serpents, and scorpions, and drought, where there was no water; who brought thee forth water out of the rock of flint."

Drove[1] – 4x., n. [A.D. 934, < OE. (n.) **draf** (< (v.) **drifan** (see 'Drove' [2])) = 'a number of domestic animals (such as sheep or cows) driven in a group'] Thus, a **drove** is 'a number of domestic animals, driven in one big group'. Eg. Gen.32:16 "And he delivered them into the hand of his servants, every drove by themselves; and said unto his servants, Pass over before me, and put a space betwixt drove and drove."

Drove[2] – 9x., v. pret. [A.D. 1300(?), < E. **drive** < OE. **drifan** = 'to send with impelling force'] Thus, **drove** means 'the past-tense action of sending with a powerful, impelling force.' Eg. Jn.2:15, "And when he had made a scourge of small cords, he drove them all out of the temple, and the sheep, and the oxen; and poured out the changers' money, and overthrew the tables." (NOI. 'Drove'[2] and 'drave' are similar words in meaning but different in emphasis, or intensity. A study of the five Hb. words and one Gk. word (all translated 'drove'), including their contexts, indicates that 'drave' is the stronger, more emphatic word. See also 'Drave'.) {drave 13x., drive 57x., driven 49x., driver 2x., driveth 4x., driving 4x., overdrive 1x., tot. = 139x.}

Drowsiness – 1x., n. [A.D. 1559, < (adj.) **drowsy** (< **drowse** < OE. **drūsian** = 'to sink and become sluggish') + **ness** = 'a state or condition' (see E. suffix '–ness')] Thus, **drowsiness** is 'the state or condition of heavy sluggishness' (as in 'half asleep'). Eg. Pr.23:21, "For the drunkard and the glutton shall come to poverty: and drowsiness shall clothe a man with rags."

Drunk – 30x., adj. and v. pret. [A.D. 800, < OE. (n.) **drync** = 'the state of having consumed much (usually alcoholic) beverage' (NOI. The n. came before the v. pret, **dronk** (= 'the past-tense action of drinking') which came in A.D. 1350. As a v. pret., 'drunk' and 'drank' are similar, but differ in quantity, as 'drunk' speaks of a greater amount consumed. Be aware that in Gen.43:34, the 1611 says 'drunke', whereas the KJV says 'drank'. This will slightly affect the meaning and the word-count of both words.)] Thus, as an adj., **drunk** modifies its n. as 'being intoxicated by consuming a great quantity of an alcoholic beverage'. Eg. Eph.5:18, "And be not drunk with wine, wherein is excess; but be filled with the Spirit." (NOI. The adj. 'drunk' is sometimes used figuratively of delirious, or 'out of one's mind with excitement', as in Rev.17:2.) Furthermore, as a v. pret, **drunk** means 'the past-tense action of consuming a great quantity of a beverage'. Eg. Jn.2:10, "And saith unto him, Every man at the beginning doth set forth good wine; and when men have well drunk, then that which is worse: but thou hast kept the good wine until now." {drank 19x., drink 369x., drinkers 1x., drinketh 17x., drinking 21x. drinks 1x., drunkard 5x., drunkards 6x., drunken 33x., drunkenness 7x., tot. = 509x.}

Dryshod – 1x., adj. [A.D. 1535(CB.), originally two words, **drye shod** (= 'dry shoed', i.e. 'dry shoes and feet')] Thus, **dryshod** modifies its n. (in this case 'men') as 'having dry shoes and feet'. Eg. Isa.11:15, "And the LORD shall utterly destroy the tongue of the Egyptian sea; and with his mighty wind shall he shake his hand over the river, and shall smite it in the seven streams, and make men go over dryshod."

Dues – 1x., n. pl. [A.D. 1430, < E. **due** (< OF. *deu* = 'owed or owing' < L. *debere* = 'to owe' or 'to be indebted') + **s** = forms the pl.] Thus, **dues** are 'two or more things that are owed to other people'. Eg. Rom.13:7, "Render therefore to all their dues: tribute to whom tribute is due; custom to whom custom; fear to whom fear; honour to whom honour." {due 31x., tot. = 32x.}

Duke – 43x., adj. [A.D. 1129, < ME. **duc** < OF. *duc* < ML. *duke* < L. *dux* (= 'leader') < *ducere* = 'to lead' (NOI. In LL., a *dux* was the governor of a province. In a monarchy, 'duke' was applied to a nobleman of the highest rank, just below the prince.)] Thus, a **duke** is 'a leader of a tribe or territory'. Eg. Gen.36:18, "And these are the sons of Aholibamah Esau's wife; duke Jeush, duke Jaalam, duke Korah: these were the dukes that came of Aholibamah the daughter of Anah, Esau's wife." {dukes 15., tot. = 58x.}

Dulcimer – 3x., adj. [A.D. 1475, < OF. *doulcemer* (probably from L. *dulce melos* = 'pleasant song') = 'pleasant sounding instrument' (NOI. Some say the 1611 is in error, and should have said 'bagpipe', or some wind instrument, yet the Hb. word is סיפניא (*ciyphonya*), which is supposed to be from Gk. συμφωνία (*sumphonia*) = 'a symphony' or 'harmony of sounds'. However, the 1611 itself has a marginal note, "*singing, Chaldee symphony*", indicating that the translators were well aware of this. The WB. and the CB. both say 'symphonies' instead of dulcimer, but the BB. and the GB. both say 'dulcimer'. The 'dulcimer' is considered to be the ancestor of the modern piano, and was much in use during the 1600's. The 'dulcimer', like the piano, is able to produce a 'harmony of sounds', and this may be why the BB. and GB. and 1611 all chose 'dulcimer'.)] Thus, a **dulcimer** 'is a sound box over which strings were stretched and hit to make harmonious, musical sounds'. Eg. Dan.3:5, "That at what time ye hear the sound of the cornet, flute, harp, sackbut, psaltery, dulcimer, and all kinds of musick, ye fall down and worship the golden image that Nebuchadnezzar the king hath set up."

Dull – 3x., adj. [A.D. 975(RG.), < ME. **dul** (probably from OE. **dyl** < OE. **dol** = 'foolish, stupid') = 'not quick to learn, but slow of understanding'] Thus, **dull** modifies its n. as 'being slow to understand words, thoughts, doctrine, etc.' Eg. Mt.13:15, "For this people's heart is waxed gross, and their ears are dull of hearing, and their eyes they have closed; lest at any time they should see with their eyes, and hear with their ears, and should understand with their heart, and should be converted, and I should heal them."

Dumb –29x., adj. and n. [A.D. 1000(ASG.), < OE. **dumb** (akin to Ice. *dumbr* and Goth. *dumbs*) = 'mute' (NOI. The Ger. *dumm* and Du. *dum* both mean 'stupid, dull', which is where our E. 'dumb', as in 'stupid' comes from.)] Thus, as an adj., **dumb** modifies its n. as 'being mute and unable to speak'. Eg. Ps.38:13, "But I, as a deaf man, heard not; and I was as a dumb man that openeth not his mouth." Furthermore, as a n., **dumb** is 'the state or condition of not being able to speak'. Eg. Mt.9:33, "And when the devil was cast out, the dumb spake: and the multitudes marvelled, saying, It was never so seen in Israel."

Dung –28x., n. and v. [A.D. 1000, < OE. **dung** < oo., but refers to 'the excrement or waste matter from the body' (NOI. The 'dung gate' (Neh.3:13) was the gate in Jerusalem through which the dung and other garbage was removed.)] Thus, as a n., **dung** is 'the solid waste matter discharged from the bodies of humans and animals'. Eg. Ex.29:14, "But the flesh of the bullock, and his skin, and his dung, shalt thou burn with fire without the camp: it is a sin offering." Furthermore, as a v., **dung** means 'the action of fertilizing soil with manure'. Eg. Lk.13:8, "And he answering said unto him, Lord, let it alone this year also, till I shall dig about it, and dung it." (NOI. Animal waste has a much higher content of nitrogen, potassium and phosphorus, than does human waste, and therefore makes a far better fertilizer for plants. Animal dung was also used as a fire-fuel for cooking food, and had value during a famine. See 2Ki.6:25.) {dunghill 7x., dunghills 1x., tot. = 36x.}

Dungeon – 13x., adj. [A.D. 1300, < OF. *donjon* (= 'keep') < ML. *domnio* (= 'domain') < L. *dominus* = 'master' (NOI. The English understood a 'dungeon' to be a large tower, in the center of the court, where prisoners were kept in cells, usually below ground, but sometimes in cells above. The Hb. word is בור (*bowr*) and means 'a pit or large hole in the ground', signifying a dungeon below ground. Sometimes בור (*bowr*) was coupled with בית (*bayith*), which means 'a house or prison house', thereby meaning a dungeon cell above ground.)] Thus, a **dungeon** is 'a secure facility in which prisoners were kept in cells, either above or (usually) below ground'. Eg. Jer.38:13, "So they drew up Jeremiah with cords, and took him up out of the dungeon: and Jeremiah remained in the court of the prison."

Dunghill –7x., adj. [A.D. 1320, < E. **dung** (see 'Dung') + **hill** = 'a natural elevation in the earth's surface' or 'an artificial heap or pile' (see 'Hill') (NOI. The 'dunghill' was part of the garbage-dump area outside of the city, where not only rodents lived, but also beggars. In 17th c. England, dunghills were common sites in and around the little villages.)] Thus, a **dunghill** was 'a place where dung was taken to and heaped up into a pile'. Eg. 1Sam.2:8, "He raiseth up the poor out of the dust, and lifteth up the beggar from the dunghill, to set them among princes, and to make them inherit the throne of glory: for the pillars of the earth are the LORD'S, and he hath set the world upon them."

Dureth –1x., v. [A.D. 1275, 3rd pers. sing. pres. act. ind. of E.

dure (= 'to last') < OF. *durer* < L. *durare* = 'to harden' (i.e. 'to last, endure')] Thus, **dureth** means 'the 3rd pers. sing. pres. act. ind. action of enduring'. Eg. Mt.13:21, "Yet hath he not root in himself, but dureth for a while: for when tribulation or persecution ariseth because of the word, by and by he is offended."

Durst – 9x., v. pret. [A.D. 888, < E. **dare** (see 'Dare')] Thus, **durst** means 'the past-tense action of daring'. Eg. Mt.22:46, "And no man was able to answer him a word, neither durst any man from that day forth ask him any more questions." {dare 5x., tot. = 14x.}

Duty – 8x., n. [A.D. 1297, < ME. **duetee** (< **due** < OF. *deu* = 'owed or owing' < L. *debere* = 'to owe' or 'to be indebted') = 'conduct owed to another person, or to God, as if it were a debt (NOI. 'Duty' can involve obedience and respect, as in people towards God, or children towards parents, or citizens towards government. Good character requires us to perform what is expected of us, and when we do, it is still no great matter. Jesus said we have merely performed our duty. See Lk.17:10.)] Thus, **duty** is 'the conduct of obedience and respect that is owed to another'. Eg. Ecc.12:13, "Let us hear the conclusion of the whole matter: Fear God, and keep his commandments: for this is the whole duty of man." {duties 1x., tot. = 9x.}

Dwarf – 1x., n. [A.D. 700, < OE. **dweorg** = 'a small human adult' (NOI. There are approximately 200 recorded different types of dwarfism, 'achondroplasia' (< Gk. ἀχονδρος (*achondros*) = 'without cartilage' + πλασις (*plasis*) = 'conforming'; thus, 'an abnormal formation of cartilage') being the most common. This is characterized by short arms and legs, a slightly enlarged head and an average sized trunk. The total height is usually around 4 ft. 10 in. (1.47 m.). The most famous dwarf in the Bible was Zacchaeus, in Lk.19:3. Please note: the term 'midget', when applied to someone affected with dwarfism, is an insult, and was first recorded in

A.D. 1865. 'Midge' (= 'a small insect') + et (= 'an E. suffix denoting a smaller size' (as in 'cigar' and 'cigarette')). This derogatory term was coined when circuses would display a little person as a curiosity. For more information, see www.lpaonline.org.)] Thus, a **dwarf** is 'a human whose height is far below what is considered a normal average'. Eg. Lev.21:20, "Or crookbackt, or a dwarf, or that hath a blemish in his eye, or be scurvy, or scabbed, or hath his stones broken."

E

Eagle –23x., n. [A.D. 1380(in a sermon by Wycliffe), < ME. **egle** < OF. *aigle* < L. *aquila* = 'an eagle' < L. *aquilus* = 'dark brown color' (i.e. in reference to the color of the bird) (NOI. An 'eagle' is one of several species of large, meat-eating birds, having a wingspan from about 43-98 in. (1.09-2.49 m.). It is known for its soaring flight, keen vision and powerful claws. Eagles catch their prey with their feet, while their powerful claws close together, killing their victims. After eating, they spit out pellets containing undigested feathers, hair, and bone fragments. They mate for life, the females being slightly larger than the males, and lay from one to four eggs each year. There are bout 7 different species of eagles known to Israel. (The life spans recorded here are an estimate in their natural habitat and not in captivity, which is always longer.) These include: #1. Lesser Spotted Eagle (*Aquila pomarina*, weighing as little as 2.6 lb. (about 1.2 kilo.), and lives about 26 years); #2. Greater Spotted Eagle (*Aquila clanga*, very rare, weighing up to 5 lb. (about 2.3 kilo.), and lives about 20 (?) years); #3. Steppe Eagle (*Aquila nipalensis*, weighs up to 8.8 lb. (about 4.0 kilo.), and lives about 20(?) years), #4. Eastern Imperial Eagle (*Aquila heliaca*, very rare and weighing as much as 10 lb. (about 4.5 kilo.), and lives about 21 years), #5. Golden Eagle (*Aquila chrysaetos*, weighs up to 14.5 lb. (about 6.6 kilo.), and lives about 26 years. The best known in Europe and the most commonly known in Britain until about A.D. 1658), #6. Bonelli's Eagle (*Hieraaetus fasciatus*, weighing up to 4.4 lb. (about 2.0 kilo.), and lives about 20(?) years) #7. Booted Eagle (*Hieraaetus pennatus* weighing as little as

1.5 lb. (about 700 grams), and lives about 12 years). The majestic "Bald Eagle" (*Haliaeetus leucocephalus* weighing up to 13.2 lb. (about 6.0 kilo.), and lives about 22 years) is found only in North America. The NT. name 'Aquila' (Act.18:2) is from the Gk. Ακυλας (*Akulas*) = 'eagle'.)] Thus, an **eagle** is 'a majestic bird of prey, dark brown in color, weighing as much as 14.5 lb. (about 6.6 kilo.), having a wingspan up to 98 in. (2.49 m.) and known for its soaring flight'. Eg. Pr.23:5, "Wilt thou set thine eyes upon that which is not? for riches certainly make themselves wings; they fly away as an eagle toward heaven." {eagle's 2x., eagles 7x., eagles' 2x., tot. = 34x.}

Ear[1] –1116x., n. [A.D. 825(VP), < OE. **eare** (akin to L. *auris* = 'ear') and refers to the sensory organ of hearing on humans and animals (NOI. The human ear is divided into 3 separate parts. The external-ear catches the sound waves and channels them into the ear, amplifying those in the range of human voice. The middle-ear transforms the sound waves into mechanical vibrations. The inner-ear consists of 3 coiled chambers, filled with fluid, which pulsates with the mechanical vibrations from the middle-ear. Attached to the chambers are thousands of sensory hair-cells, to which are attached thousands of nerve-fibers that carry the information to the brain. The human ear can detect a difference of just 2 degrees in the direction of a source of sound. It can pick out a particular sound in a room full of noise, and it recognize at least 400,000 different sounds and matches them to memories in the brain. The earlobe is that elongated 'lobe' at the base of the ear. It is often used as a place for decoration, but it is also used as a telltale for certain diseases, such as methahemoglobinemia' (excessive methahemoglobin in the blood), 'Raynaud's phenomenon' (a disorder of the small blood vessels of extremities such as fingers, toes and ears) and 'Chilblain' (skin inflammation, usually in cold weather). Medical researchers argue whether a crease in the lobe is a sign of a heart problem, or not.)] Thus, an **ear** is 'the organ of hearing consisting of

3 parts, external-ear, middle-ear and inner-ear'. Eg. Ex.21:6, "Then his master shall bring him unto the judges; he shall also bring him to the door, or unto the door post; and his master shall bore his ear through with an aul; and he shall serve him for ever." (NOI. Sometimes, 'ear' is used figuratively to mean 'listen carefully', as in Ex.15:26 and Pr.18:15.) {earring 5x., earrings 12x., ears 129x., tot. = 262x.}

Ear [2] – 3x., n. [A.D. 800 < OE. **ear** (akin to Du. *aar* and Ger. *ahre* and L. *acus* = 'husks of grain') = 'an ear of a cereal plant'] Thus, an **ear** is 'the spike or head-part of a cereal plant, such as wheat or barley, which contains the actual grain'. Eg. Ex.9:31, "And the flax and the barley was smitten: for the barley was in the ear, and the flax was bolled." {ears 22x., tot. = 25x.}

Ear [3] – 1x., v. [A.D. 888 < OE. **erian** (akin to L. *arare* = 'to produce by plowing' < Gk. αρουν (*aroun*) = 'plow')] Thus, **ear** means 'the action of plowing or tilling the soil'. Eg. 1Sam.8:12, "And he will appoint him captains over thousands, and captains over fifties; and will set them to ear his ground, and to reap his harvest, and to make his instruments of war, and instruments of his chariots." {eared 1x., earing 2x., tot. = 4x.}

Earing – 2x., vbl.n. [A.D. 1440, < E. **ear** (see 'Ear'[3]) + **ing** = forms the vbl.n. (see E. suffix '–ing'[1])] Thus, **earing** is 'the plowing of a field into long furrows, ready for sowing'. Eg. Gen.45:6, "For these two years hath the famine been in the land: and yet there are five years, in the which there shall neither be earing nor harvest." {ear 1x., eared 1x. tot. = 4x.}

Early – 86x. adj. and adv. [A.D. 950(LfG.), < ME. **earlich** < OE. **rlice** (< **ere** = 'sooner' (see 'Ere') + **lice** = 'like') = 'sooner-like', as in 'the first part of some period of time'] Thus, as an adj., **early** modifies its n. as 'being connected to the first part of some period of time'. Eg. Hos.13:3, "Therefore they shall be as the morning cloud, and as the early dew that passeth away, as the chaff that is driven with the whirlwind out of the floor, and as the smoke out of the chimney." (Here, the **dew** (n.) is modified as being **early** (adj.).) Furthermore, as an adv., **early** modifies its v. as 'happening in the first part of period division of time', such as a day, a year or a life. Eg. Gen.28:18, "And Jacob rose up early in the morning, and took the stone that he had put for his pillows, and set it up for a pillar, and poured oil upon the top of it." (See also 'Betimes'.)

Earnest [1] – 5x., adj. [A.D. 1000, < OE. **eorneste** = 'serious in purpose or intention'] Thus, **earnest** modifies its n. as 'being very serious in its purpose or intention'. Eg. Heb.2:1, "Therefore we ought to give the more earnest heed to the things which we have heard, lest at any time we should let them slip." {earnestly 16x., tot. = 21x.}

Earnest [2] –3x., n. [A.D. 1225, < ME. **ernes** (< oo., but probably from OE. **erles** < OF. *erle* < L. *arrhula* = 'a token payment made on an account' < Gk. αρραβων (*arrhabon*) (which is a business word, meaning 'a pledge' or 'a deposit') < Hb. ערבון (*arabown*) = 'a pledge' as a show of good faith that the buyer will make full payment later (NOI. In modern Gk., αρραβων (*arrhabon*) means 'an engagement ring', given to a woman as a promise that one day she will receive the husband!)] Thus, an **earnest** is 'a partial payment (or down payment) as a promise that full payment will later be made'. Eg. Eph.1:14, "Which is the earnest of our inheritance until the redemption of the purchased possession, unto the praise of his glory." (Here, the Holy Spirit (vs. 13) is given the believer as the 'earnest' or 'down payment' towards a full inheritance in heaven.)

Earthen – 10x., adj. [A.D. 1225, < E. **earth** < OE. **eorthe**

(= 'ground or soil') + **en** = forms the adj. (see E. suffix '–en'[3])] Thus, **earthen** modifies its n. as 'being made of earth, soil or earthy-matter', such as clay. Eg. Lev.14:50, "And he shall kill the one of the birds in an earthen vessel over running water." (NOI. 'Earthen' is once used as part of a figure of speech to describe the human body. See 2Cor.4:7. Cp. also 1Cor.15:47.) {earth 987x., tot. = 997x.}

East – 157x., adj., adv. and n. [A.D. 890, < OE. **east** or **eastan** < early Ger. *austral* = 'to shine' or 'towards the sun rising' (akin to L. *aurora* = 'dawn' or *Aurora* 'the goddess of the dawn') (NOI. The 'east wind' was always a hot, scorching, blasting or vehement wind with devastating effects (cp. Eze.19:12).) and Eoς (*Eos*) was the Gk. goddess of dawn (who was the mother of Eυρoς (*Euros*), the god of the east-wind)] Thus, as an adj., **east** modifies its n. as 'being in the direction toward or from the rising of the sun'. Eg. Gen.41:6, "And, behold, seven thin ears and blasted with the east wind sprung up after them." Furthermore, as an adv., **east** modifies its v. as 'happening in a direction toward or coming from the rising of the sun'. Eg. Gen.13:11, "Then Lot chose him all the plain of Jordan; and Lot journeyed east: and they separated themselves the one from the other." Finally, as a n., **east** is 'a geographic place in the direction of the rising of the sun', from the perspective of Israel. Eg. Mt.2:2, "Saying, Where is he that is born King of the Jews? for we have seen his star in the east, and are come to worship him." {eastward 40x., tot. = 197x.}

Easter – 1x., n. [A.D. 890, < OE. **astre** < **ostre** = 'the ancient pagan 'goddess of dawn' of the north European Saxons'. She was the goddess of fertility and sunrise, to whom a feast was celebrated at springtime.(NOI. The Gk. word in Act.12:4, (πασχα (*paskah*) translated 'Easter'), is translated as 'Passover' 28x. elsewhere. Because of this, some feel the 1611 is in error. However, the word 'Passover' was unknown in the E. language until Tyndale invented it in A.D. 1525 (see

'Passover'). Till then, the only other E. Bible was WB., and it followed the LV., using '*paskah*'. The common man in England, in Tyndale's day, was Biblically-ignorant and didn't know what *paskah* meant, but he certainly understood (probably from his Roman Catholic upbringing) that 'Easter' (or so he thought) was the celebration of Christ's death, burial and resurrection. So, of the 29x., πασχα (*paskah*) is used in the NT., Tyndale translated it 'Easter' 14x., 'Easter-lamb' 11x., 'paschal lamb' 3x., and 'easterfest' 1x., However, the next 86 years witnessed the Reformation, the starting of the Church of England and a tremendous increase in Biblical knowledge for the common English man. People began understanding what the 'Passover' was, and what the word 'Easter' really meant. Therefore, the E. Bible translations that followed Tyndale's, began using 'Passover' more and more (and 'Easter' less and less), until the translators of the 1611 used 'Passover' 28x., and 'Easter' only once – in Act.12:4. Why? First, notice that the timing of Peter's arrest was during "the days of unleavened bread" (Act.12:3), which came after the Passover (cp. Deut.16:1-3; Ezr.6:19,22). Therefore, πασχα (*paskah*) in Act.12:4 cannot refer to the Jewish Passover, because technically, it was now over. Secondly, it must be remembered that Herod was a pagan idol-worshipper and had no interest whatsoever in celebrating the Jewish Passover. But there were other religious celebrations going on in the Roman world at that time including one for a pagan fertility goddess, known to Herod as '*Aurora*', which came after the Jewish "*days of unleavened bread*". Some believe the pagan goddess to be the Chaldean '*Astarte*', or the Assyrian '*Ishtar*'. However, the 'Venerable Bede' (A.D. 672-735), a Benedictine monk, wrote in his book '*De Ratione Temporum*' (The Reckoning of Time) that **ostre** (see beginning of this entry) was named after Εος (*Eos*) the Gk. goddess of dawn, springtime and fertility (the very same is *Aurora*, the Roman goddess of dawn, one of Herod's pagan gods). The Romans borrowed most of their pagan gods from the Greeks, and simply changed their names.

(Shakespeare even mentions *Aurora* in Romeo and Juliet (Act 1, Scene 1).) Therefore, if these things be true, then the 1611 was correct in rendering Act.12:4 as the pagan 'Easter' and not the Jewish 'Passover'.)] Thus, **<u>Easter</u>** is 'a pagan, springtime celebration to a fertility goddess who bears many similar names to Easter'. Eg. Act.12:4, "And when he had apprehended him, he put him in prison, and delivered him to four quaternions of soldiers to keep him; intending after Easter to bring him forth to the people."

Ebony –1x., n. [A.D. 1382(WB.), < ME. **hebenyf** < **ebon** < OF. *ebene* (= 'the black wood called heben') < L. *hebenus* < Gk. εβενος (*ebenos*) < Hb. הָבְן (*hoben*) = from an unused root meaning 'to be hard' (NOI. 'Ebony' is a rare and expensive wood that (in Ezekiel's time) came from Africa and India. It has a very dense grain and a coarse texture and is used in making expensive cabinets (and modern piano keys), however, ebony sawdust has been known to cause respiratory problems.)] Thus, **<u>ebony</u>** is 'a hard, dark, expensive wood from Africa and India'. Eg. Eze.27:15, "The men of Dedan were thy merchants; many isles were the merchandise of thine hand: they brought thee for a present horns of ivory and ebony."

Ed – 1x., pn. [A.D. 1568(BB.), trans. < Hb. עֵד (*ed*) = 'witness' < עוּד (*uwd*) = 'testify'] Thus, **<u>Ed</u>** is 'the name (meaning 'a witness') of an altar that was built by the Reubenites, the Gadites and ½ the tribe of Manasseh'. Eg. Josh.22:34, "And the children of Reuben and the children of Gad called the altar Ed: for it shall be a witness between us that the LORD is God." (NOI. Some have suggested that 'altar' should have been translated 'monument', yet 'altar' is the better translation, for it describes what the rest of Israel thought these 2 ½ tribes were going to use it for. However, it was not meant for sacrifice (vs. 23) but as a witness or testimony (vs. 28).)

Eden – 20x., pn. [A.D. 1225, trans. < Hb. עדן (*Eden*) = 'pleasure, delight' (NOI. 'Eden' was also the name of a son of Joah (2Chr.29:12), and a region conquered by the Assyrians that produced valuable goods (Eze.27:23; 2Ki.19:12; Isa.37:12). However, this entry will only deal with the area where the garden was. Seekins, in his book 'Hebrew Word Pictures', pg. 138, suggests 'Eden' means either 'to see the judge' (the one who offers justice) or 'eternal life'.)] Thus, **Eden** is 'the name (meaning 'pleasure') of an unknown geographic region of the Middle East, wherein God planted a garden, and where He put our first parents, Adam and Eve'. Eg. Gen.2:8. "And the LORD God planted a garden eastward in Eden; and there he put the man whom he had formed." (NOI. We sometimes speak of the 'garden of Eden' as if it were all one big garden. In fact, Eden was the area, and the garden was in the eastern part of Eden. Some speculate that Eden was in Armenia or Babylonia, but we do not know.)

Edification –4x., [A.D. 1382(WB.), < L. *aedificatio* (='the act of building') < *aedificare* = 'to build' (NOI. This is equal to the E. **edify** (< OF. *edifier* < L. *aedificare* = 'to build'.) + **ation** = 'a state or condition' (see E. suffix '–tion') (NOI. The NT. Gk. word is οικοδομη (*oikodome*) = 'to build up (< οικος (*oikos*) = 'house or home' + δωμα (*doma*) = 'a roof top'). The top of the average home in the Middle East was flat and used for socializing and, for the believers, for prayer and meditation, as in Act.10:9. A believer's well-used rooftop might then have been a good sign that things were strong between him and the Lord. The term οικοδομη is appropriate, as believers are referred to as a "spiritual house" in 1Pt.2:5, and a house needs 'edification'... building up and strengthening. Also, the use of edification and its variants in the NT. leads us to believe that it is something we do for others, rather than something we seek for ourselves. It's as we minister to others that we ourselves receive a blessing. See Rom.14:19 and Act.20:35. The opposite of edification would be 'destruction' (the pulling apart of the house) as in 2Cor.13:10.)] Thus, **edification** is 'the act or state of building up another's happiness and spiritual well-being through spiritual service to that individual'. Eg. 1Cor.14:3, "But he that prophesieth speaketh unto men to edification, and exhortation, and comfort." {edified 2x., edifieth 3x., edify 3x., edifying 8x., tot. = 20x.}

Effect – 14x., n. and v. [A.D. 1385, < OF. *effect* < L. *effectus* < *efficere*, *ex* = 'out' (see L. prefix '*ex*–') + *facere* = 'to make or do'] Thus, as a n., an **effect** is 'the thing accomplished or produced by some cause'. Eg. Gal.5:4 "Christ is become of no effect unto you, whosoever of you are justified by the law; ye are fallen from grace." (Here, the 'effect' referred to is 'salvation by grace'.) Furthermore, as a v., **effect**, means 'the action of bringing about a result or an accomplishment, and generally points to an object'. Eg. Jer.48:30, "...his lies shall not so effect it." (See also 'Affect' and 'Cause'.) {effected 1x., effectual 6x., effectually 2x., tot. = 23x.}

Effectual – 6x., adj. [A.D. 1386, < ME. **effectuell** < OF. *effectuel* < ML. *effectualis* < L. *effectus* = 'to accomplish' or 'to bring about' (See 'Effect'.)] Thus, **effectual** modifies its n. as 'being capable of producing a planned or intended effect'. Eg. Eph.3:7, "Whereof I was made a minister, according to the gift of the grace of God given unto me by the effectual working of his power." {effect 14x., tot. = 20x.}

Effeminate – 1x., adj. [A.D. 1393, < L. *effeminatus* = 'womanish' (which is pp. of) *effeminare* = 'to make womanish' < *femina* = 'woman' (NOI. The NT. Gk. word is μαλακος (*malakos*) = 'soft to the touch', and in classical Gk. it was a term of shame when applied to men. Socrates, in Plato's book, 'The Republic', made the comment that too much music makes a man effeminate. However, the word μαλακος is also used in Mt.11:8 and Lk.7:25 in reference to 'soft' clothing.] Thus, **effeminate** modifies its masculine n. as 'being soft and woman-like'. Eg. 1Cor.6:9, "Know ye not that the unrighteous shall not inherit the kingdom of God? Be not deceived: neither fornicators, nor idolaters, nor adulterers, nor effeminate, nor abusers of themselves with mankind."

Elder –20x., adj. and n. [A.D. 888, < OE. **eldra** (a comparative word meaning 'older') < **ald** = 'old' (= 'age', as in 'duration of life')] Thus, as an adj., **elder** modifies its n. as 'being older'. Eg. Lk.15:25, "Now his elder son was in the field: and as he came and drew nigh to the house, he heard musick and dancing." Furthermore, as a n., an **elder** is 'an older person, a senior, either physically or spiritually'. Eg. 1Pt.5:5, "Likewise, ye younger, submit yourselves unto the elder. Yea, all of you be subject one to another, and be clothed with humility: for God resisteth the proud, and giveth grace to the humble." (NOI. Another important usage of 'elder' in the NT. is the office of elder, as in 1Pt.5:1. Some understand this to be the same office as pastor, while others see it as a separate office in the church. (C. H. Spurgeon saw it as a separate office.) Elders were used in OT. Israel as men with authority, as seen in Ex.3:16 and Mt.16:21, and were 'ordained' in the NT. (as in Act.14:23 χειροτονεω (*cheirotoneo*) = 'to vote by the raising of the hand').) {elders 179x., eldest 14x., tot. = 213x.}

Elect –17x., adj. and n. [A.D. 1398, < L. *electus* = 'picked' or 'chosen' (which is pp. of) *eligere* = 'to pick out' or 'to choose' (< *e* = 'out' (see L. prefix '*ex*–') + *legere* = 'to select, gather or choose, by deliberate action, from a group') (NOI. The NT. Gk. word εκλεκτος (*eklektos*), translated '**elect**', is also translated '**chosen**' 7x. Theologians attach various theological meanings to the words '**elect**' and '**election**', but this dictionary is only concerned with the basic meaning of the words in english.)] Thus, as an adj., **elect** modifies its n. as 'having been chosen or picked out of a group'. Eg. 1Tim.5:21, "I charge thee before God, and the Lord Jesus Christ, and the elect angels, that thou observe these things without preferring one before another, doing nothing by partiality." Furthermore, as a n., the **elect** are 'those who have been chosen or picked out of a group'. Eg. Rom.8:33, "Who shall lay any thing to the charge of God's elect? It is God that justifieth." {elect's 3x., elected 1x., election 6x., tot. = 27x.}

Election –6x., n. [A.D. 1270, < E. (v.) **elect** = 'to pick out of a group' (see 'Elect') + **tion** = 'the state or condition' (see E. suffix '–tion')] Thus, an **election** is 'the state or condition of deliberate choosing of certain ones from a group'. Eg. Rom.11:5, "Even so then at this present time also there is a remnant according to the election of grace." {elect 17x., elect's 3x., elected 1x., tot. = 27x.}

Elements –4x., n. pl. [A.D. 1300, < E. **element** (< OF. *element* < L. *elementum* = 'a first principle') + **s** = forms the pl. (NOI. The Greeks and Romans considered the elements, or 'building blocks of the universe', to be: earth, water, fire and air. Today, these 4 are often used as principles of astrology, mysticism and some holistic healing. The Gk. word στοιχειον (*stoicheion*) = 'a principle', and it primarily deals with physical things; but as a secondary meaning, it deals with the first principles of any art, science or religion.)] Thus, primarily, **elements** are 'two or more basic or first principles, or building blocks, of this universe'. Eg. 2Pt.3:10, "But the day of the Lord will come as a thief in the night; in the which the heavens shall pass away with a great noise, and the elements shall melt with fervent heat, the earth also and the works that are therein shall be burned up." (NOI. These primary 'elements' are composed of certain matter, for it says (vs. 11) they shall 'dissolve' (λυω (*luo*) = 'to loose' or 'to break into small particles'). Also, in a secondary sense, 'elements' are the first principles of religion, such as the laws and obedience, but do not include grace and faith. See Gal.4:9.)

Eloquent –3x., adj. [A.D. 1393, < OF. *eloquent* < L. *eloquens* = 'speak out' (which is prp. of) *eloqui* = 'to speak out', < *e* = 'out' (see L. prefix '*ex–*') + *loqui* = 'to speak' (i.e. 'having the power of speech') (NOI. Lawyers, actors, business men and politicians all require powers of speech or debate in order to persuade and convince others. Apollos was an eloquent man (Act.18:24).)] Thus, **eloquent** modifies its n. as 'being gifted in fluent, forceful power of speech'. Eg. Isa.3:3, "The captain of fifty, and the honourable man, and the counsellor, and the cunning artificer, and the eloquent orator."

Embalm –1x., v. [A.D. 1340, < ME. **enbaume** < OF. *embaumer*, < *em* (< L. *in* = 'in' (see L. prefix '*in–*')) + *baume* = 'balm' (see 'Balm') (NOI. Embalming had its origins in Egypt where 'mummification' may have been thought to assist the departed dead in a 'physical afterlife'. This concept is further attested to by the discovery of food and utensils placed in the graves alongside the bodies. The art of embalming seemed to reach its height in about the days of Joseph. After this, the careful art of embalming deteriorated until bodies were merely treated with molten resin, which destroyed the tissues. Frederick Ruysch (A.D. 1638-1731) is considered the first to embalm by injecting a preservative into the blood vessels. Modern embalming involves injecting several gal. of embalming solution into the body through an artery, and forcing out the blood through a tube. For further study in Egyptian mummification, the reader is directed to the Encyclopedia Britannica, volume 15, pg. 948. See Bibliography at end.)] Thus, **embalm** means 'the action of putting balm or spices into a dead body to preserve it from decay'. Eg. Gen.50:2, "And Joseph commanded his servants the physicians to embalm his father: and the physicians embalmed Israel." {embalmed 3x., tot. = 4x.}

Emboldeneth – 1x., v. [A.D. 1571, < E. **embolden** (< **em** = 'in' (see E. prefix 'em–') + **bold** (= 'courage' (see 'Bold'))

\+ **en** = forms the v. (see E. suffix '–en'[4])) = 'to add in courage' + **eth** = forms the pres. ind. 3rd pers. sing. (see E. suffix '–eth')] Thus, **emboldeneth** means 'the pres. ind. 3rd pers. sing. action of adding in boldness or courage'. Eg. Job.16:3, "Shall vain words have an end? or what emboldeneth thee that thou answerest?" {bold 11x., boldly 13x., boldness 10x., emboldened 1x., tot. = 36x.}

Embrace – 8x., v. [A.D. 1360, < OF. embracier < ML. *imbrachiare* < *im* = 'in', with intensity (see L. prefix '*in–*'[2]) + *brachium* (or *bracchium*) = 'the arm' (NOI. This is usually an action of affection.)] Thus, **embrace** means 'the intensive action of taking into one's arm or arms'. Eg. SoS.2:6, "His left hand is under my head, and his right hand doth embrace me." {embraced 5x., embracing 2x., tot. = 15x.}

Embroider – 1x., v. [A.D. 1420(?), < ME. **em** = 'in, into' (see E. prefix 'em–') + **broider** = 'to decorate with fancy stitching' (see 'Broidered')] Thus, **embroider** means 'the action of adding in fancy or decorative stitching'. Eg. Ex.28:39, "And thou shalt embroider the coat of fine linen, and thou shalt make the mitre of fine linen, and thou shalt make the girdle of needlework." {broided 1x., broidered 8x., embroiderer 2x., tot. = 12x.}

Emerald – 5x., n. [A.D. 1300, < OF. *esmeraude* < L. *smaragdus* < Gk. σμαραγδος (*smaragdos*) = 'a green precious stone' (NOI. The 'emerald' is a highly valued gem stone, and is actually a variety of 'beryl' (see 'Beryl'), having a clear, deep green color, which is caused by the presence of chromium rather than aluminum. Ancient civilizations believed it to have medicinal value, such as being good for eyesight, protection against epilepsy and could drive away evil spirits. The emerald was used as the first stone in the second row on the High Priest's breastplate (Ex.28:18), and will be used to garnish the fourth foundation of the wall of the New Jerusalem

(Rev.21:19). The Spanish female name, 'Esmeralda' means 'emerald'.)] Thus, an **emerald** is 'a transparent, precious gem stone, having a deep green color'. Eg. Ex.28:18, "And the second row shall be an emerald, a sapphire, and a diamond." {emeralds 1x., tot. = 6x.}

Emerods –8x., n. pl. [A.D. 1400, < L. pl. *haemorrhoides* < Gk. pl. άιμορροίδες (*haemorroides*) < Gk. sing. άιμορροίς (*haemorrois*), άιμα (*haema*) = 'blood' + ρειν (*rein*) = 'flow' (NOI. An 'emerod' is basically a varicose, or bulging, vein (or blood-vessel) located at the anus. Bowel movements often cause the vein to tear, causing a flow of blood. The OT. Hb. word is טחרים (*techorim*) < an unused root word, meaning 'to burn', which describes the burning pain that sufferers describe. The word 'emerods' was a trans. of the L., but was also spelled, 'emeraudes', 'emerodes', 'emeroids' and 'emrods'.)] Thus, **emerods** are 'two or more swollen blood-vessels at the anus, which cause much pain and produce a flow of blood should the blood-vessel become torn'. Eg. 1Sam.5:9, "And it was so, that, after they had carried it about, the hand of the LORD was against the city with a very great destruction: and he smote the men of the city, both small and great, and they had emerods in their secret parts."

Eminent –4x., adj. [A.D. 1420, < L. *eminens* (which is prp. of) *eminere* (= 'to stand out'), < *e* = 'out' (see L. prefix '*ex–*') + *minere* = 'to project' (NOI. The L. *minere* is close to *minari* = 'to threaten'. When the prefix '*e*' is added, it amplifies the concept of 'project' to huge proportions.)] Thus, **eminent** modifies its n. as 'being very prominent and out front, so that all can see it'. Eg. Eze.16:31, "In that thou buildest thine eminent place in the head of every way, and makest thine high place in every street..."

Emulation –1x., n. [A.D. 1552, < L. *aemulatio* = 'unfriendly rivalry' (as in 'a jealous or envious desire to equal or surpass someone else in status or possessions') < *aemulus* = 'rival'] Thus, an **emulation** is 'a jealous rivalry to equal or surpass someone'. Eg. Rom.11:14, "If by any means I may provoke to emulation them which are my flesh, and might save some of them." (NOI. It was Paul's desire to see his fellow Jews spiritually saved through the gospel of Messiah Jesus. He mentions that their fall has brought salvation to the Gentiles, which made the Jews jealous (vs. 11). Cp. Also Act.13:45.) {emulations 1x., tot. = 2x.}

Encamp – 11x., v. [A.D. 1549, < E. **en** = 'into' (see E. prefix 'em–') + **camp** (< L. *campus* = 'a field, or plain' (see 'Camp')) = 'a place where an army would set up their tents for temporary rest'] Thus, **encamp** means 'the action of setting up tents into a camp-like formation, or military fashion'. Eg. 2Sam.12:28, "Now therefore gather the rest of the people together, and encamp against the city, and take it: lest I take the city, and it be called after my name." {camp 136x., camped 1x., camps 7x., encamped 33x., encampeth 2x., encamping 1x., tot. = 191x}

Enchantment – 3x., n. [A.D. 1297, < OF. *enchantement* < *enchanter* (= 'to bewitch, or charm') < L. *incantare* (= 'to chant a magical formula'), *in* = 'against' (see L. prefix '*in*–'[1]) + *cantare* = 'to sing' (NOI. The idea of 'singing against someone' is to be understood as doing it against their will with the goal of gaining control over them. Greek mythology tells the story of Sirens (creatures with the head of a female and body of a bird), which inhabited the island of *Sirenum scopuli*. By using their irresistible, charming song, they lured sailors to their death and destruction on the rocks that surrounded their island. This is what is meant by 'singing against' someone.)] Thus, an **enchantment** is 'the act or state of enchanting someone' (as in 'bewitching them with a song'). Eg. Lev.19:26, "Ye shall not eat any thing with the blood: neither shall ye use enchantment, nor observe times." (NOI. Music and song can be a powerful force. Some singers on stage appear to 'enchant' their audience. 2Ki.21:6 illustrates other things that enchantment is used along with.) {enchanter 1x., enchanters 1x., enchantments 10x., tot. = 15x.}

Encourage – 4x., v. [A.D. 1483, < OF. *encoragier* < *en* = ‘in’ (same as L. *in* (see L. prefix ‘*in–*’[2])) + *corage* = ‘heart’ (< L. *cor* = *‘heart’)* (see ‘Courage’)] Thus, **encourage** means ‘the action of adding courage, or heart, to a person so that they can face danger’. Eg. Deut.3:28, “But charge Joshua, and encourage him, and strengthen him: for he shall go over before this people, and he shall cause them to inherit the land which thou shalt see.” {encouraged 5x., tot. = 9x.}

Endamage – 1x., v. [A.D. 1374, < E. **en** = ‘into’ (see E. prefix ‘em–’) + **damage** = ‘injury, loss or harm’ (< L. *damnum*, see ‘Damage’)] Thus, **endamage** means ‘the action of bringing in, or causing, harm or loss to something’. Eg. Ezr.4:13. “Be it known now unto the king, that, if this city be builded, and the walls set up again, then will they not pay toll, tribute, and custom, and so thou shalt endamage the revenue of the kings.” {damage 6x., tot. = 7x.}

Endeavour – 1x., v. [A.D. 1400, < OF. (two words) *en devoir* (= ‘in duty’), < *en* = ‘in’ (same as E. prefix ‘em–’) + *devoir* < L. *debere* = ‘to owe’ (as in a debt of some kind)] Thus, **endeavour** means ‘the action of exerting oneself to achieve or accomplish something, out of a sense of duty’. Eg. 2Pt.1:15, “Moreover I will endeavour that ye may be able after my decease to have these things always in remembrance.” {endeavoured 2x., endeavouring 1x., endeavours 1x., tot. = 5x.}

Endow – 1x., v. [A.D. 1420, < OF. *endouer*, < *en* = ‘in’ (same as E. prefix ‘em–’) + *douer* < L. *dotare* = ‘to provide with a dowry’ (see ‘Dowry’)] Thus, **endow** means ‘the action of providing a dowry, or payment, to or for a woman, for the purpose of marriage’. Eg. Ex.22:16, “And if a man entice a maid that is not betrothed, and lie with her, he shall surely endow her to be his wife." (NOI. If a man defiled a young, single girl, he was to marry her and provide her with a dowry. If the father refused the marriage, then he was to give money to the father as a satisfaction for the disgrace done. See Ex.22:17.)

Endued —5x. v. pret. [A.D. 1400, < ME. **endue** (< OF. *enduire* < L. *inducere*, *in* = 'in', having intensity (see L. prefix '*in–*'[2]) + *ducere* = 'to lead') + **ed** = forms the pret.] Thus, **endued** means 'the past-tense action of bringing or leading something into someone or something'. Eg. Jam.3:13, "Who is a wise man and endued with knowledge among you? let him shew out of a good conversation his works with meekness of wisdom."

Endure —29x., v. [A.D. 1325, < OF. *endurer* < L. *indurare* (= 'to make hard'), *in* = 'in', having intensity (see L. prefix '*in–*'[2]) < durus = *'hard'*] Thus, **endure** means 'the action of hardening oneself, or something, against adverse forces that could overcome and destroy'. Eg. Jam.5:11, "Behold, we count them happy which endure. Ye have heard of the patience of Job, and have seen the end of the Lord; that the Lord is very pitiful, and of tender mercy." {endured 8x., endureth 59x., enduring 3x., tot. = 99x.}

Enemy — 107x., n. [A.D. 1300, < OF. *ennemi* (= 'a male foe' (NOI. *Ennemie* = 'a female foe'.)) < L. *inimicus* (= 'not a friend'), *in* = 'not' (se L. prefix '*in–*'[1]) + *amicus* = 'a friend'] Thus, an **enemy** is 'a person who is not a friend' (i.e. 'a foe'). Eg. Jam.4:4, "Ye adulterers and adulteresses, know ye not that the friendship of the world is enmity with God? whosoever therefore will be a friend of the world is the enemy of God." (NOI. Notice that 'enemy' and 'enmity' both have a similar root word. See 'Enmity'.) {enemies 266x., enemies' 3x., enemy's 3x., tot. = 379x.}

Engines —2x., n. pl. [A.D. 1300, < ME. **engin** (< OF. *engin* < L.

ingenium = 'a talent or cleverness' (NOI. By A.D. 200-500, *ingenium* meant 'a mechanical contrivance'.) < *in* = 'in', (see L. prefix '*in*–'[2]) + *gen* = 'to beget, or produce') + **s** = forms the pl. (NOI. An 'engineer' is one who invents or plans'. 'Ingenious' (note: prefix 'in' and 'en' are the same) means 'cleverness' or 'skillful at contriving something'.)] Thus, **engines** are 'two or more clever, mechanical devices' (used in the Bible as weapons of warfare). Eg. 2Chr.26:15, "And he made in Jerusalem engines, invented by cunning men, to be on the towers and upon the bulwarks, to shoot arrows and great stones withal..."

Engrafted – 1x., p. [A.D. 1600, < ME. (v.) **engraft** (< **en** = 'in' (see E. prefix 'em–') + **graft** = 'the action of inserting a branch from one plant into another plant') + **ed** = forms the p. (see E. suffix '–ed'[4])] Thus, **engrafted** modifies its n. (in this case, 'the word') as 'having been grafted in, or implanted in'. Eg. Jam.1:21, "Wherefore lay apart all filthiness and superfluity of naughtiness, and receive with meekness the engrafted word, which is able to save your souls." (NOI. Tyndale translated it, "the word that is grafted in you.")

Engrave – 2x., v. [A.D. 1509, < E. **en** (= 'in' (see E. prefix 'em–') + **grave** (< OE. **grafan** = 'to dig')] Thus, **engrave** means 'the action of digging in, or carving in' (as in 'carving in writing, or a design'). Eg. Ex.28:11, "With the work of an engraver in stone, like the engravings of a signet, shalt thou engrave the two stones with the names of the children of Israel: thou shalt make them to be set in ouches of gold." (NOI. The onyx stone has a hardness of 7-out-of-10 on the 'Mohs Scale of Mineral Hardness' (devised in A.D. 1812 by German mineralogist Frederich Mohs), which means it can be scratched with tools. The Jews in the wilderness had metal engraving tools and diamond (10 on the Mohs scale) (see Ex.28:18), and would have used it for all their engraving needs.) {engraven 1x., engraver 3x., engravings 5x., tot. = 11x.}

Enjoin – 1x., v. [A.D. 1225, < OF. *enjoindre* < L. *injungere* (= 'to join into'), *in* = 'in', having intensity (see L. prefix '*in–*'[2]) + *jungere* = 'to join' (NOI. 'Enjoin' is a much stronger word than 'join'.)] Thus, **enjoin** means 'the intensive action of joining together two things'. Eg. Phi.1:8, "Wherefore, though I might be much bold in Christ to enjoin thee that which is convenient." {enjoined 3x., tot. = 4x.}

Enlargement – 1x., n. [A.D. 1540, < ME. **enlarge** (< OF. *enlarger* (= 'to make larger'), *en* = 'in' (same as E. prefix 'em–') + *large* < L. *largus* = 'abundant or plentiful') + **ment** = 'the result or product of an action' (see E. suffix '–ment')] Thus, an **enlargement** is 'the result of making something larger and more abundant'. Eg. Est.4:14, "For if thou altogether holdest thy peace at this time, then shall there enlargement and deliverance arise to the Jews from another place..." (NOI. The 'enlargement' here refers to 'room to live, grow and prosper', the Hb. word being רוח (*revach*) = 'large space'.) {enlarge 10x., tot. = 11x.}

Enlighten –1x., v. [A.D. 1382(WB.), < E. **en** = 'in' (see E. prefix 'em–') + (v.) **lighten** (= 'to illuminate' or 'to shed light upon'), < (adj.) **light** = 'bright or luminous' + **en** = forms the v. (see E. suffix '–en'[4]) (NOI. The Hb. word is נגה (*nagah*) = 'to shine'.)] Thus, **enlighten** means 'the intensive action of bringing light into a situation'. Eg. Ps.18:28, "For thou wilt light my candle: the LORD my God will enlighten my darkness." {enlightened 6x., enlightening 1x., tot. = 8x.}

Enmity –8x., n. [A.D. 1300, < OF. *ennemistie* < L. *inimicus* (see 'Enemy') < VL. *inimicitas* = 'deep hatred'] Thus, **enmity** is 'a feeling of deep hatred between two persons'. Eg. Gen.3:15, "And I will put enmity between thee and the woman, and between thy seed and her seed; it shall bruise thy head, and thou shalt bruise his heel."

Enough —32x., adj., adv. and n. [A.D. 888, < OE. **genog** (akin to D. *genoeg*, and Ger. *genug*), < **ge** = 'with, together' + **nog** < **nah** = 'to reach or attain'] Thus, as an adj., **enough** modifies its n. as 'being fully reached in quantity or quality'. Eg. Gen.24:25, "She said moreover unto him, We have both straw and provender enough, and room to lodge in." Furthermore, as an adv., **enough** modifies its v. as 'having brought about a full measure of action'. Eg. Deut.1:6, "The LORD our God spake unto us in Horeb, saying, Ye have dwelt long enough in this mount." Finally, as a n., **enough** is 'a quantity of something that is sufficient to meet certain needs or demands'. Eg. Gen.33:9, "And Esau said, I have enough, my brother; keep that thou hast unto thyself."

Enquire — 52x., v. [A.D. 1290 (spelled in the 1611 as both '**enquire**' (49x.) and '**inquire**' (3x.)), < OF. *enquerre* < L. *inquirere* (= 'to examine, seek or search'), < *in* = 'in' (see L. prefix '*in–*'[2]) + *quaerere* = 'to ask, or seek' (NOI. The OED. notes that some modern dictionaries suggest 'inquire' meant a general research, whereas 'enquire' meant asking a specific question. This may or may not have been true when it comes to the 1611, as we find examples of 'inquire' (in the 1611) used in the context of specific questioning (eg. Act.9:11), rather than general research. After careful comparisons, it seems (to this author) that both forms were used interchangeably, similar to **entreat** and **intreat**. Both E. prefixes '**en**' and '**in**' mean the same (see E. prefix 'em–'). Of the 89 occurrences in the 1611, only 10 use the '**in**' prefix, and this may have simply been the typesetter ran short on the letter 'e', and used 'i' instead. The Cambridge KJV does not use 'inquire', yet the Scrivener edition uses it rather than 'enquire'.)] Thus, **enquire** means 'the action of searching into something, usually by the asking of questions'. Eg. Deut.13:14, "Then shalt thou enquire, and make search, and ask diligently; and, behold, if it be truth, and the thing certain, that such abomination is wrought among you." {enquired (spelled both 'enquired' and 'inquired' (5x.) in the 1611) 34x., enquirest 1x., enquiry (spelled 'inquirie' in the 1611) 2x., tot. = 89x.}

Ensample —3x., n. [A.D. 1250, < OF. *ensample* or *essample* = 'a sample, used as a pattern or a warning' (NOI. Was 'ensample' and 'example' the very same word in the Bible? Some dictionaries say yes. The case for similarity is further strengthened by the fact that 'ensample' is used to translate two different Gk. words (τυπος (*tupos*) = 'a mark made by an impression'; and υποδειγμα (*hupodeigma*) = 'a pattern'), both of which are also translated elsewhere as 'example'. Yet there still appears to be a difference between the two E. words. 'Ensample' was a common word in ME. and used by such writers as Chaucer, Gower, Caxton and Morley, though not used by Shakespeare. After careful study and comparison, it seems (to this author) that the prefix 'ex' or 'en' determines the direction of the root word 'sample'. An 'ex-ample' would be a sample taken out-of something (ex = 'out' (see L. prefix '*ex–*')), whereas an 'en-sample' would be a sample put-into something (en = 'into' (see E. prefix 'em–')). See also 'Example'.)] Thus, an **ensample** is 'a sample of something that has been put into something else for others to see'. Eg. 2Pt.2:6, "And turning the cities of Sodom and Gomorrha into ashes condemned them with an overthrow, making them an ensample unto those that after should live ungodly." (Here, a sample of God's judgment was put into Sodom and Gomorrah for others to see.) {ensamples 3x., tot. = 6x.}

Ensign —8x., n. [A.D. 1375, < OF. *enseigne* < L. *insignia, in* = 'in', having intensity (see L. prefix '*in–*'[2]) + *signum* = 'a sign or mark'] Thus, an **ensign** is 'a special sign signifying some authority or something important'. Eg. Num.2:2, "Every man of the children of Israel shall pitch by his own standard, with the ensign of their father's house: far off about the tabernacle of the congregation shall they pitch." {ensigns 1x., tot. = 9x.}

Ensue —1x., v. [A.D. 1398, < OF. *ensuivre* < L. *insequi* (= 'to follow in'), *in* = 'into' (see L. prefix '*in*–'[2]) + *sequi* = 'to follow' or 'to aim at'] Thus, **ensue** means 'the action of following something right in to where it is'. Eg. 1Pt.3:11, "Let him eschew evil, and do good; let him seek peace, and ensue it." (Cp. also 'Pursue'.)

Enterprise —1x., n. [A.D. 1430, < OF. *entreprise* < *entreprendre* (= 'to take in hand'), < L. *interprehendere* (= 'to take hold, occupy or seize'), *inter* = 'between or among' + *prehendere* = 'to seize or take'] Thus, an **enterprise** is 'a project, or piece of work, taken in hand to be completed'. Eg. Job.5:12, "He disappointeth the devices of the crafty, so that their hands cannot perform their enterprise."

Entertain —1x., v. [A.D. 1475, < ME. entertene < OF. *entretenir* (= 'to hold together or support') < L. *intertenere* (= 'to hold up, support or preserve'), *inter* = 'between or among' + *tenere* = 'to hold' (NOI. The association with amusement began in A.D. 1626. An 'entertainer', then, is one who can hold up or support the imagination or amusements of others.)] Thus, **entertain** means 'the action of supporting, preserving or maintaining someone or something'. Eg. Heb.13:2, "Be not forgetful to entertain strangers: for thereby some have entertained angels unawares." {entertained 1x., tot. = 2x.}

Entice —8x., v. [A.D. 1297, < OF. *enticier* (= 'to set on fire') < VL. *intitiare* (= 'to set on fire'), *in* = 'into' (see L. prefix '*in*–'[2]) + *titio* = 'a firebrand' (NOI. 'Entice' is used in an evil sense. The ME. 'tice' meant 'to attract through pleasure or enflamed passion'.)] Thus, **entice** means 'the action of setting on fire one's emotions and passions, for some evil purpose'. Eg. Pr.1:10, "My son, if sinners entice thee, consent thou not." {enticed 3x., enticeth 1x., enticing 2x., tot. = 14x.}

Entreat — 2x., [A.D. 1340 (spelled 'intreat' both times

in the 1611), < OF. *entraitier, en* = 'in' (see E. prefix 'em–') + *traitier* < L. *tractare* = 'to drag, handle or manage' (the frequentative form of L. *trahere* = 'to draw or drag', from which we get our E. 'tractor' and 'traction') (NOI. A comparison of the 1611 and the KJV reveals no discernable difference between **entreat** and **intreat**, neither does a study of other ME. writings. It seems then (to this author) that both words were used interchangeably, similar to **enquire** and **inquire**. Both E. prefixes '**en**' and '**in**' mean the same (see E. prefix 'em–'). The only perceptible difference between them in the KJV (but not the 1611) is that '**entreat**' is almost always done by an enemy and results in ill-favor, whereas '**intreat**' is always done by a friend. See also 'Intreat'.)] Thus, **entreat** means 'the action of handling or managing a people-situation'. Eg. Act.7:6, "And God spake on this wise, That his seed should sojourn in a strange land; and that they should bring them into bondage, and entreat them evil four hundred years." {entreated 9x., entreateth 1x., tot. = 12x.}

Environ –1x., v. [A.D. 1340, < OF. *environner* (= 'to encompass' or 'to hedge in on all sides') < *environ* (= 'around or about'), < *en* = 'in' (see E. prefix 'em–') *viron* = 'a circle or circuit' (NOI. Our E. word 'environment' means 'the surrounding things or conditions'.)] Thus, **environ** means 'the action of surrounding, or forming a circle around someone or something'. Eg. Josh.7:9, "For the Canaanites and all the inhabitants of the land shall hear of it, and shall environ us round, and cut off our name from the earth: and what wilt thou do unto thy great name?"

Envy –20x., n. and v. [A.D. 1280, < OF. *envie* (= 'a lust unto, or longing after' or 'a malicious emulation') < L. *invidia* (= 'hatred or envy') < *invidere* (= 'to view with ill-will, or hatred'; lit. 'to look against'), *in* = 'against' (see L. prefix '*in*–'[1]) + *videre* = 'to look or view'] Thus, as a n., **envy** is 'a condition of ill-will, or hatred, brought about by looking 'against' someone or something'. Eg. Mk.15:10, "For he knew that the chief priests had delivered him for envy." Furthermore, as a v., **envy** means 'the action of looking 'against' something or someone with feelings of hatred or ill-will'. Eg. Pr.23:17, "Let not thine heart envy sinners: but be thou in the fear of the LORD all the day long." {envied 6x., envies 1x., enviest 1x., envieth 1x., envious 4x., envying 5x., envyings 2x., tot. = 40x.}

Ephah – 39x., n. [A.D. 1398, trans. < Hb. איפה (*eyphah*) probably < Egyptian *'pt* = 'a container for measuring grain' (NOI. The Jews would have become accustomed to the *'pt* while in Egypt. There were also 3 people in the Bible with the name 'Ephah', but they have a different Hb. word, עיפה (*Eyphah*), meaning 'gloomy'.)] Thus, an **ephah** is 'a unit of dry measure, such as for wheat, which holds the same as a 'bath', which is approximately 8 US (dry) gal. (about 35 litres)'. Eg. Eze.45:11, "The ephah and the bath shall be of one measure, that the bath may contain the tenth part of an homer, and the ephah the tenth part of an homer: the measure thereof shall be after the homer."

Ephod – 52x., n. [A.D. 1382(WB.), trans. < Hb. אפוד (*ephowd*) < oo., but possibly 'to bind' or 'to wrap up' (NOI. The **ephod** was normally a short, sleeveless coat made of linen and worn by Jewish priests and the High Priest (who wore a very fine one), yet we find Samuel, as a very young boy, wearing one in 1Sam.2:18. In fact, King David danced in one, in 2Sam.6:14, possibly so he could feel very close to God. 'Ephod' was also a man's name in Num.34:23.)] Thus, an **ephod** was 'a religious article of clothing, resembling a short coat without sleeves, and normally worn by Jewish priests overtop of their other clothes'. Eg. 1Sam.2:28, "And did I choose him out of all the tribes of Israel to be my priest, to offer upon mine altar, to burn incense, to wear an ephod before me?..."

Epicureans – 1x., n. pl. [A.D. 1382(WB.), trans. < Gk. Επικουρειος (*Epikoureios*) = 'the followers of Επικουρος' (*Epikouros*) = the name of a famous Gk. philosopher (whose name come from the Gk. επικουρια (*epikouria*) = 'a maid who comes in to help') (NOI. Επικουρος (or Epicurus as his name is usually spelled) lived from 341-270 B.C. and taught that pleasure (as in freedom from pain of body and mind) is the goal of man, for when he dies he ceases to exist. His school was co-ed (consisting of both men and women), which later gave rise to scandalous rumors.)] Thus, **Epicureans** were 'people who followed the philosophical freedom and pleasure-seeking teachings of Epicurus'. Eg. Act.17:18, "Then certain philosophers of the Epicureans, and of the Stoicks, encountered him. And some said, What will this babbler say? other some, He seemeth to be a setter forth of strange gods: because he preached unto them Jesus, and the resurrection." (NOI. It's no wonder that the Epicurean philosophers thought Paul's teaching on the resurrection to be strange, as they believed in cessation after death.)

Epistle —19*x., n. [A.D. 893, < OF. *epistle* < L. *epistola* < Gk. επιστολη (*epistole*) (= 'a letter or message'), < επιστελλειν (*epistellein*) (= 'send to'), επι (*epi*) = 'to' or 'on' (see Gk. prefix 'επι') + στελλειν (*stellein*) = 'to send' (NOI. There are a few times when επιστολη is translated 'letter' (eg. Act.23:25 and 2Cor.7:8) but the translators decided that an 'epistle' was different from a 'letter' in that it was part of the NT. canon of scripture, thereby making it of eternal value. The difference can be seen in 2Cor.3:1, the **epistle** being written to them and the letter being written by them. See also 'Letter'.)] Thus, an **epistle** is 'a letter written by an apostle, which became part of the NT. canon of scripture'. Eg. 1Ths.5:27, "I charge you by the Lord that this epistle be read unto all the holy brethren." (NOI. Figuratively, **epistle** was used in reference to the believers in the church at Corinth, showing their eternal value and worth. See 2Cor.3:2.) (*includes ps. in 1Cor., 2Cor., 1Ths., 2Ths., and 2Tim.) {epistles 2x. tot = 21x.}

Equal – 21x., adj. and v. [A.D. 1391, < L. *aequalis* (= 'equivalent, identical') < *aequus* = 'level, fair, even or calm'] Thus, as an adj., **equal** modifies its n. as 'being of an identical value, amount etc. as something or someone else'. Eg. Jn.5:18, "Therefore the Jews sought the more to kill him, because he not only had broken the sabbath, but said also that God was his Father, making himself equal with God." Furthermore, as a v., **equal** means 'the action of making something or someone identical to someone or something else'. Eg. Job.28:19, "The topaz of Ethiopia shall not equal it, neither shall it be valued with pure gold." {equality 2x., equally 1x., equals 1x., unequal 2x., unequally 1x., tot. = 28x.}

Equity – 10x., n. [A.D. 1315, < OF. *equite* (= 'equality or evenness' in a moral or legal sense) < L. *aequitas* (= 'justice, evenness or sameness') < *aequus* (see 'Equal') (NOI. 'Equity' is a quality.)] Thus, **equity** is 'the quality of impartial fairness in a moral or legal sense'. Eg. Ps.98:9, "Before the LORD; for he cometh to judge the earth: with righteousness shall he judge the world, and the people with equity."

Erected – 1x., v. pret. [A.D. 1417, < ME. **erect** (< L. *erectus* (which is pp. of) *erigere* = 'to set upright' or 'to build' (< *e* = 'out of' (see L. Prefix '*ex–*') + *regere* = 'to direct')) + **ed** = forms the pret.] Thus, **erected** means 'the past-tense action of building something (or setting it) in an upright position'. Eg. Gen.33:20, "And he erected there an altar, and called it Elelohe-Israel."

Err – 24x., v. [A.D. 1303, < OF. *errer* (= 'to transgress by wandering') < L. *errare* = 'to stray, wander' (NOI. '**Err**' was used in a moral sense, when someone wandered away from that which is right and proper.)] Thus, **err** means 'the action of a moral wandering away from what is right and proper'. Eg. Ps.95:10, "Forty years long was I grieved with this generation, and said, It is a people that do err in their heart, and they have not known my ways." (NOI. The Sadducees wandered away from a proper 'literal-grammatical-historical-method' of interpreting the Scriptures, as in Mt.22:29, and not taking the Scriptures for what they said.) {erred 12x., erreth 2x., error 13x., errors 4x., tot. = 55x.}

Error –13x., n. [A.D. 1300, < OF. *error* (modern Fr. *erreur*) (= 'a wandering out of the right way') < L. *error* < *errare* (see 'Err') (NOI. '**Error**' is the n. whereas '**err**' is the v. The use of **error** suggest an ignorance by the wanderer, i.e. he/she is committing the sin through foolish mistake rather than cold-hearted calculation. An example of this is Uzzah in 2Sam.6:7.] Thus, an **error** is 'a sin or transgression caused by foolish wandering'. Eg. Jam.5:20, "Let him know, that he which converteth the sinner from the error of his way shall save a soul from death, and shall hide a multitude of sins." {err 24x., erred 12x., erreth 2x., errors 4x., tot. = 55x. tot.}

Escape –59x., v. [A.D. 1292, < OF. *escaper* < LL. *excappare* (= 'to slip out of a cape or cloak'), *ex* = 'out of' (see L. prefix '*ex–*') + *cappa* = 'a cape' (NOI. A person, when caught, would try to slip out of his cape and be gone. This is illustrated in Mk.14:51-52.)] Thus, **escape** means 'the action of gaining liberty by trying to slip away from one's captors and run to safety'. Eg. 1Sam.27:1, "And David said in his heart, I shall now perish one day by the hand of Saul: there is nothing better for me than that I should speedily escape into the land of the Philistines; and Saul shall despair of me, to seek me any more in any coast of Israel: so shall I escape out of his hand." {escaped 58x., escapeth 6x., escaping 1x., tot. = 124x.}

Eschew – 1x., v. [A.D. 1340, < OF. *eschuer* (= 'to avoid') (modern Fr. *esquiver* = 'to dodge') (akin to E. 'shy' = 'to keep away' or 'to avoid') (NOI. The Gk. word is εκκλινω (*ekklino*) = 'to turn aside' or 'to get out of the way'.)] Thus,

eschew means 'the action of avoiding, or getting out of the way of'. Eg. 1Pt.3:11, "Let him eschew evil, and do good; let him seek peace, and ensue it." {eschewed 1x., escheweth 2x., tot. = 4x.}

Especially –5x., adv. [A.D. 1400, < E. (adj.) **especial** (< OF. *especial* < L. *specialis* (= 'special, particular' as opposed to general (Lewis and Short describe *specialis* as, "the particular thing, among many, to which the looks are turned.")) < *specere* = 'to look at') = 'special (as in 'special purpose or design') of a particular type' + **ly** = forms the adv. (see E. suffix '–ly'[2]) ((NOI. For some reason, people often forget that '**especially**' is an adv. (not an adj.) and modifies verbs, not nouns. Always look for the verb in the sentence that it modifies.)] Thus, **especially** modifies its v. as 'happening in an especial, or particular, manner'. Eg. 2Tim.4:13, "The cloke that I left at Troas with Carpus, when thou comest, bring with thee, and the books, but especially the parchments." {special 2x., tot. = 7x.}

Espied –2x., v. pret. [A.D. 1225 < E. **espy** (see 'Espy')] Thus, **espied** means 'the past-tense action of espy'. Eg. Gen.42:27, "And as one of them opened his sack to give his ass provender in the inn, he espied his money; for, behold, it was in his sack's mouth." {spy 12x., tot. = 14x.}

Espousals – 2x., n. pl. [A.D. 1393, < E. **espousal** (< OF. *espousaille* (usually the pl. *espousailles*) (= 'a wedding, marriage') < L. *sponsalia* (= 'a betrothal' or 'a wedding')) + **s** = forms the pl. (NOI. This was normally a pl. word because the wedding ceremony often lasted for 7 days. Cp. Gen.29:27-28 and Jud.14:10-12. See also 'Betroth'.)] Thus, **espousals** refer to 'the days of the marriage ceremony'. Eg. SoS.3:11, "Go forth, O ye daughters of Zion, and behold king Solomon with the crown wherewith his mother crowned him in the day of his espousals, and in the day of the gladness of his heart." (NOI. Scholars speculate that the crown here was a wedding wreath given to Solomon by his mother Bathsheba.) {espoused 5x., tot. = 7x.}

Espy —2x., v. [A.D. 1225, < OF. *espier* (= 'to watch from a distance' or 'to observe narrowly') akin to E. **spy** (= 'to make secret observations' (see 'Spy')) and L. *specere* (= 'to look at')] Thus, **espy** means 'the action of observing from a distance and making secret observations'. Eg. Josh.14:7, "Forty years old was I when Moses the servant of the LORD sent me from Kadeshbarnea to espy out the land; and I brought him word again as it was in mine heart." {spy 12x., tot. = 14x.}

Establish —44x., v. [A.D. 1374, < ME. **establisse** < OF. *establiss* or *establir* (= 'to settle' or 'to fix in place') < L. *stabilire* = 'to make firm' (< *stabilis* = 'firm')] Thus, **establish** means 'the action of making something firm or stable'. Eg. Lev.26:9, "For I will have respect unto you, and make you fruitful, and multiply you, and establish my covenant with you." {established 74x., establisheth 3x., establishment 1x., tot. = 122x.}

Estate — 17x., n. [A.D. 1225, < OF. *estat* < L. *status* = ('posture, position or way of standing') < *stare* = 'to stand'] Thus, an **estate** is 'an office, realm or a set of special conditions in which a person lives and functions'. Eg. Eze.16:55, "When thy sisters, Sodom and her daughters, shall return to their former estate, and Samaria and her daughters shall return to their former estate, then thou and thy daughters shall return to your former estate." {estates 2x., tot. = 19x.}

Esteem —5x., v. [A.D. 1450, < OF. *estimer* (= 'to respect' or 'to hold dear') < L. *æstimare* = 'to judge, or place, the value of something' (see 'Estimate') (NOI. '**Esteem**' deals with a moral value.)] Thus, **esteem** means 'the action of placing a moral value on something or someone'. Eg. Phil.2:3, "Let nothing be done through strife or vainglory; but in lowliness of mind let each esteem other better than themselves." {esteemed 11x., esteemeth 4x., esteeming 1x., tot. = 21x.}

Estimate —2x., v. [A.D. 1374, < L. *æstimatus* (= 'a valuation, reckoning') < *æstimare* (= 'to judge, or place, the value of something') (NOI. '**Estimate**' deals with a financial value.] Thus, **estimate** means 'the action of establishing a financial value on something'. Eg. Lev.27:14, "And when a man shall sanctify his house to be holy unto the LORD, then the priest shall estimate it, whether it be good or bad: as the priest shall estimate it, so shall it stand." {estimation 23x., tot. = 25x.}

Estranged —5x., p. [A.D. 1552, < E. (v.) **estrange** (< OF. *estrangier* < ML. *extraneare* (= 'to treat as strange or foreign') < L. *extraneus* = 'stranger, external' or 'not of one's household', < *extra* = 'outside') + **ed** = forms the p. (see E. suffix '–ed' [4])] Thus, **estranged** modifies its n. as 'having become as a stranger or foreigner'. Eg. Ps.58:3, "The wicked are estranged from the womb: they go astray as soon as they be born, speaking lies."

Eternal —47x., adj. [A.D. 1386, < OF. *eternal* < LL. *æternalis* < L. *æternus* (= 'perpetual' or 'having no beginning nor ending') (NOI. The main Gk. word of the NT. is (adj.) αιωνιος (*aionios*) = 'eternal, everlasting' < αιων (*aion*) = 'life', which originally meant 'time allotted to a being'. Eventually, Gk. writers began linking αιων with a preposition (such as απο (*apo*) = 'away from') to get the idea of 'eternity', then they simply began using αιωνιος. Because God is eternal (Deut.33:27), ζωη αιωνιος (*zoe aionios*) (ζωη = 'fullness of life') represents that quality of life (outside the boundaries of time) that God enjoys, which, by the way, is offered to the whole world as a free gift. See Jn.3:16.)] Thus, **eternal** modifies its n. as 'being outside the boundaries of time, thereby having, as we would understand, an unbroken perpetuity of time'. Eg. Mt.25:46, "And these shall go away into everlasting punishment: but the righteous into life eternal." {eternity 1x., tot. = 48x.}

Eternity – 1x., n. [A.D. 1374, < OF. *eternite* < L. *æternitas* < L. *æternus* (see 'Eternal')] Thus, **eternity** is 'the state or condition of being outside the boundaries of time as we know it' (i.e. 'eternal existence'). Eg. Isa.57:15, "For thus saith the high and lofty One that inhabiteth eternity, whose name is Holy; I dwell in the high and holy place, with him also that is of a contrite and humble spirit..." {eternal 47x., tot. = 48x.}

Eunuch – 7x., n. [A.D. 1387, < L. *eunuchus* < Gk. ευνουχος (*eunouchos*) (= 'a bed-chamber attendant or guard') < ευνη (*eune*) = 'a bed' + εχειν (*ekein*) = 'to hold, keep' (NOI. A '**eunuch**' was usually a castrated male (done before puberty to prevent the development of masculine characteristics, although sometimes the patient died from infection caused by the surgery), and employed as a harem-keeper, a chamberlain or given some other affairs of state, such as military or financial. The practice goes back thousands of years to ancient Egypt, China and India.)] Thus, a **eunuch** is 'a castrated male who was employed as a trusted man in the inner courts of a kingdom'. Eg. Act.8:27, "And he arose and went: and, behold, a man of Ethiopia, an eunuch of great authority under Candace queen of the Ethiopians, who had the charge of all her treasure, and had come to Jerusalem for to worship." {eunuchs 20x., tot. = 27x.}

Euroclydon – 1x pn. [A.D. 1587(GB.), trans. < Gk. Ευροκλυδων (*Eurokludon*) (= 'a violent agitation') < ευρος (*euros*) = 'east wind' (see 'East') + κλυδων (*kludon*) = 'a billow, wave' (NOI. During the winter months, from about mid-November till mid-February, storms on the Mediterranean Sea were common as east winds caused huge waves.)] Thus,

Euroclydon was 'the name of a tempestuous east wind on the Mediterranean Sea, causing violent storms during the winter months'. Eg. Act.27:14, "But not long after there arose against it a tempestuous wind, called Euroclydon."

Evangelist —2x., n. [A.D. 1175, < L. *evangelista* < Gk. ευαγγελιστης (*euaggelistes*) < ευαγγελιζεσθαι (*euaggelizesthai*) (= 'to preach good news') < ευ (*eu*) = 'well, good' + αγγελος (*aggelos*) = 'a messenger' (NOI. An '**evangelist**' was a man whose job it was to preach, or proclaim, to others the gospel tidings; that being the death, burial and resurrection of Jesus Christ, repentance from sin and faith in Christ as Savior in order to secure eternal life. The office of **evangelist** is seen in Eph.4:11. The **evangelist** also helps the people of a church in learning how to evangelize.)] Thus, an **evangelist** is 'a man who is called of God to preach the good news of the gospel'. Eg. 2Tim.4:5, "But watch thou in all things, endure afflictions, do the work of an evangelist, make full proof of thy ministry." {evangelists 1x., tot. = 3x.}

Eve —4x., pn. [A.D. 1525(TNT.), < L. *Eva* < Gk. Ευα (*Eua*) < Hb. חוה (*Chavvah*) = 'life, living' (NOI. Some scholars wonder whether the name '**Eve**' (life) was a play on words, since she led Adam into the first sin, which brought about death. However, there is no indication of this in the Bible, so we must assume than Adam simply chose a good name for her.)] Thus, **Eve** is 'the name Adam gave to his wife, after their fall into sin, meaning 'life''. Eg. Gen.3:20, "And Adam called his wife's name Eve; because she was the mother of all living."

Even [1] — 1314*x., adj. and adv. [A.D. 697, < OE. **efen** = 'level' (as in 'level ground') (NOI. '**Even**' has shades of meaning in E., but can be divided into two basic classifications. (As a v., **even** is not used in the KJV.) Its function is usually to make comparisons, similar to how we use 'like' and 'as'.) (*incl. title of Ps.39. The 1611 has an extra '**even**' in Josh.3:11 (which would make the total count 1385x.), where the KJV does not.)] Thus, as an adj., **even** modifies its n. as 'being like-or-as something else'. Eg. 1Ths.2:7, "But we were gentle among you, even as a nurse cherisheth her children." Furthermore, as an adv., **even** modifies its v. as 'happening in a fashion similar to something else'. Eg. Jn.20:21, "Then said Jesus to them again, Peace be unto you: as my Father hath sent me, even so send I you."

Even [2] —80x., n. [A.D. 950, < OE. **fen** (akin to Du. *avond* and Ger. *abend*) = 'end of the day' i.e. when the sun is setting and the light rays become level with the ground] Thus, **even** is 'the closing part of the work day, as the sun is just disappearing'. Eg. Jud.19:16, "And, behold, there came an old man from his work out of the field at even, which was also of mount Ephraim; and he sojourned in Gibeah: but the men of the place were Benjamites." {evening 60x., evenings 1x., eveningtide 2x., eventide 5x., tot. = 148x.}

Evening — 60x., n. [A.D. 1000(AT.), < OE. **fnung** < **fnian** (= 'to draw towards even') (NOI. '**Evening**' started before **even** until just after **even**.)] Thus, **evening** is 'the condition of when shadows on the ground become long (late afternoon?), until when there is no more light from the sun'. Eg. Mt.14:15, "And when it was evening, his disciples came to him, saying, This is a desert place, and the time is now past; send the multitude away, that they may go into the villages, and buy themselves victuals." (Here, evening was starting to happen, but had not fully come until vs. 23.) {even 80x., evenings 1x., eveningtide 2x., eventide 5x., tot. = 148x.}

Eveningtide — 2x., n. [A.D. 1568(BB.), < E. **evening** (see 'Evening') + **tide** = 'time' (NOI. The addition of '**tide**' puts more emphasis on the time frame.)] Thus, **eveningtide** is 'the time frame at the end of the day, when shadows lengthen, until after the sun sets and there is no more light'. Eg. 2Sam.11:2, "And it came to pass in an eveningtide, that David arose from off his bed, and walked upon the roof of the king's house: and from the roof he saw a woman washing herself; and the woman was very beautiful to look upon." (see also 'Eventide' and 'Noontide'.) {even 80x., evening 60x., evenings 1x., eventide 5x., tot. = 148x.}

Eventide – 5x., n. [A.D. 950(LfG.), < OE. **fentid, fen** = 'even' (see 'Even'[2]) + **tide** = 'time' (NOI. The addition of '**tide**' puts more emphasis on the time frame.)] Thus, **eventide** is 'the time frame of even, when the sun is just setting'. Eg. Josh.8:29, "And the king of Ai he hanged on a tree until eventide: and as soon as the sun was down, Joshua commanded that they should take his carcase down from the tree, and cast it at the entering of the gate of the city, and raise thereon a great heap of stones, that remaineth unto this day." (See also 'Eveningtide' and 'Noontide'.) {even 80x., evening 60x., evenings 1x., eveningtide 2x., tot. = 148x.}

Everlasting – 97x., adj. and n. [A.D. 1340, < E. **ever** (adv.) (< OE. **fre** = 'at all times') + **lasting** (vbl.n.) (= 'a continuing, permanent duration')] Thus, as an adj., **everlasting** modifies its n. as 'being at all times of a continuing, permanent duration'. Eg. Jn.3:16, "For God so loved the world, that he gave his only begotten Son, that whosoever believeth in him should not perish, but have everlasting life." Furthermore, as a n. **everlasting** is 'the condition of eternity, outside the restrictions of time'. Eg. Ps.90:2, "Before the mountains were brought forth, or ever thou hadst formed the earth and the world, even from everlasting to everlasting, thou art God." {ever 476x., last 85x., lasting 1x., tot. = 659x.}

Evermore –26x., adv. [A.D. 1205, < E. **ever** (adv.) (< OE. **fre**

= 'at all times') + **more** = 'greater, larger or superior' (NOI. Originally, **evermore** came from the OE. ' **fre ma**' the **ma** simply adding emphasis to the **fre**. Later, the **ma** was replaced with **more**, which became the modern way of adding emphasis.)] Thus, **evermore** modifies its v. as 'happening for ever, or throughout all future time'. Eg. 1Ths.5:16, "Rejoice evermore." {ever 476x., more 686x., tot. = 1188x.}

Evidence —7x., n. [A.D. 1300, < OF. *evidence* (= 'a manifestation') < L. *evidentia* (= 'apparent, clearness') < *evidens* = 'clear', < *e* = 'out' (see L. prefix '*ex*–') + *videns* (which is prp. of) *videre* = 'to see'] Thus, an **evidence** is 'a manifestation, or something that can be clearly seen'. Eg. Heb.11:1, "Now faith is the substance of things hoped for, the evidence of things not seen." {evidences 2x., tot. = 9x.}

Evidently —2x., adv. [A.D. 1374, < E. **evident** (< OF. *evident* < L. *evidens* (see 'Evidence')) + **ly** = forms the adv. (see E. suffix '–ly'[2])] Thus, **evidently** modifies its v. as 'happening in a clearly visible manner'. Eg. Gal.3:1, "O foolish Galatians, who hath bewitched you, that ye should not obey the truth, before whose eyes Jesus Christ hath been evidently set forth, crucified among you? " (Just as in a court of law the evidence is clearly set before the jury, so also the clear 'proof-of-fact' concerning the crucifixion of Christ was set before the Galatians.) {evident 5x., tot. = 7x.}

Evil — 613x., adj., adv. and n. [A.D. 825(VP.), < OE. **yfel** < oo., but possibly from Teut. *ubilo* = 'up or over'; i.e. 'overstepping proper limits' (as in something that is morally bad). However, if **evil** means 'morally bad' or 'sinful', as some suggest, then Gen.37:20 means that certain beasts are sinful. Ex.32:14 and Isa.45:7 would also suggest that God has bad morals, and this is obviously not the Bible meaning of **evil**. A careful study of how **evil** is used in the Bible indicates a basic meaning of 'purposing to cause loss or destruction'. (NOI. When man chooses his own way and rejects God's way, it always ends in destruction, as seen in Pr.16:25 and Isa.55:9. Man's way can therefore be termed **evil**, because it causes damage and loss, according to the Bible.)] Thus, as an adj., **evil** modifies its n. as 'being of a destructive nature'. Eg. Jer.24:3, "Then said the LORD unto me, What seest thou, Jeremiah? And I said, Figs; the good figs, very good; and the evil, very evil, that cannot be eaten, they are so evil." Furthermore, as an adv., **evil** modifies its v. as 'happening in a destructive manner'. Eg. Deut.26:6, "And the Egyptians evil entreated us, and afflicted us, and laid upon us hard bondage." Finally, as a n., an **evil** is 'something (or someone) which is destructive in its ways and causes loss and damage in the sight of God'. Eg. Pr.3:7, "Be not wise in thine own eyes: fear the LORD, and depart from evil." (See also 'Iniquity', 'Sin', 'Transgression', 'Trespass' and 'Wicked'.) {evildoer 2x., evildoers 12x., evil-favouredness 1x., evils 9x., tot. = 637x.}

Evilfavouredness —1x., n. [A.D. 1535(CB.), < E. **evil** (adj.) (see 'Evil') + **favour** (n.) (< OF. *favor* < L. *favor* = 'bias, applause' (See 'Favour'[1])) + **ed** (= forms the adj. (see E. suffix '–ed'[5])) + **ness** (= 'the quality or condition of' (see E. suffix '–ness'))] Thus, an **evilfavouredness** is 'a condition that tends toward weakness, malfunction or disease'. Eg. Deut.17:1, "Thou shalt not sacrifice unto the LORD thy God any bullock, or sheep, wherein is blemish, or any evilfavouredness: for that is an abomination unto the LORD thy God."

Ewe —7x., n. [A.D. 700, < OE. **eowu** (= 'a female sheep') akin to L. *ovis* (= 'a female sheep') and Gk. οις (*ois*) (= 'sheep') and Sans. *avi* (= 'a sheep')] Thus, a **ewe** is 'a female sheep'. Eg. 2Sam.12:3, "But the poor man had nothing, save one little ewe lamb, which he had bought and nourished up: and it grew up together with him, and with his children; it did eat of his own meat, and drank of his own cup, and lay in his bosom, and was unto him as a daughter." (Cp. also Ps.78:71) {ewes 3x., tot. = 10x.}

Exact – 8x., v. [A.D. 1529, < L. *exactus* (which is pp. of) *exigere* (= 'to drive out' or 'to force out'), < *ex* = 'out' (see L. prefix '*ex*–') + *agere* = 'to drive, do'] Thus, **exact** means 'the action of forcing something out of something or someone'. Eg. **Lk**.3:13, "And he said unto them, Exact no more than that which is appointed you." {exacted 2x., exacteth 1x., exaction 1x., exactions 1x., exactors 1x., tot. = 14x.}

Exalt –26x., v. [A.D. 1400, < L. *exaltare* (< *ex* (='out' (see L. prefix '*ex*–')) + *altus* (= 'high')) = 'to lift up high' (NOI. **Exalt** is used in a figurative sense, although other variations may be used literally, such as **exalted** in 2Ki.19:22.) (NOI. **Exalt** seems like it can be used of God or man, whereas 'extol' is only used of God. See 'Extol'.)] Thus, **exalt** means 'the action of elevating in glory, honor, rank, etc.'. Eg. 1Pt.5:6, "Humble yourselves therefore under the mighty hand of God, that he may exalt you in due time." {exalted 64x., exaltest 1x., exalteth 9x., tot. = 100x.}

Examine –5x., v. [A.D. 1303, < OF. *examiner* < L. *examinare* < *examen* = 'a consideration' or 'a weighing of a situation'] Thus, **examine** means 'the action of carefully weighing, testing or interrogating a situation, according to the its details or facts, for the purpose of arriving at a conclusion'. Eg. Ezr.10:16, "And the children of the captivity did so. And Ezra the priest, with certain chief of the fathers, after the house of their fathers, and all of them by their names, were separated, and sat down in the first day of the tenth month to examine the matter." {examination 1x., examined 6x., examining 1x., tot. = 13x.}

Example –8x., n. [A.D. 1386, < OF. *example* < L. *exemplum* (= 'a sample that has been taken out for use as a pattern or a warning') < *eximere* (= 'to take out'), *ex* = 'out of' (see L. prefix '*ex–*') + *mere* = 'to take, buy or gain' (See also 'Ensample' for the difference between the two.)] Thus, an **ex-ample** is 'a sample of a larger thing, which has been taken out for use as a pattern or a warning'. Eg. 1Tim.4:12, "Let no man despise thy youth; but be thou an example of the believers, in word, in conversation, in charity, in spirit, in faith, in purity." (Here, Timothy was to be a sample, taken out of the larger group of believers, to all men.) {examples 1x., tot. = 9x.}

Exceed –4x., v. [A.D. 1374, < OF. *exceder* (= 'to pass, go beyond') < L. *excedere* (= 'to pass'), < *ex* = 'out of', as in 'beyond' (see L. prefix '*ex–*') + *cedere* = 'to go'] Thus, **exceed** means 'the action of going beyond a limit or boundary'. Eg. Deut.25:3, "Forty stripes he may give him, and not exceed: lest, if he should exceed, and beat him above these with many stripes, then thy brother should seem vile unto thee." {exceeded 3x., exceedest 1x., exceedeth 1x., exceeding 59x., exceedingly 39x., tot. = 107x.}

Excel –5x., v. [A.D. 1430, < L. *excellere* (= 'to stand out' or 'to be very prominent'), < *ex* = 'out' (see L. prefix '*ex–*') + *cellere* = 'to rise' (NOI. The OED. suggests the L. root to be *celsus* = 'lofty'. This is not 'celsius', the centigrade thermometer, named after Mr. Anders Celsius its inventor in A.D. 1742.)] Thus, **excel** means 'the action of rising above others' (as in 'superior achievement'). Eg. Ps.103:20, "Bless the LORD, ye his angels, that excel in strength, that do his commandments, hearkening unto the voice of his word." {excelled 1x., excellency 26x., excellent 34x., excellest 1x., excelleth 3x., tot. = 70x.}

Except –74x., subordinating conj., and prep. [A.D. 1377, < L. *exceptus* (which is pp. of) *excipere* (*ex* = 'out' (see L. prefix '*ex–*') + *capere* = 'to take') = 'to take out of something', which is under consideration (NOI. Some people substitute

except with 'unless', however, 'unless' is a different word, meaning 'on-the-less'. See 'Unless'.)] Thus, as a subordinating conj., **except** 'joins and subordinates a dependent thought to a main thought by taking out the main thought'. Eg. Jn.3:3, "Jesus answered and said unto him, Verily, verily, I say unto thee, Except a man be born again, he cannot see the kingdom of God." (Here, the main thought is 'a man be born again' and it is taken-out by the subordinating conj. **except**.) Furthermore, as a prep., **except** 'shows the position or relationship of a noun in a sentence to other nouns by taking it out of a group'. Eg. Act.8:1, "And Saul was consenting unto his death. And at that time there was a great persecution against the church which was at Jerusalem; and they were all scattered abroad throughout the regions of Judaea and Samaria, except the apostles." (Here, the apostles were taken-out of the group of other believers by the prep. **except**.) {excepted 1x., tot. = 75x.}

Exchange[1] —6x., n. [A.D. 1374, < ME. **eschaunge** OF. *eschange* (= 'an exchange' or 'a barter') < LL. *excambium* < L. *excambiare* (= 'to out-change'), < *ex* = 'out' (see L. prefix '*ex–*') + *cambiare* = 'to change' or 'to barter for something of equal worth' (NOI. In Italy, the 'money-exchanger' is called a '*Cambio*' (< L. *cambiare*). Whereas 'change' may be of unequal value, **exchange** is of an equal value.)] Thus, an **exchange** is 'the act of barter, in which something is changed for something of equal value'. Eg. Mk.8:37, "Or what shall a man give in exchange for his soul?" {exchangers 1x., tot. = 7x.}

Exchange[2] —1x., v. [A.D. 1300, < OF. *eschanger* (= 'to change one for another') < L. *excambiare* (see 'Exchange'[1])] Thus, **exchange** means 'the action of bartering or changing one item for something else of equal value'. Eg. Eze.48:14, "And they shall not sell of it, neither exchange, nor alienate the firstfruits of the land: for it is holy unto the LORD."

Excuse[1] —2x., n. [A.D. 1374, < OF. *excuse* < L. *excusare*, *ex* = 'out' (see L. prefix '*ex–*') +*causa* = 'cause', used in a legal sense, i.e. 'an accusation' (lit. 'to release from an accusation') (see also 'Cause')] Thus, an **excuse** is 'an attempt to release oneself from an accusation or obligation'. Eg. Lk.14:18, "And they all with one consent began to make excuse. The first said unto him, I have bought a piece of ground, and I must needs go and see it: I pray thee have me excused."

Excuse[2] —1x., v. [A.D. 1225, < OF. *excuser* < L. *excusare* (see 'Excuse'[1])] Thus, **excuse** means 'the action of releasing oneself from an accusation or obligation'. Eg. 2Cor.12:19, "Again, think ye that we excuse ourselves unto you? we speak before God in Christ: but we do all things, dearly beloved, for your edifying." {excused 2x., excusing 1x., tot. = 4x.}

Execration —2x., n. [A.D. 1382(WB.), < L. *execratio* (= 'the act of cursing or calling down evil upon'), < *exsecrari*, *ex* = 'out' (see L. prefix '*ex–*') + *sacrare* = 'to consecrate' (lit. 'to make un-sacred')] Thus, an **execration** is 'the state or condition of cursing or making abominate'. Eg. Jer.42:18, "... so shall my fury be poured forth upon you, when ye shall enter into Egypt: and ye shall be an execration, and an astonishment, and a curse, and a reproach; and ye shall see this place no more."

Execute —32x., v. [A.D. 1386, < OF. *executer* < L. *executus* (which is pp. of) *exsequi* (= 'to follow out', as in 'to the very end'), < *ex* = 'out' (see L. prefix '*ex–*') + *sequi* = 'to follow'] Thus, **execute** means 'the action of following right to the end some act of service, duty or judgment'. Eg. Num.8:11, "And Aaron shall offer the Levites before the LORD for an offering of the children of Israel, that they may execute the service of the LORD." {executed 20x., executedst 1x., executest 1x., executeth 6x., executing 3x., execution 1x., executioner 1x., tot. = 65x.}

Exhort —16x., v. [A.D. 1400, < L. *exhortari* < *ex* = 'out' (in a thorough sense) (see L. prefix '*ex–*') + *hortari* = 'to urge, encourage'] Thus, **exhort** means 'the action of thoroughly urging someone'. Eg. Act.2:40, "And with many other words did he testify and exhort, saying, Save yourselves from this untoward generation." {exhortation 10x., exhorted 3x., exhorteth 1x., exhorting 4x., tot. = 34x.}

Exile —2x., n. [A.D. 1300, < OF. *exil* (= 'banishment') < L. *exilium* (= 'banishment'), < *ex* = 'out' (see L. prefix '*ex–*') + *salire* = 'to leap' (< *sal* (akin to Sans. *sar* = 'to go'))] Thus, an **exile** is 'a person who has been officially banished from their native country'. Eg. Isa.51:14, "The captive exile hasteneth that he may be loosed, and that he should not die in the pit, nor that his bread should fail."

Exorcists —1x. n. pl. [A.D. 1382(WB.), < E. **exorcist** (< LL. *exorcista* < Gk. εξορκιστης (*exorkistes*) (= 'one who uses a formula to expel evil spirits) < εξορκιζω (*exorkizo*) < εξ (*ex*) = 'out of' (see Gk. prefix 'εκ–') + ορκιζω (*horkizo*) = 'to force someone to take an oath' or 'to adjure them' (see 'Adjure') (< ορκος (*horkos*) = 'an oath or pledge')) + **s** = forms the pl. (NOI. Cases of demonic possession, oppression and exorcism are recorded in the Bible. David used good music to rid King Saul of repeated attacks by an evil spirit, 1Sam.16:23. Jesus referred to Jewish exorcists in Mt.12:27, He cast out demons Himself (Mk.1:34) and allowed His disciples to do the same (Mk.6:13). Historically, **exorcists** have tried various methods of casting out evil spirits, but normally relied on words and phrases.)] Thus, **exorcists** are 'two or more people whose job it is to force evil spirits out of a victim by binding them under an oath to God, or some other holy thing or person'. Eg. Act.19:13, "Then certain of the vagabond Jews, exorcists, took upon them to call over them which had evil spirits the name of the Lord Jesus, saying, We adjure you by Jesus whom Paul preacheth."

Expectation —14x., n. [A.D. 1536, < L. *expectatio*, (= 'to look out', as in 'looking to see something') < *ex* = 'out of' (see L. prefix '*ex*–') + *spectare* = 'to look' (NOI. Expect has the idea of anticipating something favorable to happen.)] Thus, an **expectation** is 'the state or condition of looking forward to something'. Eg. Ps.62:5, "My soul, wait thou only upon God; for my expectation is from him." {expected 1x., expecting 2x., tot. = 17x.}

Expedient —7x., adj. [A.D. 1398, < Fr. *expédient* < L. *expedient* (= 'be disengaging') < *expedire* (= 'to disengage' or 'to free the foot') < *ex*, = 'out of' (see L. prefix '*ex*–') + *pedis* (or *pes*) = 'a foot' (NOI. When ones foot is entangled, progress is hampered, but when the foot is freed, then progress resumes. Expedite (v.) means 'to help go forward, or send off; or help attain some end result'. See also 'Impediment'.)] Thus, **expedient** modifies its n. as 'being helped forward in life'. Eg. 2Cor.8:10, "And herein I give my advice: for this is expedient for you, who have begun before, not only to do, but also to be forward a year ago."

Experience —4x., n. [A.D. 1377, < Fr. *expérience* < L. *experientia* (= 'test, find out') < *experient* (which is prp. of) *experiri* (= 'to test or prove') < *ex*, = 'out of' (see L. prefix '*ex*–') + *peritus* = 'skilled'] Thus, an **experience** is 'the state or condition of proving something by careful testing and trial'. Eg. Gen.30:27, "And Laban said unto him, I pray thee, if I have found favour in thine eyes, tarry: for I have learned by experience that the LORD hath blessed me for thy sake."

Experiment —1x., n. [A.D. 1362, < OF. *experiment* < L. *experimentum* (= 'a testing or trial') < *experiri* (see 'Experience')] Thus, an **experiment** is 'a test for the purpose of discovering something unknown'. Eg. 2Cor.9:13, "Whiles by the experiment of this ministration they glorify God for your professed subjection unto the gospel of Christ, and for your liberal distribution unto them, and unto all men." (Here, the experiment was, ultimately, sent by God so that the results might be seen by the other believers as well as the Corinthians themselves.)

Expert – 6x., adj. [A.D. 1374, < OF. *expert* < L. *expertus* (= 'tested and well proven') (which is pp. of) *experiri* (see 'Experience')] Thus, **expert** modifies its n. as 'being tested and well proven in a certain area or skill'. Eg. Act.26:3, "Especially because I know thee to be expert in all customs and questions which are among the Jews: wherefore I beseech thee to hear me patiently." (The year was about A.D. 62 when Paul (perhaps close to 60 years of age) stood before King Agrippa (A.D. 27-100) who was about 35 years old, yet was a proselyte to Judaism and was well versed in Jewish teachings.)

Expired – 9x., pp. [A.D. 1400, < E. (v.) **expire** < Fr. *expirer* < L. *expirare* (= 'to breath out'), < *ex*, = 'out of' (see L. prefix '*ex–*') + *spirare* = 'to breath' (NOI. Cp. LL. *inspiratio* found in 'Inspiration'.) + **d** = forms the pp. (see E. suffix '–ed'[3])] Thus, **expired** modifies its n. as 'having breathed out its last bit of life' (i.e. 'completely finished'). Eg. Act.7:30, "And when forty years were expired, there appeared to him in the wilderness of mount Sina an angel of the Lord in a flame of fire in a bush."

Exploits – 2x., n. pl. [A.D. 1393 < E. **exploit** (< OF. *esploit* < L. *explicitum* < *explicare* (= 'to unfold, set forth'), < *ex*, = 'out of' (see L. prefix '*ex–*') + *plicare* = 'to fold') + **s** = forms the pl.] Thus, **exploits** are 'two or more heroic achievements of honorable or notable character'. Eg. Dan.11:32, "And such as do wickedly against the covenant shall he corrupt by flatteries: but the people that do know their God shall be strong, and do exploits."

Expound —1x., v. [A.D. 1300, < ME. **expoune** < OF. *espondre* < L. *exponere* (= 'to expose, explain' or set forth), < *ex*, = 'out of' (see L. prefix '*ex–*') + *ponere* = 'to place or put'] Thus, **expound** means 'the action of putting forth an explanation in detail'. Eg. Jud.14:14, "And he said unto them, Out of the eater came forth meat, and out of the strong came forth sweetness. And they could not in three days expound the riddle." {expounded 6x., tot. = 7x.}

Extol —4x., v. [A.D. 1494, < L. *extollere* (= 'to exalt, lift up or praise'), < *ex*, = 'out of' (see L. prefix '*ex–*') + *tollere* = 'to lift, raise' (NOI. **Extol** appears only to be used when praising God in the deepest sense of worship. See also 'Exalt'.)] Thus, **extol** means 'the action of lifting up the Name, honor and glory of the Lord'. Eg. Ps.145:1, "I will extol thee, my God, O king; and I will bless thy name for ever and ever." {extolled 2x., tot. = 6x.}

Extortion —2x., n. [A.D. 1300, < ML. *extortio* < L. *extortus* (which is pp. of) *extorquere* (= 'to twist away with violence'), < *ex*, = 'out of' (see L. prefix '*ex–*') + *torquere* = 'to twist'] Thus, an **extortion** is 'a state or condition whereby something is violently twisted away from someone else'. Eg. Eze.22:12, "In thee have they taken gifts to shed blood; thou hast taken usury and increase, and thou hast greedily gained of thy neighbours by extortion, and hast forgotten me, saith the Lord GOD." (NOI. Extortion is usually a brow-beating or an under-handed legal action, rather than a physical act, such as torture.) {extortioner 3x., extortioners 3x., tot. = 8x.}

Extreme —1x., adj. [A.D. 1460, < OF. *extreme* < L. *extremus* (which is a superlative of) (adj.) *exterus* < *extra* = 'outer'] Thus, **extreme** modifies its n. (in this case, 'burning') as 'happening to its most outer limits'. Eg. Deut.28:22, "The LORD shall smite thee with a consumption, and with a fever, and with an inflammation, and with an extreme burning, and with the sword, and with blasting, and with mildew; and they shall pursue thee until thou perish." {extremity 1x., tot. = 2x.}

Eye – 116x., n. [A.D. 700, < OE. **eage** = 'the organ of sight' (akin to Du. *oog*, Ger. *auge* and Goth. *augo*) (NOI. The experience of 'sight' requires more than just an eyeball, but also the multiplicity of optic nerves and the nervous system itself all work together to convert radiant energy (called light waves) into electrical impulses, which are sent to the brain and interpreted as images of various size, shape and color. The human eyeball has compound lenses which change their shape allowing for focus, the ability to adjust itself for brighter or dimmer light conditions, and a self-washing system using tear ducts and the eyelid. Being a very delicate organ, the eye is well protected by the hard socket in which it rests, the eyelid and the nose. Those who study the eye are amazed with its masterful design. The eye is such a perfect instrument, that Charles Darwin wrote (in a letter to Asa Gray, April 03, 1860) that it made him "*cold all over*", meaning he could not explain its evolution. This author believes the eye shows the design work of an Almighty Creator.)] Thus, an **eye** is the organ, or device, the causes one to see things'. Eg. Job.7:8, "The eye of him that hath seen me shall see me no more: thine eyes are upon me, and I am not." {eye's 1x., eyebrows 1x., eyed 2x., eyelids 9x., eyes 501x., eyesalve 1x., eyeservice 2x., eyesight 1x., eyewitnesses 2x. tot. = 636x.}

Eyesalve – 1x., n. [A.D. 1000, < E. **eye** (see 'Eye') + **slave** (< OE. **sealf** (akin to Du. *zalf* and OHG. *salpa*) < oo., but possibly Sans. *sarpis* = 'clear butter') = 'a soothing ointment meant for comfort and healing' (NOI. The Gk. word is κολλουριον (*kollourion*) < κολλουρα (*kolloura*) = 'a cake' (< κολλαω (*kollao*) = 'to glue') Laodicea had a famous school of medicine, which made **eyesalve**. The Gk. physician Claudius Galen (A.D. 129-216) describes it as being made from various ingredients and applied like a paste to the eyes. When first made, it was probably let to harden in a little cake-form (hence the κολλουρα), then, when taken up for use, was softened into a paste with warm water. Notice that it is never called 'eyebalm'. See 'Balm'.)] Thus, **eyesalve** is 'an ointment, applied to tired and sore eyes, for comfort and well-being'. Eg. Rev.3:18, "I counsel thee to buy of me gold tried in the fire, that thou mayest be rich; and white raiment, that thou mayest be clothed, and that the shame of thy nakedness do not appear; and anoint thine eyes with eyesalve, that thou mayest see." {eye 116x., tot. = 117x.}

Eyeservice – 2x., n. [A.D. 1525(TNT.), < E. **eye** (see 'Eye) + **service** (= 'the occupation of serving' (see 'Service')) (NOI. Wycliffe translated it, "not serving at eye" (modern spelling).] Thus, an **eyeservice** is 'a properly done service only when carefully watched by the eye of a master or boss'. Eg. Col.3:22, "Servants, obey in all things your masters according to the flesh; not with eyeservice, as menpleasers; but in singleness of heart, fearing God." {eye 116x., serve 209x., tot. = 327x.}

Eyewitnesses – 2x. n. pl. [A.D. 1539,< E. **eye** (see 'Eye') + **witness** (= 'testimony or evidence given by one who observed something' (see 'Witness')) + **es** = the pl.] Thus, **eyewitnesses** are 'two or more people who saw something with their eyes and can thereby give evidence as to what actually happened'. Eg. 2Pt.1:16, "For we have not followed cunningly devised fables, when we made known unto you the power and coming of our Lord Jesus Christ, but were eyewitnesses of his majesty."

Bibliography

The KJV (by Cambridge University Press)
The 1611 Authorized Version (a photostat copy of an original 1611 'He Bible', Greyden Press)
The New Testament (1526) Translated by William Tyndale (The British Library)
The New Testament (The Greek Text Underlying the English Authorised Version) (Trinitarian Bible Society)
SEPTUAGINTA (Id est Vetus Testamentum graece iuxta LXX interpretes) (© 1935, 1982 Deutsche Bibelgesellschaft Stuttgart)

A Concise Anglo-Saxon Dictionary (by J.R. Clark Hall, © 1984, University of Toronto Press)
A Dictionarie of French and English Tongues (by Randale Cotgrave © 1611, reprinted by Adam Islip)
A Glossary of Terms Used in English Architecture (by Thomas Atkinson, © 1906, W.T Comstock)
A Greek-English Lexicon of the New Testament and other Early Christian Literature (by Walter Bauer © 1957, University of Chicago Press)
A New and Concise Bible Dictionary (© 1890, G. Morrish)
All The Plants of the Bible (by Winifred Walker © 1957, Doubleday & Company Inc.)
Allen and Greenough's New Latin Grammar (edited by Greenough, Kitteredge, Howard & D'ooge © 1903, Ginn & Company Publishers)
American Dictionary of the English Language by Noah Webster (1828, edition on CD)
Analytical Greek Lexicon , The (edited by Harold K. Moulton © 1978, Zondervan Corp.)
Analytical Hebrew and Chaldee Lexicon, The (by Benjamin Davidson © 1848, Hendrickson Publishers)
Archaic Words and the Authorized Version (by Laurence Vance © 1996, Vance Publications)
Bible Almanac, The (edited by James Packer © 1980, Thomas Nelson Publishers)
Bible Versions (by Eldred Thomas © 1978, Research Education Foundation Inc.)

Business In The Bible (by W.G. Barnes © 1926, Vir Publishing Company)
Cambridge Bible Handbook, The (© 1996, Cambridge University Press)
Cassell's German Dictionary (by Karl Breul © 1933, Cassell and Company Ltd.)
Defending the King James Bible (by D.A. Waite © 1999, Bible For Today Press)
Early Modern English (by Charles Barber © 1976, 1997, Edinburgh University Press)
Encyclopedia Britannica (© 1960, Encyclopedia Britannica Inc.)
Etymological Dictionary of the English Language (by Walter Skeat © 1882, Macmillan and Co.)
Everyone in the Bible (by William P. Barker © 1966, Fleming H. Revell Co.)
Fundamentals of Insect Life (by C.L. Metcalf and W.P. Flint © 1932, McGraw-Hill Book Company)
Funk and Wagnall's Standard Dictionary (© 1959, by Encyclopedia Britannica)
Gems and Mineral of the Bible (by Wright & Chadbourne © 1970, Harper and Row)
Hebrew English Lexicon (23rd Edition) (Samuel Bagster & Sons Ltd., London, 1928)
Hellas—Civilizations of Ancient Greece (© 1980, by McGraw-Hill, New York)
Introduction to Early Modern English (by Manfred Gorlach © 1991, Cambridge Univ. Press)
Josephus (complete works) (translated by William Whiston © 1960, Kregel Press)
King's English, The (by H.W & F.G. Fowler © 1993, Wordsworth Editions Ltd.)
Legacy of Our English Bible, The (by John Wesley Sawyer © 2003, John Wesley Sawyer)
Machines, Buildings and Weaponry of Biblical Times (by Max Schwartz © 1990, Fleming H. Revell Co.)
MacMillan Bible Atlas, The (by Yahanan Aharoni and Michael Avi-Yonah © 1968, Macmillan Publishing Company.
New Century Dictionary, The (© 1952, by Appleton-Century-Crofts Inc.)
New Testament Times (by Merrill Tenney © 1965, William Eerdmans Publishing Company)
Old French—A concise Handbook (by E. Einhorn © 1975, Cambridge University Press)
Only Grammar Book You'll Ever Need, The (by Susan Thurman © 2003, Adams Media Corp.)
Origins – The Encyclopedia of Words (by Eric Partridge © 1958,

The Macmillan Co.)
Oxford English Dictionary, The (2nd Edition on CD Rom © 2002, Oxford University Press)
Purified Seven Times - the Miracle of the English Bible (by Bill Bradley © 2001, Landmark Baptist Press)
Sailor's Word-Book, The (by Admiral W.H. Smyth ©1867, Blackie Son)
Science and the Bible (by Henry Morris © 1986, Moody Press)
Strauss Dictionary of New Testament Terms (by Dr. Lehman Strauss © 1981, Biola University)
Strongest Strong's Exhaustive Concordance of the Bible, The (by John Kohlenberger & James Swanson © 2001, Zondervan)
Theological Dictionary of the New Testament (in ten volumes) (by WM. B. Eerdmans)
Thereby Hangs a Tale - Stories of Curious Word Origins (by Charles Earle Funk © 1950, Harper & Row Publishers)
Unger's Bible Dictionary (by Merrill Unger © 1957, Moody Press)
Usage And Abusage (by Eric Partridge © 1942, WW Norton & Company)
Way of Life Encyclopedia of the Bible and Christianity (by D. Cloud © 2002, Way of Life Literature)
Weather & The Bible (by Donald B. DeYoung © 1992, Baker Book House)
Webster's 1828 Dictionary on CD
Which Version is the Bible (by Floyd Nolen Jones © 1989 – 1999, Floyd Jones Ministries Inc.)
Wimples and Crisping Pins – being studies in the coiffure and ornaments of women (by Theodore Child © 1894, Harper Brothers)
Word Origins - and Their Romantic Stories (by Wilfred Funk © 1950, Bell Publishing Co.)
Word Study Concordance (by George Wigram, Tyndale House Pubishing)
Wycliffe Bible Encyclopedia (in two volumes) (by Moody Bible Press)
Wycliffe Historical Geography of Bible Lands, The (by Charles Pfeiffer and Howard Vos ©1967, Moody Press)
Zondervan Pictorial Bible Dictionary, The (by Merrill C. Tenney ©, Zondervan)
Zondervan Pictorial Encyclopedia of the Bible, The (in five volumes) (edited by Merrill C. Tenney © 1975, Zondervan)

<u>Online Bibliography</u>

Merriam-Webster's Online Dictionary, 10th Edition
King James Search Engine
(http://www.lib.uchicago.edu/efts/ARTFL/public/bibles/kjv.
Dictionary of English
The Wordsmyth English Dictionary-Thesaurus
The American Heritage® Dictionary of the English Language
Infoplease Dictionary
Lewis and Short Latin Dictionary
(http://www.sms.org/mdl-indx/lsearch.htm#LATDICT)
Dictionary.com
UltraLingua English Dictionary
Cambridge Dictionary of American English
Online Plain Text English Dictionary
Webster's Revised Unabridged, 1913 Edition
Webster's 1828 Dictionary
AllWords.com Multi-Lingual Dictionary
Etymonline.com

APPENDIX I

Word Origins

The following table will give the reader a birds-eye view of when each word entry, listed in this dictionary, was first recorded in the English language. This information helps the reader to see the development of the English language all the way up to A.D. 1611.

The column on the left indicates the approximate year in which the word was first recorded. The column in the middle shows if the word entry was first used in a copy of the Scriptures, and if so, there will be an abbreviated form of where it was found. A list of these abbreviations may be found at the beginning of this dictionary. Where there is no abbreviation, only a blank space, this means that the word entry was first recorded in a source other than the Scriptures. The column on the right gives the word entry.

Year	Bible	Word
696		church
697		even[1]
700		apes
700		clouts
700		corn
700		crop
700		ewe
700		eye
700		dwarf
800		answer

Year	Bible	Word
800		anvil
800		beetle
800		bellow
800		bellows
800		bird
800		calf
800		churl
800		clothes
800		cluster
800		cow
800		dale
800		ear[2]
800		devil

Year	Bible	Word
800		dew
800		drunk
825	VP.	arise
825	VP.	ark
825	VP.	behold
825	VP.	cheek
825	VP.	cherub
825	VP.	cherubims
825	VP.	cymbal
825	VP.	deaf
825	VP.	deed
825	VP.	ear[1]
825	VP.	evil
825(?)		doest
825(?)		doeth
825(?)		dost
825(?)		doth
826		beam
835		arrow
854		cliff
872		book
880		about
880		anchor
880		angle
885		adamant
885		alway
885		apple
885		ask

Year	Bible	Word
885		aul
885		bare[1]
888		bereave
888		cleave[2]
888		craft
888		creep
888		dare
888		ear[3]
888		elder
888		enough
888		dim
888		durst
890		Almighty
890		behoved
890		between
890		bier
890		bishoprick
890		bruise
890		chapmen
890		east
890		Easter
891		boat
893		bear[1]
893		besom
893		bid
893		bishop
893		bit[1]
893		bow[2]
893		breath
893		crafty
893		deadly

Year	Bible	Word
893		epistle
894		again
897		befall
897		cock
897		cummin
898		afore
900		deacon
900		disciple
910		cleave[1]
931		betwixt
934		drove[1]
940		aileth
950		adder
950		aloes
950		amen
950		angel
950	LfG.	apostle
950		ashes
950		beacon
950	LfG.	beckoned
950	LfG.	Beelzebub
950		belly
950	LfG.	bless
950	LfG.	bread
950	LfG.	camel
950	LfG.	child

Year	Bible	Word
950	LfG.	Christ
950	LfG.	cripple
950	LfG.	crown
950		day
950	LfG.	early
950		even[2]
950	LfG.	eventide
963		cross
966		barley
970		aright
971		before
971		bind
971		bitter
971		bosom
971		broad
971		burden
975		acre
975	RG.	blind
975	RG.	crumbs
975	RG.	dull
995		bed
1000	LfG.	abide
1000	LfG.	affright
1000	AT.	afterward
1000	ASG.	alms
1000	AT.	altar
1000	ASG.	among
1000		anon

Year	Bible	Word
1000		ant
1000	AT.	archangel
1000	ASG.	art[2]
1000		ashamed
1000	AT.	ass
1000	ASG.	assunder
1000		athirst
1000	AT.	bake
1000	AT.	bare[2]
1000		bathe
1000		bear[2]
1000		begat
1000		beget
1000	ASP.	belch
1000	AT.	belied
1000	AT.	bemoan
1000	ASG.	bethink
1000		bite
1000		bittern
1000		blains
1000		blast
1000	ASG.	blood
1000		bloody
1000		boil[1]
1000	ASG.	bold
1000		bolster
1000		bore
1000	ASG.	borrow
1000	ASG.	bough
1000	AT.	bow[1]
1000	AT.	bramble
1000	LP.	brasen
1000		brass
1000		breach
1000		breast

Year	Bible	Word
1000	ASG.	bride
1000		bridle
1000		brier
1000		brood
1000		broth
1000		bullock
1000	ASG.	calvary
1000		calve
1000		canker
1000	ASG.	care[1]
1000		care[2]
1000		careless
1000	ASG.	cassia
1000	ASG.	castle
1000	ASG.	cedar
1000	ASG.	chaff
1000	AT.	chide
1000		churlish
1000		circle
1000		clouted
1000	ASG.	cockle
1000	AT.	colt
1000	ASP.	comely
1000		coulter
1000		crane
1000		craveth
1000		crib
1000	ASG.	crow
1000	ASP.	crystal
1000		cud
1000	ASG.	daughter
1000		earnest[1]
1000	AT.	evening
1000		eyesalve
1000		den

Year	Bible	Word
1000		diddest
1000		didst
1000		distaff
1000	AT.	drank
1000		drought
1000	ASG.	dumb
1000		dung
1025		bond[2]
1045		ditch
1050		byword
1050		dog
1050(?)		curse[1]
1050(?)		curse[2]
1066		chancellor
1095		aware
1123		accord
1125		council
1129		duke
1140		altogether
1154		against
1154		asleep
1154		charity
1175		afar
1175		backbiting

Year	Bible	Word
1175		beseech
1175		blessed
1175		circumcision
1175		evangelist
1175		dread
1175(?)		besought
1199		damsel
1200		anger
1200		awe
1200		band[1]
1200		bank[1]
1200		barren
1200		begotten
1200		believe
1200		blame
1200		booth
1200		bull
1200		cart
1200		cast
1200		chaste
1200		clothed
1200		coney
1200		custom
1200		draught
1205		another
1205		ball
1205		bewitched
1205		breeches
1205		brim
1205		evermore
1205		dote

Year	Bible	Word
1210		beast
1215		amerce
1220		accursed
1220		amend
1220		anguish
1220		balm
1220		bason
1220		cave
1220		dragon
1225		art[1]
1225		beguile
1225		Belial
1225		bestead
1225		blasphemy
1225		boil[2]
1225		bond[1]
1225		buffet
1225		case
1225		cause
1225		chamber
1225		chamberlain
1225		chapel
1225		charge[1]
1225		charge[2]
1225		chatter
1225		cheer
1225		city
1225		cogitations
1225		comfort
1225		conscience
1225		consent[2]
1225		counsel[1]
1225		covet
1225		cruel
1225		cry
1225		dainty
1225		danger
1225		debt
1225		debtor
1225		earnest[2]
1225		earthen
1225		Eden
1225		enjoin
1225		espied
1225		espy
1225		estate
1225		excuse[2]
1225		delight
1225		deliver
1225		depart
1225		desert[2]
1225		destroy
1225		devotions
1225		devout
1225		diet
1225		dignities
1225		dignity
1225		discomfited
1225		dispute
1225		double[1]
1225		doubt[1]
1225		doubt[2]
1230		acquit
1230		adventure
1230		adversity
1230		affection

Year	Bible	Word
1230		always
1230		amazed
1230		assault
1230		authority
1230		babbling
1230		bag
1230		banner
1230		cake
1230		carbuncle
1230		conquer
1230		degree
1230		desire
1230		discord
1240		cuckow
1250		abode
1250		amiss
1250		amongst
1250		apparel
1250		appear
1250		assemble
1250		attire
1250		betray
1250		bounty
1250		butler
1250		censer
1250		circumcise
1250		commandment
1250		company[1]
1250		contrary
1250		dearth
1250		ensample
1250		divers
1250		dream

Year	Bible	Word
1260		abroad
1260		account[2]
1260		alas
1270		election
1275		balance
1275		balances
1275		cattle
1275		centurion
1275		chrysoprasus
1275		cloke
1275		country
1275		deceit
1275		delay
1275		doleful
1275		dureth
1280		ado
1280		ah
1280		envy
1280		dromedary
1285		Christian
1290		amethyst
1290		colour
1290		confirm
1290		confound
1290		confusion
1290		contain
1290		counsel[2]
1290		countenance
1290		cousin
1290		creature

Year Bible	Word
1290	dash
1290	enquire
1290	demand
1290	despite
1290	device
1290	diadem
1290	distress
1290	double[2]
1290	dropsy
1292	escape
1292	deserve
1292	detain
1297	accuse
1297	acquaint
1297	advise
1297	allied
1297	ancestors
1297	appeal
1297	archer
1297	arches
1297	armour
1297	array
1297	assent
1297	baptize
1297	bastard
1297	battle
1297	besiege
1297	boast
1297	branch
1297	certain
1297	chance
1297	chief
1297	common

Year Bible	Word
1297	commune
1297	companion
1297	compass[2]
1297	concubine
1297	covenant
1297	dam
1297	enchantment
1297	entice
1297	desert[1]
1297	despise
1297	dine
1297	dismayed
1297	diverse
1297	duty
1300	allow
1300	almond
1300	ambush
1300	anise
1300	antichrist
1300	asswage
1300	astray
1300	attain
1300	attend
1300	author
1300	availeth
1300	avoid
1300	axletrees
1300	bade
1300	barked
1300	barrel
1300	bat
1300	beeves
1300	beryl
1300	bewail

Year	Bible	Word
1300		bewray
1300		bit[2]
1300		bondage
1300		bosses
1300		bowels
1300		bray[2]
1300		breathe
1300		brimstone
1300		brink
1300		buckler
1300		bushel
1300		buttocks
1300		caldron
1300		cease
1300		chrysolite
1300		cistern
1300		clad
1300		clave[1]
1300		clave[2]
1300		cleft
1300		clift
1300		coast
1300		coat
1300		coffer
1300		command
1300		compass[1]
1300		conceive
1300		conception
1300		conclude
1300		concord
1300		condemn
1300		consent[1]
1300		convert
1300		corban
1300		corrupt[2]
1300		courage
1300		covetous
1300		crag
1300		crucify
1300		cumbereth
1300		cure[1]
1300		current
1300		cypress
1300		damnation
1300		dance
1300		dayspring
1300		debate
1300		deceive
1300		deemed
1300		defy
1300		elements
1300		emerald
1300		enemy
1300		engines
1300		enmity
1300		error
1300		evidence
1300		exchange[2]
1300		exile
1300		expound
1300		extortion
1300		denounce
1300		deny
1300		deposed
1300		descend
1300		descry
1300		devise
1300		dirt
1300		discover
1300		dishonour

Year	Bible	Word
1300		dissension
1300		drave
1300		dungeon
1300(?)		dress
1300(?)		drove[2]
1303		account[1]
1303		affinity
1303		anoint
1303		appetite
1303		behalf
1303		betroth
1303		chronicles
1303		covert
1303		cumbrance
1303		decree
1303		err
1303		examine
1303		deliciously
1303		discretion
1303		doctor
1305		approach
1305		chalcedony
1305		charger
1307		aprons
1310		diamond
1313		camphire
1314		agone
1314		amends
1314		betimes

Year	Bible	Word
1314		check
1314		citizen
1314		dart
1315		administration
1315		bestow
1315		corpse
1315		equity
1315		devour
1320		cormorant
1320		dunghill
1321		bill
1325		abomination
1325		admonish
1325		alarm
1325		although
1325		angry
1325		assembly
1325		baken
1325		base[2]
1325		battlement
1325		blemish
1325		blot
1325		blush
1325		brandish
1325		burnished
1325		captivity
1325		carpenter
1325		chapt
1325		chariot
1325		chastise
1325		commend

Year	Bible	Word
1325		corrupt[1]
1325		cubit
1325		cunning
1325		curious
1325		daub
1325		declare
1325		decline
1325		defile
1325		endure
1325		deprived
1325		despair
1325		disguise
1327		caul
1327		cauls
1330		advantage
1330		adversary
1330		affirm
1330		afraid
1330		alien
1330		appease
1330		assay
1330		austere
1330		byways
1330		certify
1330		chafed
1330		chimney
1330		coffin
1330		couch[2]
1330		countervail
1330		decease
1330		discharge
1330		disease
1330		dowry

Year	Bible	Word
1340		advocate
1340		ancient
1340		approve
1340		asp
1340		blaspheme
1340		carcase
1340		chameleon
1340	HP.	charmer
1340		closet
1340		company[2]
1340		compassion
1340		comprehend
1340		concupiscence
1340		condescend
1340		confess
1340		congregation
1340	HP.	constrain
1340		continual
1340	HP.	contrite
1340	HP.	conversant
1340	HP.	conversation
1340	HP.	conversion
1340		correct
1340	HP.	corruption
1340		couch[1]
1340		embalm
1340		entreat
1340		environ
1340		eschew
1340		everlasting
1340		difference
1340		diligence
1340		diligent
1340		diligently
1340		discreet

Year	Bible Word
1340	diviners
1350	amiable
1350	astonied
1350	displease
1360	accept
1360	eagle
1360	embrace
1362	chop
1362	collops
1362	defraud
1362	experiment
1366	abominable
1366	adultery
1366	agree
1366	apothecary
1369	aside
1370	assure
1374	abound
1374	adorn
1374	affect
1374	albeit
1374	alter
1374	ambassador
1374	appoint
1374	Arcturus
1374	assurance
1374	astrologer

Year	Bible Word
1374	attentive
1374	audience
1374	bay[3]
1374	captive
1374	complain
1374	complete
1374	conceit
1374	consolation
1374	convenient
1374	delicacies
1374	endamage
1374	establish
1374	estimate
1374	eternity
1374	evidently
1374	exceed
1374	exchange[1]
1374	excuse[1]
1374	expert
1374	delicates
1374	desolate
1374	determine
1374	direct
1374	discern
1374	dispensation
1374	disposition
1374	distill
1374	divination
1374	division
1375	alabaster
1375	avenge
1375	bonnets
1375	bottle

Year	Bible	Word
1375		captain
1375		carriage
1375		compare
1375		consider
1375		dagger
1375		defer
1375		ensign
1377		ague
1377		benefit
1377		botch
1377		brawler
1377		cure[2]
1377		defied
1377		except
1377		experience
1377		delicate
1377		delicately
1377		divorce
1378		college
1380		abstain
1380		already
1380		antiquity
1380		bleating
1380		commission
1380		compel
1380		disdained
1380		disposing
1382	WB.	aceldama
1382	WB.	adjure
1382	WB.	adoption
1382	WB.	agony

Year	Bible	Word
1382	WB.	allegory
1382	WB.	alleluia
1382	WB.	Alpha
1382	WB.	Armageddon
1382	WB.	ascend
1382	WB.	ascribe
1382	WB.	Ashtaroth
1382	WB.	Baal
1382	WB.	Baalim
1382	WB.	bdellium
1382	WB.	Behemoth
1382	WB.	Bel
1382	WB.	birthday
1382		bray[1]
1382	WB.	Caesar
1382	WB.	choler
1382	WB.	circuit
1382	WB.	clamour
1382	WB.	cockatrice
1382	WB.	colony
1382	WB.	communion
1382	WB.	concision
1382	WB.	concourse
1382	WB.	consecration
1382	WB.	consume
1382	WB.	controversy
1382	WB.	curdled
1382	WB.	Dagon
1382	WB.	ebony
1382	WB.	edification
1382	WB.	enlighten
1382	WB.	ephod
1382	WB.	Epicureans
1382	WB.	execration
1382	WB.	exorcists

Year	Bible	Word
1382	WB.	deputed
1382	WB.	destitute
1382	WB.	doctrine
1382	WB.	doubletongued
1384		benevolence
1384		blaze
1384		celestial
1384		congealed
1384		dissimulation
1385		bay[2]
1385		effect
1386		accomplish
1386		aha
1386		appertain
1386		artillery
1386		bakemeats
1386		breastplate
1386		bribe
1386		broided
1386		chalkstones
1386		chant
1386		cinnamon
1386		commit
1386		conspiracy
1386		constant
1386		cottage
1386		create
1386		effectual
1386		eternal
1386		example
1386		execute
1387		confection

Year	Bible	Word
1387		confederate
1387		consecrate
1387		contribution
1387		convocation
1387		eunuch
1388	WB.	calamus
1388	WB.	cor
1388	WB.	coriander
1388	WB.	crew
1388		drag
1391		equal
1393		abase
1393		afflict
1393		artificer
1393		avouched
1393		babe
1393		base[1]
1393		contempt
1393		effeminate
1393		eloquent
1393		espousals
1393		exploits
1394		band[2]
1395	WB.	Augustus
1395	WB.	Baalzebub
1398		agreement
1398		amber
1398		apprehend
1398		apt

Year	Bible	Word
1398		bath
1398		bay[1]
1398		cane
1398		clods
1398		compact
1398		consumption
1398		crush
1398		elect
1398		ensue
1398		ephah
1398		expedient
1400		apparently
1400		augment
1400		beggarly
1400		carnal
1400		champaign
1400		conduct
1400		content[1]
1400		copulation
1400		cornet
1400		creditor
1400		crimson
1400		crisping (pins)
1400		delectable
1400		emerods
1400		endeavour
1400		endued
1400		especially
1400		exalt
1400		exhort
1400		expired
1400		disobedience
1401		allure

Year	Bible	Word
1405		deputy
1413		abuse
1417		erected
1417		diminish
1418		bulwarks
1418		content[2]
1420		commodius
1420		cruse
1420		eminent
1420		endow
1420		delusion
1420(?)		embroider
1422		circumspect
1425		chapiter
1425		clovenfooted
1430		abjects
1430		advertise
1430		aforehand
1430		alienate
1430		casement
1430		cieled
1430		confidence
1430		conflict
1430		contentious
1430		cumbered
1430		enterprise
1430		excel
1430		dominion

Year	Bible	Word
1430		dues
1434		distribute
1438		bracelet
1440		bedstead
1440		behave
1440		broiled
1440		bulrushes
1440		caterpiller
1440		causeway
1440		churning
1440		cracknels
1440		earing
1440		drams
1449		abhor
1449		chambering
1450		alleging
1450		broidered
1450		bruit
1450		concern
1450		contemn
1450		crossway
1450		esteem
1450		disinherit
1450		disperse
1456		brigandine
1460		blasting
1460		brute
1460		decay
1460		extreme

Year	Bible	Word
1465		apiece
1470		commonwealth
1471		commotion
1474		bank[2]
1474		boisterous
1474		booty
1474		defamed
1475		entertain
1475		dulcimer
1481		acknowledge
1481		brickkiln
1483		banquet
1483		cupbearer
1483		custody
1483		encourage
1485		affliction
1489		daysman
1490		abolish
1490		admiration
1490		band[3]
1490		calamity
1490		decision
1494		benefactors
1494		crookbackt
1494		extol
1494		disannul

Year	Bible	Word
1494		dispossess
1494		divide
1495		calkers
1507		banishment
1509		afresh
1509		engrave
1511		conformable
1513		astonished
1513		atonement
1513		deck
1513		describe
1513		dissembleth
1514		contend
1517		dispatch
1519		chesnut
1523		breadth
1525	TNT.	Adria
1525	TNT.	busybody
1525		camp
1525	TNT.	castaway
1525	TNT.	Castor
1525	TNT.	Eve
1525	TNT.	eyeservice
1526	TNT.	anathema

Year	Bible	Word
1526		barbarous
1526		beautiful
1526		chasten
1526		communicate
1526		consist
1526		divorcement
1529		arrogancy
1529		exact
1530		cankerworm
1530		convince
1530		dandled
1530		dedicate
1530		deride
1530		disquiet
1532		aloof
1533		detest
1534		abated
1534		addicted
1534		celebrate
1535	CB.	Beulah
1535	CB.	birthright
1535	CB.	bloodguiltiness
1535	CB.	bolled
1535	CB.	cab
1535	CB.	chode
1535	CB.	evilfavouredness
1535		doorkeeper
1535	CB.	dryshod

Year	Bible	Word
1536		expectation
1539		eyewitnesses
1540		consult
1540		enlargement
1542		booties
1543		confiscation
1548		ambassage
1548		answerable
1548		bravery
1548		congratulate
1549		barbarian
1549		crackling
1549		encamp
1549		disgrace
1552		backsliding
1552		billows
1552		decently
1552		emulation
1552		estranged
1553		clemency
1559		drowsiness
1565		debase
1568	BB.	Ed
1568	BB.	Eveningtide

Year	Bible	Word
1570		agate
1571		emboldeneth
1578	GB.	algum
1579		bridechamber
1586		devote
1587		ancients
1587	GB.	Chemosh
1587	GB.	Euroclydon
1595		amazement
1595		convicted
1597		averse
1599		confectionaries
1600		borne
1600		engrafted
1601		coping
1611	HB.	almug
1611	HB.	Areopagus
1611	HB.	Ashtoreth
1611	HB.	bekah
1611	HB.	couchingplace

APPENDIX II

Scriptures Used

The following table is a valuable resource for those doing general research on Bible verses. The column on the left is a list of the Bible verses used in this dictionary. The column on the right tells the reader where to look in the dictionary in order to find the reference.

Verse	Word Entry
Gen.1:24	creature
Gen.2:7	breath
Gen.2:12	bdellium
Gen.2:24	cleave[2]
Gen.3:7	aprons
Gen.3:8	amongst
Gen.3:10	afraid
Gen.3:15	bruise
Gen.3:24	cherubims
Gen.4:8	against
Gen.4:13	bear[1]
Gen.4:22	artificer
Gen.4:25	another
Gen.5:4	begotten
Gen.6:14	ark
Gen.6:15	breadth
Gen.8:3	abated
Gen.8:7	calf
Gen.8:20	altar
Gen.8:22	cease
Gen.9:4	blood
Gen.9:10	creature
Gen.9:13	bow[1]
Gen.11:7	confound
Gen.11:30	barren
Gen.12:3	bless
Gen.13:2	cattle
Gen.14:13	confeder-ate
Gen.14:14	captive
Gen.15:17	between
Gen.16:15	begotten
Gen.17:11	circumcise
Gen.18:19	command
Gen.19:3	bread
Gen.19:24	brimstone
Gen.19:30	cave
Gen.21:17	aileth
Gen.23:9	cave
Gen.24:4	country
Gen.30:32	cattle
Gen.31:36	chode
Gen.31:39	bare[2]
Gen.31:51	cast
Gen.31:51	betwixt
Gen.32:15	colt
Gen.32:20	appease
Gen.34:6	commune
Gen.37:3	coat
Gen.38:42	child

Verse	Word Entry
Gen.40:13	butler
Gen.40:17	bakemeats
Gen.43:9	blame
Gen.43:33	birthright
Gen.49:4	couch[1]
Gen.49:17	adder
Gen.49:22	bough
Gen.50:26	coffin
Ex.2:2	child
Ex.2:3	bulrushes
Ex.2:3	ark
Ex.2:6	babe
Ex.3:9	cry
Ex.9:3-6	cattle
Ex.9:9	blains
Ex.9:9	boil[1]
Ex.9:31	bolled
Ex.12:16	convocation
Ex.12:29	captive
Ex.12:35-36	borrow
Ex.15:8	blast
Ex.15:8	congealed
Ex.16:31	coriander
Ex.17:2	chide
Ex.20:14	adultery
Ex.20:17	ass
Ex.20:17	covet
Ex.21:6	aul
Ex.21:6	bore
Ex.21:8-9	betroth
Ex.22:29	delay
Ex.23:5	burden
Ex.23:13	circumspect

Verse	Word Entry
Ex.23:22	adversary
Ex.25:21	ark
Ex.25:33-36	almond
Ex.25:33-36	branch
Ex.26:31	cunning
Ex.27:1	broad
Ex.27:4	brasen
Ex.27:5	compass[1]
Ex.28:4	breastplate
Ex.28:19	amethyst
Ex.28:19	agate
Ex.28:20	beryl
Ex.28:42	breeches
Ex.29:11	bullock
Ex.29:13	caul
Ex.30:23	calamus
Ex.30:26	anoint
Ex.30:30	consecrate
Ex.30:35	apothecary
Ex.30:35	confection
Ex.32:10	brandish
Ex.32:33	blot
Ex.33:22	clift
Ex.35:1	congregation
Ex.38:18	answerable
Ex.38:26	bekah
Ex.39:10	carbuncle
Ex.39:23	band[2]
Lev.1:17	cleave[1]
Lev.5:15	amends
Lev.8:31	boil[2]
Lev.8:33	consecration
Lev.11:3	cud

Verse	Word Entry
Lev.11:3	cloven-footed
Lev.11:5	coney
Lev.11:16	cuckow
Lev.11:17	cormorant
Lev.11:19	bat
Lev.11:22	beetle
Lev.11:29	creep
Lev.11:30	chameleon
Lev.11:39	carcase
Lev.13:55	colour
Lev.15:16	copulation
Lev.15:27	bathe
Lev.18:23	confusion
Lev.21:20	crookbackt
Lev.22:19	beeves
Lev.23:41	celebrate
Lev.25:21	bless
Lev.25:35	decay
Lev.26:16	ague
Lev.26:21	contrary
Lev.26:26	bake
Lev.26:45	ancestors
Lev.27:28	anathema
Num.5:22	belly
Num.10:5	alarm
Num.12:8	apparently
Num.13:24	cluster
Num.15:20	cake
Num.16:18	censer
Num.16:30	appertain
Num.16:31	clave[1]
Num.16:48	between
Num.17:6	apiece

Verse	Word Entry
Num.21:6	bit[2]
Num.22:25	crush
Num.24:14	advertise
Num.31:32	booty
Num.32:14	augment
Num.34:5	compass[2]
Deut.1:4	Ashtaroth
Deut.1:12	cumbrance
Deut.2:9	contend
Deut.2:18	coast
Deut.3:11	bedstead
Deut.3:11	cubit
Deut.7:14	barren
Deut.7:26	abomination
Deut.10:16	circumcise
Deut.11:30	champaign
Deut.13:14	ask
Deut.14:6	beast
Deut.14:6	cleft
Deut.16:3	bread
Deut.18:11	charmer
Deut.19:4	case
Deut.20:7	betroth
Deut.20:19	besiege
Deut.20:20	bulwarks
Deut.21:20,21	crucify
Deut.22:8	battlement
Deut.22:19	amerce
Deut.24:10-13	borrow
Deut.25:1	controversy
Deut.26:17	avouched
Deut.27:16	amen
Deut.28:12	borrow

Verse	Word Entry
Deut.28:22	consumption
Deut.28:26	carcase
Deut.28:30	betroth
Deut.28:35	botch
Deut.28:37	byword
Deut.28:42	consume
Deut.28:58	book
Deut.31:17	befall
Deut.31:23	charge[1]
Deut.32:3	ascribe
Josh.3:8	brink
Josh.6:4	compass[2]
Josh.8:2	ambush
Josh.8:9	ambush
Josh.8:29	corpse
Josh.8:29	carcase
Josh.9:10	Ashtaroth
Josh.9:5	clouted
Josh.10:16	cave
Josh.11:11	breathe
Josh.15:2	bay[2]
Jud.1:15	bless
Jud.2:11	Baalim
Jud.3:24	chamber
Jud.5:6	byways
Jud.6:19	broth
Jud.6:25	bullock
Jud.7:13	cake
Jud.8:10	about
Jud.11:6	captain
Jud.11:24	Chemosh
Jud.13:3	conceive
Jud.15:18	athirst
Jud.16:19	afflict
Jud.16:29	borne
Jud.18:7	careless
Jud.20:5	concubine
Jud.20:20	array
Rut.4:13	conception
Rut.4:16	bosom
1Sam.1:16	babbling
1Sam.2:14	caldron
1Sam.6:8	coffer
1Sam.6:9	chance
1Sam.6:18	country
1Sam.7:10	battle
1Sam.7:16	circuit
1Sam.8:3	bribe
1Sam.8:13	confectionaries
1Sam.9:20	agone
1Sam.12:3	blind
1Sam.13:20	coulter
1Sam.14:14	acre
1Sam.14:28	adjure
1Sam.15:14	bleating
1Sam.17:7	beam
1Sam.17:10	defy
1Sam.17:22	carriage
1Sam.17:29	cause
1Sam.17:34	bear[2]
1Sam.17:38	brass
1Sam.18:13	captain
1Sam.20:40	artillery
1Sam.24:13	ancients

Verse	Word Entry
1Sam.25:3	churlish
1Sam.25:15	conversant
1Sam.26:7	bolster
1Sam.26:12	cruse
1Sam.30:12	cake
1Sam.30:13	agone
1Sam.31:10	Ashtaroth
2Sam.1:10	bracelet
2Sam.5:23	compass[2]
2Sam.6:3	cart
2Sam.6:19	cake
2Sam.17:8	chafed
2Sam.18:3	care[2]
2Sam.18:5	captain
2Sam.19:15	conduct
2Sam.20:4-5	assemble
2Sam.24:10	beseech
2Sam.24:13	advise
1Ki.4:28	barley
1Ki.7:9	coping
1Ki.7:16	chapiter
1Ki.7:20	belly
1Ki.7:27	base[2]
1Ki.7:32	axletrees
1Ki.7:33	chariot
1Ki.8:47	bethink
1Ki.9:8	astonished
1Ki.10:11	almug
1Ki.10:22	apes
1Ki.11:5	Ashtoreth
1Ki.11:29	clad
1Ki.12:28-29	chapel
1Ki.14:3	cracknels
1Ki.14:19	chronicles
1Ki.16:32	Baal
1Ki.17:12	barrel
1Ki.18:25	bullock
1Ki.18:27	babbling
1Ki.19:6	baken
2Ki.1:2	Baalzebub
2Ki.1:9	captain
2Ki.1:10	consume
2Ki.4:7	debt
2Ki.4:10	chamber
2Ki.5:23	crisping-(pins)
2Ki.6:5	alas
2Ki.6:25	cab
2Ki.9:11	babbling
2Ki.12:20	conspiracy
2Ki.14:28	chamber
2Ki.18:6	clave[2]
2Ki.20:4	afore
1Chr.5:5	Baal
1Chr.5:18	buckler
1Chr.8:30	Baal
1Chr.11:5	castle
1Chr.15:28	cornet
1Chr.18:10	congratulate
1Chr.19:13	behave
1Chr.20:7	defied
1Chr.23:29	baken
1Chr.26:16	causeway
1Chr.26:27	dedicate
1Chr.27:33	companion

Verse	Word Entry
1Chr.28:7	constant
2Chr.2:8	algum
2Chr.3:6	cieled
2Chr.3:12	cherub
2Chr.9:14	chapmen
2Chr.15:8	abominable
2Chr.16:9	behalf
2Chr.18:12	assent
2Chr.18:15	adjure
2Chr.20:16	cliff
2Chr.21:18	bowels
2Chr.32:18	affright
2Chr.34:22	college
2Chr.36:15	betimes
Ezr.2:59	cherub
Ezr.4:8	chancellor
Ezr.7:26	banishment
Ezr.7:26	confiscation
Ezr.9:14	affinity
Ezr.9:3	astonied
Ezr.9:6	blush
Neh.1:8	abroad
Neh.1:11	cupbearer
Neh.2:2	countenance
Neh.4:23	clothes
Neh.5:3	dearth
Neh.13:1	audience
Neh.13:4	allied

Verse	Word Entry
Est.2:14	chamberlain
Est.5:1	apparel
Est.6:9	array
Est.7:4	countervail
Est.8:11	assault
Job.4:2	assay
Job.6:5	bray[2]
Job.6:12	brass
Job.7:11	complain
Job.15:26	bosses
Job.15:27	collops
Job.15:35	belly
Job.16:5	asswage
Job.17:6	byword
Job.19:15	alien
Job.20:3	check
Job.21:10	cow
Job.21:10	bull
Job.21:26	coffin
Job.22:21	acquaint
Job.30:8	base[1]
Job.31:40	cockle
Job.33:15	bed
Job.36:2	behalf
Job.38:32	Arcturus
Job.38:40	covert
Job.38:40	couch[2]
Job.39:10	calve
Job.39:10	band[1]
Job.39:28	crag
Job.40:10	deck
Job.40:15	Behemoth
Job.42:10	captivity

Verse	Word Entry
Ps.1:4	chaff
Ps.7:11	angry
Ps.7:12	bow[1]
Ps.10:13	contemn
Ps.18:10	cherub
Ps.18:18	calamity
Ps.19:1	declare
Ps.19:9	altogether
Ps.22:1	crucify
Ps.23:5	abound
Ps.27:12	breathe
Ps.32:9	bit[1]
Ps.32:9	bridle
Ps.33:8	awe
Ps.34:2	boast
Ps.34:18	contrite
Ps.35:15	abjects
Ps.35:16	backbiting
Ps.37:35	bay[1]
Ps.38:5	corrupt[1]
Ps.38:11	aloof
Ps.38:13	deaf
Ps.40:15	aha
Ps.44:8	boast
Ps.44:26	arise
Ps.45:8	cassia
Ps.48:13	bulwarks
Ps.50:23	aright
Ps.51:3	acknowledge
Ps.51:14	bloodguiltiness
Ps.51:17	contrite
Ps.57:2	cry
Ps.58:4	adder

Verse	Word Entry
Ps.59:7	belch
Ps.60:4	banner
Ps.62:4	consult
Ps.62:9	degree
Ps.65:4	approach
Ps.68:9	confirm
Ps.76:6	chariot
Ps.78:33	consume
Ps.80:5	bread
Ps.83:5	confederate
Ps.84:1	amiable
Ps.89:34	alter
Ps.91:1	abide
Ps.91:5	arrow
Ps.92:12	cedar
Ps.104:13	chamber
Ps.104:20	creep
Ps.106:48	alleluia
Ps.122:3	compact
Ps.123:4	contempt
Ps.137:5	cunning
Ps.139:8	bed
Ps.139:8	ascend
Ps.147:9	cry
Pr.1:5	attain
Pr.3:6	acknowledge
Pr.4:20	attend
Pr.5:4	bitter
Pr.5:9	cruel
Pr.5:15	cistern
Pr.6:6	ant
Pr.6:6	consider

Verse	Word Entry	Verse	Word Entry
Pr.6:15	calamity	Pr.30:33	churning
Pr.7:6	casement	Pr.31:14	afar
Pr.7:17	aloes	Pr.31:21	clothed
Pr.7:17	cinnamon		
Pr.7:20	bag	Ecc.1:6	about
Pr.7:25	decline	Ecc.2:7	cattle
Pr.8:7	abomina-tion	Ecc.5:4	defer
		Ecc.6:3	beget
Pr.8:13	arrogancy	Ecc.7:6	crackling
Pr.8:14	counsel[1]	Ecc.10:8	bite
Pr.8:15	decree	Ecc.10:20	bird
Pr.9:7	blot	Ecc.11:9	cheer
Pr.10:22	bless		
Pr.14:4	crib	Sos.1:14	camphire
Pr.15:19	causeway	Sos.2:3	apple
Pr.16:26	craveth	SoS.2:6	embrace
Pr.17:17	adversity	SoS.3:11	espousals
Pr.18:5	accept		
Pr.19:18	chasten	Isa.1:8	cottage
Pr.22:28	ancient	Isa.1:18	crimson
Pr.23:2	appetite	Isa.2:18	abolish
Pr.23:29	babbling	Isa.3:2	ancient
Pr.23:31	aright	Isa.3:18	cauls
Pr.23:32	cockatrice	Isa.3:18	bravery
Pr.25:9	debate	Isa.3:22	crisping-(pins)
Pr.25:23	backbiting		
Pr.26:12	conceit	Isa.6:10	conversion
Pr.26:21	contentious	Isa.6:10	convert
Pr.27:15	continual	Isa.8:21	bestead
Pr.27:22	bray[1]	Isa.11:8	asp
Pr.28:1	courage	Isa.14:23	besom
Pr.28:20	abound	Isa.14:29	cockatrice
Pr.29:17	correct	Isa.16:3	bewray
Pr.30:25	ant	Isa.18:5	afore
Pr.30:26	coney	Isa.19:8	angle

Verse	Word Entry
Isa.20:4	buttocks
Isa.22:18	ball
Isa.23:7	antiquity
Isa.27:9	chalk-stones
Isa.28:1	crown
Isa.28:24	clods
Isa.28:27	cummin
Isa.30:17	beacon
Isa.32:5	churl
Isa.34:7	bull
Isa.35:5	blind
Isa.36:16	agreement
Isa.37:33	bank[1]
Isa.38:8	degree
Isa.38:14	crane
Isa.38:14	chatter
Isa.40:22	circle
Isa.41:7	anvil
Isa.43:24	cane
Isa.44:9	delectable
Isa.44:13	compass[1]
Isa.44:13	carpenter
Isa.44:15	chafed
Isa.46:5	compare
Isa.46:6	balance
Isa.47:2	bare[1]
Isa.52:7	beautiful
Isa.54:1	barren
Isa.55:11	accomplish
Isa.57:9	debase
Isa.57:15	contrite
Isa.59:17	clad
Isa.61:1	bind
Isa.62:4	Beulah

Verse	Word Entry
Isa.62:5	bride
Isa.65:17	create
Isa.66:2	contrite
Isa.66:13	comfort
Jer.1:11	almond
Jer.2:32	attire
Jer.5:12	belied
Jer.6:2	comely
Jer.6:29	bellows
Jer.8:22	balm
Jer.10:22	bruit
Jer.10:22	commotion
Jer.14:4	chapt
Jer.14:9	astonied
Jer.15:7	bereave
Jer.18:10	benefit
Jer.19:1	bottle
Jer.22:10	bemoan
Jer.22:14	cieled
Jer.22:18	ah
Jer.26:13	amend
Jer.30:12	bruise
Jer.31:18	bullock
Jer.33:15	branch
Jer.34:13	covenant
Jer.38:12	clouts
Jer.43:9	brickkiln
Jer.50:11	bellow
Jer.50:24	aware
Jer.51:3	archer
Jer.51:3	brigandine
Jer.51:8	balm
Jer.51:44	Bel

Verse	Word Entry
Lam.1:15	crush
Lam.4:3	breast
Eze.1:7	burnished
Eze.1:13,20	creature
Eze.1:16	beryl
Eze.1:27	amber
Eze.3:9	adamant
Eze.4:16	care[1]
Eze.7:23	bloody
Eze.13:7	albeit
Eze.14:18	bonnets
Eze.16:13	broidered
Eze.16:34	contrary
Eze.23:41	bed
Eze.25:3,6	aha
Eze.25:5	couching-place
Eze.26:10	breach
Eze.27:9	calkers
Eze.28:24	brier
Eze.31:8	chesnut
Eze.40:5	cubit
Eze.40:30	arches
Eze.43:13	cubit
Eze.45:11	bath
Eze.45:14	cor
Eze.47:12	bdellium
Eze.48;14	alienate
Dan.2:10	astrologer
Dan.4:37	abase
Dan.5:10	banquet
Dan.5:27	balances
Dan.7:9	ancient

Verse	Word Entry
Dan.7:28	cogitations
Dan.11:11	choler
Hos.4:16	backsliding
Hos.7:8	cake
Hos.13:3	chimney
Hos.13:8	caul
Hos.14:4	backsliding
Joe.1:4	caterpiller
Joe.1:4	canker-worm
Joe.1:7	barked
Joe.2:16	closet
Joe.3:14	decision
Amo.5:12	bribe
Amo.6:5	chant
Amo.7:13	chapel
Oba.1:14	crossway
Jon.2:3	billows
Jon.4:5	booth
Mic.1:4	cleft
Mic.2:8	averse
Mic.3:3	chop
Nah.1:3	acquit
Nah.3:15	canker-worm
Hab.2:7	booties
Zep.2:14	bittern

Verse	Word Entry	Verse	Word Entry
Hag.2:17	blasting	Mt.24:32	branch
		Mt.25:36	clothed
Zec.6:3	bay[3]	Mt.26:7	alabaster
Zec.7:12	adamant	Mt.26:73	bewray
Zec.9:6	bastard	Mt.27:37	cross
		Mt.27:40	cross
Mt.1:16	Christ		
Mt.2:4	Christ	Mk.1:37	bull
Mt.3:11	baptize	Mk.1:45	blaze
Mt.4:2	afterward	Mk.2:19	bride-chamber
Mt.6:4	alms		
Mt.6:13	amen	Mk.3:2	accuse
Mt.6:16	appear	Mk.4:39	abated
Mt.6:19	corrupt[2]	Mk.5:39	ado
Mt.7:28	astonished	Mk.6:21	birthday
Mt.8:9	authority	Mk.6:29	corpse
Mt.8:24	asleep	Mk.6:29	carcase
Mt.9:2	bed	Mk.7:11	corban
Mt.10:17	council	Mk.12:17	Caesar
Mt.10:38	cross	Mk.14:1	craft
Mt.11:25	babe	Mk.14:8	aforehand
Mt.12:31	blasphemy	Mk.14:18	betray
Mt.13:3	byword	Mk.14:29	although
Mt.13:20	anon	Mk.14:30	crow
Mt.14:6	birthday	Mk.14:65	buffet
Mt.14:8	charger	Mk.14:72	crew
Mt.14:30	boisterous	Mk.15:1	council
Mt.15:27	crumbs	Mk.15:15	content[2]
Mt.16:24	cross	Mk.15:21	compel
Mt.18:19	agree	Mk.15:29	ah
Mt.20:19	crucify	Mk.16:18	deadly
Mt.22:46	answer		
Mt.23:23	cummin	Lk.1:19	angel
Mt.23:23	anise	Lk.1:36	cousin
Mt.23:24	camel	Lk.1:44	babe

Verse	Word Entry	Verse	Word Entry
Lk.2:1	Augustus	Lk.22:44	agony
Lk.2:1	decree	Lk.23:16	chastise
Lk.2:49	about	Lk.23:33	calvary
Lk.3:17	chaff	Lk.23:41	amiss
Lk.5:26	amazed	Lk.23:46	commend
Lk.6:24	consolation	Lk.24:42	broiled
Lk.6:29	cloke	Lk.24:46	behoved
Lk.6:44	bramble		
Lk.7:14	bier	Jn.1:29	Christ
Lk.7:41	creditor	Jn.1:48	before
Lk.8:56	astonished	Jn.2:2	belly
Lk.10:33	compas-sion	Jn.2:7	brim
		Jn.3:7	again
Lk.10:40	bid	Jn.3:16	begotten
Lk.10:40	cumbered	Jn.4:52	amend
Lk.11:15	Beelzebub	Jn.6:38	bread
Lk.11:22	armour	Jn.8:11	condemn
Lk.11:33	bushel	Jn.8:44	abode
Lk.11:48	allow	Jn.8:9	convicted
Lk.12:18	bestow	Jn.9:6	blind
Lk.13:7	cumbereth	Jn.10:18	corpse
Lk.13:16	bond[1]	Jn.11:1	castle
Lk.13:34	brood	Jn.12:15	colt
Lk.14:18	consent[1]	Jn.12:24	corn
Lk.14:32	ambassage	Jn.12:37	before
Lk.15:15	citizen	Jn.13:5	bason
Lk.16:7	bill	Jn.14:23	abode
Lk.16:22	bosom	Jn.18:27	cock
Lk.18:9	certain	Jn.19:9	answer
Lk.19:8-9	amends	Jn.20:21	apostle
Lk.19:21	austere	Jn.20:27	behold
Lk.19:23	bank[2]	Jn.21:20	breast
Lk.19:48	attentive	Jn.21:25	amen
Lk.22:25	benefac-tors		
		Act.1:8	assunder

Verse	Word Entry	Verse	Word Entry
Act.1:14	accord	Act.17:19	Areopagus
Act.1:19	aceldama	Act.17:22	Areopagus
Act.1:20	bishoprick	Act.17:3	alleging
Act.2:22	approve	Act.18:3	craft
Act.2:44	common	Act.19:31	adventure
Act.3:2	beautiful	Act.19:32	church
Act.3:3	about	Act.19:39	church
Act.3:19	conversion	Act.19:40	concourse
Act.4:9	deed	Act.19:41	church
Act.4:23	company[1]	Act.21:39	city
Act.5:14	baptize	Act.23:8	confess
Act.6:3	appoint	Act.24:4	clemency
Act.7:8	circumci-	Act.24:16	conscience
	sion	Act.25:17	delay
Act.7:8	begat	Act.25:21	Augustus
Act.7:34	affliction	Act.26:12	commis-
Act.7:60	asleep		sion
Act.8:11	bewitched	Act.26:28	Christian
Act.8:27	chamber-	Act.27:12	commodius
	lain	Act.27:26	certain
Act.10:1	centurion	Act.27:27	Adria
Act.10:1	band[3]	Act:27:27	deemed
Act.10:45	circumci-	Act.27:30	boat
	sion	Act.27:30	colour
Act.10:9	battlement	Act.27:36	cheer
Act.11:12	bade	Act.28:2	barbarous
Act.11:26	Christian	Act.28:8	bloody
Act.12:8	bind	Act.28:11	Castor
Act.13:10	child	Act.28:15	courage
Act.14:5	assault	Act.28:19	appeal
Act.14:8	cripple	Act.28:31	concern
Act.15:3	conversion		
Act.16:12	colony	Rom.1:1	apostle
Act.16:15	besought	Rom.1:14	barbarian
Act.16:31	believe	Rom.1:14	debtor

Verse	Word Entry	Verse	Word Entry
Rom.1:29	debate	1Cor.10:16	communion
Rom.2:29	circumci-sion	1Cor.12:31	covet
		1Cor.13:1	brass
Rom.3:28	conclude	1Cor.13:11	child
Rom.5:11	atonement	1Cor.13:13	charity
Rom.8:7	carnal	1Cor.14:3	comfort
Rom.10:9	confess	1Cor.14:8	battle
Rom.12:1-2	altar	1Cor.14:11	barbarian
Rom.12:9	abhor	1Cor.14:39	covet
Rom.12:16	conde-scend	1Cor.14:40	decently
		1Cor.15:37	chance
Rom.12:19	avenge	1Cor.15:40	celestial
Rom.13:12	aforehand	1Cor.15:51	behold
Rom.13:13	chamber-ing	1Cor.15:58	always
		1Cor.16:2	anathema
Rom.15:7	cousin	1Cor.16:12	convenient
Rom.15:26	contribution	1Cor.16:15	addicted
Rom.16:23	chamber-lain		
		2Cor.1:15	benefit
		2Cor.2:4	anguish
1Cor.3:1	babe	2Cor.2:11	advantage
1Cor.3:4	carnal	2Cor.5:17	creature
1Cor.3:17	defile	2Cor.6:7	armour
1Cor.4:13	defamed	2Cor.6:15	Belial
1Cor.5:9	company[2]	2Cor.6:15	concord
1Cor.6:20	Christian	2Cor.8:10	before
1Cor.7:3	benevo-lence	2Cor.8:20	blame
		2Cor.9:5	bounty
1Cor.7:9	contain	2Cor.9:12	administra-tion
1Cor.7:23	Christian		
1Cor.8:1	charity	2Cor.11:2	betroth
1Cor.8:7	conscience	2Cor.11:28	care[1]
1Cor.9:11	carnal	2Cor.11:32	apprehend
1Cor.9:18	abuse	2Cor.12:16	crafty
1Cor.9:27	castaway	2Cor.12:16	burden

Verse	Word Entry
Gal.1:8	accursed
Gal.1:11	certify
Gal.1:13	conversation
Gal.3:13	crucify
Gal.4:9	beggarly
Gal.4:17	affect
Gal.4:24	allegory
Gal.5:15	bite
Gal.6:12	constrain
Eph.1:5	adoption
Eph.2:8-9	confess
Eph.2:12	commonwealth
Eph.3:3	afore
Eph.3:9	create
Eph.3:14	bow^2
Eph.3:18	comprehend
Eph.4:14	deceive
Eph.4:26	angry
Eph.4:31	clamour
Eph.5:5	covetous
Eph.5:27	blemish
Eph.6:4	breastplate
Eph.6:8	bond^2
Eph.6:11	armour
Eph.6:20	ambassador
Phil.1:10	approve
Phil.1:14	bold
Phil.1:23	betwixt
Phil.1:29	behalf
Phil.2:20	care^2
Phil.3:2	concision
Phil.3:10	conformable
Phil.3:12	apprehend
Phil.3:12	already
Phil.4:4	alway
Col.1:17	consist
Col.2:4	beguile
Col.2:8	deceit
Col.2:10	complete
Col.2:10	conflict
Col.3:2	affection
Col.3:21	anger
Col.4:16	church
1Ths.4:5	concupiscence
1Ths.4:6	defraud
1Ths.5:8	breastplate
1Ths.5:12	admonish
1Ths.5:14	comfort
1Ths.5:22	abstain
1Tim.1:5	conscience
1Tim.1:10	contrary
1Tim.1:15	chief
1Tim.1:15	Christ
1Tim.2:9	broided
1Tim.2:9	crisping-(pins)
1Tim.2:9	array
1Tim.3:2	bishop

Verse	Word Entry
1Tim.3:3	brawler
1Tim.4:2	conscience
1Tim.5:21	charge[2]
1Tim.6:3	consent[2]
1Tim.6:8	content[1]
1Tim.6:18	communi-cate
2Tim.2:2	commit
2Tim.2:15	approve
2Tim.2:17	canker
2Tim.2:23	avoid
2Tim.2:24	apt
2Tim.4:8	crown
Ti.1:9	convince
Ti.2:10	adorn
Ti.2:13	blessed
Ti.3:8	affirm
Phi.1:12	bowels
Phi.1:18	account[2]
Heb.3:1	apostle
Heb.5:9	author
Heb.6:6	afresh
Heb.6:19	anchor
Heb.10:22	assurance
Heb.10:27	certain
Heb.10:35	confidence
Heb.11:17	begotten
Heb.11:20	blessed
Heb.11:36	cruel
Heb.12:1	aside

Verse	Word Entry
Jam.2:2	assembly
Jam.2:18	believe
Jam.3:2	bridle
Jam.5:16	availeth
1Pt.2:16	cloke
1Pt.2:25	astray
1Pt.2:25	bishop
1Pt.3:2	chaste
1Pt.3:6	amaze-ment
1Pt.4:15	busybody
1Pt.4:16	ashamed
1Pt.5:4	chief
1Pt.5:8	aware
1Pt.5:14	charity
2Pt.1:8	barren
2Pt.1:15	decease
2Pt.2:6	ashes
2Pt.2:12	brute
2Pt.2:18	allure
2Pt.2:19	bondage
2Pt.3:15	account[1]
1Jn.1:9	confess
1Jn.2:2	advocate
1Jn.2:18	antichrist
1Jn.3:17	bowels
1Jn.3:19	assure
1Jn.3:23	command-ment
2Jn.1:7	antichrist
3Jn.1:9	among

Verse	Word Entry
Jude.1:9	archangel
Jude.1:12	charity
Rev.2:1	angel
Rev.3:14	amen
Rev.3:18	counsel[2]
Rev.4:6	crystal
Rev.4:7	beast
Rev.4:8	Almighty
Rev.4:11	create
Rev.6:2	conquer
Rev.6:5	balances
Rev.9:11	angel
Rev.12:10	accuse
Rev.13:1-4	beast

Verse	Word Entry
Rev.13:6	blaspheme
Rev.13:11-14	beast
Rev.14:14	crown
Rev.16:5	angel
Rev.16:16	Armageddon
Rev.17:6	admiration
Rev.18:3	delicacies
Rev.18:9	bewail
Rev.19:1	alleluia
Rev.21:8	brimstone
Rev.21:9	bride
Rev.21:19	chalcedony
Rev.21:20	beryl
Rev.21:20	chrysolite
Rev.22:13	Alpha